I0825777

INTERPERSONAL COMMUNICATION

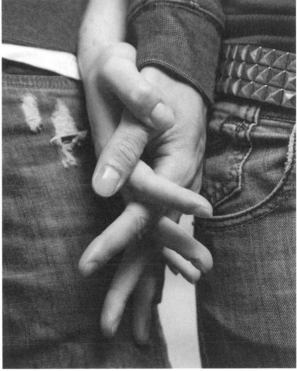

Navigating Relationships in a Changing World

Fourth Edition

Carrie C. Hutchinson

macmillan learning
curriculum solutions

Copyright © 2017 by Carrie C. Hutchinson
Copyright © 2017 by Hayden-McNeil, LLC on illustrations provided
Photos provided by Hayden-McNeil, LLC are owned or used under license

All rights reserved.

Permission in writing must be obtained from the publisher before any part of this work may
be reproduced or transmitted in any form or by any means, electronic or mechanical, including photocopying and recording, or by any information storage or retrieval system.

Printed in the United States of America

10 9 8 7 6 5 4 3 2 1

ISBN 978-0-7380-9623-0

Macmillan Learning Curriculum Solutions
14903 Pilot Drive
Plymouth, MI 48170
www.macmillanlearning.com

Hutchinson 9623-0 F17

 macmillan learning
curriculum solutions

Sustainability
Hayden-McNeil's standard paper stock uses a minimum of 30% post-
consumer waste. We offer higher % options by request, including a 100%
recycled stock. Additionally, Hayden-McNeil Custom Digital provides authors
with the opportunity to convert print products to a digital format. Hayden-
McNeil is part of a larger sustainability initiative through Macmillan Learning.
Visit http://sustainability.macmillan.com to learn more.

bedford/st. martin's • hayden-mcneil
w.h. freeman • worth publishers

This book is dedicated to the indigenous people on whose land our colleges and universities now sit, who were the original authors of all great theories about interpersonal communication and social harmony.

TABLE OF CONTENTS

SECTION 1

An Introduction to Interpersonal Communication

CHAPTER 1

Defining Interpersonal Communication

"To know how much there is to know is the beginning of learning to live."
—Dorothy West

Learning Objectives

After studying this chapter, you should be able to:

1. Define interpersonal communication and explain what distinguishes it from impersonal communication.
2. Explain the characteristics of an interpersonal relationship.
3. Explain the evolution of the models for understanding interpersonal communication.
4. Explain why it is useful to study interpersonal communication.
5. Understand what is meant by communication competence and assess your own competence.

It is impossible to get through life without communicating. It is estimated that 80–90% of your waking hours are spent communicating in some way. From the moment you are born, your very survival depends on being able to communicate your needs to others. In fact, some people believe that even newborn baby language is much more specific and meaningful than we originally thought. Although there is debate about when exactly we start constructing meaningful messages, we know that without these messages we would perish. We communicate our needs consciously, subconsciously, directly and indirectly, but we are always communicating something. As long as there is more than one person around, communication is occurring.

Most people would like to improve their communication with one or more people in their lives, be it a family member, friend, lover, or all of the above. This process begins with metacommunication, or communicating about how we communicate. Sometimes communicating about how we communicate can be awkward and difficult, which is one of the reasons we stick to our old habits and tend to shy away from pursuing a deeper understanding of how our tendencies and patterns affect those around us.

One way to make the challenge of improving your communication a bit less daunting is to break it into parts; therefore each chapter of the first half of this book will be dedicated to understanding a particular part of the communication process. This chapter is dedicated to helping you understand the topic of interpersonal communication so that you are better prepared to enter into your personal study of it as it applies to your life. After reading this chapter you should have a better understanding of what will be studied in this course.

First, you will learn the definition of interpersonal communication and how it compares and contrasts with other types of communication. Then, the principles of interpersonal communication will be explained in order for you to learn about some "facts of life" that apply to our interactions. The last section of this chapter is dedicated to explaining why it is useful to study interpersonal communication and what you can gain from the adventure upon which you are about to embark. From this section you will be able to understand what is meant by communication competence and assess your own competence before you proceed with the course.

WHAT DOES IT MEAN TO STUDY "COMMUNICATION"?

When browsing through your school's course catalog you probably came across several courses in the field of "communication." It may have been unclear to you what distinguished one topic in communication studies from another. You may have even wondered what "communication" really means as a field of study. In 1972, Dance and Larson found more than 120 published definitions of the term "communication."[1] So, which is the correct one we use today? If you are trying to choose your major this question is especially important. Even if you are just looking for a good course to take, you should know exactly what awaits you in a course on interpersonal communication, and what makes it different from any other course.

First, it is important to define **communication**, which is simply the process of acting on information. Following this definition, computers communicate, animals communicate, and anything that responds to a stimulus communicates. More specifically, **human communication** is the process of making sense out of the world around us and attempting to share that sense with others. What separates humans from all other species is our ability to analytically and logically make sense of the stimulus we receive from the environment. For example, when someone pays you a compliment, you have the ability to wonder what his or her motivation was, whether or not it was sincere, or to contemplate if your response was appropriate. Although many other species react to the environment, humans' ability to create and negotiate meaning is what makes human communication unique.

The field of human communication can be complicated by the fact that it is studied under a different name at different institutions. For example, at University of California, Santa Barbara, the study of communication occurs in the "Communication Department." At California State University Fullerton, the same topics are studied in the "Department of Human Communication

Studies." Still yet, many universities teach communication classes in the "Department of Speech Communication," even though nonverbal communication is a large component of the field. How you label the study of human communication often depends on where you study it.

AREAS OF STUDY IN THE FIELD OF COMMUNICATION

Scholars are not always in agreement as to what topics should *not* be included in human communication studies. Some institutions consider public relations, advertising, and journalism as included in the field of communication, but typically these fields are referred to as "communications" (with an "s"). In addition, some institutions consider rhetoric and critical theory (which study the creation and dissemination of persuasive messages, often through film, literature, and other social artifacts) as part of the field of communication. English and Literature scholars also study these subjects. In sum, there is no one simple definition of what constitutes the field of communication. Regardless of these differences in labels, you will typically find some specific areas of study under the larger umbrella of "communication."

Some studies of communication are categorized by the particular context in which the interactions occur. **Intergroup communication** is communication between people from two different social, cultural, or demographic groups (such as different ages, genders, or teams). Included in intergroup communication is **intercultural communication**, which occurs specifically between people from two different cultures. **Business/organizational communication** is communication that occurs in the workplace or in professional settings.

Other areas of study in the field are determined by how many people are present in the interaction. **Public communication**, sometimes called public speaking, is the communication that occurs when a speaker addresses a large audience in person, for example when giving a presidential address. **Mass communication** is the type of communication that occurs when one sender delivers the same message to many receivers at once in *non-face-to-face settings*, which offer little or no opportunity for listener feedback. Mass communication includes public address that is televised or broadcast via radio, but also includes journalism and advertising messages.

Small group communication is yet another area of study, which attempts to analyze communication between three to fifteen people who meet to interact with a common purpose to solve a problem, make a decision, or just have fun. Examples of small group communication contexts may include a club gathering, a business meeting, a small dinner party, or interaction between members of a family. *Intra*personal (not *inter*personal) **communication** is communication with yourself, otherwise known as thinking or self-talk. This form of communication has major implications for your interpersonal relationships, which is why it will be addressed in depth in a later chapter. When there are two people communicating the interaction is considered **interpersonal**, which is the focus of this book. For an interaction to be considered interpersonal it must fit a number of other criteria, which you'll learn about next.

Review! Types of Communication Studies	
Intercultural communication: Communication that occurs between people of different cultures.	**Business/Organizational communication:** Communication in the workplace.
Intergroup communication: Communication between people from two different social, cultural, or demographic groups.	**Small group communication:** Communication between three to fifteen people.
Public communication: When a speaker addresses a large audience in person.	**Mass communication:** When one source sends the same message to many people at once through a mediated channel.
Interpersonal communication: Interactions in which there are only two communicators.	**Intrapersonal communication:** Communication with yourself.

WHAT IS INTERPERSONAL COMMUNICATION?

At this point you may have questions about what constitutes interpersonal communication. Based on what you know so far, ask yourself whether each of the following would be considered an interpersonal context:

- A conversation in an Internet chat room

- A tutoring session with the librarian at your school

- A chat with your professor during office hours

- A conversation with your stylist at a hair salon

- An interview with a potential employer

This section will help you narrow the parameters of our subject and determine if your answers were correct.

DISTINGUISHING INTERPERSONAL FROM IMPERSONAL COMMUNICATION

When we use the term "interpersonal communication" to describe any interaction between two people, we are referring to an interaction that is contextually interpersonal. However, when we use the term "interpersonal communication" to refer to the interactions between people who have some kind of meaningful relationship, we are using the term to describe interactions that are qualitatively interpersonal. For our purpose in this course, **interpersonal communication** is a process of two individuals interacting and mutually influencing each other simultaneously, usually for the purpose of managing relationships.[2] Rather than referring to every one-on-one interaction we have with others, the subject of this course is a special form of communication that occurs when you treat others as unique, irreplaceable individuals. These interactions are therefore distinct from **impersonal communication**, which occurs when you relate to people based

on their roles, or as a means to an end. In impersonal communication, interactions are scripted and predictable, and the people interacting are replaceable. To distinguish the two, imagine your interactions with the checkout clerk at the grocery store (impersonal) versus your interactions with a friend (interpersonal).

You are expected to have a wide variety of relationship types. Not all interactions are meant to be interpersonal because impersonal communication is a normal and necessary function of everyday life. **Interpersonal relationships,** on the other hand are defined as the ongoing connections we maintain through interpersonal communication with the important people in our lives. They have a much greater impact on us than impersonal relationships.

One way to understand the difference between impersonal and interpersonal communication is to place all of your relationships on a scale ranging from impersonal to interpersonal, based on the depth and breadth of communication you have in each. Take a moment to place at least three relationships in your life on the scale below, depending on how interpersonal they are.

Interpersonal   Impersonal

Figure 1.0. Relationships types range from interpersonal to impersonal.

CHARACTERISTICS OF AN INTERPERSONAL RELATIONSHIP

To help you understand the characteristics of interpersonal communication, ask yourself what makes your relationship with a friend different from that with an acquaintance. The characteristics that define a relationship as a "friendship" are the very things that make it an interpersonal relationship versus an impersonal one. These characteristics are interdependence, relational maintenance, and rule-governed behaviors. The next section will cover each of these to help you better define what makes your relationships interpersonal.

Interdependence

Both individuals in an interpersonal relationship have a somewhat mutual investment in the relationship; therefore you each expect a certain level of honesty, a reasonable amount of disclosure, and some degree of loyalty. The depth and degree of these features depend entirely on the nature and status of the interpersonal relationship; new relationships have different expectations than mature ones, and friendships carry different expectations than sibling relationships. What makes the relationship **interdependent** is that the status is constantly negotiated between two parties that are both affected in some way by its outcome. If one person pushes you back or pulls you forward, you have no choice but to be affected by, and to react in some way, to his or her action. As such, we study communication from the perspective of **systems theory**, which acknowledges that an interpersonal system is synergistic; rather than being a sum of its parts, a relationship is a complex system of intertwined pieces that affect each other.

Relational Maintenance

We generally expect that most of our interpersonal relationships will have a future. We continue to invest effort in a friendship or romantic relationship because we want to see it last. The desire to have a relationship succeed motivates us to perform regular **maintenance strategies** such as telling someone when they've hurt our feelings or made us mad, or even making sure we fulfill the mutually expected amount of time together. Of course these maintenance behaviors would be inappropriate if applied to your relationship with the checkout clerk, which is why they are evidence of an interpersonal relationship, rather than an impersonal one!

Rules of Behavior

Interpersonal communication helps individuals establish and maintain rules of behavior that serve the needs of the individuals in the relationship. A **rule** is a prescription that indicates what behavior is obligated, preferred, or prohibited in certain communication situations or contexts.[3] Rules help us to define appropriate and inappropriate communication in a given situation. Although impersonal relationships are also governed by rules, in an interpersonal relationship the rules are developed by those involved in the interaction and by the climate in which they are communicating. For example, in a romantic relationship couples may have rules about how often they should talk on the phone, what topics are taboo, or whether they are allowed to use profanity when fighting. Rules can be **implicit**, meaning that they are unspoken but mutually understood, or they can be **explicit**, meaning that there has been some verbal agreement about the rule. Rules for communication are mutually renegotiated as the relationship develops over time. For example, the rules about how often a dating couple sees each other will change as the relationship intensifies.

PRINCIPLES OF INTERPERSONAL COMMUNICATION

There are several principles upon which the study of interpersonal communication is founded.[4] **Principles** are fundamental ideas that are assumed to be true, from which all other knowledge derives. Understanding these principles will help you further define and identify interpersonal communication as it occurs in your life. As you read each principle think of an example from your life that demonstrates it.

INTERPERSONAL COMMUNICATION IS INESCAPABLE

This principle is derived from a popular axiom in the field, which states: "One cannot not communicate." Human communication occurs even when you are not conscious of what you are doing. You may be minding your own business in a coffee shop, typing away on your computer or reading the paper, but those around you are receiving some kind of message from your behavior. Even the *absence* of behavior communicates a message. If your instructor entered the room and stood staring out into the class without saying a word or making a single gesture, the class members would each interpret a message from the lack of expected behavior. Although these examples are from impersonal interactions, the same occurs in your interpersonal relationships. If one spouse comes home from work and does not say a word to the other, a message has been delivered. One side effect of this principle is that messages can be intentional or unintentional. Remember, you are *always* communicating something, and the message sent is not always the message received.

INTERPERSONAL COMMUNICATION IS IRREVERSIBLE

Have you ever asked someone to *"take it back"* when he or she has said something cruel, unfair, or untrue? The only reasonable answer to this demand is, "I can't." The truth is that you can never take back your communication. You can clarify or apologize, you can say you did not mean it, but you simply cannot take it back. This is evidenced by the fact that the comment may linger in the mind of the recipient long after it occurred, even though it was "taken back." It may even resurface in a later interaction, even though you supposedly "took it back." Simply put, interpersonal communication is irreversible. Once it comes out, it's out there.

INTERPERSONAL COMMUNICATION IS UNREPEATABLE

Each interaction between two people is so entirely unique that it cannot occur the same way twice. Even if you agree to re-enact a communication episode with someone, you are literally a different person the second time it occurs. In the re-enactment, you are now a person who has already experienced this particular situation, whereas before you were not. Constant new knowledge, emotions, moods, and insights make each episode entirely new because no two people are the same as they were in the previous moment. In this sense, every interpersonal relationship is dynamic and ever changing.

Review! Characteristics of Interpersonal Communication	
Interpersonal communication is characterized by:	—Interdependence —Rules of behavior —Relational maintenance
Principles of interpersonal communication:	—Interpersonal communication is inescapable —Interpersonal communication is irreversible —Interpersonal communication is unrepeatable

STUDYING INTERPERSONAL COMMUNICATION

COMPONENTS OF THE INTERPERSONAL PROCESS

Although each interaction is entirely unique, any given communication encounter includes the same components. When we study interactions we usually refer to each one as an episode. An **episode** is any communication encounter during which there is a source, a receiver, and a message. The **source** is the person attempting to communicate an idea, thought, or emotion. The source's role is to **encode** the message, or to translate ideas, thoughts, and feelings into a verbal or nonverbal code. The **message** is the cumulative written, spoken, and unspoken elements of communication to which people assign meaning, which is sent through the **channel**, or medium. Face-to-face interactions include multiple channels, both verbal and nonverbal. Mediated communication, however, travels through some form of technology, such as a telephone or computer, which can limit the message. The **receiver** is the person who attempts to make sense of the message from the source by **decoding**, or interpreting ideas, feelings, and thoughts that have been translated into a verbal or nonverbal code.

Although this process seems simple enough, there are other components in each episode that are less obvious. **Noise** is anything that interferes and keeps a message from being understood completely and achieving its intended effect. **Physical noise** can be an external sound, such as a car driving by. Equally distracting, **psychological noise** occurs internally, such as preoccupation, fears, or thoughts of any kind. **Feedback** is the ongoing verbal or nonverbal responses to a message sent, which can be intentional or unintentional. The receiver of a message is constantly giving feedback throughout the entire episode, whether consciously or unconsciously. Finally, the **context** is the particular environment within which the communication takes place. Context includes the **physical environment,** the number of people present, the relationship between communicators, the communication goal, and the impact of culture, gender, and other group memberships.

Review! Components of the Communication Process	
Episode:	Any communication encounter during which there is a source, receiver, and message.
Receiver:	The person who attempts to make sense of the message from the source.
Source:	The originator of a thought or emotion.
Message:	The cumulative written, spoken, and unspoken elements of communication to which people assign meaning.
Channel:	The pathway through which the messages are sent.
Context:	The particular environment within which the communication takes place.
Feedback:	The ongoing verbal or nonverbal responses to a message sent, which can be intentional or unintentional.
Noise:	Anything that interferes and keeps a message from being understood completely and achieving its intended effect.

Theorists have developed several models that demonstrate the relationship of the above components. The explanation of each of these models coming up in the next section will help you see how our understanding of communication has changed and improved over time.

MODELS FOR UNDERSTANDING INTERPERSONAL COMMUNICATION

As the field of interpersonal communication has evolved over time, theorists have created and adapted various models to depict the process of communication. The earliest communication model was the **Message Transfer Model,** which showed human communication as an *action*.[5] This model was originally devised by the Bell Telephone Laboratories to help examine the accuracy of message transmission, which explains why it characterizes communication as a linear, step by-step sequence rather than as a simultaneous process of constant influence between senders and receivers.

Figure 1.1. The Message Transfer Model of communication.

The next model that attempted to more accurately depict the process of human communication was the **Message Exchange Model**,[6] which gets closer to reality by showing human communication as an *interaction.* This model is an improvement on the one-way model because it includes feedback from the receiver to the sender. Another important addition to this model is context. The context in which any interaction occurs greatly influences all of the other components. However, even though this model shows communication as an interactive process, it still overlooks the complexities of real-life human communication.

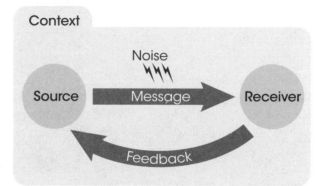

Figure 1.2. The Message Exchange Model of communication.

The **Message Creation Model** shows human communication as a *transaction.[7]* It is the most current model used to understand communication. In the model, represented below, you can see that the message is continuously going back and forth between the sender and receiver, showing that feedback never stops, and each person is both the sender and receiver simultaneously. Of course it also includes all the components from the older models such as noise and context.

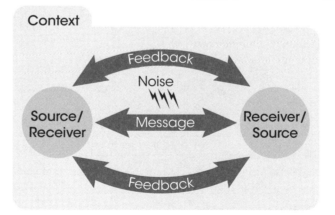

Figure 1.3. The Message Creation Model of communication.

Review! Progress in Communication Models	
Message transfer:	One-way action.
Message exchange:	Two-way interaction, includes feedback.
Message creation:	Simultaneous transaction.

CHARACTERISTICS OF MEDIATED INTERPERSONAL COMMUNICATION

Now that you've learned about the traditional ways in which interpersonal communication was studied, let's talk about what's new. Our changing world requires that we constantly re-consider our notions of what it means to communicate interpersonally. Traditional definitions and models insisted that to qualify as interpersonal communication any given interaction had to occur face-to-face, in real time. New tools for communicating provided to us by communication technology

have expanded the traditional definition of interpersonal communication. Many of our interactions occur over other channels, and these interactions impact our interpersonal relationships.

Mediated communication is any communication that does not take place face-to-face, but instead is transmitted through some other channel such as the Internet or a cell phone. Researchers often use the term **computer-mediated-communication** (CMC) to refer to online interpersonal interactions, while they use the term **electronically mediated communication** (EMC) to refer to communication using devices other than computers, such as texting. Whereas mass communication refers to communication that is unidirectional and sent from one person to many receivers with no chance for feedback, mediated communication usually includes the opportunity for feedback, and can be multidirectional (many-to-many).

Even though it is not face-to-face and even sometimes includes a delay, mediated communication often *feels* interpersonal, and it certainly fulfils many of the criteria that would qualify it as interpersonal; that is, it involves relational development and maintenance, and it is bound by interpersonally established implicit and explicit norms and rules. In today's world, much of our relational development, maintenance, and even relational deterioration occur through mediated channels.

From your own experience you know that there are many other ways in which mediated communication can differ greatly from face-to-face communication. As you'll learn throughout the upcoming chapters, mediated interpersonal communication carries some unique features that affect our interactions. Each chapter will highlight these characteristics and the current research being done to discover how our choice of communication channel (face-to-face, cell phone, Internet) affects our relationships. For now, here are some general ways in which mediated interpersonal communication is significantly different than that which occurs face-to-face.

VISIBILITY

One characteristic of mediated interpersonal communication is that it often occurs over channels that are public. Of particular interest to researchers is the most popular new channel of mediated communication known as social media. **Social media** can be defined as communication channels that allow for mediated interactions between multiple people and an infinite amount of receivers for the purpose of information exchange and social interaction. Social media, therefore, blur the line between interpersonal, small group, and public communication. For example, your boyfriend may post a sweet message on your Facebook page, but your best friend may comment on it.

The concept of social media is somewhat amorphous because of the rapid rate at which new communication technology is being invented. The ways in which social media are used seem to evolve daily. Social media share many characteristics with mass media, but are more interpersonal in several important ways:

- The audience reached by social media is *variable*, meaning the message can go out to one, a few, or millions of receivers.

- Social media are *interactive*. There is usually an opportunity for the receivers to respond by simply clicking "reply," posting on an associated message board, or blogging.

ANONYMITY

Mediated interactions can be anonymous: you may not always know who is on the other end of your interaction. You may receive a text from a friend's phone number, but someone else may have intercepted the phone and sent you the message. When you enter into a chat room you have no idea who you are dealing with, and research indicates that the likelihood of encountering people using false identities is exceptionally high. When it comes to deception detection a mediated environment can create an enormous problem because there are fewer leakage cues available, making it easier to be deceived, and since there is a sense of anonymity people feel less accountable for their actions. Because of this, researchers believe that there is a greater frequency of deception in online interactions than in those that occur face-to-face.

DISTANCE

Another characteristic of mediated interpersonal communication that distinguishes it from face-to-face communication is that there typically exists a greater distance between people communicating. This distance can range from the space between two separate tables at a café to the distance between two continents. If mediated communication is occurring between two continents, it's likely that it is occurring between two time zones, which leads to another way in which mediated interpersonal communication is unique: it is often asynchronous, meaning that your messages are not necessarily received at the time you send them. When you send an email or text message, your communication will be received at the convenience of the other person, who may or may not respond immediately.

PERMANENCE

Mediated messages are more permanent than face-to-face messages. Mediated interactions often have a "paper trail," which means you can track them down, retrieve them and view them days, months, and even years after they occurred. Although there is often no real "paper" involved, this phrase depicts the permanence of mediated communication. Emails can be retrieved from archives when you thought they had been deleted, text messages can be obtained from cell phone companies, and even online chats are often recorded and stored without the user's knowledge. You may have felt the effect of this permanence when someone forwarded you an old email to remind you of what you had written, or when you read old emails from someone else that were stored away safely in your account. In this sense, we can "replay" mediated messages in a way that we cannot with face-to-face interactions.

Review! Characteristics of Mediated Interpersonal Communication	
Visibility:	Although the interaction may feel intimate, other people are often privy to what's happening.
Anonymity:	You may not be able to know who is sending or receiving a message if vocal cues or facial cues are absent.
Distance:	Mediated channels allow for greater distance between communicators.
Permanence:	There is usually a permanent record of the communication.

MINDFUL MEDIATED COMMUNICATION

Sexting and the Downside of Permanence

Most adults cringe at the sight of their old yearbook photo, hardly believing that they are the same person smiling awkwardly on those glossy pages. Assuming they have grown up a bit since high school, today's adults are grateful to have endured those years relatively unscathed. Fortunately for them, all evidence of their questionable, odd, or rebellious behavior is tucked away in those dusty yearbooks, never to be seen by their current friends and coworkers. This will not be the case for modern teenagers, however, who may be forever haunted by adolescent mistakes in the form of digital photos. The axiom that states, "Communication is irreversible" has never been truer, especially when it comes to the recent phenomenon of sexting. Sexting, defined as "creating, sharing and forwarding of sexually suggestive nude or nearly nude images,"[8] is a term known by most young people today. A poll conducted by MTV in partnership with the Associated Press found that 10% of young adults between the ages of 14 and 24 have texted or emailed a nude or partially nude image of themselves to someone else and 15% have received nude pictures or videos of someone else they know. Perhaps even scarier, 8% reported that they had been forwarded nude or partially nude images of someone they knew.[9]

One teen respondent in the study recounted this incident: "This girl sent pictures to her boyfriend, then they broke up and he sent them to his friend, who sent them to like everyone in my school. Then she was supposed to come to my school because she got kicked out of her school...it ruined high school for her." This

phenomenon is so widespread that it led to the development of Snapchat, a photo-sharing app that destroys photos a few seconds after they are sent. Recently Snapchat came under fire as users learned that it doesn't actually destroy the photos, it just changes how they are labeled so that the operating system can no longer find them. Hackers have had no problem digging up archived photos that users thought were long gone.

Unfortunately these mistakes can last a lifetime, and the consequences can be far more severe than embarrassment alone. Eighteen-year-old Jesse Logan hanged herself after months of torment from classmates who were forwarded a sexually explicit photo she sent to a boy. The tormenters were other girls in her class.

Because of the potential harm involved in sexting, some states are starting to implement laws to deter teens from the practice. In some places, police and lawyers have even begun prosecuting teens involved in sexting because they are in violation of laws pertaining to the production and distribution of child pornography. To grasp the severity of these charges, consider the incident in Florida, where an 18-year-old sent friends nude images of his 16-year-old girlfriend after an argument, was then convicted and is now listed as registered sex offender for the next 25 years. The permanence of mediated communication messages should not be underestimated by users of email, texting, and even chat rooms. If you plan on sharing any information with someone that you wouldn't want the whole world to know or see, best to keep your sharing face-to-face.

WHY IS IT IMPORTANT TO LEARN ABOUT INTERPERSONAL COMMUNICATION?

According to Schutz,[10] there are three primary social needs that affect our degree of communication with others. The need for **inclusion** is the interpersonal need to be sought out, considered, and included in social activities and the need to seek out and include others. The need for **control** is the interpersonal need for some degree of dominance in our relationships, as well as the need to be controlled by others. The need for **affection** is the interpersonal need to give and receive physical affection, and verbal praise and approval. The greater a person's interpersonal needs for inclusion, control, and affection, the more actively they will pursue interpersonal relationships. People will have varying degrees of each of these needs in different situations and with different people. These needs are dynamic and ever changing. The main motivation for learning about interpersonal communication is that it can offer insight into our own needs, ways of thinking, and ways of behaving. Only when these needs are understood can they be successfully met in healthy and effective ways.

Our own sense of identity is highly integrated in our social ties with others, and lack of necessary social support and interaction can have extremely detrimental consequences to our sense of well-being, which affects our physical health. Studies indicate that terminally ill patients with limited social support die sooner than those with stronger ties to friendships.[11] Similarly, grief-stricken spouses are more likely than others to die prematurely, especially around the time of the departed spouse's birthday or their anniversary.[12] Harlow's famous maternal deprivation studies show that this need starts at infanthood. In one study this researcher took infant monkeys away from their mothers and raised them in isolation cages, which resulted in severe mental psychoses and growth retardation.[13]

FAMILY COMMUNICATION

One context where it is exceptionally important to understand communication behavior is in the *family*. Although you are born or adopted into your family, you have a choice about how your relationships with family members develop. You can consider family members circumstantial relationships about which you have no control, or you can make them relationships of choice whereby you seek and receive intimacy and fulfillment. Identifying family communication patterns can make relationships of circumstance relationships of choice.

In addition to creating positive relationships with family members, learning about family communication can help you understand relationships outside of the family. The patterns of communication you learn from your family will affect your relationships throughout your life. You will carry with you the behaviors taught to you by your parents and impose these norms onto other people in other contexts. Becoming aware of how your family communicates allows you to control which patterns you want to keep, and which you would like to change in your other relationships.

ROMANTIC RELATIONSHIPS

Learning about interpersonal communication can help you more successfully navigate your romantic relationships. You may have heard that half of all marriages will end in divorce. New data suggest that divorce rates are actually on the decline, but still, many partnerships fail. Relational termination is one of the most stressful events a person can endure, which is why it is advantageous to learn skills that will help your *romantic relationships* through conflict, or even allow a peaceful end to a relationship that is not meant to continue. Having confidence that you handled a relationship well allows for closure that is otherwise very difficult to achieve when a relationship ends. Likewise, resolving a conflict in a healthy and constructive way allows an enduring relationship to flourish and for both parties to grow together.

FRIENDSHIPS

Whether or not you are in a romantic relationship, you certainly have friends. As the typical age at first marriage becomes older and older, friendships have become a central focus of the interpersonal literature. Our relationships with friends can be just as, if not more, rewarding than our familial and romantic relationships. We often take our friendships for granted, failing to recognize that friendships need the same amount of care and investment as do other relationships in our lives. Most everything you learn about interpersonal communication in this text can be applied to your friendship relationships.

WORKPLACE RELATIONSHIPS

A final important interpersonal context is the workplace. Understanding how relationships develop at work can help you decrease overall stress, manage conflict, and increase your sense of satisfaction

with your job. Having satisfying work relationships creates peace of mind outside of the office, as well. People often take their work problems home, and dwell on their relationship problems at the office, which means that our work relationships and our personal relationships are intertwined. Furthermore, success and promotions often hinge upon how well we relate with supervisors and peers. The ability to listen, manage conflict, and have good interpersonal relationships with clients and co-workers are at the top of the list of skills that employers are seeking.[14] Demonstrating interpersonal skills can often get you a job, allow you to succeed at that job, and keep you satisfied in your job, no matter what career path you choose.

BUILDING CULTURAL COMPETENCE

When Minorities Become Majorities

In today's global village it's imperative to embrace diversity. We meet people from diverse backgrounds every day. In fact, demographers predict that by the middle of the century one in five residents of the United States will be an immigrant. Here is what experts predict our country will look like at a mid-century:

Changing population trends	2050
Non-Hispanic Whites	46%
Hispanics	30%
African Americans	15%
Asian Americans	9%

In the next few years, ethnic and racial minority students are expected to make up almost 50% of the college student population.[15] Facts like these make it clear that learning how to communicate with a variety of people is no longer an option, it's a necessity!

HOW CAN YOU IMPROVE YOUR OWN INTERPERSONAL COMMUNICATION?

Many people take a course in communication expecting to "master" their own communication, which may include learning how to express themselves effectively at all times, being in control of all their relationships, and becoming mind readers of nonverbal cues. However, none of these are indicators of communication competence. This section will describe what is meant by communication competence, and what are considered realistic expectations for the outcomes of studying this topic.

HOW MUCH CAN YOU CONTROL?

Scholars differ in their ideas about how much control people have over their own behavior. The **communibiological approach** to communication is a theoretical perspective that suggests peoples' communication behavior can be predicted based on personal traits and characteristics that result from their genetic makeup.[16] This perspective allows for little change beyond how we are each pre-programmed to behave. In contrast, **social learning theory** suggests that while biology plays a large role in how we each behave, we adapt and adjust our behavior toward others based on our own personal experiences.[17] There is a large body of research that demonstrates how strongly we respond to social learning. Bandura's famous Bobo Doll studies[18] show that children will behave violently toward a doll after watching an adult model behave violently, especially if the adult modeling the behavior is the same sex as the child.[19] It should come as no surprise that you have learned many of your own behavioral tendencies from watching people around you such as your parents, siblings, and friends.

HOW DOES ONE ACHIEVE COMMUNICATION COMPETENCE?

In order to evaluate your own behavior as competent or incompetent, you must become aware of the criteria for evaluation. There are several indicators of competent communication, including that it is effective, appropriate, adaptive, and involved.

Competent Communication Is Effective

Competent communicators can make their goals become realized by communicating them well to others. For this to happen your message must be understood, meaning that it should be clear, not ambiguous. Furthermore, to be effective means that your message must achieve its intended effect. A receiver not only has to understand what you need and want, but also has to agree to participate in its fruition. Goals are not always selfish; your goals can include the development or improvement of a relationship, the desire to help an important cause, to empathize with others, or to be a good employee. No matter what your goals are, your communication competence can be measured, in part, by your effectiveness in meeting the outcomes you desire.

Competent Communication Is Appropriate

To be appropriate, your message should consider time, place, and the overall context in which your communication is occurring. Clearly your *effectiveness* and *appropriateness* are inextricably linked: you will not be effective if you are inappropriate. This includes sensitivity to the feelings and attitudes of the listener. Sometimes we tend to be **egocentric communicators**, meaning that we are so wrapped up in our goals and needs that we create messages without giving much thought to the person who is listening. **Other-oriented communication** suggests that you consider the needs, goals, desires, and motives of your partner when sending a message. Occasionally this will include deciding to wait, and delivering a message at a better place and time.

Competent Communication Is Adaptive

Adaptability requires that you change what is not working. Often times we blame the receiver when our messages are misunderstood, but if you begin to see a pattern in people's responses to your communication, you may consider taking responsibility for the problem and making some changes. Adaptability includes the ability to try new things, which can be scary. Many of the communication strategies discussed in this text will not appeal to you because you may feel uncomfortable when trying them. However, in order to develop competence you must change what is not working and learn new strategies that are more effective.

Competent Communication Is Involved

Competent communicators know how to engage in conversation that is mutually satisfying by applying appropriate turn-taking norms, self-disclosure, and feedback. We all have experience with "conversational hijackers," people who are so self-absorbed that they dictate the entire conversation, leaving the other person feeling empty and dissatisfied. When one person feels dissatisfied with the interaction, it is usually because the roles are uneven: one person is talking too much, revealing significantly more than the other, interrupting, or not giving nonverbal feedback when the other person is talking. Learning how to manage a conversation so that both people feel equally understood and satisfied is one way to demonstrate communication competence.

WATCH AND LEARN

View a TED Talk on the importance of interpersonal communication and relationship choices by typing this into your browser: TED Talk 30 is not the new 20.

SKILL BUILDING EXERCISE

Assessing Your Communication Competence

It's difficult to assess your own communication competence when you haven't taken a class on interpersonal communication yet. Here is a short list of considerations for you to start with as you begin to evaluate your own communication with others.

Circle "yes" or "no" to each statement to help identify your strengths and weaknesses.

1. I know how to effectively open a discussion.   YES   (NO)

2. I allow the other to complete his or her thoughts/statements.   (YES)   NO

3. I establish and maintain a personal connection throughout the   (YES)   NO
    conversation (i.e., avoid distractions).

4. I use questions to enhance my understanding of what the other is saying. (YES) NO

5. I summarize and/or paraphrase information I am receiving to check my understanding. YES (NO)

6. I actively listen using nonverbal communication (e.g., eye contact, body position). (YES) NO

7. I acknowledge and respond to the other's ideas, feelings, and values. (YES) NO

8. I use words and a speaking style that the other can understand (based on culture, age, etc.). (YES) NO

9. I share information about myself and my opinions, feelings, and values. YES (NO)

10. I use effective closing statements to end the conversation. (YES) NO

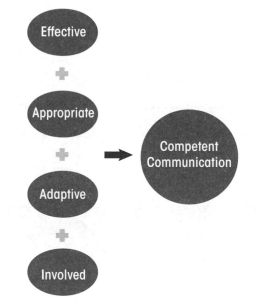

Figure 1.4. The components of competent communication.

WHAT SHOULD I EXPECT?

A MODEL OF COMMUNICATION COMPETENCE

One model of communication competence suggests that there are three main pieces to achieving competence,[20] which are knowledge, motivation, and skills. The **knowledge component** is the information you need to know in order to understand how you and others communicate, and what it means to communicate effectively. From reading the above, you now "know" what it takes to be

a good communicator. This does not mean you necessarily want to be an effective communicator, or have the necessary skills. The second piece, the **motivational component**, is the desire to improve your communication. However, just because you have the desire and the knowledge, does not mean you know "how" to do it. Thus, the **skills component** is the set of behaviors, often learned, that you can use to improve your communication with others. Like with any skill, communication skills take practice; they do not always come naturally.

These different pieces combine to form four levels of communication competence.[21] The first stage is called **unconscious incompetence**, which is when you are not aware of the deficits in your skill set. This may describe your level of competence before taking this class. Think about when you were a child and you were a passenger in your parent's car. You did not know how to drive, but driving was not required of you, so you did not think about it much; you had unconscious incompetence.

The second stage, **conscious incompetence**, is when you are aware of the areas in which you lack skills, but are not sure how to improve. Some people taking this course are in this stage. Imagine when you were about to turn the age where you would get a driver's learning permit. You knew you did not know how to drive, but were ready to learn; you were consciously incompetent.

Stage three is termed **conscious competence**, which occurs when you are aware of how to improve and you actively employ these strategies. You will reach this stage during this class, and it will likely feel awkward to use your new skills. Following the driving example, when you were learning to drive with a permit you had to actively apply your skills with great thought and attention. Do you remember the first time you drove on the highway? You had to pay close attention just to stay in the proper lane; your conscious competence now seems laughable!

Finally, the last stage is **unconscious competence**, when you are so accustomed to using your learned skills that they come naturally. This stage is where you will be long after this course is over and you continue to use the skills in your everyday life. It may take years to achieve this stage, and many people never achieve it. This is when you drive to work without even thinking about it. Sometimes you pull in to the parking lot and realize you haven't been paying any attention to how you got there, but somehow your unconscious competence managed to help you arrive effectively (and safely)!

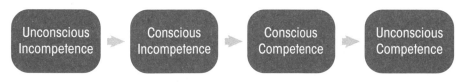

Figure 1.5. Stages of communication competence.

Review! The Process of Communication Competence	
Unconscious incompetence:	A communicator is incompetent and is unaware of this fact.
Conscious incompetence:	A communicator is incompetent, but is willing to learn how to become more competent.
Conscious competence:	A communicator is aware of his or her new communication skills and is able to demonstrate them proficiently.
Unconscious competence:	A communicator demonstrates competence without being aware that he or she is doing so.

INTERPERSONAL SKILLS ACROSS CONTEXTS

Parent-Child Communication

Parents are known for their famous mantra "Do as I say, not as I do." Unfortunately this expectation is not only unrealistic, but also harmful. As most people could probably guess, parents' actions shape their children far more than their words of wisdom ever will. Children look to their parents as role models of appropriate behavior, especially when it comes to communication. Even the most subtle verbal and nonverbal messages sent by parents are heard loud and clear by children, and end up in their communication repertoire as adults. One study shows how children actually pick up on their parents' communication competence, and use what they learn to manage their interactions with others. A team of researchers sought to understand this phenomenon and its implications for children's physical health, mental well-being, and the quality of their relationships.[22]

The study concluded that adolescents who believe their parents possess good communication skills were better able to manage stressful communication interactions than adolescents who believed their parents were communicatively unskilled. The sample of 118 adolescents were asked how they perceive their parents' communication skills, and also asked to discuss something stressful. Adolescents who believed their parents were unskilled communicators were much more likely to overreact, show no reaction, or downplay their feelings during a stressful conversation with another person. On the contrary, those who considered their parents to be communicatively competent were much more able to manage a stressful discussion. Furthermore, the participants who tended to overreact during a stressful conversation had notably poorer health indices, poorer psychological well-being, and lower relationship quality than those who did not overreact.

As it turns out, the way parents communicate is a strong indicator of how their children will begin to navigate relationships of their own. If you are a parent now or plan to be one someday, keep in mind that your communication is under the watchful eye of your child, and your competence has an enormous impact on his or her future relationships.

MINDFULNESS VERSUS AUTOPILOT

The term "mindfulness" may conjure up images of the self-help section in your local bookstore. In fact, the study of mindfulness is a legitimate and burgeoning area of both cognitive and behavioral

sciences. Early studies of mindfulness equated the practice with thoughtful, conscious communication, but current research indicates that it's more about how we think than how we speak. One scholar explains, "Mindfulness in the field of communication has mainly been considered in terms of how consciously people plan their approach to a communication exchange… which differs substantially from the construct of mindfulness within the fields of psychology and medicine."[23] Recently scientific fields have been merging, finding the same conclusions across disciplines: People who are self-reflective, open-minded, and unattached to communicative outcomes experience better relationships and overall personal health. In contrast, folks who operate on "autopilot," not considering how they construct their own realities through their own thought patterns, are often dissatisfied with their relationships because they tend to repeat the same ineffective communication behaviors over and over again. To this end, a large portion of this text is dedicated not to how you speak, but how you think. Our cognitive processes birth our communication, so in order to communicate effectively you must first learn the thoughts behind your words and actions. Otherwise, using communication skills is simply an exercise in planning messages, not changing relationships. To learn anything from this course, you must first attempt to shut off autopilot and begin to engage in mindfulness.

DEVELOPING REALISTIC EXPECTATIONS

Part of communication competence is having realistic expectations. This course can help you in certain ways and not in others. As stated above, *you should not expect to obtain unconscious competence during the span of this course.* Instead, consider this class an experiment where you are learning new strategies and testing them to determine whether you would like to keep them.

Another important expectation is realizing that just because you are learning about communication does not mean every one around you wants to learn, as well. *Do not plan to teach your partner, friend, or family members these skills, unless they ask you to.* Most people want to learn how to communicate better, but they do not want to be "taught" by their communication partner. In fact, most people become quite resentful when their communication partner takes on the role of "communication expert" simply because they are taking a class.

Something else to keep in mind as you enter into this course is that you should not expect to be responsible for more than your share of the relationship. *The most you can do in any interpersonal relationship is 100% of your 50%.* Nothing more. You cannot do someone else's work for him or her, and each person has to be responsible for his or her half of the relationship. If another person is completely unwilling to do his or her share of work, there is nothing you can do except decide whether or not the situation is acceptable to you.

In light of these considerations, it's also worth pointing out that more communication is not necessarily better. There is such a thing as "over communicating." We are often tempted to send every message that comes to mind because the modern world offers so many methods for communication: text message, email, IM, and Twitter, just to name a few. Throughout this text you'll read about some challenges presented by these new communication technologies as we try to achieve communication competence.

One final thing to remember is that *learning about interpersonal communication will not solve all of the problems in a relationship*. Not all problems in relationships are communication problems. There are certain relationships that cannot work out despite strong efforts by both parties. On the other hand, there are many otherwise wonderful relationships that could be dramatically improved with the addition of a few basic skills for communicating. Hopefully the information you learn here will give you a choice about what kind of communicator you want to be, and give you the tools you need to create the kinds of relationships you desire in your life.

INTERPERSONAL COMMUNICATION FOR SOCIAL CHANGE

The Great Divide

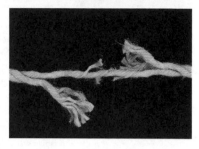

It was only October and Rebecca was already starting to think about the upcoming holidays. Every time she thought about going home to visit her family, she vacillated between feelings of dread and panic. One thing was for sure, if she decided to go home at all this year she wouldn't be bringing her boyfriend, Raul. There's no way she could endure another discussion at the dinner table with her conservative uncle, knowing that Raul's parents were undocumented. And how was she supposed to tolerate her grandma, with all her religious pro-life rhetoric? Just thinking about it made Rebecca want to scream. How could she even be related to these people?

It's an interesting time to be alive in America. With no end in sight to our tumultuous political climate, people across the country report feeling more tense than ever. Regardless of which side they are on, most folks seem to agree that they feel concerned about the future of our divided nation.

College and university classrooms are natural arenas for debate and discussion, so teachers across academic disciplines have been giving a lot of thought to our roles as facilitators and educators in these strange times. Bayard Rustin, civil rights activist, summarized the role of teachers, writing, "The chief task now, it seems to me, is for teachers to ensure quality education, to foster the ideal of communication and compassion among all the young people of our society, and to view the teaching process as an integral part of the effort to bring about social change and social justice in our society."

This call to action is especially relevant to those of us who study and teach interpersonal communication because a natural side effect of greater tolerance and understanding in our interpersonal relationships is improved tolerance and understanding in our society as a whole. This sidebar, Interpersonal Communication for Social Change (ICSC), will underscore the link between interpersonal skills and intergroup harmony. In each chapter, the ICSC sidebar will try to explain how communication changes we make at the micro level (in our interpersonal relationships), can affect what occurs at the macro level (in society). The following diagram shows how real change must first occur at the personal and interpersonal levels before societies and cultures can permanently change for the better.

Four Levels of Change[24]

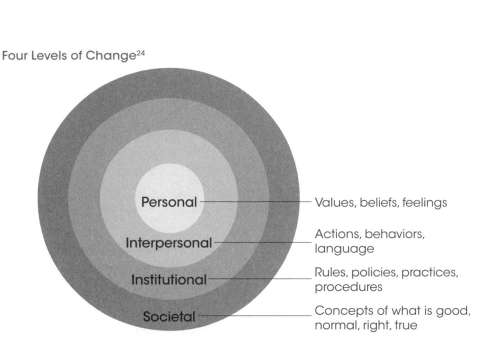

Personal —————— Values, beliefs, feelings

Interpersonal —————— Actions, behaviors, language

Institutional —————— Rules, policies, practices, procedures

Societal —————— Concepts of what is good, normal, right, true

To be clear, we shouldn't wait for interpersonal change in order to implement policy changes that will create a more equitable society. However, the diagram above shows that actions, behaviors, and language at the interpersonal level ultimately affect what we consider good, normal, right, and true in our society. Masterful communicators have known this for centuries. Take, for example, one of the greatest teachers of conflict resolution in history: Nelson Mandela. Mandela worked with both Black and White South Africans to end more than fifty years of legalized racial oppression and injustice known as Apartheid. Mandela even found a way to reconcile with his oppressors after being unjustly jailed for seventeen years. His unique approach to managing societal conflict was actually interpersonal. Mandela believed that each individual must first strive to improve his or her own values and beliefs at the personal level, then apply these values in the form of actions and behaviors in interpersonal relationships. Finally, he believed that these personal and interpersonal practices could be applied to tense and contemptuous relationships between dissimilar groups of people.

Taking this course will not turn you into a master mediator of Mandela's caliber. However, as you navigate the shift from unconscious incompetence to conscious competence, the changes in your communication will have an impact beyond your interpersonal relationships. Please make sure to read the Interpersonal Communication for Social Change sidebar in each chapter to learn how.

Reflection

1. Think of a person in your life whose perspective you have a hard time understanding.

2. Think about someone who seems to have a hard time seeing things from your perspective.

3. Do you tend to believe that it's better to cut ties with people with whom we strongly disagree on important things (de-friend them on Facebook, stop sending holiday cards, etc.)?

4. Do you think people can coexist peacefully even though they have fundamentally different sets of values?

CHAPTER SUMMARY

Learning about interpersonal communication can be a daunting process if you do not know what to expect. This chapter outlined what is meant by the study of interpersonal communication. You learned how it compares with other forms of communication we study in the field such as small group communication, intercultural communication, and public speaking. Interpersonal communication is unique because it involves interactions with significant others in your life with whom you have meaningful relationships. We discussed the characteristics of interpersonal relationships, namely that they are interdependent, involve relational maintenance, and are governed by behavioral rules. The principles of interpersonal communication were explained, specifically that it is inescapable, irreversible, and unrepeatable.

The second half of the chapter described the evolution of communication models, showing that over time our understanding of interpersonal communication has changed from viewing it as a simple send/receive process to a complex, multi-channeled process of simultaneous influence, complicated by both noise and context. Lastly, the concept of communication competence was explained, so that you can assess where you are in the four-phase process of becoming a competent communicator. The chapter concluded with guidelines for establishing realistic expectations for what you will get out of a course in interpersonal communication.

CHAPTER ACTIVITIES

TEST YOUR UNDERSTANDING

True or False

_T_ 1. Conscious competence is when you behave competently, but it takes a lot of effort.

_T_ 2. The Message Transfer Model of communication views communication as a linear process.

_T_ 3. In the next few years, ethnic and racial minority students are expected to make up almost 50% of the college student population.

Multiple Choice: Circle the best answer choice.

1. Ways of improving your own interpersonal communication include all of the following EXCEPT:

    A. Considering your effectiveness

    B. Becoming a more egocentric communicator

    C. Considering your appropriateness

    D. Becoming more adaptable

    E. All of the above are ways to improve interpersonal communication

2. "Sexting" or sending sexually explicit words or images over text messages can result in:

    A. Child pornography charges for senders under 18 or recipients of their messages

    B. Appearance on the sex offender registration for people over 18 who receive a sext from someone under 18 or send a sext to someone under 18

    C. Public humiliation

    D. A permanent record of the message

    E. All of the above

3. Mindfulness includes all of the following EXCEPT:

    A. Being unattached to communication outcomes

    B. Being self-reflective

    C. Creating pre-formulated messages

    D. Being open-minded

    E. Adapting to the situation

**Answers are listed at the end of this section before the references.

Short Answer

1. Describe at least three different areas of study in the field of communication.

   • Intrapersonal Comm, Communication w/ yourself throug thinking e Self talking.

   _____

   _____

   _____

   _____

   _____

   _____

   _____

   _____

   _____

2. Define interpersonal communication and compare and contrast it with impersonal communication.

   _____

   _____

   _____

   _____

   _____

   _____

   _____

   _____

   _____

   _____

   _____

   _____

3. Explain the characteristics of interpersonal communication.

    _____

    _____

    _____

    _____

    _____

    _____

    _____

    _____

    _____

    _____

    _____

    _____

4. Compare and contrast the three models used to describe the process of interpersonal communication.

    _____

    _____

    _____

    _____

    _____

    _____

    _____

    _____

    _____

    _____

5. Explain why it is useful to study interpersonal communication.

_____

_____

_____

_____

_____

_____

_____

_____

_____

_____

_____

_____

_____

_____

_____

_____

_____

_____

_____

_____

_____

_____

IN-CLASS ACTIVITY

Pre-Course Relationship Analysis

Think of two important interpersonal relationships in your life.

Relationship 1 (list person): _____

What specific improvements could be made in this relationship?

_____

_____

_____

Which improvements can you control?

_____

_____

_____

Which improvements can you not control?

_____

_____

_____

Assess your own communication competence in this relationship (1 is poor, 5 is excellent)

My communication with_____

...is effective (I get what I need and want from our interactions)

     1   2   3   4   5

...is appropriate (I am sincere, I do not regret my communication)

     1   2   3   4   5

...demonstrates adaptability (I do not have a pre-formulated approach, I change my communication depending on its effectiveness)

     1   2   3   4   5

...shows conversational involvement (I show that I care with verbal statements and nonverbal feedback)

     1   2   3   4   5

...shows good conversational management (I ask questions, I make sure the other person speaks as much as I do)

     1   2   3   4   5

Relationship 2 (list person): _____

What specific improvements could be made in this relationship?

_____

_____

_____

_____

Which improvements can you control?

_____

_____

_____

_____

Which improvements can you not control?

_____

_____

_____

_____

Assess your own communication competence in this relationship (1 is poor, 5 is excellent)

My communication with _____

...is effective (I get what I need and want from our interactions)

     1   2   3   4   5

...is appropriate (I am sincere, I do not regret my communication)

     1   2   3   4   5

...demonstrates adaptability (I do not have a pre-formulated approach, I change my communication depending on its effectiveness)

     1   2   3   4   5

...shows conversational involvement (I show that I care with verbal statements and nonverbal feedback)

     1   2   3   4   5

...shows good conversational management (I ask questions, I make sure the other person speaks as much as I do)

     1   2   3   4   5

SKILL PRACTICE: ASKING FOR FEEDBACK ABOUT YOUR COMMUNICATION

What Is the Goal of Asking for Feedback About Your Communication?

Asking others how they perceive your communication will allow for a more thorough understanding of your own strengths and weaknesses. In addition, learning to ask others about their perception is the first step of many skills you'll learn later in this class, so this is excellent practice.

How Do You Do It?

1. Ask someone you trust if he or she would be willing to help you analyze your communication so that you can identify your strengths and areas that need improvement.

   Who is the person you chose? _My Mom_

2. Instead of opening the floor for a general critique of your communication, tell your partner that you are interested in feedback on four particular aspects of your communication:

   - Is it *effective* (i.e., do you make your point or your desired outcome clear)?

   What did he/she say? _Yes, but you are very quiet._

   - Is it *appropriate* (i.e., are you sensitive and responsive to the feelings and attitude of the listener)?

   What did he/she say? _absolutley_

   - Is it *adaptive* (i.e., do you change what isn't working and are you open to new approaches)?

   What did he/she say? _"You're very easy going, If you know something isn't working you change it, you're very open minded"_

   - Is it *involved* (i.e., do you give nonverbal feedback, self-disclose, and ask questions)?

   What did he/she say? _I always answer, I ask a cot of questions_

3. Identify which particular areas you'd like to improve, based on the feedback from your trusted partner. You may want to compare your partner's perception with your own assessment in the Skill Building section of this chapter.

   _____

   _____

   _____

_____ _____
Name   Instructor

HOMEWORK ACTIVITY

VISITING A CHAT ROOM

Interpersonal communication is governed by rules, and these rules can be extended to online interaction, as well. Select a chat room and log on to observe for a while. When you are comfortable with the environment, look for evidence of a social rule. Next, enter the chat and get involved. If possible, create an opportunity to break the rule you have observed. List your findings here and bring them to class for discussion.

_____

_____

_____

_____

_____

_____

_____

_____

_____

_____

_____

_____

Answers to True/False and Multiple Choice

1. True

2. True

3. True

1. B

2. E

3. C

REFERENCES

[1]Dance, F. & Larson, C.E. (1972). *Speech communication: Concepts and behaviors*. New York: Holt, Rinehart and Winston, Inc.

[2]Duck, S. (1985). Social and personal relationships. In M.L. Knapp and G.R. Miller (Eds.) *Handbook of interpersonal communication* (pp. 665–686). Beverly Hills, CA: Sage.

[3]Shimanoff, S. (1980). *Communication rules: Theory and research*. Beverly Hills: Sage Publications.

[4]Watzlawick, P., Beavin, J., and Jackson, D. (1967). *Pragmatics of human communication*. New York: Norton.

[5]Shannon, C.E. & Weaver, W. (1949): *A mathematical model of communication*. Urbana, IL: University of Illinois Press.

[6]Schramm, W. (1954). How communication works. In W. Schramm (Ed.), *The process and effects of mass communication*. Urbana, IL: University of Illinois Press.

[7]Watzlawick, P., Beavin, J., & Jackson, D. (1967). *Pragmatics of human communication*. New York: W. W. Norton.

[8]Lenhart, A. (December, 2009). Teens and Sexting. *The Pew Internet and American Life Project*. Retrieved January 10, 2009 from http://www.pewinternet.org/Reports/2009/Teens-and-Sexting.aspx

[9]MTV-AP Digital Abuse Study, Executive Summary (2009). Retrieved January 10, 2009 from http://www.athinline.org/MTV-AP_Digital_Abuse_Study_Executive_Summary.pdf

[10]Schutz, W. (1958). FIRO: *A three-dimensional theory of interpersonal behavior.* New York: Holt, Rinehart & Winston.

[11]Korbin, F.E. & Hendershot, G.E. (1977). Do family ties reduce mortality? *Journal of Marriage and the Family 59*, 143–155.

[12]Phillips, D. P. (1972). Deathday and birthday: an unexpected connection. In J. M. Tanur (Ed.): *Statistics: A guide to the unknown*. San Francisco, CA: Holden-Day.

[13]Harlow, H.F. (1964). Early social deprivation and later behavior in the monkey. In A. Abrams, H.H. Gurner & J.E.P. Tomal (Eds.) *Unfinished tasks in the behavioral sciences*. Baltimore: Williams & Wilkins.

[14]Winsor, J.L., Curtis, D.B., & Stephens, R.D. (1997). National preferences in business and communication education: A survey update. *Journal of the Association for Communication Administrators, 3*, 170–179.

[15]Carnevale, A.P. & Frye, R.A. (2000). *Crossing the Great Divide: Can We Achieve Equity When Generation Y Goes to College?* Princeton, NJ: Educational Testing Services.

[16]Beatty, M. J., McCroskey, J. C., & Heisel, A. D. (1998). Communication apprehension as temperamental expression: A communibiological paradigm. *Communication Monographs, 65*, 197–219.

[17]Bandura, A. (1977). *Social learning theory*. New York: General Learning Press.

[18]Bandura, A., Ross, D., & Ross, S. A. (1961). Transmission of aggressions through imitation of aggressive models. *Journal of Abnormal and Social Psychology, 63*, 575–582.

[19]See http://www3.georgetown.edu/departments/psychology/resources/researchmethods/examples/9304.html

[20]Spitzberg, B. H., & Cupach, W. R. (1984). *Interpersonal communication competence*. Beverly Hills, CA: Sage.

[21]Howell, W.C. & Fleishman, E.A. (Eds.) (1982). *Human performance and productivity. Vol. 2: Information processing and decision making*. Hillsdale, NJ: Erlbaum.

[22]Affifi, T.D., Granger, D.A., Denes, A., Joseph, A. & Aldeis, D. (2011). Parents' communication skills and adolescents' salivary a-Amylase and Cortisol response patterns. *Communication Monographs, 78*, 273–295.

[23]Huston, D.C., Garland, E.L., & Farb, A.S. (2011). Mechanisms of mindfulness in communication training. *Journal of Applied Communication Research, 39*(4), 407.

[24]Adapted from Pace, K. (July, 2016) Can the practice of mindfulness reduce unconscious racial bias? Retrieved from http://msue.anr.msu.edu/news/can_the_practice_of_mindfulness_reduce_unconscious_racial_bias

CHAPTER 2

Nonverbal Messages

One must view the world through the eye in one's heart rather than just trust the eyes in one's head.
—Mary Crow Dog

Learning Objectives

After studying this chapter, you should be able to:

1. *Explain the differences between the verbal and nonverbal channels of interpersonal communication.*
2. *Explain the characteristics of nonverbal communication.*
3. *Describe the nonverbal channels of interpersonal communication.*
4. *Describe how culture and gender impact our use and interpretation of nonverbal communication.*
5. *Explain how media richness affects nonverbal communication.*

Many people use the term "body language" as synonymous with nonverbal communication, but nonverbal communication is much more complex than this. **Nonverbal communication** is any communicative behavior other than written or spoken language that creates meaning for someone. It makes sense with this broad definition that nonverbal behaviors comprise the majority of our messages. Communication theorists have tried to account for the specific percentage of meaning derived from the verbal and nonverbal channels. Mehrabian concluded that as little as 7% of the emotional meaning of our messages is communicated explicitly through verbal channels, meaning that up to 93% of our meaning is transmitted nonverbally.[25] Regardless of the specific percentage, scholars unanimously agree that the majority of our messages come through nonverbal channels.

This chapter will outline how nonverbal communication is distinct, and highlight some of the types of nonverbal behaviors that we use to transmit messages both intentionally and unintentionally. You'll learn some specific information about nonverbal channels such as the face and body, and some of the meanings we assign to various nonverbal behaviors. Finally, an analysis of mediated interpersonal communication will help you understand the challenges that occur as we lose access to nonverbal cues through such mediated channels as the telephone, email, and instant messaging.

FUNCTIONS OF NONVERBAL BEHAVIOR

Nonverbal behavior serves several communicative functions to help us get messages across effectively.[26] Of course, nonverbal behaviors can work by themselves by *substituting* for a spoken message. When someone asks you a question and you shrug your shoulders in response without saying a word, you have substituted a verbal response for a nonverbal one. Even more often, nonverbal messages can help clarify the verbal message through repeating, complementing and accenting. Nonverbal behaviors are *repeating* when they communicate the exact same thing as the verbal message. For example, when you say "The beach is North of here," you may also point your finger in the direction to which you are referring. Nonverbals can also be *complementing*, meaning that they add meaning in addition to what is being said verbally. When you tell a friend you ate a huge piece of cake and you make the size of the slice with your hands, you are complementing the spoken message. We also use nonverbals for *accenting* the verbal message by emphasizing a word, touching the person with whom we are communicating, or pounding our fist to make the point. A final way we use nonverbals to ensure smooth communication is by *regulating*. Regulating behaviors are nonverbals that help the flow of conversation. You may lean forward to show when you want to say something; if you are bored by the other person, you may yawn or look at your watch; if you disagree you might furrow your brow.

Nonverbal behaviors can also be used in ways that may add confusion to the message. Often nonverbals are *contradicting*, meaning that they send the opposite message of what someone is saying with words. If you roll your eyes while you say you are sorry, you are contradicting the verbal message with your obvious display of annoyance or insincerity. Finally, nonverbals can be used for *deceiving*, or sending an intentionally false message. If you smile and nod when a friend asks if you like her hideous dress, you are deceiving with your nonverbals. You'll learn more about deceptive communication in the next section.

CHARACTERISTICS OF NONVERBAL COMMUNICATION

NONVERBAL MESSAGES ARE BELIEVABLE

Although they operate together, there are some characteristics that make nonverbal communication different than spoken words. For one, nonverbal messages are more believable. We have learned through experience that people do not always say what they mean, and we often think that we can detect someone's "real" meaning if we pay close attention to **leakage cues**, or nonverbal behaviors that indicate someone might be lying. This idea has been especially popular in the deception detection literature. During the Clinton-Lewinsky scandal when former President Bill Clinton made his televised statement to the American public that he "Did not have sexual relations with that woman," experts and novices alike were scrounging to detect anything in his behavior that revealed dishonesty. Unfortunately, it is very difficult to become an expert in deception detection for several reasons. First, good liars often know which nonverbal cues to control, which they have conveniently learned from experience (when your mom told you to look her in the eye to show her you weren't lying, you made a mental note to maintain eye contact when lying in the future!). Second, we are usually only good at detecting dishonesty from people we know, because we sense when their behavior is different from normal; we have no foundation for what is normal for people we don't know and could easily mistake their normal behavior for lying, or their lying behavior for truth. Finally, people are so unique that each individual's leakage cues are different. Some people might tend to include too many details when they are lying, others will say "um" too much (again, another reason why knowing the "normal" behavior of the person helps).

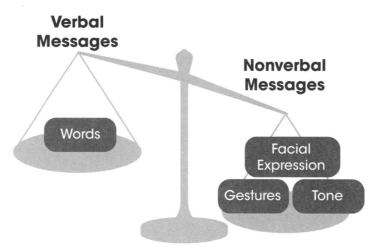

Figure 2.0. Nonverbal messages often carry more meaning than verbal messages.

There are some cues that are worth considering when trying to decode deception. Although most people have learned to look their target in the eye when they are lying, there are other less conscious eye behaviors that can give away a liar. Research suggests that liars blink less often than normal when lying and more often than normal immediately after they have told the lie.[27] This clue depends on your knowledge of what is "normal" for the person you suspect is lying. Being

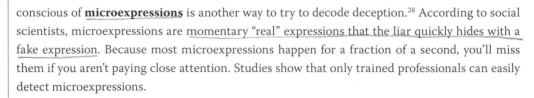

conscious of **microexpressions** is another way to try to decode deception.[28] According to social scientists, microexpressions are momentary "real" expressions that the liar quickly hides with a fake expression. Because most microexpressions happen for a fraction of a second, you'll miss them if you aren't paying close attention. Studies show that only trained professionals can easily detect microexpressions.

Because of our personal idiosyncrasies, there is no dictionary of nonverbal behavior that the average person can study to detect lying across the board (although some pop-psychology books would have you believe so). If you intend to become a lay lie detector, try to utilize these suggestions, but keep in mind that there is no certainty when it comes to uncovering untruthful behavior:

- Realize that to detect deception, you must know what the target does when he or she is *not* lying. This is called baseline behavior.

- Try to look for behaviors that are less likely to be overtly controlled by the liar, such as blinking.

- Look for small instances of microexpressions that are different from the controlled expression that lasts longer.

NONVERBAL MESSAGES ARE CONTINUOUS

Another way in which nonverbal and verbal messages differ is that nonverbal messages are continuous. Words are discrete entities that have a beginning and an end; that is, we can easily point out when someone is talking and when they are not. In contrast, nonverbal cues occur in a continuous stream that has no set beginning and end, so they are difficult to categorize and interpret. You may stop using your tone of voice, but all the while you are still gesturing. Once you stop gesturing, you are still communicating nonverbally through your posture, use of space, and what you are wearing. As such, there is no end to your nonverbal communication, which goes hand in hand with the next characteristic.

NONVERBAL MESSAGES ARE MULTI-CHANNELED

An additional reason why nonverbal messages are distinct is that nonverbal cues are multi-channeled; they come from a variety of sources simultaneously. Although you develop an overall "impression" of the message being delivered through the combination of channels, you can only actually attend to one nonverbal cue at a time when you are trying to categorize them. This may explain why nonverbal messages speak more "loudly" than messages from the verbal channel: there are more channels occurring at once and therefore there is more information, even when we cannot pinpoint exactly where it is coming from.

By now, nonverbal communication may seem quite complicated. One way to make it easier to understand is to break it down into sub-channels, or categories of nonverbal cues. The next section will highlight the various categories of nonverbal communication so that you can better understand your own and other's nonverbal messages.

Review! Characteristics of Nonverbal Communication	
Nonverbal communication is more believable than verbal communication:	We often pay greater attention to it when trying to determine the real meaning of someone's message.
Nonverbal communication is continuous:	There is no start and stop to it.
Nonverbal communication is multi-channeled:	It comes through several channels at once.

INFORMATION WE GATHER FROM NONVERBAL CUES

As you've learned, nonverbal communication is particularly revealing because it is a *less conscious* reflection of one's attitude toward others. Although we gain lots of information from nonverbal cues, we synthesize and interpret these cues along three primary dimensions: immediacy, arousal, and dominance.[29]

IMMEDIACY

We tend to take note of the immediacy shown by other peoples' nonverbal behaviors. **Immediacy cues** are behaviors that communicate friendliness, attraction, and liking. We gravitate toward people and things we like and nonverbally move away from those we dislike. There are several dimensions of immediacy. *Involvement* is indicated by directness of gaze and body orientation, closer distance, and positive feedback, such as nodding of the head and smiling. Altercentrism, or *pleasantness*, is the level of attentiveness, receptiveness, and adaptability toward the other during conversation. Pleasantness is communicated through a warm and friendly voice and interested body orientation as well as an absence of nonverbal hostility (such as aggressive gestures), contempt (such as eye rolling), and defensiveness (such as putting hands up). *Expressiveness* is the degree to which communicators are dynamic and animated. Nonverbal behaviors that elicit positive evaluations of expressiveness include facial and gestural animation.[30] Non-immediacy behaviors can include closed body orientation, crossed arms, or tense facial expressions, among others.

INTERPERSONAL SKILLS ACROSS CONTEXTS

Communicating with Elderly Patients

Elderly people face a likelihood of increasingly frequent exposure to doctors and healthcare providers as they age. Communication researchers are interested in discovering how healthcare experiences can either help or harm elderly patients. Recent studies reveal a strong link between health care providers' nonverbal communication and the efficacy of their therapy with older patients.[31] In one study, physical therapists were videotaped during a session with a client. A team of non-experts rated the therapists nonverbal communication on levels of expressiveness and distancing. Expressiveness was defined as facial changes, smiling, nodding and frowning. Distancing included patterns of not smiling and frequent looking away from the client. The judges' ratings were then correlated with the clients' physical, cognitive, and psychological functioning during three stages of treatment: at admission, at discharge, and at 3 months after discharge. Researchers found that the therapists' nonverbal distancing behaviors were strongly correlated with short-term and long-term decreases in their clients' functioning both physically and cognitively, while expressiveness was associated with improvements in functioning.

AROUSAL

We can also detect the arousal of our communication partners. **Arousal cues** show interest and excitement through vocal cues, facial expressions, and gestures. Arousal is communicated through forward lean, eyebrow raise, and a nod of the head. There are also other cues of arousal that are less easily detected, such as increased heart rate, sweating, and dilated pupils. When you are nonverbally aroused it means that your nonverbal behaviors are reactive to what the other person says and does. Imagine the scenario of a person talking to her partner at the dinner table about a problem at work while the partner browses a magazine, uttering "Sure, uh huh." This is a non-reactive response, showing lack of interest and excitement.

In contrast, researchers find that too much arousal indicates an anxious or nervous communication environment. The level of anxiety, or the *relaxedness*, refers to the level of tension and discomfort communicated by the participants. When someone is tense it often manifests as vocal and postural rigidity and the use of adaptors, such as fidgeting.[32] From these cues we may detect nervousness, anxiety, or dishonesty.

DOMINANCE

Finally, **dominance cues** communicate status, position, importance, and control.[33] We communicate dominance through the increased use of space, more direct eye contact, initiating touch, increased vocal volume, lower pitch, greater range of pitch, and increased interruptions. Dominant body orientation can include pointing, hovering over the other, standing with hands on hips, and an expanded chest. When one partner approaches the other to talk about a conflict with her hands on her hips, speaking in a loud voice, while pointing her finger, she is showing dominance. We often avoid dominance cues when we like someone because we want to send a message of equality. Thus, dominant nonverbal behaviors are often considered unfriendly or aggressive.

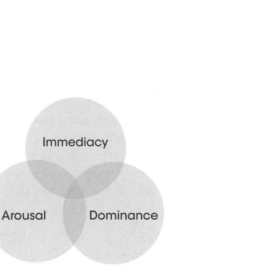

Figure 2.1. Nonverbal immediacy cues, arousal cues, and dominance cues sometimes overlap.

WATCH AND LEARN

View a TED Talk on nonverbal communication by typing this into your browser: TED Talk body language shapes who you are.

Review! Information We Gather from Nonverbal Cues	
Immediacy cues:	Nonverbal behaviors that communicate liking and involvement.
Arousal cues:	Nonverbal behaviors that show feelings of interest and excitement.
Dominance cues:	Nonverbal behaviors that communicate status, position, importance, and control.

MINDFUL MEDIATED COMMUNICATION

Safety First

Many of the safety issues surrounding the use of technology have to do with "paying attention," otherwise known as engaging in nonverbal arousal. Perhaps you've found yourself in situations like these:

- Even though you know it's a bad idea, you answer a cell phone call while driving and nearly hit a cyclist.
- While walking down the street texting, you bump into a pedestrian.

Neither of these situations would have existed a generation ago. New communication technologies call for an amendment to our traditional notions of arousal. Paying attention to what's in front of you, *instead* of paying attention to the person with whom you are communicating via technology, could mean the difference between life and death.

Talking on a cell phone while driving is just as dangerous as driving under the influence of alcohol or drugs. Cell phone use while driving (hand held or hands free) lengthens a driver's reaction as much as having a blood alcohol concentration at the legal limit of .08%.[34] In the U.S. alone, drivers distracted by cell phones cause 2,600 deaths and 330,000 injuries every year.[35] Even a hands-free device doesn't eliminate the risks of DWT (driving while texting). Drivers carrying on a phone conversation are 18% slower to react to brake lights. They also take 17% longer to regain the speed they lost when they braked.[36]

Text messaging has posed an even greater hazard on the road than conversing. One-fifth of experienced adult drivers in the United States send text messages while driving.[37] Studies have found that texting while driving causes a 400% increase in time spent with eyes off the road. Drivers who are sending or reading a text message spent about five seconds looking at their devices before a crash or near crash, allowing them to travel more than 100 yards at typical highway speeds with their eyes off the road.[38] There are clearly some serious considerations for proper use of communication technology. The continuing development of new technologies makes it even more important to think critically when choosing your own behavior. Risking offending someone on the other end of the text or phone is worth it if it means paying attention and reacting quickly to what's in front of you.

CATEGORIES OF NONVERBAL BEHAVIOR

KINESICS

When people use the term "body language," they are referring to **kinesics**, which is the study of human movement, posture, and gesture. Kinesics can be further divided into several categories, according to researchers Ekman & Friesen, who spent an extensive amount of time analyzing human body movement.[39]

Emblems are bodily cues—often in the form of hand gestures—that have a specific and commonly understood meaning in a given culture and may even substitute for a word or phrase. The "peace" sign (✌) is an example of an emblem. Note, however, that this emblem is culturally relative, which is typical of emblems: they usually mean something different depending on the culture in which they are used. This particular emblem can actually be quite offensive in some cultures, signifying a derogatory slur or insult. Other emblems that are culturally relative include the thumbs-up sign and the a-okay sign. President Nixon make a historical emblematic faux pas when he used the OK sign (👌) to a Latin American audience, and quickly learned that it meant something quite dirty to his hosts. Make sure you ask the meaning of these gestures before you use them on foreign soil!

Another category of bodily cues called **illustrators** are nonverbal behaviors that accompany a verbal message and either contradict, accent, or complement it. A typical example of an illustrator is when someone uses their hands to emphasize the words "this big," (for example, in describing the fish you caught, or slice of pie you ate). Illustrators actually help encoders remember their own

messages better. In one study, people who used illustrators to emphasize their verbal message were able to recall the message up to 20% more than those who communicated without illustrating the message nonverbally.[40]

Adaptors are bodily cues that help people adapt to a situation by channeling excess energy, such as excitement or nervousness, through a bodily movement. When someone taps a pencil on his desk or twirls her hair, they are using adaptors. Adaptors are often habitual, meaning we tend to latch onto a particular behavior and repeat it. Think for a moment about what adaptors you use when you have too much energy or anxiety, such as when you are speaking to someone who makes you nervous.

Regulators are nonverbal messages that help to control the flow of communication between people during an interaction. In a formal, larger context, raising one's hand to ask a question would act as a regulator, but in interpersonal interactions we use other cues to regulate the conversation such as opening your mouth as if ready to speak, furrowing your brow when you'd like to express that you are about to disagree, or leaning forward to show you have something to contribute.

Finally, **affect displays** are nonverbal bodily behaviors that communicate emotion. Emotion can come through a combination of nonverbal channels, such as the way you walk, hold your arms, or posture yourself. We pay special attention to affect displays, whether consciously or unconsciously. People who are not comfortable saying how they really feel often use affect displays to get their message across. When the nonverbal message intentionally contradicts the verbal message, it can come across as passive aggressive.

FACIAL CUES

The head and face are obviously a part of the body, and some of the examples of kinesics given earlier take place in the facial channel. This channel is so expressive; however, that it deserves a category of its own, called **facial cues.** Your face is capable of producing over 250,000 different expressions, according to researchers Ekman and Friesen. These scholars tested the universality of emotional expression by showing pictures of various expressions to people all over the world, asking them what emotion was signified by the expression they were seeing. From their studies they concluded that all facial expressions are derived from six primary emotions, and each of these six are recognized universally: sadness, anger, disgust, fear, surprise, and happiness. However, cultures vary in their level of expressiveness of these emotions. For example, members of Japanese culture are often encouraged to show less emotion through their facial expressions, while North Americans tend to value facial animation and expressiveness.[41] Regarding sex differences in facial expression, research indicates that women tend to be slightly better judges of the meaning behind a person's facial cues.[42]

Perhaps the most expressive part of the face is the eye area, which is why the study of nonverbal eye behavior has its own name: **oculesics.** Not only does the shape we make with our eyes reveal

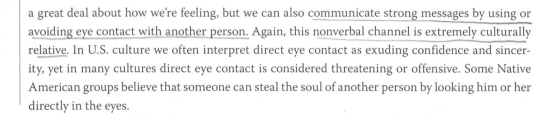

a great deal about how we're feeling, but we can also communicate strong messages by using or avoiding eye contact with another person. Again, this nonverbal channel is extremely culturally relative. In U.S. culture we often interpret direct eye contact as exuding confidence and sincerity, yet in many cultures direct eye contact is considered threatening or offensive. Some Native American groups believe that someone can steal the soul of another person by looking him or her directly in the eyes.

PROXEMICS

Proxemics are how we communicate meaning through our use of personal distance. Edward Hall identified four zones that people in Western cultures use to define their relationships with others.[43] **Intimate space** is the zone of space most often reserved for intimate interactions, and it ranges from zero to one and one-half feet from the individual. **Personal space** is the zone of space normally used in a conversation with friends, families,

colleagues, and even sometimes strangers, which ranges from one and one-half to four feet from the individual. **Social space** is the zone of distance typically used during group interactions, ranging from four feet to twelve feet. Finally, **public space** is the distance most often used in one-to-many interactions, such as public speaking, which extends twelve feet or more from the individual. The zone we choose communicates our relationship with another person, our interactive goals, and the spatial norms of our culture. The spatial zones you find comfortable may also have to do with your unique personality. You may have heard people refer to their individual tolerance for closeness with others as their "personal bubble." Think about the size of your personal bubble and how that affects your interactions with others.

Figure 2.2. Hall's Spatial Zones.

HAPTICS

Haptics, or touch, is another nonverbal channel through which we communicate meaning. We use touch to emphasize our words, to communicate affection, to assert ourselves or dominate others, and to manage interactions.

Each individual has a different tolerance and need for touch, just as we each have a differently sized "personal bubble." You probably have friends whom you consider very affectionate, and others who are noticeably "stand offish" when it comes to touch. Researchers have found that *touch avoidance* tends to correlate with some other communication problems such as communication apprehension and low self-disclosure. These tendencies are only problematic insofar as they impede the desired development of interpersonal relationships.[44]

Recent research suggests that physical touch can "speak" volumes, even if it lasts only a few seconds. A supportive pat on the back, a high five, or even an inappropriate graze can be more powerful than words, eliciting a strong emotional reaction in the receiver. Experts argue that when it comes to touch, actions speak louder than words because touch is the first language we learn as infants.[45]

The evidence supporting the power of touch spans across contexts. Research shows that massage can alleviate negative states of mind and strengthen bonds between loved ones.[46] At school, students are twice as likely to volunteer and speak up in class if they have received supportive touch on the back or arm from their teacher. Even successful sports teams tend to engage in more touching of teammates than unsuccessful teams. One study ranked the touchiest teams, discovering that league's top teams, the Boston Celtics and the Los Angeles Lakers, touched each other most often, while the highly unsuccessful Sacramento Kings and Charlotte Bobcats ranked amongst the lowest in touch.[47]

APPEARANCE AND ARTIFACTS

Appearance serves as yet another category in the nonverbal channel. American culture places a high value upon how much people weigh, the style of their hair, and the clothes they wear. In fact, in dating scenarios, appearance is usually assessed within the first three seconds of meeting, and plays a larger role in determining a second date than common interests and values.

Height seems to make an especially "big" impression. Research shows that tall presidential candidates are historically more likely to win than short ones, and tall interviewees are more likely to get the job than their short competitors.[48] If you happen to be on the shorter side, you may find hope in new research conducted at the Virtual Human Interaction Lab at Stanford. These studies show that people who create a tall avatar are more persuasive in virtual reality interactions even if they are short in real life. Furthermore, once two communicators enter back into the "real" world, the person who had the taller avatar continues to be more persuasive, regardless of real-life height.[49]

One part of appearance is **artifacts**, which includes anything in addition to your own physical body that communicates something about you. Artifacts can include jewelry, a cell phone (what *kind* of cell phone, of course), a car (what *kind* of car, of course), your purse, backpack, hat, or any other item on your person from which people receive a message about you. Nonverbal communication through

artifacts also occurs in one's surrounding environment. The way people arrange their things in the space in which they live and work sends strong messages. Even the way buildings, offices, and residences are arranged is a form of nonverbal communication referred to as the **physical environment**, a field of study that bridges artifacts and proxemics with other communication factors.

Understanding the role of appearance and artifacts is critical to remembering that not all messages you send are intentional, and not all of the messages people interpret about you are accurate. Nonetheless, part of the reason for the axiom "you cannot *not* communicate" is due to the fact that we all display artifacts, almost all the time.

VOCALICS

Vocal cues, or **vocalics**, are the final and perhaps most misunderstood category among the nonverbal channels. Just because vocal cues come out of your mouth does not mean they are considered verbal. Remember, verbal communication is based on words and language. Vocalics include the tone, rate/speed, pitch, and volume of your words. In sum, vocalics are anything included in *how* you say what you say. As you are probably aware, *how* you say your message carries a lot more meaning than *what* you say. You can communicate any emotion with just a small inflection of your voice, including anger, disgust, sarcasm, excitement, confusion, and infinitely more. Try communicating each of the previously listed emotions using the same words: "I just love it when you do that." As you can see, we are well equipped to greatly vary the meaning of our message simply by adjusting our vocalics.

INTERPERSONAL COMMUNICATION FOR SOCIAL CHANGE

Speak No Evil, Hear No Evil

Amanda: "I just don't trust a politician with a Southern drawl. I feel like he's the kind of person who would have a Confederate flag waving outside his house."

Jonas: "I'd rather listen to that all day than endure my statistics teacher's accent. I can't understand a word he says. His voice sounds like nails on a chalkboard."

Since the 1960s researchers have been studying the effects of accents on perceptions of a speaker, concluding that people are more likely to dislike someone who has an accent different from their own. In fact, children as young as five months show discernable differences in their reactions to adults based on whether or not they have an accent, even though the baby can't speak! As children grow, their reactions to accents turn into discrimination, often deciding who they befriend. One study showed that when presented with photographs and voice recordings of potential friends, five-year-old children chose to be friends with native speakers of their own language who had no accent rather than foreign-accented speakers. Even more interesting, when asked to select the children with whom they would most want to be friends, children chose a same-race child based on photos only, but when audio was added and the same-race child spoke with an accent, they chose an other-race child with no accent. These findings suggest that an accent makes an even stronger impression than race when determining our similarities with others.

Studies on adolescents and adults show that we use accents to infer additional unrelated traits such as intelligence, warmth, and even height for individuals we have never met.[50] In one recent study, adolescents in Southern California evaluated U.S. American English–accented speakers as having more favorable personality characteristics than English speakers with a Spanish accent.[51]

This information reveals that our judgement of accents goes far beyond whether their sound is favorable or unpleasant. An accent tells us whether someone is an ingroup or outgroup member, which affects how we evaluate their personality and likability (you'll learn more about this in Chapter 5). We are less likely to evaluate someone positively if they have an accent unlike our own, which means we are also less likely to hire them, befriend them, believe them, or speak favorably about them. Think about your own perceptions of people who have an accent that is different from yours, and how it may affect your interpretations and even your communication behavior.

Reflection

1. Which accents do you find unpleasant sounding?

2. Do you ever attribute personality characteristics to a speaker because of his or her accent?

3. How would you summarize the information you just learned if you were trying to explain it to someone who was judging a speaker based on his or her accent?

4. Why do you think evil characters in movies often have a British accent? Perform an Internet search to find out!

OLFACTICS

One nonverbal channel that is becoming a central focus in attraction research is **olfactics**, which is our sense of smell. Humans can detect as many as ten thousand different compounds by smell, making us more sensitive to smell than most other mammals.[52] Unfortunately, we work against our natural drive to decipher information from smell by masking the natural smells of the body through chemical fragrances and perfumes. In doing so, we disable part of our nonverbal code, since human smells are meant to give off information that helps in mate selection and procreation. Research indicates that women tend to be the most sensitive to odors during ovulation, and that we are attracted to the smells of other people with whom our genes are most compatible.[53] You may have heard of the famous "T-shirt studies" whereby people sniff well-worn T-shirts and rate the attractiveness of the wearer based entirely on the smell. Women are most attracted to the smell of men possessing their opposite immune system, a partnership that is ideal for creating offspring with the strongest resilience to disease. Men are most attracted to the T-shirts worn by women who are ovulating, and even experience an on-the-spot increase in testosterone when sniffing the T-shirt worn by an ovulating woman.[54]

Smell is also used to inhibit attraction. Historically marginalized groups have been accused of smelling bad, an accusation that their oppressors use as evidence of their genetic or moral inferiority. Even school children use smell to evaluate each other. Calling someone "smelly" or accusing a child of stinking is the oldest form of interpersonal bullying.

Associations with smell are almost always culturally relative. Members of any given culture often share perceptions of what smells are putrid and which ones are pleasant. Americans in particular are preoccupied with smell, causing us to have a global reputation of having a non-human, or "antiseptic," smell due to our attempt to suppress natural bodily odors. Members of a cattle farming group in Ethiopia known as the Dassanetch have such a positive association with the smell of cattle that Dassanetch men are known to wash their hands in the urine of the cattle and even smear cow manure on their bodies to communicate status and fertility. Some cultures find certain foods so appealing that they use scents such as onions to perfume their bodies.[55]

We communicate a lot when we adhere to or deviate from social rules regarding smells. Like many nonverbal messages, what we communicate may or may not be intentional.

Review! The Study of Nonverbal Communication	
Kinesics:	Human bodily movement, including gestures.
Facial cues:	Communication that comes from the face through over 250,000 different expressions.
Proxemics:	Personal distance.
Haptics:	Human touch.
Appearance:	How you look, both naturally and with effort.
Artifacts:	Anything you possess or display that communicates something about you.
Vocalics:	The tone, rate/speed, pitch, and volume of your words and all non-language that comes out of your mouth.
Olfactics:	Messages we receive through smell.

NONVERBAL COMMUNICATION STYLES

Each person has a unique way of using nonverbal communication, and it's part of what makes up our individual personalities. In addition to our idiosyncratic differences, we tend to use different styles based on our culture and sometimes our gender.

CULTURE AND NONVERBAL COMMUNICATION

The culture that you associate with has an enormous impact on the meaning you assign to nonverbal cues. **Display rules** are the implicit rules we use to measure the appropriateness of different nonverbal behaviors. For example, it is a commonly understood "rule" in many Central and South American cultures that strong emotional displays are encouraged. However, in many Asian cultures, emotional displays are understood to be inappropriate. Unfortunately, we are often unaware of the display rules of cultures other than our own, so nonverbal misperceptions are common in intercultural communication settings. Here are some examples to illustrate our differences:[56]

- Proxemics: Some Middle Eastern cultures believe that two communicators should be close enough to smell each other's breath. Standing too far apart may indicate something is wrong in the relationship.

- Eye contact: Countries with greater power distance such as Japan and China engage in less direct eye contact, especially toward a superior or elder.

- Facial expression: Many Asian cultures believe that facial expression should be kept to a minimum so as not to stand out from others.

- Haptics: British citizens are cited as engaging in the least amount of touch, while Italians and Brazilians are rated as using touch the most.

- Vocalics: Although some of this pitch variance can be attributed to the size of the larynx, it has been suggested that women who live in less egalitarian cultures tend to have even higher vocal pitch than normal, and that the more a culture focuses on youth and femininity the more likely it is that the women will intentionally speak more like children than adults.

BUILDING CULTURAL COMPETENCE

The *Hijab*: A Nonverbal Statement

Standpoint theory argues that two people will likely never experience the same thing in the same way. While people who share the same gender identity, culture, or socioeconomic status may also share a similar life experience, we each have a unique "standpoint" from which we see the world. More specifically, when group memberships and attributes such as gender and culture are not shared, it's nearly impossible to see the world from the perspective of the other. An excellent example of standpoint theory in practice is the non-Muslim perception of the *hijab*, the traditional head covering worn by Muslim women. Most non-Muslim women consider the *hijab* a forced practice that acts as a tool to oppress Muslim women, but studies find that this perspective is extremely one-sided.

Thirteen Muslim American women were interviewed and asked to express their opinions and experiences with wearing the *hijab*. Each woman had both personal and social reasons for preferring to wear it, including helping to express and define their Muslim identity, reminding them of appropriate behavior, helping to resist sexual objectification, affording them more respect, helping to preserve their intimate relationships, and providing them with freedom. Two of these reasons seem in direct contrast with the non-Muslim perception of the practice: namely, resisting objectification and providing freedom.[57]

In contrast to the dominant Western perception that the *hijab* strips women of their own identity and therefore creates objectification, the women interviewed believed that by wearing the *hijab* they escaped objectification by men. By removing the emphasis on their physical appearance, these women believed that they are seen as people, as opposed to objects of desire. To them, the *hijab* eliminates the distractions created by superficial appearances and allows members of their group to focus more deeply on each other as people.

The other sentiment that non-Muslim Americans may find surprising is the women's connection between wearing the *hijab* and having freedom. Specifically, they each felt that the fashion industry controls women by dictating what they should wear and creating standards by which they are judged. The types of clothes and accessories women are expected to wear are often objectifying and exploitative, and focus too heavily on materialism and a perfect physique.

From the standpoint of the thirteen Muslim-American women interviewed, the *hijab* looks quite different than how it may be viewed by non-Muslims. By wearing the *hijab*, these women believe that they are making a nonverbal statement about their values and beliefs, which honors both their religion and their personal sense of values. From their standpoint, who are the real victims of oppression?

GENDER AND NONVERBAL COMMUNICATION

Research indicates that there are several categories of nonverbal behavior that are affected by gender. Although gender does not necessarily correlate with biological sex, most of the nonverbal research at this time still looks for differences between men and women, rather than "masculine" or "feminine" communicators. Some of the findings on the differences between men and women are the following:[58]

- Proxemics: When it comes to space, women tend to sit or stand more closely to others, and both sexes approach women more closely than they approach men. Men tend to use more space, which can be attributed to space as a function of relative power; because men have traditionally had more power in society, they have become accustomed to taking up more space.

- Eye contact: In their use of eye contact, women are more likely to prolong their gaze during conversation in a way that communicates affiliation, but men are more likely to use eye contact as a form of power through staring or glaring. Prolonged eye contact (longer than 1.18 seconds)[59] has been identified by researchers as one of the main ways LGBTQ folks indicate interest in someone of the same sex.[60]

- Facial expression: Women tend to smile more than men, and their facial expressions tend to be more expressive overall (they are also a little better at interpreting people's expressions, particularly negative ones such as anger).

- Haptics: When it comes to touch women are less likely than men to initiate it, but they use it more often to communicate support and warmth. Men are more likely to use touch to demonstrate power or status.

- Vocalics: Women generally speak at a higher pitch and a softer volume than men. Even though these differences can be physiological, often this vocalic difference stems from the caretaking nature of feminine communicators. Research shows that people are more relaxed and comforted by a higher pitch female voice than a lower pitch male voice.[61]

Now that you have gained a greater understanding of the differences between verbal and nonverbal communication, and know a little about how they combine to send messages between people, it's

time to consider what happens when one or more of these forms of communication is taken away. How does our communication change when certain nonverbal cues are absent? Questions such as this arise from the ever-changing world of technology, which both assists and hinders our ability to communicate interpersonally. Next, you'll become even more familiar about a topic with which you probably already have quite a bit of experience: mediated nonverbal communication.

SKILL BUILDING EXERCISE

Identifying Gender Expectations

Think about the most feminine and most masculine communicators you know. List the differences in their communication in each of the nonverbal channels listed:

	Masculine	Feminine
Kinesics	_____	_____
Facial Cues	_____	_____
Proxemics	_____	_____
Haptics	_____	_____
Appearance/Artifacts	_____	_____
Vocalics	_____	_____

Now consider how your expectations for masculine and feminine nonverbal behaviors affect your interpretations of others. Can you think of a recent situation where someone's nonverbal communication was not "typical" or not expected based on his or her sex?

_____

_____

_____

_____

What impact did that have on the impression you formed of this person?

_____

_____

_____

_____

MEDIATED NONVERBAL COMMUNICATION

As you learned in the first chapter, **mediated communication** is communication with others through media such as email, phone, IM or text, rather than through face-to-face encounters. Mediated communication is part verbal and part nonverbal.

MEDIA RICHNESS

Mediated communication is different from face-to-face interaction because there is less or no emphasis on nonverbal cues. If you are leaving a voicemail you still can decode vocalics, and if you are using a webcam you can decode some kinesics and facial expression. However, if you are texting or emailing, you are limited by language. To overcome this difficulty, people have developed emojis to compensate for the lack of nonverbal cues and increase shared meaning.

In addition to using emojis, people have also learned to utilize SHOUTING and *italics* to replace nonverbal vocalics. These codes are useful, but the mediated channel is still more limited than face-to-face communication when it comes to decoding another person's message.

To make sense of how these limitations affect the interpersonal nature of our communication with others, we can examine the various communication media in terms of their "richness."[62] Any given medium can be placed on a scale ranging from "high richness" to "low richness" based on four criteria: 1) the amount of feedback the communicators can receive, 2) the number of nonverbal cues the channel allows for, 3) the variety of language that communicators can use, and 4) the potential for expressing emotions and feelings. The face-to-face medium is the richest because it allows for encoding and decoding in all the channels discussed in the previous section: kinesics, facial expression, proxemics, haptics, appearance, and vocalics. Once each of these channels is unavailable, a medium starts to lose its richness. Recent research shows that even tech-savvy communicators still prefer richer channels when dealing with important interpersonal relationship issues. In long-distance relationships people commonly use email for staying in touch, but they still seem to prefer that important personal matters are discussed on the phone rather than online.[63]

The prevalence of new communication technology has resulted in an ongoing debate about the limitations of mediated communication. Many young people who feel extremely comfortable communicating via email, text, or IM find that their communication feels richer in these media than those who are not accustomed to the medium. Becoming literate and fluent in mediated communication is almost like learning a second language. **Cues-filtered-out theory** suggests that emotional expression is severely restricted in online communication no matter how good you are at it. However, **social information-processing theory** suggests that we can communicate relational and emotional messages via technology, but it just may take longer to express messages that are typically communicated with facial expressions and tone of voice. Each of these theories represents the different opinions regarding how various channels affect communication.

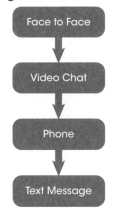

High Media Richness

Face to Face

↓

Video Chat

↓

Phone

↓

Text Message

Low Media Richness

Figure 2.3. Different communication media carry different levels of richness.

FRESH FROM THE LAB: COMMUNICATION RESEARCHERS AT WORK

Virtually Romantic

As mediated communication becomes the norm, online romantic connections are on the rise. Researchers have defined online close relationships as those that were initiated over a computer and that are primarily maintained that way.[64] Experts have mixed opinions about whether online relationships have the ability to foster true intimacy. Robert Craig notes, "These devices seem to wall us off from one another in some ways while both intensifying and yet perhaps also trivializing interpersonal contact in other ways."[65] Although some researchers and theorists argue that online relationships are somehow inauthentic,[66] more recent research indicates that devices can help foster intimacy. Specifically, Walther's hyperpersonal model[67] suggests that online interpersonal communication is more conducive to rapid relationship development because it tends to involve greater disclosure, which equals more intimacy, than face-to-face (FTF) communication.

Even if "real" relationships can develop in a virtual environment, researchers are interested in learning more about this unique context and exactly what distinguishes online romantic relational development from regular face-to-face relational escalation. Similarities found between electronically mediated communication (EMC) and FTF communication include the strategies people use to initiate relationships, as well as the reasons cited for attraction. As with FTF encounters, people in online environments are more attracted to those who are similar to them.

One difference between the two contexts is that online relationships move toward rather than away from richer mediums where they end up having less control over what information is revealed. For example, two people may meet online, but eventually talk on the phone, and then finally meet in person. The opposite is true of FTF relationships, where people start out in the context that provides the most information (face-to-face), and slowly include less rich forms of communication as forms of relational maintenance. For example, two people may meet at a bar and then decide to chat online later in the week. Another important distinguishing factor between FTF and mediated relational development is the type of information exchange that occurs. In online relationships senders are able to strategically reveal information in a way that FTF communicators are not. One researcher explains, "In the online environment individuals are able to carefully pick and choose the aspects of themselves that they want to present. Since people have a natural tendency to want to 'put their best foot forward,' the self that is constructed on-line may not be an exact replica of the self they are off-line."[68] One participant admits, "I had just started working out when we met, and I held off on the photos until I built up a little bulk. That way, in her mind, I have always been buff—she doesn't need to know about the fat decades."[69]

This phenomenon may explain one reason that many mediated relationships dissolve after they become FTF relationships. In one study 68% of respondents reported that their online relationship terminated due to their first face-to-face interaction going poorly.[70] Relationships that succeeded after becoming face-to-face reported that increased communication is what held them together. It appears that good communication is the glue of a good relationship, no matter where it starts.

Paying attention to the medium of communication is especially important as new technologies change the way we communicate every day. Misunderstandings due to inadequate media richness are common, and the ability to encode and decode accurately and appropriately can be affected by the medium in which the interaction occurs. Furthermore, individuals have very different levels of expertise and experience with different media.

WATCH AND LEARN

View a TED Talk on the effect of mediated communication by typing this into your browser: TED Talk alone together.

CHAPTER SUMMARY

In this chapter you learned that nonverbal channels include any non-linguistic form of communication. Nonverbal communication differs from verbal communication in that it is continuous and multi-channeled, making it harder to study but even more communicative than verbal messages. The various categories of nonverbal behavior were outlined to show how complex nonverbal communication is, including bodily cues, facial cues, distance, touch, appearance and artifacts, and the voice. The information we derive from nonverbal cues includes level of arousal, immediacy and dominance. However, all information we perceive depends on our own gender and culture: nonverbal norms vary greatly between people who are either masculine or feminine communicators, and especially those from different cultural backgrounds. The last part of this chapter concluded with a discussion of the special problems created by the mediated channels of interpersonal communication, suggesting that media richness plays a large role in how our messages get across when using technology to communicate.

Name _____   Instructor _____

CHAPTER ACTIVITIES

TEST YOUR UNDERSTANDING

True or False

_____1. The study of touch is called chronemics.

_____2. Kyle and Ryan were sitting next to each other at the table having a conversation. This zone would be considered personal space.

_____3. When Muslim women wear a *hijab*, this is a form of nonverbal communication.

Multiple Choice: Circle the best answer choice.

1. Tapping a pencil repetitively is considered to be a/an:

    A. Emblem

    B. Adapter

    C. Illustrator

    D. Display

    E. None of the above

2. Similarities found between relationships initiated over computer-mediated communication (CMC) and those initiated face-to-face (FTF) include:

    A. The statements people use to initiate relationships

    B. The reasons cited for attraction

    C. The tendency to move away from richer mediums as the relationship progresses

    D. All of the above

    E. A and B only

3. Which of the following is NOT one of the categories of space:

    A. Personal zone

    B. Social zone

    C. Impersonal zone

    D. Intimate zone

    E. Public zone

**Answers are listed at the end of this section before the references.

Short Answer

1. Explain the characteristics of nonverbal communication.

   _____

   _____

   _____

   _____

2. Describe the nonverbal channels of interpersonal communication.

   _____

   _____

   _____

   _____

3. Describe the differences in nonverbal communication patterns of masculine and feminine communicators.

   _____

   _____

   _____

   _____

4. Describe cultural differences in nonverbal behaviors.

   _____

   _____

   _____

   _____

5. Explain how media richness affects interpersonal communication.

   _____

   _____

   _____

   _____

IN-CLASS ACTIVITY

Mediated Messages

Take out your cell phone and text a message to someone you know can respond immediately. Simply type a happy face: :)

What was the person's response? How would you have sent this message differently if it were face-to-face, and how would the person have responded differently? Would you have been more or less satisfied with the interaction? Are there any situations where an emoticon is MORE effective than a face-to-face expression?

_____

_____

_____

_____

_____

_____

Now text another person you know can respond immediately. Simply type a sad face: :(

Compare the response you get with the response you received from a happy face.

_____

_____

_____

_____

_____

_____

Describe a time when a text message you sent was completely misinterpreted by the recipient.

_____

_____

_____

_____

_____

_____

SKILL PRACTICE: NONVERBAL DECODING ACUITY

What Is the Goal of Increasing Nonverbal Decoding Acuity?

Training yourself to focus on nonverbal behavior will increase your ability to decode nonverbal messages more accurately, and also increase your ability to send nonverbal messages more effectively.

How Do You Do It?

In the next meaningful conversation you have with an interpersonal partner (friend, family member, or romantic partner), try to focus on each channel of nonverbal communication, while staying tuned into the verbal message. See if you can glean any additional information other than what is being stated. This is an exercise in effective listening and understanding, so don't forget to perception check your findings (i.e., ask the person if they are feeling a certain way, instead of assuming that your interpretation is correct).

What did you notice?

Kinesics:

_____

_____

Proxemics:

_____

_____

Haptics:

_____

_____

Vocalics:

_____

_____

Facial Expression:

_____

_____

What did you find out when you checked your perceptions by asking if your interpretation of his/her nonverbal communication was correct?

_____

_____

_____

Name

Instructor

HOMEWORK ACTIVITY

THE LYING GAME

Ask a friend to lie to you at some point in the next two days in order to see whether you can detect dishonesty from someone you know. After he or she presents the lie, make sure you debrief together. How were you able to tell it was a lie? If you were not able to tell, why not?

_____

_____

_____

_____

_____

_____

Answers to True/False and Multiple Choice

1. False

2. True

3. True

1. B

2. E

3. C

REFERENCES

[25]Mehrabian, A. (1972). *Nonverbal communication*. Chicago, Illinois: Aldine-Atherton.

[26]M. Knapp & E. Hall (1996). *Nonverbal behavior in human interaction* (3rd ed.). New York: Holt, Rinehart, & Winston.

[27]Leal, S. & Vrij, A. (2008). Blinking during and after lying. *Journal of Nonverbal Behavior, 32,* 187–194.

[28]Ekman, P. (1985). *Telling lies: Clues to deceit in the marketplace, politics, and marriage.* New York: W. W. Norton & Company.

[29]Mehrabian, A. (1972). *Nonverbal communication*. Chicago, Illinois: Aldine-Atherton.

[30]Ibid.

[31]Ambady, N., Koo, J., Rosenthal, R. & Winograd, C. H. (2002). Physical therapists' nonverbal communication predicts geriatric patients' health outcomes. *Psychology and Aging, 17*(3), 443–452.

[32]Le Poire, B.A., Shepard, C., & Duggan, A. (1999). Nonverbal involvement, expressiveness, and pleasantness as predicted by parental and partner attachment style. *Communication Monographs, 66,* 293–311.

[33]Argyle, M. (1988). *Bodily communication.* New York: Methuen & Co.

[34]Strayer, D.L., Drews, F.A., Crouch, D. J. & Johnston, W.A. (2005). Why do cell phone conversations interfere with driving? In W. R. Walker and D. Herrmann (Eds.) *Cognitive Technology: Transforming Thought and Society,* 51–68. McFarland & Company Inc., Jefferson, NC.

[35]Cohen, J.T. & Graham, J.D. (2003). A revised economic analysis of restrictions on the use of cell phones while driving. *Harvard Center for Risk Analysis, 23,* 5–17.

[36]Strayer, D.L. & Drew, F.A. (2004). Profiles in driver distraction: Effects of cell phone conversations on younger and older drivers. *Human Factors, 46,* 640–649.

[37]Nationwide Mutual Insurance Company. (2007). NMIC Report. Retrieved January 10, 2010 from http://www.nationwide.com/newsroom/nationwide-fights-dwd.jsp

[38]Virginia Tech News. (2009). Virginia Tech Transportation Institute Study. Retrieved January 10, 2009 from http://www.vtnews.vt.edu/story.php?relyear=2009&itemno=571

[39]Ekman, P., & Friesen, W. V. (1969). The repertoire of nonverbal behavior: Categories, origins, usage, and coding. *Semiotica,* 1, 49–98.

[40]Goldin-Meadow, S. Nusbaum, H., Kelly, S.D. & S. Wagner (2001). Gesture–Psychological aspects. *Psychological Science, 12,* 516–522.

[41]Miller, R.A. (1992). *Japan's modern myth: The language and beyond.* Tokyo: Weatherhill.

[42]Rosenthal, R., Archer, D., Koivumaki, J.H., DiMattee, M.R., and Rogers, D.L. (1974). Assessing sensitivity to nonverbal communication: The PONS Test. *Division 8 Newsletter of the Division of Personality and Social Psychology of the American Psychological Association,* 1–3.

[43]Hall, E.T. (1963). A system for the notation of proxemic behavior. *American Anthropologist, 65,* 1003–1026.

[44]Hall, E. (1996). Touch, status, and gender at professional meetings. *Journal of Nonverbal Behavior, 20,* 23–44.

[45]Keltner, D. (2009). *Born to be good: The science of a meaningful life.* New York: W. W. Norton & Company.

[46]Field, T., Lasko, D., Mundy, P., Henteleff, T., Kabat, S., Talpins, S. & Dowling, M. (1997). Brief report: Autistic children's attentiveness and responsivity improve after touch therapy. *Journal of Autism and Developmental Disorders, 27,* 333–338.

[47]Kraus, M.W., Huang, C. & Keltner, D. (2010). Tactile communication, cooperation, and performance: An ethological study of the NBA. *Emotion, 10,* 745–749.

[48]Guerrero, L.K. & Hecht, M.L. (2008) *The nonverbal communication reader: Classic and contemporary readings* (3rd ed.). Long Grove, IL: Waveland Press.

[49]Yee, N. & Bailenson, J.N. (2008). A method for longitudinal behavioral data collection in Second Life. *Presence, 17,* 594–596.

[50] Giles, H., Billings, A. (2004). Language attitudes. In A. Davies & E. Elder (Eds.), *The Handbook of Applied Linguistics* (187–209). Oxford: Blackwell.

[51] Dailey, R., Giles, H., & Jansma, L. (2005). Language attitudes in an Anglo-Hispanic context: The role of the linguistic landscape. *Language & Communication, 25,* 27–38.

[52]Shepherd, G.M. (2004). "The Human Sense of Smell: Are We Better Than We Think?" *PLOS Biology 2*(5). Ed 146.

[53]Herz, R.S. (2002). Sex differences in response to physical and social factors involved in human mate selection: The importance of smell for women. *Evolution and Human Behavior 23*(5), 359–364.

[54]Miller, S.L., & Maner, J.K. (2010). Scent of a woman: Men's responses to olfactory ovulation cues. *Psychological Science, 21,* 276–283.

[55]Classen, C., Howes, D. & Synnott, A. (1994). *Aroma: The Cultural History of Smell.* London and New York: Routledge.

[56]Storti, C. (1999). *Figuring Foreigners Out: A Practical Guide.* Boston: Intercultural Press.

[57]Droogsma, R.A. (2007). Redefining *hijab*: American Muslim women's standpoints on veiling. *Journal of Applied Communication Research, 35,* 294–319.

[58]Tannen, D. (1990), *You just don't understand: Women and men in conversation.* William Morrow/Ballantine, New York, NY.

[59]Argyle, M. (1998). *Bodily communication* (2nd ed.) New York: Methuen.

[60]Lawson, W. (2005). Blips on the gaydar. *Psychology Today, 38,* 30.

[61]Imhof, M. (2010). Listening to voices and judging people. *The International Journal of Listening, 24.*

[62]Daft, R. L., and Lengel, R. H. (1984). Information richness: A new approach to managerial behavior and organizational design. In L. L. Cummings and B. M. Staw (Eds.) *Research in Organizational Behavior*, 191–233. Homewood, IL: JAI Press.

[63]Utz, S. (2007). Media use in long-distance friendships. *Information, Communication & Society, 10*(5), 694–713.

[64]Wildermuth, S.M. (2001). Love on the line: Participants' descriptions of computer-mediated close relationships. *Communication Quarterly, 49*, 90–95.

[65]Craig, R.T. (2007). Issue forum introduction: Mobile media and communication: what are the important questions? *Communication Monographs, 74*, 386–388.

[66]Anderson, T.L., & Emmers-Sommer, T.M. (2006). Predictors of relationship satisfaction in online romantic relationships. *Communication Studies, 57*, 153–172.

[67]Walther, J.B. (1996). Computer-mediated communication: Impersonal, interpersonal, and hyper-personal interaction. *Communication Research, 23*, 3–43.

[68]Wildermuth (2001), p. 93.

[69]Ibid, p. 91.

[70]Ibid.

CHAPTER 3

Language and Relationships

"Language, belief, perception, and action are all intimately interrelated. The words we use shape what we perceive, which in turn shapes how we act."

—AnaLouise Keating

Learning Objectives

After studying this chapter, you should be able to:

1. *Explain the arbitrary and rule-based nature of words.*
2. *Explain the power of words, and the two types of meaning.*
3. *Explain the different ways in which language can be confusing or unclear.*
4. *Describe how culture and gender impact our use and interpretation of verbal communication.*
5. *Demonstrate the ability to change "You Language" to "I Language" to improve shared meaning in interpersonal relationships.*

How many times today did you stop and wonder if the message you were intending to send was the same message someone was receiving? Probably infrequently, if at all. We tend to operate as if the use of a common language between two people will guarantee "shared meaning," or the same understanding of each other's thoughts. When we add mediated messages into the mix, an accurate understanding of verbal communication can be quite a challenge. Shared meaning, which will be referred to throughout this book, is unfortunately uncommon in both mediated and face-to-face interpersonal contexts.

Interestingly, when you're having a heated argument with someone else it suddenly becomes clear how difficult it is to get your meaning across accurately and efficiently. You may say things that the other person "takes the wrong way," or both people may admit, "I just don't get you!" or "You're not making any sense!" When two people are fighting each can see how difficult it is to understand the other, but when things are going well each of us generally assumes that we are

being understood, although this is not usually the case. Finnish communication scholar Osmo Wiio, presents several maxims that offer a bleak perspective on finding shared meaning between two people.[71] His maxims state:

1. Communication usually fails, except by accident.

    1.1 If communication can fail, it will.

    1.2 If communication cannot fail, it still most usually fails.

    1.3 If communication seems to succeed in the intended way, there's a misunderstanding.

2. If a message can be interpreted in several ways, it will be interpreted in a manner that maximizes the damage.

3. There is always someone who knows better than you what you meant by your message.

4. The more we communicate, the faster misunderstandings propagate.

You may be curious about *why* we have such a hard time getting our thoughts back and forth to each other in a way that ensures understanding. This chapter will introduce you to the characteristics of the verbal channel of communication so that you can gain a better understanding of the nature of language, then we'll talk about some specific problems that lead to miscommunication and even conflict.

WORDS ARE ARBITRARY SYMBOLS

What is verbal communication? The most important characteristic that makes communication "verbal" is that it is based on a language. Therefore, American Sign Language is considered verbal communication. So are text messages, emails, and chats online, as long as words are being used in some form.

Language is perhaps the most taken for granted tool for communication. We rarely think about the fact that language is just an invented system to help send our thoughts to another person. It is important to remember that language is simply a tool, or a set of *symbols* we use to *refer* to our *thoughts*; language has no real meaning beyond the agreed upon meaning that we give it. Furthermore, symbols can have multiple meanings and interpretations when used by different people.

THE TRIANGLE OF MEANING

The **triangle of meaning,** also known as the **semantic triangle,** explains the arbitrary nature of language by outlining the relationship between referents, thoughts, and symbols.[72] A **symbol** is a word, or visual device that represents a thing, idea or experience. For example, imagine that you recently went on a plane ride. You would describe your aircraft as a P-L-A-N-E. The **referent** is the thing that a symbol represents, which in this example is the *actual* plane. The **thought,** or **reference,** is the mental process of imagining the thing, idea or experience triggered by the symbol; thus, the mental image of the plane that comes to mind when you say or hear the word is the *thought.* Interpersonal relationships often include shared meaning for certain words; however, since we are all unique individuals with our own life experiences, the meanings of most words are still individualized. When you say the word "plane," the thought that emerges for you is different from someone else's thought.

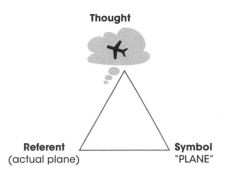

Thought

Referent
(actual plane)

Symbol
"PLANE"

Figure 3.0. The triangle of meaning.

Understanding the difference between a thought, symbol and referent is key to understanding the nature of language. As with most symbols, the words that comprise our language are arbitrary. The arbitrary nature of most words means that there is no inherent meaning in a word; there is not necessarily a logical connection between the referent and the symbol we use to signify it. The only exception to this is the *onomatopoeia*, which is a word or group of words whose sound imitates or replicates it's meaning, such as *"buzz."*

WORDS HAVE RULES

Language rules are used to help the flow of conversation, meet goals, and navigate relationships. We don't give the rules much thought, that is, until those rules are violated. We definitely notice when someone uses incorrect, inappropriate, or inaccurate language. These rules tend to fall into three categories: phonological, syntactic, and pragmatic rules.

PHONOLOGICAL RULES

Phonological rules are the rules that dictate how letters and words should sound when they are pronounced. For example, the words schedule and aluminum are pronounced differently in the United States and in Great Britain, even though they are spelled the same and they are both from the English language. English in particular has some tricky phonological rules that make it an enigma to non-native speakers.

Non-native speakers have special trouble with words that are spelled the same but have a different pronunciation depending on the meaning:

Farmers from the country produce the best produce.

I did not object to the object.

I shed a tear when I found a tear in my jeans.

Other difficulties in pronunciation occur because words spelled differently are pronounced the same:

Where will you wear that?

I have the right to write.

Which witch was the good one and which was the bad witch?

SYNTACTIC RULES

Another set of rules determines how we create sentences. **Syntactic rules** govern the way symbols can be arranged to create the intended meaning. English syntax requires that the verb goes before the noun, as in "Are you going to the mall" instead of "Are you the mall going to?" In contrast, the syntactic rules of many other languages require that the noun is stated before the verb. Unless you are a scholar of linguistics you may not be able to list the syntactic rules of your native language, but you certainly can identify when the rules are violated because it sounds wrong.

PRAGMATIC RULES

In addition to structural and pronunciation rules, there are rules for what is considered "appropriate" during regular interpersonal conversations. **Pragmatic rules** determine how we adapt our language in different social and cultural contexts to follow the implicit rules and expectations of our conversational partners. One way to examine pragmatic rules is to consider what types of statements are expected as we manage regular interactions.

Conversational management is the process of initiating, maintaining, and closing a conversation with another person. We manage our conversations with others by using several easily identifiable cues and rules that help each person play their respective role throughout the conversation.[73]

Rules for Beginning and Ending Conversations

When it comes to initiating conversations, we use specific strategies to get the ball rolling. *Self-reference* is a statement about yourself that implies interest in a conversation, such as, "I'm Dana, I'm new in town." People often use self-deprecation as a conversation starter because it is a non-

intimidating way to approach someone. A self-deprecating comment is a subtle insult delivered to oneself, such as "I hate these parties, I never know how to make small talk." *Referring to the other person* is also a typical conversation starter. For example, you can refer to someone's possessions ("Nice car"), someone's culture or gender ("Must be tough being the only woman in this office"), someone's behaviors ("I see you know how to enjoy a martini"), or any other number of things you notice about the other. *References*

to the relationship between the participants are also common, such as "Mind if I sit down?" or "Can I ask you a question?" Finally, *context references* are the mention of something going on at the time or place of the budding conversation, such as "Sure is cold out here!" or "Who knew they had curry on the menu?"

We tend to close the conversation with equally predictable strategies. We often make a *direct reference to the end*, such as "I gotta go." Other times we *reflect on the conversation* to signal it's ending by saying something like, "I'm really glad we talked, I feel a lot better now." We may make a *reference to the future*, such as "Hey let's talk about this later," or even make a direct *request for closure* by stating, "Are we done here?" The last linguistic strategy for ending a conversation is the *pleasantry*, which is a statement of closure such as "It was nice chatting with you."

SKILL BUILDING EXERCISE

Opening and Closing Conversations

In each of the following scenarios, what would be an effective way to open a conversation, based on the conversation openers from this chapter?

You are the second person to arrive at a social event, and the other person there is sitting alone.

_____

_____

You want to visit a professor in office hours but you don't have a specific question.

_____

_____

You decide to share a taxi with a stranger to save money, so you are both sitting together in the backseat for 10–20 minutes.

_____

_____

In each of the following scenarios, what would be an effective way to close the conversation, based on the conversation enders from this chapter?

You are on a long plane ride and the person seated next to you is trying to engage in conversation when you want to tune into a movie.

_____

_____

You are working out on an exercise machine when an acquaintance spots you and approaches to talk. After a couple of minutes of chatting there is nothing else to say and you'd really prefer to put your earphones back in.

_____

_____

You are at a party and you want to mingle but the person you are talking to seems intent on continuing a one-on-one conversation with you.

_____

_____

Rules for Maintaining Conversations

The rules for beginning and ending conversations are easy to use and commonly understood. However, throughout the duration of a conversation there are even more rules we use to manage the interaction, and there tends to be greater skill required to use them. These rules can be categorized into three principles: turn taking, dialogue, and cooperation.

The Principle of Turn Taking explains that in a proper conversation each person should play both the listener and speaker roles, and spend about an equal amount of time doing each. As you may have experienced, some people aren't very skilled at following this principle. People who don't easily adopt the listening role and instead insist on playing the speaker throughout the conversation are guilty of **stage-hogging**. Stage-hoggers often use the other person's story or comments to go off on a tangent about their own personal story. You may recall from Chapter 1 that recognizing turn-taking cues and listening effectively are measures of communication competence.

The Principle of Dialogue is somewhat related to turn taking, but emphasizes the presence of each participant. This principle states that in an effective, satisfying conversation both people actively participate even if that just means paying attention and caring about what the other is saying. Anyone can engage in a *monologue*, or a unidirectional stream of self-expression with no attention paid to feedback from the other. *Dialogue* requires involvement in the dynamic between the two people conversing, paying attention to the impact and clarity of what you are saying and hearing, and taking into account the other person's feedback. As you've already learned, conversations that are based on scripts where neither person really cares much about the other are considered *impersonal*; in contrast, interpersonal conversations should be dialogic in nature.

Finally, the *Principle of Cooperation* suggests that each person in a conversation is striving toward understanding and will cooperate with the other to achieve shared meaning.[74] This principle includes four maxims, or rules of engagement. First, the *information load* should be appropriate, meaning that the person speaking should include enough information that the other understands him or her, but should not over-inform and cause confusion. Next, the *quality* of the information should be truthful and accurate. *Relevance* is also important; that is, each communicator should keep on topic and not fly off on tangents that are unrelated to the conversation at hand. Finally, *clarity* should be considered. Speakers should not intentionally use words the listener does not understand. Next you'll learn about some additional characteristics of words that naturally work against the principle of clarity in our struggle for shared meaning.

WORDS ARE POWERFUL

Even though words are arbitrary creations that have no meaning other than that which we assign them, once we assign meaning they have enormous power. The meanings we place on words can elicit powerful emotions, cause conflict, and prevent us from seeing things clearly.

SAPIR-WHORF HYPOTHESIS

We rarely think about how our language shapes what we actually "see" in the world around us. According to linguistic determinists who developed the **Sapir-Whorf hypothesis**,[75] words have the power to actually create our reality by serving as the tools we use to name and label what we experience. Author Deborah Tannen describes this process, writing:

> *When we think we are using language, language is using us...the terms in which we talk about something shape the way we think about it—and even what we see.*[76]

For example, linguists point out that our language has a disproportionate amount of negative terms to describe the sexually "promiscuous" behavior of women versus that of men. It should come as no surprise, then, that female sexual promiscuity is "viewed" more negatively than male promiscuity: we have more tools with which to describe it as such.

Because our language inevitably determines our thoughts and perceptions, with each different language comes different experience. When comparing languages, linguists find that most languages do indeed include some words that have no direct translation to other languages, a concept known as **linguistic relativity**. For example, the Swedish word "lagom" does not have an equivalent word in English. Attempts at defining this word seem to fall short; for example, one traveler tried to explain the word in his Internet blog as meaning "something like all good, 'cause more would be too much, less would be too little."[77] Ask a Swede to tell you the English version of this word and you are likely to get a similarly confusing answer because it simply doesn't translate.

It's difficult to find examples of the Sapir-Whorf hypothesis in action because we are too ingrained in our own language to identify it. We use our language without giving it much thought at all, failing to recognize our own role in perpetuating the reality we've created with our words. Try and think about how your language shapes your experience. For example, how did our culture view "hyperactive" children before we invented the term "attention deficit?" How does that term shape the way we perceive children today? What about the words "depression" and "terrorist?" How would our experience of the world be different if these words were not in our language?

Scholars are constantly searching for words that cannot be translated from one language to another in order to exemplify the Sapir-Whorf hypothesis. However, Frijda, Markam, Sato, and Wiers concluded that there actually exists a high degree of similarity and overlap in words used to describe emotions across different languages.[78] In fact, there is a relatively small set of common emotional word categories across languages. This team of researchers had groups of subjects in 11 different cultures (Belgium, France, Switzerland, Italy, Netherlands, England, Canada, Indonesia, Japan, Surinam, and Turkey) list as many emotion words as they could in a span of five minutes. They then created a table of the most frequently mentioned words for each of the groups. Words for joy/happiness, sadness, anger, fear, and love appeared across all languages. However, the English equivalent of "hate" was not found across cultures. Semin and his colleagues suggest that the variations in emotional words probably reflect the social differences across cultures.[79] In cultures that value individualism, words to describe emotions are more likely to be "self" centered, because individual needs prevail over group needs. It's possible that the word "hate" is too strong or socially inappropriate to be used in collectivistic cultures.

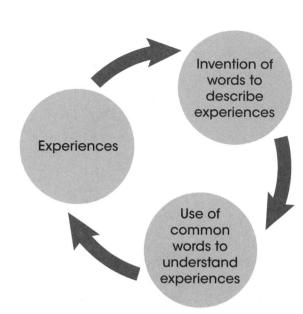

Figure 3.1. The Sapir-Whorf hypothesis suggests that the words we invent to describe our experiences then serve as the lens through which we experience.

WATCH AND LEARN

View a TED Talk on the power of language by typing this into your browser: TED Talk grammar, identity, and the dark side.

WORDS CARRY CONTENT AND RELATIONAL MEANING

Another very important characteristic that lends power to language is that it always contains meaning on two levels: the content level and the relational level. Content refers to the informational component of words. Sometimes referred to as the **denotative** meaning, the content is the

word's literal meaning that would be found if you looked it up in the dictionary.

The relationship dimension of the message is more implied and includes the emotion, attitudes, and intentions of the speaker. Sometimes referred to as the **connotative** level of meaning, the relationship dimension conveys feelings and includes the personal or subjective meaning of the verbal and nonverbal behavior.

Most interpersonal conflict centers not around the literal meaning of a word someone used, but on what they "meant" by it. If you are human, you've probably had an argument where one person used a word that the other person did not like, and an entire conflict erupted based on what was "meant" by the word. Connotative meaning is unique to the context and the relationship, which is why these fights can't be resolved by consulting a dictionary.

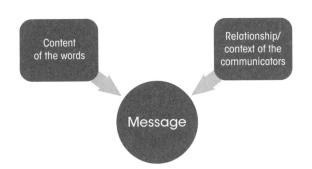

Figure 3.2. A message is composed of both the literal, denotative meaning of the words used, and the connotative meaning of the words based on the relationship of the communicators and the context in which they are communicating.

INTERPERSONAL COMMUNICATION FOR SOCIAL CHANGE

What's in a Name?

Researchers in Massachusetts scoured the registry of babies born between 1974 and 1979 to discover the most common names for female and male babies from both White and Black racial groups. The winners were Lakisha, Greg, Jamal, and Emily. Can you guess which names were from which category? Of course you can—and so can employers, landlords, and a variety of other people who can impact the economic well-being of others.

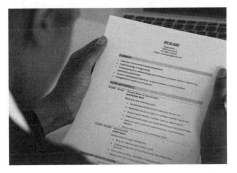

These same researchers crafted a resume and made only one change by listing the applicant's name as either Lakisha Washington, Jamal Jones, Emily Walsh, or Greg Baker. The resumes with "White sounding" names spurred 50 percent more callbacks from employers than the ones with "Black sounding" names.[80]

In another study from 2017, researchers analyzed email resume submissions for 3,225 jobs in Toronto and Montreal, tracking which ones received calls for interviews. Resumes with Chinese, Indian, or Pakistani names were 28 percent less likely to generate a call for an interview than those where the applicant listed an Anglo-sounding name, even when qualifications were identical.[81]

A different team of researchers sent 1,115 emails responding to advertisements for apartment vacancies in Los Angeles County over 10 weeks, randomly assigning names that implied either Arab, African American, or White ethnicity. Arab-sounding names received significantly fewer positive responses than the White-sounding names, but the African American–sounding names received the fewest positive responses of all.[82]

Reflection

1. Think about the interpretations you make based only on someone's name.

2. What do you think your name says to others about you?

3. If new parents were aware of this information, do you think it would affect how they name their babies?

4. Can you think of any reasons why adapting babies names based on social expectations could be a poor solution to this problem?

WORDS RANGE IN CLARITY

Considering what you've learned so far about language, it's a wonder we can communicate at all! If you reflect back on Wiio's Maxims of Communication from the beginning of the chapter, you'll recall that shared meaning is the exception to the rule when it comes to interpersonal interactions. This section explains how our word choices contribute to our inability to get accurate and effective meaning across to our communication partners.

VAGUE LANGUAGE

One characteristic of language that makes it so complex is that words can be placed along a continuum from abstract to concrete. We usually call a word *concrete* if we can experience its referent with one of our senses, such as cold or blue. If we cannot experience the referent with our senses then the word is usually considered *abstract*, such as phantom or heaven. Furthermore, all ideas can be expressed in a variety of ways that range in level of abstraction. For example, I can tell you about my house in several ways, including:

- My house

- My small house

- My small yellow cottage

- My small yellow cottage downtown

As the specificity of the language increases, so does the likelihood of one person's thoughts accurately getting across to the other person. When I described "my house," you may have had an entirely different image in your mind than when I described it as "my small yellow cottage downtown." In general, the more concrete terms we use in our communication the easier it is for others to understand, and the more abstract our language is, the greater likelihood for confusion and misunderstanding.

Often times when a speaker is worried about offending others or is uncomfortable uttering a particular word, he or she will use a **euphemism**, or a term that acts as a substitute for a word that may not be socially acceptable in a given context. Bathroom behavior is an especially touchy subject that easily offends, which is why there are numerous euphemisms to describe what is a completely natural human process. Some examples used to refer to the process include:

- Go potty

- Go number one

- Make a pit stop

- Powder my nose

- Answer Mother Nature's call

- See a man about a horse

Euphemisms can be problematic only if the desire to tiptoe around the topic prevents others from understanding. You may be unfamiliar with that last euphemism listed above because it's older than the others. If I told you I needed to step out of a meeting to "see a man about a horse" you might think I was nuts. In sum, words are not inherently understood between communicators just because they come from the same language: they range in abstraction and clarity to such a degree that confusion is typical.

Occasionally speakers intentionally use abstract or vague language in order to reduce their own responsibility or avoid the truth. An **equivocation** is an intentionally evasive statement that can be interpreted in many ways. If a curious boyfriend asks, "Was your ex-boyfriend at the party last night?" and his girlfriend replies, "There were mostly people I didn't know" her intentional evasiveness is clear. Equivocal language from one partner can be an enormous barrier to shared meaning, and create a spiral of misunderstanding.

FRESH FROM THE LAB: COMMUNICATION RESEARCHERS AT WORK

What the @$*&!?

A useful example of the difference between connotative and denotative meaning in interpersonal relationships comes from the study of profanity. How do you react when someone unexpectedly drops the "F" bomb during normal conversation? Are you offended, surprised, or perhaps intrigued? It's likely that your reaction stems from your relationship with the offender. Like all verbal messages, swear words speak volumes beyond their literal meaning.

First, a little background. Profanity is considered one of the oldest forms of spoken language and has provoked curiosity from as early as 1901. Even our more conservative ancestors were familiar with all seven categories we still use today:[83]

- Names of deities ("God almighty!")

- Names referring to the hurts of deities ("For the love of Jesus!")

- Names of saints ("Holy Saint Christopher!")

- Names of sacred locations ("On my mother's grave!")

- References to an afterlife ("In heaven's name!," also including "Damn!" which is short for damnation)

- Vulgar language that is considered socially impolite ("Shit!")

- Expletives that have exaggerated force ("Mercy!")

Yet not all cuss words are created equal. There are two general categories a foul mouth can choose from, depending on the goal.[84] Assertive swearing is intended to attract attention from the listener and emphasize the speaker's point with more assertion and certainty. This category includes exclamations such as, "Hell, yes!" or "I told you, damnit!" On the other hand, ejaculatory swearing is a simple exclamation used for its own sake, such as "Damn!" or "Bastard!"

This breakdown of linguistic categories represents the denotative component of swear words, or the "literal" meaning. However, according to recent research, using profanity serves several relational purposes as well. Not only are we more likely to swear in the company of people we trust and know, but also swearing often indicates a level of comfort and acceptance of the other.[85] We use swearing intentionally (although sometimes subconsciously) to create relational boundaries; that is, we demonstrate whom we consider "members" of our group by our language selection. Young adults use profanity toward one another as a display of affiliation or closeness. Researchers also find that some African-Americans use the "n" word to describe close ingroup members, while the same word would be unacceptable from an outgroup member.[86] Profanity, like all language, contains information about the goals, intentions, and expectations of the speaker. Over time the denotative component loses all meaning, and what's left is strictly relational.

EXAGGERATED LANGUAGE

One set of verbal behaviors that disrupt shared meaning has to do with thinking in extremes. **Allness** is the tendency to use language to make sweeping and often untrue generalizations about a person or situation, such as "You *always* leave the kitchen a mess," or "*All* men are such slobs."

Polarization is another use of extreme language, whereby you describe and evaluate what you observe in terms of black and white: everything is *either* good or bad, right or wrong, terrible or perfect. By describing things in extremes and leaving out the possibility that most things are complex and multi-faceted, your language does not accurately reflect reality. An example of polarization may occur when you are on vacation with your friend who, at the first sign of inconvenience states, "The plane is late! I knew this trip was going to be a total disaster." A more common example occurs when you select one behavior from someone and make extreme conclusions from that one behavior, such as, "You were late to dinner. I knew you were too good to be true."

LANGUAGE MISTAKES

Public figures like politicians are an easy target when it comes to pointing out errors in speech. Critics of the former president of the United States, George W. Bush, enjoyed pointing out his tendency to commit a **malapropism**, or the confusion of one word for another word that has a different meaning but sounds similar. In one speech the former president stated, "We cannot let terrorists and rogue nations hold this nation hostile or hold our allies hostile." We're pretty sure he meant to use the word "hostage." Occasionally word choice is so off the mark that the word used doesn't even sound like the intended word, such as when former President Barack Obama defended himself during the presidential campaign by saying he wasn't as "green behind the ears" as his running mates were suggesting. He meant to say, "wet behind the ears." When someone commits a malapropism it can prevent the listener from understanding the message, or simply draw attention away from the message to the mistake.

The use of language is further complicated by another language mistake referred to as bypassing. **Bypassing** is when the same word means something different to each person in the conversation. Bypassing occurs everyday in interpersonal conversations and can be relatively benign and even humorous when it happens. However, if the topic is serious, bypassing can create enormous conflict.

People in developing relationships often discover that the words "I love you" have different meanings for each person. When one person hears "I love you," he or she might assume the relationship is headed toward marriage, while another person may think it simply means, "I'm developing strong feelings for you." The word "love" has so many meanings and uses in our language that it is commonly cited as causing great confusion in all types of relationships.

IDENTITY LANGUAGE

Have you ever wondered why there isn't a "universal" language? Imagine getting off a plane in any country in the world and communicating effortlessly with the locals. As international travel becomes commonplace, it seems like someone would have thought of this already. It turns out they did. You may be surprised to learn that there is in fact a universal language, and it's over 100 years old. Esperanto, invented in the late 1870s by Dr. Ludovic Lazarus Zamenhof, has been coined the world's only universal language. It is estimated that anywhere from 100,000 to 2 million people across the world speak the language fluently. Several organizations use Esperanto as their primary language, there are hundreds of books published in Esperanto, and even a few feature-length films where only Esperanto is spoken (including Incubus, starring William Shatner). Free lessons are not hard to find, in fact promoters of the language argue that the average person can reach fluency in a little over two weeks.

If a simple Google search generates over half a million hits for the term "Esperanto" then why haven't you heard of this universal language? Well, unfortunately the language didn't catch on with quite the contagion its supporters hoped it would. Verbal communication helps us express our unique identities, which include our memberships in certain groups. Just as groups are attached to their "inside jokes" and unique verbal codes, countries are attached to their languages, and subsets of countries are attached to their particular dialects. We use our unique languages to communicate who we are, and frankly, we don't want to be the same as everyone else. Very few people would willingly replace their native tongue with a universal language because it would take away part of their identity. Even if we all spoke the same language, people would inevitably feel the need to personalize it through jargon and slang, and pretty soon the language wouldn't be universal at all.

Jargon, sometimes referred to as a "restricted code," is vocabulary that is shared by members of a particular group, but that others outside that group may not understand.[87] Sometimes people use jargon intentionally, to demonstrate their knowledge of a subject or membership in a specialized group. When communicating with other members of that special group jargon can be used to show similarity, understanding, and cohesion. However, jargon can also be used as a tool to alienate outsiders who are not members of a group. Here's a small sampling of jargon used by the police, which is just one of many careers where specialized terms are a large part of the language used on the job:

- clanlab: a facility where methamphetamines are made

- cop the plate: get the license plate number

- deuce: a drunk driver

- mahaska: concealed firearm

- mups: missing person's database

Slang is another type of unique vocabulary used by people who share some kind of group membership, but may confuse others who are not in that group. Slang is different from jargon because jargon is usually technical or field-specific, whereas slang is based on similar interests and experience. Slang is also more temporary than jargon; it tends to become popular quickly, then loses popularity over time and eventually becomes extinct. Here are some slang terms you may or may not be familiar with:

- lit

- sick

- AF

- woke

After a slang term enjoys a certain degree of longevity, it becomes a more normalized term and often makes its way into a traditional dictionary. Even Merriam-Webster's dictionary features the slang term "phat," since it's become so common. You can access the most up-to-date additions to the English language at www.urbandictionary.com, where bloggers add new terms they hear every day.

MINDFUL MEDIATED COMMUNICATION:

Cyberbullying and the Power of Words

The ease of treating others badly with little face-to-face consequence has caused cyberbullying to become a widespread phenomenon, often with dire consequences. On October 10, 2012, Amanda Todd hanged herself in her home after being blackmailed with photos she had been conned into sharing. One month before her suicide she posted the now famous YouTube video "My story: Struggling, bullying, suicide, self harm," a brave effort to force a national conversation about cyberbullying and suicide. With over 20 million views and counting, her effort was successful even though she didn't live to see it.

From 1993 to 2012 school-aged suicide trends were relatively constant. However, starting in 2014 suicide rates in the United States were 24 percent higher than they were 15 years prior for both males and females.[88] The number of reported cases where cyberbullying was a factor is also on the rise, a sobering fact considering that 81 percent of cyberbullies surveyed in the U.S. admitted their only reason for toying with the power of words was because "it's funny."[89] Even more alarming, one study reports that 95 percent of teen social media users who have witnessed cruel behavior on social media sites say they have seen others ignore the mean behavior, two-thirds of teenagers who have witnessed online cruelty have also witnessed others joining in, and 21 percent of teens admitted that they have joined the harassment themselves.[90]

Review! Unclear Language	
Abstract words:	Words we cannot experience with our senses, or words that lack descriptive detail.
Euphemism:	A term that acts as a substitute for a word that may not be socially acceptable in a given context.
Equivocation:	An intentionally evasive statement that can be interpreted in many ways.
Allness:	The tendency to use language to make sweeping and often untrue generalizations about a person or situation.
Polarization:	The use of language that describes events and people in polarized extremes with no opportunity for grey area.
Malapropism:	The confusion of one word for another word that has a different meaning but sounds similar.
Bypassing:	When the same word means something different to each person in the conversation.
Jargon:	Vocabulary that is shared by members of a particular group, but that others outside that group may not understand. Usually field or trade specific.
Slang:	A unique vocabulary used by people who share some kind of group membership, usually based on shared activities or interests.

Each of these features of our linguistic system make shared meaning a challenge. Abstract language infused with jargon and slang can certainly prevent one person from understanding another either intentionally or unintentionally. The final characteristic of language will show how our individual and group differences are yet another barrier to shared meaning.

LANGUAGE HAS STYLE

A final characteristic of language is that its users have different styles. When you choose how to communicate, your choices are based especially on your age, culture, and gender. Because of these differences between us, we can have a hard time understanding one another.

AGE AND LANGUAGE

One contextual factor that affects language is time. We are bound by the words of our generation, and our place in history. It is especially difficult for people of different ages to effortlessly create shared meaning, mainly because they use different words and often have different meanings for the same words. Think of the impact someone's age might have on his or her understanding of the word "gay" or the word "dope." Read the following list and contrast the meaning you have for each word with the meaning someone in his or her 90s would have:

- bail

- bounce

- tight

- sweet

- FOMO

- fly

CULTURE AND LANGUAGE

Another important context that affects the meaning of words is culture. **Culture** consists of the rules, norms, and values of a group of people that have been learned, adapted, and passed from one generation to the next. Part of this learned knowledge includes the specific meanings of words, but another part includes *when* and *how* to use language (and when not to use it).

High-Context Communication

Each culture not only has unique words in its vocabulary, but also has certain rules for how language is used. **Cultural context** is the degree to which meaning is communicated through explicit language or through implicit meanings and nonverbal cues. **High-context cultures** derive most communicative information from nonverbal cues, such as space, eye contact, and body movement.[91] These cultures focus on the connotative meaning of language, or the implied, subtle and relational meaning as opposed to the denotative, or literal meaning. Japan is an example of a country where interactions are based on high-context communication. The desire to "save face," or reduce embarrassment, is far more important than stating how you feel, thus people will often communicate their messages by using channels other than the verbal channel. When the verbal channel is used, statements are less firm and less assertive than those used by low-context communicators.

Low-Context Communication

In contrast, **low-context cultures** derive most information from the explicitly stated and literal meaning of language, and they tend to pay less attention to subtle information from nonverbal and environmental cues.[92] The United States is an example of a country where low-context communication is the norm. This is shown by such common phrases as "don't beat around the bush," "tell it like it is," and "cut to the chase," which all demonstrate the goal of efficiency and clarity.

One misconception of the difference between high-context and low-context cultures is that high-context cultures are less *direct*. However, high-context cultures are actually no less "direct" than low-context cultures: people raised in a high-context culture understand this method of communication perfectly. High-context forms of communication may *seem* less direct to people accustomed to communicating in a low-context way, but it's all relative.

When we examine differences in business negotiations between U.S. and Japanese companies we can see a typical example of the difference between high and low-context communication norms. Because Japan is a high-context culture, Japanese business people are unlikely to say "no" to a deal because this will cause the other party to lose "face," or dignity. Instead, they might say they will discuss it privately, will consider it in the future, or they are not sure. If they were dealing with another Japanese company, both parties would understand that this meant "no." However, Americans may be confused by what they perceive as a "wishy washy" form of negotiating. U.S.

business people regularly say "no" as a form of hardball: they welcome competition and are often aggressive when negotiating. Japanese business people have been known to find this method of communication offensive and unnecessary.[93] As shown by this example, the difference between these two cultural contexts lies more in the method of communication than in the directness. The form of communication only becomes problematic when people from high-context and low-context cultures are trying to communicate with each other!

GENDER AND LANGUAGE

In addition to your age and culture dictating the words you use, your gender may affect your verbal communication patterns as well. Keep in mind that gender does not necessarily correlate with sex. Some females communicate in a masculine way and some males communicate in a feminine way. Your **gender** is defined as the psychological and emotional characteristics that make you masculine, feminine, or androgynous, according to the characteristics that define these labels. If you are a masculine woman, you probably enjoy competition and aren't as "feely" as your feminine counterparts. If you are a feminine man you may be an excellent listener and aren't as forward or demanding as your masculine friends. Being a masculine woman or a feminine man does not necessarily have anything to do with your biological sex, sexual orientation, or even your gender identity; it simple means that you tend not to adhere to the behavioral stereotypes of your sex. In fact, much of the current research is inconclusive regarding the degree of difference between the sexes when it comes to communication. One study debunked a common myth that women speak *more* than men.[94] It turns out that we both average about 16,000 words per day. However, there are many ways in which gender, not necessarily sex, affects communication. Masculine and feminine communication styles are different, and these differences show up in verbal communication.

Masculine Speech

People who use masculine speech tend to value achievement and assertiveness, which means they often compete in conversation. In addition, they view communication as information exchange, which has been coined by researcher Deborah Tannen as "report talk."[95] Most masculine individuals base their friendships more on sharing activities than on talking.

Feminine Speech

In contrast, people who are stereotypically feminine value relationships, caring for others, and overall quality of life; thus they are usually supportive rather than competitive in conversation. They often approach communication for the purpose of relating, and to know and be known by others. Tannen terms this type of conversation "rapport talk," because the goal is to build rapport with the other. Feminine speech is also characterized by the use of hedges, disclaimers, and tag questions. Here are some examples of each:

Hedging statement:	"Maybe we could call the client?"
Regular statement:	"Let's call the client."
Disclaimer:	"I might be crazy, but I don't think they are open on Saturdays."
Regular statement:	"I don't think they are open on Saturdays."

Tag question:	"We're going to wrap up now, okay?"
Regular statement:	"We're going to wrap up now."

Neither masculine nor feminine styles are necessarily better. Each is more suited for certain situations. For example, in a debate or actual competition, a masculine speech style can be more effective. However, in situation when you are required to console a friend or share your feelings, a feminine style may be more appropriate. Most experts agree that the ability to adapt your style depending on the situation is required for communication competence. Whether your style is masculine or feminine, high or low context, the next section will give you some guidance for creating more effective verbal messages.

VERBAL MESSAGES IN MEDIATED CONTEXTS

Because verbal communication is any communication using language, when we text, email, blog, or tweet we are technically using verbal communication even though our messages are not spoken. Several trends emerge in mediated communication contexts, many of which overlap with the findings you just read about.

Most research confirms that when using computer-mediated communication (CMC) the people interacting can infer the gender of their conversational partners only from the language used.[96] This finding suggests that gender differences that appear in face-to-face (FTF) communication also persist in CMC environments. In fact, some researchers believe that absence of nonverbal cues in CMC only accentuates gender differences in language, and therefore creates greater instances of conflicts and harassment.[97]

What are some of the specific gender-based language differences that surface in CMC contexts? As with face-to-face communication, females using CMC tend to use non-assertiveness in the form of powerless language. For example, females are less likely to argue than males, and apologize more often than males.[98] Also similar to FTF communication, female CMC is more supportive and rapport building, more empathetic and uses a more cooperative tone.[99] As part of rapport building females include more mentions of families and spouses.[100] Females also use more "I" statements, and tend to be more expressive,[101] using more exclamation points to show friendly interaction.[102] Like in FTF contexts, females using CMC are more skilled at sending and decoding nonverbal messages.[103]

Like face-to-face communication, male CMC behaviors show an attempt to establish dominance.[104] Males studied tend to be more confrontational, autonomous, certain, abstract, arrogant and controlling, and to use more authoritative language.[105] Males use coarser and more abusive language,

strong assertions, self promotion, put downs and challenges.[106] Males are more likely to use the opinions of others as a springboard for a challenge or debate, and are more likely to use humor and especially sarcasm.[107] Theorists speculate that male preference for authoritative language and strong assertions seem to set the stage for conflict and flaming online, and even perceptions of online sexual harassment.

Review! Characteristics of Verbal Communication
Words are *arbitrary*: There is no relationship between a referent and its symbol.
Words are *powerful*: They have the ability to shape the way we see the world around us.
Words carry *denotative meaning* (content message) and *connotative meaning* (relational message).
Words have *rules*: We use a set of commonly understood rules to navigate conversation with others.
Words range in *clarity*: Abstract language, jargon and slang are word choices that may confuse the listener.
Words communicate *identity*: We use words to show solidarity with our groups, and even to alienate others from our groups.
Words are *contextual*: Their meaning depends on who says it, when they say it, and where they say it.

IMPROVING YOUR VERBAL COMMUNICATION

You've learned a lot about the nature of language, the ways in which language can be unclear, and the differences in our styles and preferences for language. There are several ways to overcome these difficulties and barriers to understanding one another. The final section will focus on I Language, which will help you create verbal messages that communicate your perspective without putting your receiver on the defensive.

BUILDING CULTURAL COMPETENCE

I Versus We

During communication about the self, people in collectivist (i.e., group oriented) cultures frequently use the word "we" while people from individualistic (i.e., self-focused) cultures more frequently use the word "I."[108] Reflecting on the Sapir-Whorf hypothesis, this characteristic of collective language must shape the experiences of people in collectivistic cultures, and those experiences in turn reinforce their language. As such, members of collectivistic cultures may experience great difficulty trying to master the skill of I Language, and this skill may even be inapplicable or inappropriate in cultures where speaking about oneself and one's feelings are not part of the cultural paradigm. As with all communication skills, context is everything. Consider your own comfort zone, your audience, and the relationship before you attempt to apply any skill universally.

I LANGUAGE

As you've learned in this chapter we don't think about our words nearly as much as we should, considering the impact they have on others. Experts agree that you can make major changes in your interpersonal relationships by changing the way you use language. Especially when it comes to difficult conversations and conflicts, the most effective way to use language is to consider it a tool for communicating your own *feelings* and *perceptions* accurately, rather than using it to evaluate, judge, or criticize others.

When we have problems in relationships we often focus on using language to tell others what they did or are doing wrong, how they should behave differently, and in what ways they are to blame. Most of us are unconsciously incompetent with our verbal communication skills because we are accustomed to using You Language. You Language is the language of blame. For example, "It really makes me mad when you don't clean up your mess." This statement may sound perfectly fine to you because You Language is a very common way people communicate. The biggest problem with You Language is that it doesn't allow the other person any option for responding other than defensiveness. It is 99% likely that the only response that will come from one person's You Language is the other person's defense or counterargument. This pattern, known as criticism-defensiveness, rarely gets anything accomplished.[109] There is a better method, but it takes a major change in perception.

I Language is Language that focuses on the *interpretation* of the speaker as one interpretation, and not necessarily the objective truth of the situation. When you choose I Language you make a decision to tell someone how you have interpreted his or her behavior and the reaction you're experiencing because of your *interpretation*.

To learn how to use I language you'll probably need a few examples. Imagine a relationship where your partner has suddenly wanted more independence or time away from you. Let's say the person is your boyfriend, girlfriend, or spouse who has started making plans with other people on Fridays, when you had an unspoken norm of spending Fridays together until now. Depending on the relationship, you may experience one or more of these thoughts:

You don't want to spend time with me.

You don't want to be in this relationship.

You are being selfish.

I shouldn't have to put up with this.

You're going to leave me.

I should leave you.

Your verbal response to your partner's behavior stems from the above story, so it will probably include some of the following verbal statements:

"You didn't even think about what I might want to do on Friday."

"You went and made plans without even asking me."

"You don't want to spend time with me."

"You are avoiding me."

"You only care about yourself."

With these statements you are telling someone how he or she feels, and expressing your judgment of his or her intentions, goals, and desires. Instead, try explaining how you feel, not how you think he or she feels. Try following these steps:

- <u>Describe the behavior</u> you are noticing without evaluating it.
  "I noticed that you have made plans with someone else for the past two Fridays."

- <u>Describe your interpretation</u> of the behavior.
  "My interpretation is that you want to spend less time with me, or you're not into this relationship anymore."

- Describe how <u>your interpretation makes you feel</u>.
  "Because of my interpretation that you're withdrawing, I'm feeling kind of bad about myself and about our relationship."

- Describe the <u>consequences of these feelings</u>.
  "I've noticed myself becoming even clingier because I'm feeling insecure about the relationship. I hate when I'm clingy like that, it's not who I really am. Can you tell me what's really going on?"

SKILL BUILDING EXERCISE

Identifying "Real" I Language

Take each of the following "pseudo" I statements (statements that begin with the word "I" but are not I statements at all) and rephrase them so that they are actually "I" statements.

I can't get through to you.

_____

_____

I can't believe you just said that.

_____

_____

I find what you're doing really annoying.

_____

_____

I wish you weren't so selfish.

_____

_____

I know you don't trust me.

_____

_____

_____

Using I Language is more complicated than starting your sentences with the word "I." Telling someone "*I* feel like you are manipulative" is not a proper use of I Language. However, telling someone "When you don't call me back I start to worry about our relationship" is a statement that describes someone's behavior without evaluating it, and more importantly focuses on your reaction. Keep in mind that you don't have to follow the steps above in a mechanical way. Just focus on telling the other person the *interpretation* you've created for his or her behavior and your *feelings* that come from those thoughts; acknowledge that you are upset because of an interpretation you are having, not specifically because of what he or she did.

I Language takes a lot of practice before it feels natural. If at first you don't like it, consider that your aversion may be because it is a totally new way of relating to someone. As dramatic humans, we sometimes like to verbally push and shove each other a little, and it can feel powerful or exhilarating. Using I Language is not a way to avoid conflict or emotions, and you can even use I Language during a heated argument. It is simply a way to get to the root of the problem faster by giving your partner a shortcut to your innermost thoughts, while reducing the chance of a defensive response. The next section of the text will focus on how we arrive to our sometimes erroneous interpretations, and give you some additional tools for getting closer to shared meaning.

CHAPTER SUMMARY

The verbal communication channel is used when we utilize language to translate our thoughts to people around us. In interpersonal relationships it is especially difficult to decode the intended meaning of another person's ideas because of the arbitrary nature of language: words have no meaning outside of the meaning we assign them. Each language has some syntactic and phonological rules that help us to structure messages in a way that is understandable. We also have pragmatic rules for what is appropriate in conversations, and we engage in conversational management to facilitate our interpersonal interactions through conversational starters, enders, and conversational maintenance strategies. Keep in mind, though, that the context in which the communication occurs also creates a challenge:

depending on your generation, your culture, and your gender you may be "speaking a different language" than your conversational partner, even when you are both speaking the same dialect.

Words can range in abstraction and can be unclear through heavy use of jargon, slang, and euphemisms. Communication is further complicated by the enormous power that our words have, and their ability to shape the way we experience the world. The Sapir-Whorf hypothesis suggests that we are prisoners of our language in that we can't really experience things we don't have the words to describe. This chapter closed with a description of I Language, a new skill that can help communication partners understand each other better.

CHAPTER ACTIVITIES

TEST YOUR UNDERSTANDING

True or False

____1. When pitching an idea to her boss, Sarah begins by saying, "I have only thought of this recently but…" Sarah has begun her pitch with a disclaimer.

____2. Language conveys meaning on two levels: content and feeling.

____3. The English word for "hate" is found across all cultures in the world.

Multiple Choice: Circle the best answer choice.

1. The idea that suggests that the words we select and use actually help create the world that we see around us is referred to as…

    A. Linguistic idealism

    B. Encoding

    C. Verbal communication

    D. Sapir-Whorf hypothesis

    E. None of the above

2. Which of the following is a statement using I Language, according to your textbook?

    A. I find you annoying.

    B. I feel worried when you don't call me.

    C. I wish you weren't so selfish.

    D. I know you don't trust me.

    E. All of the above are I statements

3. What is the "denotative" meaning of a word?

    A. The definition you could look up in a dictionary

    B. The personal meaning each individual has for the word

    C. The way in which the technical and slang meanings of the word differ

    D. The intention of the speaker

    E. The interpretation of the listener

**Answers are listed at the end of this section before the references.

1. Summarize the differences between the verbal and nonverbal channels of interpersonal communication.

_____

_____

_____

_____

_____

_____

_____

_____

_____

_____

2. Explain how words are both arbitrary and powerful.

_____

_____

_____

_____

_____

_____

_____

_____

_____

_____

_____

3. Explain why words are inherently unclear and why shared meaning is so difficult to achieve through verbal communication.

_____

_____

_____

_____

_____

_____

_____

_____

_____

_____

_____

_____

4. Explain how we use words to communicate identity.

_____

_____

_____

_____

_____

_____

_____

_____

_____

_____

_____

_____

5. Describe the contexts that affect the meanings of words, such as culture and gender.

_____

_____

_____

_____

_____

_____

_____

_____

_____

_____

_____

_____

_____

_____

_____

_____

_____

_____

_____

_____

_____

_____

IN-CLASS ACTIVITY

Trigger Words

Without censoring yourself, list at least five words that create a strong negative emotional or physical reaction from you. List any words that you find offensive, inappropriate, or wrong. They can be words that are personal to you, or words that would cause a negative reaction from most people.

1. Word: _____

   Reaction (emotional, physical): _____

2. Word: _____

   Reaction (emotional, physical): _____

3. Word: _____

   Reaction (emotional, physical): _____

4. Word: _____

   Reaction (emotional, physical): _____

5. Word: _____

   Reaction (emotional, physical): _____

Now list at least five words that create a strong positive emotional or physical reaction from you. List any words that make you smile, get butterflies, or laugh. They can be words that are personal to you, or words that would cause a positive reaction from most people. After listing the word, write what your reaction is when you hear that word.

1. Word: _____

   Reaction (emotional, physical): _____

2. Word: _____

   Reaction (emotional, physical): _____

3. Word: _____

   Reaction (emotional, physical): _____

4. Word: _____

   Reaction (emotional, physical): _____

5. Word: _____

   Reaction (emotional, physical): _____

SKILL PRACTICE: I LANGUAGE

What Is the Goal of I Language?

The goal of I Language is to take responsibility for your own interpretations and reactions to other people's behaviors.

How Do You Do It?

1. Describe the behavior in question.
   Example: "I noticed you came home after midnight last night."

   _____

   _____

   _____

   _____

   _____

2. Describe your interpretation of the behavior.
   Example: "I immediately assumed you did it on purpose just to get me worried after our argument."

   _____

   _____

   _____

   _____

   _____

3. Describe how your interpretation makes you feel and what the consequences are of these feelings.
   Example: "That assumption left me feeling even more angry at you and now I'm having even more trouble trying to resolve this conflict with you."

   _____

   _____

   _____

   _____

   _____

HOMEWORK ACTIVITY

LINGUISTIC RELATIVISM

Interview three people who speak English as a second language (ideally from three different countries). See if you can find some words that exist in their native languages for which there is no direct English translation. Discuss how the prevalence of these words in their native language shapes their experience, based on the concept of linguistic relativism.

_____

_____

_____

_____

_____

_____

_____

_____

_____

_____

_____

_____

Answers to True/False and Multiple Choice

1. True

2. True

3. False

1. D

2. B

3. A

REFERENCES

[71]Wiio, O. (1978). *Wiio's laws~and some others*. Espoo, Finland: Welin-Goos.

[72]Ogden, C.K. & Richards, I. A. (1923). *The meaning of meaning: A study of the influence of language upon thought and of the science of symbolism*. London: Routledge & Kegan Paul.

[73]Lane, S.D. (2010). *Interpersonal communication*. Boston: Pearson.

[74]Grice, H.P (1975). Logic and conversation. In P. Cole and J.L. Morgan (Eds.) *Speech Acts: Volume 3*. New York: Academic Press.

[75]Sapir, E. (1956). *Culture, language and personality*. In D. G. Mendelbaum (Ed.), Selected essays. California: University Press.

Also see: Whorf, B. (1956) Language, thought and reality. In J.B. Carroll (Ed.), *Selected writings of Benjamin Lee Whorf*. Boston: MIT Press.

[76]Tannen, D. (1998). *The argument culture: Stopping America's war of words*. New York, New York: Ballantine Books.

[77]From personal internet blog at http://sunnybrooklyn.blogspot.com/2007/02/fight-night.html

[78]Frijda, N.H., Markam, S., Sato, K., & Wiers, R. (1995). Emotions and emotion words. In J.A. Russell, J.M. Ferdandez-Dols, A.S.R. Manstead, & J.C. Wellenkamp (Eds.), *Everyday conceptions of emotion* (pp. 121–143). Netherlands: Kluwer Academic Publishers.

[79]Semin, G.R., Gorts, C.A., Nandram, S., & Semin-Goossens, A. (2002). Cultural perspectives on the linguistic representation of emotion and emotion events. *Cognition and Emotion, 16*, 11–28.

[80]Bertrand, M. & Mullainathan, S. (July, 2003). Are Emily and Greg more employable than Lakisha and Jamal? A field experiment on labor market discrimination. *National Bureau of Economic Research*, Working Paper No. 9873.

[81]Rupa, B., Reitz, J.G., Oreopoulos, P. (2017). Do large employers treat racial minorities more fairly? A new analysis of Canadian field experiment data. Toronto: R.F. Harney Professorship and Program in Ethnic, Immigration and Pluralism Studies. Munk School of Global Affairs, University of Toronto.

[82]Carpusor, A.G. & Loges, W.E. (2006). Rental discrimination in Los Angeles: Perceptions of ethnicity in names. *Journal of Applied Social Psychology, 36*(4), 934–952.

[83]Patrick, G.T.W. (1901). The psychology of profanity. *Psychological Review, 8,* 113–127.

[84]Ibid.

[85]Winters, A.M. & Duck, S. (2009). You **@#$**&!@!!: Swearing as bonding? In K.J. Gergen, S.M. Schrader, & M. Gergen (eds.) *Constructing Worlds Together*. Boston: Pearson Education, Inc.

[86]Schwebel, D.C. (1997). Strategies of verbal dueling: How college students win a verbal battle. *Journal of Language and Social Psychology, 16*, 326–343.

[87]Lustig, M.W. and Koester, J. (2003) *Intercultural competence. Interpersonal communication across cultures (4th ed.)*. Boston: Allyn & Bacon.

[88]Curtin, S., Warner, M. & Hedegaard, H. (2016). Increase in suicide in the United States, 1999–2014. NCHS data brief, no 241. Hyattsville, MD: National Center for Health Statistics.

[89]National Crime Prevention Council (February 28, 2007). Teens and cyberbullying: Executive summary of a report on research conducted for National Crime Prevention Council.

[90]Pew Research Center (October 9, 2011). Teens, kindness and cruelty on social network sites.

[91]Hall, E.T. (1977) *Beyond culture*. New York: Doubleday.

[92]Ibid.

[93]Miller, R.A. (1992). *Japan's modern myth: The language and beyond*. Tokyo: Weatherhill.

[94]Mehl, M.R., Vazire, S., Ramírez-Esparza, N., Slatcher, R.B., & Pennebaker, J.W. (2007). Are women really more talkative than men? *Science, 317*, 5834.

[95]Tannen, D. (1998). *The argument culture: Stopping America's war of words*. New York, New York: Ballantine Books.

[96]Yates, S. (1997). Gender, identity, and CMC. *Journal of Computer Assisted Learning, 13*, 281–290.

See also Yates, S. (2001). Gender, language and CMC for education. *Learning and Instruction, 11*, 21–34.

[97]Kiesler, Siegel, J., & McGuire, T. (1984). Social psychological aspects of computer-mediated communication. *American Psychologist, 39,* 1123–1134.

[98]Savicki, V., Kelley, M. & Lingenfelter, D. (1996b). Gender and group composition in small task groups using computer-mediated communication. *Computers in Human Behavior, 12*(2), 209–224.

[99]Herring, S. (1993). Gender and democracy in computer-mediated communication. *Electronic Journal of Communication, 3*(2), 1–17.

[100]Blum, K. (1999). Gender differences in asynchronous learning in higher education: Learning styles, participation barriers and communication patterns. *Journal of Asynchronous Learning Networks, 5*(2), 18–35.

[101]Spender, D. (1995). *Nattering on the net: Women, power and cyberspace.* North Melbourne, Australia: Spinifex Press Ltd.

[102]Waseleski, C. (2006). Gender and the use of exclamation points in computer-mediated communication: An analysis of exclamations posted to two electronic discussion lists. *Journal of Computer-Mediated Communication, 11*(4).

[103]Briton, N.J. & Hall, J. (1995). Beliefs about female and male nonverbal communication. *Sex Roles, 23,* 79–90.

[104]Guadagno, R.E. & Cialdini, R.B. (2002). Online persuasion: An examination of gender differences in computer-mediated interpersonal influence. *Group Dynamics, 6*(1), 38–51.

[105]Blum. (1999).

[106]Herring. (1993).

[107]Ibid.

[108]Kashima, E.S., & Kashima, Y. (1998). Culture and language: the case of cultural dimensions and personal pronoun use. *Journal of Cross-Cultural Psychology, 29,* 461–86.

[109]Carrere, S., Buehlman, S. K. T., Gottman, J. M., Coan, J. A., & Ruhkstuhl, L (2000). Predicting marital stability and divorce in newlywed couples. *Journal of Family Psychology, 14*(1), 42–58.

Perception and
Interpersonal
Communication

CHAPTER 4

Self-Concept and Interpersonal Communication

"If you don't understand yourself you don't understand anybody else."
—Nikki Giovanni

Learning Objectives

After studying this chapter, you should be able to:

1. *Define self-concept and self-esteem.*
2. *Identify factors that shape the development and maintenance of the self-concept.*
3. *Describe the ways we identify and communicate the self.*
4. *Explain the characteristics that make up the personality and how these affect perceptions of others.*
5. *Analyze how the self-concept affects interpersonal relationships with others.*

When was the last time you described yourself? Perhaps it was when you apologized for being late sometime this week, insisting: "I'm really sorry, it's unlike me to be late!" or maybe it was when you lost your keys and said to yourself: "This is so like me! I always lose things!" We are constantly aware of who we are and how we are, whether we express it externally or internally. You also have a pretty good idea of how others would describe you. Both the way in which you describe yourself and your perception of how others see you are important components of your self-concept, and both are essential to developing satisfying and healthy relationships. In fact, this chapter precedes the other chapters because the self is the foundation of interpersonal communication. When things go wrong in relationships we tend to first blame the other person rather than taking a look at what it is about our own communication that contributes to our problems. Working toward the goal of examining ourselves first, this chapter will help you understand how your self-concept affects your communication.

WHAT IS YOUR SELF-CONCEPT?

Who are you? This question is probably not easy to answer. Your identity is so complex that it's hard to find words to accurately describe it. **Self** is defined as the sum total of who a person is; it is the place from which all thoughts stem, and consequently all communication. Your **self-concept** is your idea of this self; it is your subjective personal description of who you think you are. This description has an enormous impact on how you interact with the world around you and communicate with others.

SELF-AWARENESS

One thing that differentiates humans from most other species is the ability to observe and analyze ourselves. **Self-awareness** is your consciousness of your "self." It is your ability to "see" your own thoughts and behaviors as stemming from who you are. To demonstrate self-awareness, consider the following study. Researchers performed an experiment where children trick-or-treated one Halloween evening at a variety of different homes. At each of the homes a woman would answer the door and invite the children in. She would then instruct the children to take only one piece of candy from the candy bowl, and then she would leave the room. In the homes visited by half of the children there was a mirror strategically placed above the candy bowl so that the children could see their own reflection when taking the candy. In the homes visited by the other half of the children there was no mirror. The children who could see their own reflection took only one candy, as instructed, but the children who did not have to look at themselves sometimes violated the rule and took more candy than they were supposed to.[110] This study serves as evidence that self-awareness can be more or less present at any given time, and provoking self-awareness can have a great impact on behavior.

There are at least three kinds of self-awareness: subjective, objective and symbolic. **Subjective self-awareness** is the ability that people have to differentiate themselves from their environment, to see themselves as autonomous agents interacting with the world around them. Your belief that you are an individual entity who is unique is your subjective self-awareness. **Objective self-awareness** is the ability to be the object of one's own thoughts and attention. When you leave a party you might think, "I should have been more outgoing. Why didn't I initiate a conversation with that person who seemed interested?" or "That was a really stupid joke I told. I need to remember not to do that anymore." Here you are reflecting on yourself through objective self-awareness. **Symbolic self-awareness** is our ability not only to think about the self, but also to use language (symbols) to communicate about ourselves to others. It's likely that some of your time spent conversing with others includes analyzing your own behavior, personality, or mood; in these conversations you are using language to show that you are self-aware.

THE SIX IDENTITIES OF INTERPERSONAL INTERACTION

Because of humans' unique ability to reflect upon our "selves," when two people interact there are multiple reflections taking place at the same time. In fact, it is suggested that in any interpersonal interaction there are actually **six identities** present:[111]

1.   Who you think you are,

2.   Who you think *the other person* is,

3.   Who you think *the other person* thinks *you* are,

4.   Who the other person thinks *they* are,

5.   Who they think *you* are, and

6.   Who they think you think *they* are.

Each of these identities affects the communication that occurs between the two "real" people present. You can probably remember a time, perhaps today, when you were conversing with another person and in the back of your mind you were aware of what he or she was thinking of *you*. At the same time you were aware of what *you* were thinking of *him or her*, and of course you are always aware of what *you think of yourself*. When each person is thinking this way, that's six identities! As you add people to the mix, the number of identities present becomes exponential.

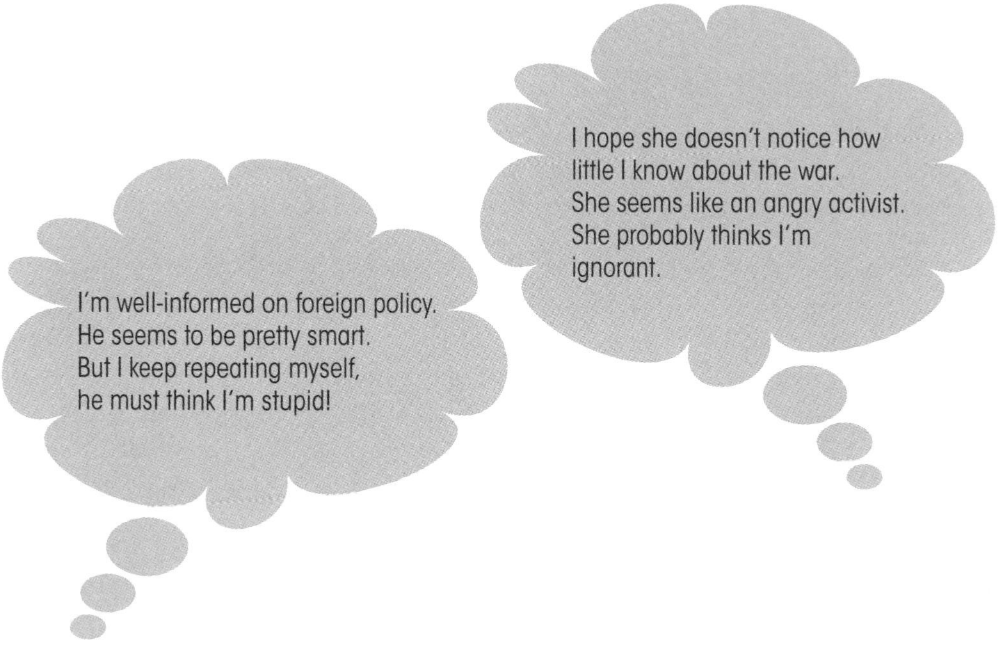

I hope she doesn't notice how little I know about the war. She seems like an angry activist. She probably thinks I'm ignorant.

I'm well-informed on foreign policy. He seems to be pretty smart. But I keep repeating myself, he must think I'm stupid!

Figure 4.0. When we interact with others we are always conscious of who we are, who they are, and what they think of us.

INTERPERSONAL COMMUNICATION FOR SOCIAL CHANGE

Stereotype Threat and the Six Identities

Interviewer: "So, Jaime, I see that you struggled through your undergraduate education."

Jaime (thinking): What is he talking about? There's only one C on my entire transcript...

Jaime (speaking): "Um, yeah, I guess I was an average student, not an Honors student or anything…"

Interviewer: "So would you say you have an 'average' work ethic, then?"

Jaime: "No, I think I have an above-average work ethic."

Interviewer: "So, you would describe your work ethic as 'above average'?"

Jaime: "No, I mean, I have a good work ethic."

Interviewer: "Well, which is it, son, or don't you know?"

Jaime: "I do know! I have a great work ethic!"

Jaime (thinking): Great, now I sound defensive. I'll never get this job.

Stereotype threat is a situation where people feel at risk of conforming to negative stereotypes about their social group, often causing them to fulfill the stereotype. Stereotype threat is one of the most widely researched topics in social psychology and helps us understand the impact of social identity on individual behavior.

The first empirical research on the effect of stereotype threat and intellectual performance was conducted in 1995 by Steele and Aronson.[112] Yet long before the first published evidence of stereotype threat, an elementary school teacher named Jane Elliott suspected that the phenomenon existed. She tested the idea in her third grade classroom by dividing children into two groups based on their eye color (brown or blue) and then convincing them that people with brown eyes were lazy and took longer to learn things. Sure enough, when she tested each group on their math facts the brown-eyed kids performed significantly worse than the blue-eyed kids, even though the scores from both groups were equal before they learned about the negative stereotype. On the next day of class Elliot reversed the groups, saying she'd been wrong and it was actually the blue-eyed kids who were less intelligent than brown-eyed kids. The performance tests showed the same result—now the blue-eyed kids did worse than the kids in the brown-eyed group![113]

Studies testing stereotype threat have focused largely on performance gaps in situations where people are aware of gender and racial stereotypes. Researchers consistently find that provoking awareness of gender and race-based stereotypes before an academic performance test creates measurable differences in scores for women and people from racial minority groups, both of whom have been targets of stereotypes related to intellectual inferiority. People from these social groups perform equally as well as others when negative

stereotypes about their groups are not primed, and can even perform higher than others when they are reminded of positive stereotypes about their ingroups (known as stereotype boost). However, when reminded about negative stereotypes surrounding their group's abilities, or even when provoked to think about it subconsciously, their performance drops significantly.[114]

In sum, the stereotypes we hold about others create expectations that can subtly or not-so-subtly leak into our interactions with them. These expectations create stereotype threat, and therefore accidental fulfillment of the stereotype. This is why stereotypes are so hard to break—once the idea is out there, they tend to fulfill themselves whether or not they are true.

Reflection

1. Which of the Six Identities described in this chapter are at play when stereotype threat is occurring?

2. Do you think people have specific stereotypes about you when they first meet you, based only on how you look or present yourself? How does your awareness of these stereotypes affect your communication?

3. Have you ever found yourself accidentally fulfilling a stereotype because you are so conscious of it?

4. Do you think you have ever communicated with someone in a certain way because you believe a stereotype about his or her group?

HOW THE SELF-CONCEPT DEVELOPS

Your self-concept develops mostly through interactions with others; it is formed over time as we "see" ourselves relating to other people. **Symbolic interaction theory**[115] explains that people make sense of the world through their interactions, which involves co-creating meaning and negotiating identities through symbols such as language. Thus, it's safe to say that without human interaction, we have little or no self-concept. Next we'll discuss two specific ways that your self-concept develops from your interactions: through the looking glass self and through social comparison.

THE LOOKING GLASS SELF

In the previous description of the "six identities," one of the identities described is "who you think the other person thinks you are." This is an extremely important component of our self-concept, called the **looking glass self**.[116] The looking glass self is the part of your self-concept that you learn based on your interaction with others who reflect your self back to you.[117] This reflection occurs in three often subconscious steps.[118] First, we imagine how others must view us. Next, we imagine the judgment included in that perspective. Finally, we believe the judgment and it gets included in our collection of thoughts about who we are. The looking glass self can be affected explicitly, when others tell us what they think of us, or implicitly, when we imagine or infer what others think of us.

The effect of the looking glass self on human behavior was demonstrated in a famous study by Rosenthal and Jacobson (1966) that took place in elementary school classrooms.[119] Teachers were given a class of students at the beginning of the school year and told to expect excellent performance from a certain group of students, and disappointing performance from another group of students. However, in reality all children were pre-tested and shown to be equally competent. Interestingly the "excellent performance" group did indeed show enormous improvement and test scores at the end of the term, whereas the "disappointing performance" group finished the term with lower test scores. In some cases improvement from the "excellent group" was about twice that shown by other children in the same class! It turns out that by expecting certain levels of performance from students, a teacher can influence the way they actually perform.

The fact that the teacher subtly engaged in behavior that brought out the worst in her "disappointing" group demonstrates the self-fulfilling prophecy. **Self-fulfilling prophecies** occur when our predictions about how things will turn out come true because we subconsciously make them come true.[120] We do so by acting in ways that bring out the behavior we are expecting. For example, the teacher likely gave more positive reinforcement to the "excellent group" but gave more criticism to the "disappointing group." Interestingly, the teachers always reported treating each group the same, which demonstrates that the self-fulfilling prophecy occurs on a very subconscious level.

SOCIAL COMPARISON

The second major way in which we form our self-concept is through social comparison. **Social comparison** is the process of noticing how you compare and contrast to other individuals with whom you interact.[121] Our self-concepts are created from social comparisons to others on two particular dimensions. First, we notice whether we are the *same or different* as the people whom we assess. Next, we notice whether we are *better or worse*. Imagine the first day of class. As you enter the room, you consciously or subconsciously survey its occupants, making interpretations about the people with whom you will spend the semester. Is there anyone "like" you? Are these people at "your level" (smarter, less intelligent, cuter, or less attractive)? These are social comparisons on the dimensions of similar/different, and better/worse.

The most common social comparisons occur by comparing yourself to people in your reference groups. Your **reference groups** are people to whom you can realistically compare yourself, such as people of your same age, gender, and social class. The **Triadic Model** proposes that people with similar attributes and opinions will be influential to each other because of their social relevance.[122] People whom you see as clearly superior or inferior to you have little influence on your self-concept because you probably consider these comparisons irrelevant or unrealistic. For example, there is no point in being authentically jealous of Mark Zuckerberg's bank account. Although you may desire his financial success, you do not beat yourself up for falling short of his measuring stick. On the other hand, if your close friend makes significantly more money than you do, this may affect how you feel about yourself.

Sometimes we can compare ourselves to inappropriate reference groups and still come out feeling okay. **Upward social comparison** occurs when individuals compare themselves to others who they consider socially better in some way. People make these comparisons because they want to believe they are similar to this superior group, and therefore want to point out similarities between themselves and the comparison group. For example, many people want to vacation where the "stars" go, so that they can feel similar to the rich and famous.

Downward social comparison occurs when a person evaluates him or herself with a comparison group that is worse off than he or she is. This tendency often serves a defense mechanism whereby ones own situation is seen as acceptable simply because it is better than someone else's situation. For example, many "soft" drug users discount their problem by comparing themselves to "hard" drug users, concluding that they are in great shape compared to some *other* people.

We engage in social comparison every time we interact with new people, and we use the outcome of our comparisons as a basis for our self-esteem.

SELF-ESTEEM

From a combination of the looking glass self and social comparisons to others we derive our **self-esteem,** or self-worth, which is an *evaluation* of personal value. Usually self-esteem includes perceptions of such traits as your skills, abilities, talents, and appearance, relative to those of other people.[123] The most important thing to remember about self-esteem is that it is filtered through your own perceptions.[124] You have probably met people who have high self-esteem, but are not stereotypically attractive or skillful. Equally, you have no doubt encountered countless people who seem flawless, but have terribly low self-esteem. Self-evaluation is a complex and subjective process that often defies logic. Self-esteem is not a permanent feature of the self. It can change through life experiences, and even age. Studies find that self-esteem levels tend to be high in childhood, drop during adolescence, and rise gradually throughout adulthood. Self-esteem tends to decline sharply in old age. These patterns hold true across gender, socioeconomic status, ethnicity, and nationality (U.S. citizens vs. non-U.S. citizens).[125]

MINDFUL MEDIATED COMMUNICATION

Seeking Perfection Through Our Avatars

The modern world gives us new options not only for how we work, but also for how we play. Entertainment companies are competing for your dollars by offering something you just can't get in the real world: a new self.

Virtual environment–based multiplayer online games such as World of Warcraft, Second Life, V-Side, and Sims give players a chance to decide on their own visual representation in the online world, otherwise known as an avatar. Second Life offers the most advanced avatar creation, allowing users to select not only their avatar's hairstyle and eye color, but also details as specific as the length of their torso and the shape of their ears.

Researchers of gaming and virtual reality have become especially interested in examining how the self-concept is invented, emphasized, or even diminished through the creation of an avatar. That is, do we create avatars that are in some way similar to our "real" selves, or do we take the opportunity of an anonymous mediated environment to create a self entirely different from our "real" persona?

One study found that gamers who created an avatar that reflected their ideal self engaged in more interactivity online with other players than those who created a replica avatar mirroring their actual self. What does this tell us about how and why we create avatars?[126]

Various theories propose that inconsistencies in the various selves we show to the world produce negative emotions. Of course our social relationships with different people bring out different aspects of our personalities, but generally we walk around in the same skin. Not true in the virtual world. Here we can actually change from an overweight person to a thin person, an unattractive person to an attractive person, a bald person to a person with hair. Research suggests that these major changes in our appearance may have the same effect as when we operate as different selves in the real world. In short, it has harmful effects on a stable self-concept and good self-esteem.

More research needs to be done in order to assess the actual damage of creating perfect avatars, and also to find out if there are some unknown beneficial effects of creating an imaginary ideal self that interacts with others in the virtual world.

SELECTIVE EXPOSURE

Another important thing to remember about self-esteem is that it is self-perpetuating. This means that we seek out situations and people that reinforce what we already believe about ourselves. We engage in **selective exposure,** which is our tendency to put ourselves in situations that reinforce who we think we are and the outcomes we expect. If you were told as a child that you were not a "math" person, you no doubt developed some anxieties about your ability to succeed in math classes. You may have even centered your entire college major on the idea that you don't like or aren't good at math. Sure enough, you end up majoring in a humanities or language based field, proving to yourself that you are more suited for non-math topics. Another example of selective exposure is that which occurs due to gender stereotypes. We learn very early which traits should go with our biological sex, and we perpetuate these stereotypes through selective exposure. By selectively exposing yourself, you are creating your own self-fulfilling prophecies, reinforcing your self-concept, and ultimately affecting your self-esteem. Because of this self-perpetuating cycle, self-esteem can be very hard to change.

WATCH AND LEARN

View a TED Talk on bullying and self-concept by typing this into your browser: TED Talk the bullied and the beautiful.

NARCISSISM

Although our culture focuses on the importance of self-esteem, too much self-esteem can impede personal development and negatively impact relationships. **Hubris**[127] is defined as exaggerated self-pride, and often comes in the form of overconfident speech or behavior. Hubris is often an indication of **narcissism**,[128] which is an inflated but fragile ego indicated by such traits as vanity, conceit, and self-centeredness. "Dorian Gray Syndrome" was coined after Oscar Wilde's famous novel *The Picture of Dorian Gray* in which a handsome young man looks at a painted portrait of himself and wishes that the image in the painting would grow old instead of himself. Gray gives his soul away in order for his wish to be granted, soon realizing that without growing old he cannot mature as a person. Although narcissism has been addressed as a problematic character flaw since the days of ancient Greek mythology, theorists have recently suggested that narcissism is on the increase due to the popularity of self-advertising in such online venues such as YouTube and Instagram. Some researchers suggest that a high degree of narcissism paired with social rejection can even lead to aggression and violence. One study reports that the Columbine High School students who went on a shooting rampage exhibited narcissistic thought patterns in their journal writings, and it may have been this characteristic combined with social humiliation that led to their severe anger and extreme violence.[129]

When it comes to self-esteem, then, it's not necessarily the case that more is better. Rather, healthy self-esteem is derived from a realistic self-concept based on social comparisons with appropriate reference groups. You shouldn't expect your self-esteem to be perfectly stable, as it ebbs and flows daily and changes over time. One day you may feel great about who you are, and the next day you may not like yourself very much. Examining your self-esteem can be difficult and emotionally challenging. However, self-esteem is a part of yourself that has an enormous impact on your interpersonal relationships, so it is worth thinking about.

Assessing Your Self-Esteem

Take the self-esteem quiz found at: testyourself.psychtests.com (go to the Lifestyle and Attitudes section and find it in the list of tests).

Are your findings consistent with your own view about your self-esteem? Is your self-esteem contextual? That is, what are some areas of your life where you have higher self-esteem? What are some contexts in which you have lower self-esteem?

_____

_____

_____

_____

_____

_____

Review! Self-Esteem	
Self-esteem:	A subjective evaluation of your personal value.
Selective exposure:	The tendency to put ourselves in situations that reinforce who we think we are and the outcomes we expect.
Hubris:	Exaggerated self-pride, often in the form of overconfident speech or behavior.
Narcissism:	Inflated but fragile self-esteem indicated by such traits as vanity, conceit, and self-centeredness.

EXPRESSION OF THE SELF

We identify and communicate the self in several common ways. In his book *The Principles of Psychology*, William James[130] identifies three components of the self that help to clarify and narrow down our multifaceted identities. Your **material self** is a total of all the "artifacts" you possess. The material self therefore encompasses your possessions, your home, and your body, and any "things" with which you surround yourself. U.S. culture places great importance on the material self. We often consider how someone looks, dresses, and what kind of car or home they have as a good indication of what type of person they are.

Your **social self** is the part of you that interacts with others. This includes your style of communicating, your level of desire for interactions, the kinds of friends and partners you choose, and your relationships with family members. Cultures where the family unit is the top priority, such as those found in Italy and Mexico, often derive much of their self-concept from the social self.

Finally, your **spiritual self** consists of internal thoughts about your values, moral standards, and beliefs, which includes your spiritual and philosophical perspectives. Cultures where religion is strongly interwoven into daily rituals and language often view the spiritual self as the most important component of the self-concept. Examples of these cultures include those found in India and Thailand.

ATTITUDES, VALUES, AND BELIEFS

Every person's self-concept has a material, social, and spiritual component. We communicate these parts of our selves by expressing how we feel about the world around us. One of these expressions takes the form of our **attitudes**, which are favorable or unfavorable predispositions to a person, situation, or thing. Attitudes generally come in the form of "liking" or "disliking" something, such as the statement, "I dislike watching golf on TV." **Beliefs** are concepts of what is true and what is false. Examples of beliefs include, "I believe in ghosts," or "I believe in God." **Values** are enduring concepts of good and bad, right and wrong, such as "Lying is wrong." Values are essentially your set of moral standards.

This quote, attributed to various sources across history, reminds us of the relationship between our thoughts and our communication:

> *"Your beliefs become your thoughts,*
> *Your thoughts become your words,*
> *Your words become your actions,*
> *Your actions become your habits,*
> *Your habits become your values,*
> *Your values become your destiny."*

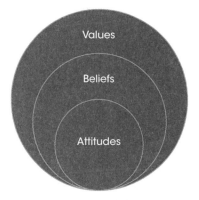

Figure 4.1. Attitudes and beliefs are both contained within your value system. In this diagram attitudes are also in the "front," because they are easiest to see. We usually have to get to know someone better before we learn their beliefs, and we often have to become even closer before we know their values.

Attitudes, beliefs, and values are socialized concepts, meaning you learn them starting at an early age and they are reinforced throughout your upbringing. Attitudes are more individualistic than beliefs and values, since your preferences may change with time and age. Beliefs and values are especially *culturally relative*, meaning that each culture has a different set of ideas about what is true and false, and right and wrong. For example, some cultures value the principle of "an eye for an eye," enforcing this moral standard through laws such as those that require thieves to have their hands cut off, while other cultures consider these laws to be inhumane. Beliefs and values are usually ingrained, which means they are so much a part of our fabric that they feel natural, and we have a hard time seeing the validity of any perspective outside of our own system.

Culturally relative concepts that are deeply ingrained create a special problem for people communicating across cultures. It is especially difficult to adapt to and respect people from another culture when your own beliefs and values are in conflict with theirs. Coping with different systems of thought is one of the greatest challenges in intercultural communication. Exposing yourself to different cultures through travel is one of the best ways to get in touch with your attitudes, values, and beliefs because they can be tricky to pinpoint when you are in familiar surroundings. Stepping outside the norms of your social groups and your own culture can help you identify and evaluate what you truly believe, think, and feel.

Review! Components of the Self	
Material self:	Your possessions, your home, and your body, and any "things" with which you surround yourself.
Social self:	The part of you that interacts with others.
Spiritual self:	Internal thoughts about your values, moral standards, and beliefs, includes your spiritual and philosophical perspectives.
Attitudes:	Favorable or unfavorable predispositions to a person, situation, or thing. Attitudes generally come in the form of "liking" or "disliking" something.
Beliefs:	Concepts of what is true and what is false.
Values:	Enduring concepts of good and bad, right and wrong, such as "lying is wrong."

PERSONALITY

The parts of the self (material, social, and spiritual) and the way the self sees the world around it (attitudes, beliefs, and values), combine to form the **personality,** or the *reaction* to one's environment based on a set of enduring internal predispositions and behavioral tendencies. Thus, your self-concept is your description of who you are, your self-esteem is your evaluation of who you are, and your personality is how you react internally and externally to the world around you.

Theorists have developed several personality types to help us understand ourselves and how we communicate with others. These taxonomies are descriptive rather than prescriptive or predictive; this means that they are used to describe how people think and behave, but they can never

predict what someone will do in any given situation, and they don't necessarily instruct on how to communicate depending on your own or others' personality types.

The Myers-Briggs typology is a personality assessment that measures four dimensions of the personality, resulting in one of sixteen possible four-letter "types."[131]

The first dimension of the personality measured by the Myers-Briggs is Introversion/Extroversion,[132] which assesses how a person is affected by the social environment around them. Specifically, this has to do with whether a person is energized or drained by social interaction. Introverts tend to get an energy depletion from social interaction, whereas extroverts tend to get an energy surplus from social interaction. One important thing to keep in mind about introverts and extroverts is that any person can flourish in a social environment, and you often cannot tell an introvert from an extrovert. What differentiates the two is how each feels *after* social interactions: if you want to go home and be alone, chances are you are an introvert; if you're the one asking, "Where's the after-party?" you are likely an extrovert.

WATCH AND LEARN

View a TED Talk on personality by typing this into your browser: TED Talk the power of introverts.

The second dimension of the Myers-Briggs typology assesses how an individual processes information, which is categorized as Intuitive or Sensing. Sensing individuals tend to trust information in the present that is tangible and concrete and can be obtained by the five senses. They generally prefer details, facts, and data. Intuitives, on the other hand, tend to be comfortable with abstract or theoretical information, and they like to improve and change things. They may be more interested in future possibilities and theories than laws and principles.

The third dimension assesses how people tend to make decisions, which determines whether they are a Thinking or Feeling type. Feelers will tend to make decisions by empathizing with the situation, and trying to find the most harmonious outcome that fits with their personal set of values. They often counsel others by encouraging them to talk about their feelings and by showing compassion. Thinking people are generally more detached in their decisions, measuring how they feel by what is reasonable, logical, and consistent. When counseling others they will usually advise. Although everyone has a bit of both tendencies, individuals will usually access their preferred style first and trust it better than if they came to a decision in another way.

The final personality dimension of the Myers-Briggs typology is the Judging versus Perceiving type. This category assesses how an individual prefers to organize his or her life. Judging individuals tend to be decisive, to start tasks well ahead of a deadline, and to have clear plans to which they tend to adhere. In contrast, perceivers are more comfortable leaving matters open, they leave tasks until close to the deadline, and they are more comfortable changing plans if new information becomes available. One stereotype of perceivers is that they tend to be "flaky," while judgers are often stereotyped as being "control freaks."

Review! Personality Types	
Introversion or **Extroversion:**	How a person is affected by the social environment around him or her.
Intuitive or **Sensing:**	How an individual processes information.
Thinking or **Feeling:**	How people tend to make decisions.
Judging or **Perceiving:**	How an individual prefers to organize his or her life.

BUILDING CULTURAL COMPETENCE

Universality of the Big Five Personality Traits

Researchers use the phrase "The Big Five" to describe the five traits that make up a person's overall personality. The Big Five are:

- Openness, or curiosity and interest in novel ideas and experiences.

- Conscientiousness, or level of discipline, organization and achievement orientation.

- Extraversion, or sociability and talkativeness.

- Agreeableness, or degree of helpfulness, cooperativeness and sympathetic tendencies.

- Neuroticism, or degree of emotional stability.

Rieman suggests that because all humans are one species and because personality has genetic roots, we should find the same personality traits across cultures.[133] Because each of The Big Five have important implications for survival in any culture, we are likely to find these measurable traits in people all over the globe.[134] Indeed, McCrae and Costa found that the same personality structure has emerged in a wide variety of cultures such as French, Japanese, Turkish, and American. While researchers caution about cultural generalizations, it may be safe to say that personality types are a universal concept.[135]

COMMUNICATION STYLE

There are several personality styles on which individuals vary. Some people believe these tendencies are genetic, while others believe they are learned; in reality they are probably a combination of both. One of these personality differences is **communication style,** or the habitual way we communicate with others. Communication style includes to what degree you are assertive, responsive and willing to communicate with others.

Assertiveness is the degree to which you pursue your own rights and best interests by making requests, asking for information, and generally expressing your needs. While some people are assertive, others are aggressive, which means that they pursue only their own rights and violate the rights and well-being of others. Still yet, some individuals are non-assertive, meaning that they always put others first, often at their own expense. You can probably imagine individuals in your own life who serve as good examples of each of these communication styles. A person who frequently lashes out at others is aggressive, while a person who rarely speaks his or her mind is

non-assertive. Someone who communicates their needs while respecting others is considered to have an assertive style.

Responsiveness is the tendency to be aware of and sensitive to the needs of others. Some individuals are highly responsive while others are non-responsive. You can probably predict the reaction of several of your friends or family members if you were to approach them with a personal problem. How sensitive is your father, mother, or sibling to your needs and feelings? You most likely make choices about who you approach based on your understanding of his or her level of responsiveness. We are often disappointed when we seek a significant other's help or attention and they are not responsive, taking it personally instead of realizing that it is part of their personality and communication style.

Willingness to communicate describes an individual's tendency to be eager for communication with others. People who readily approach others have a high willingness to communicate, while those who prefer to avoid what they consider unnecessary interaction have a low willingness to communicate. This trait is often associated with extroversion.

Communication apprehension is the fear or anxiety associated with either real or anticipated communication with other people.[136] Many people have extreme communication apprehension, which results in **shyness**, or the behavioral tendency not to talk or interact with other people. The difference between shyness and willingness to communicate is that shy people often *desire* to have more interactions, but they have a hard time starting or maintaining and interaction, whereas those who show low willingness to communicate actually prefer less communication. Everyone has some degree of communication apprehension in certain situations, such as an interview, or when giving a presentation. However, the level of communication apprehension that composes your communication style is fairly stable across situations.

Review! Communication Styles	
Assertiveness:	The degree to which you pursue our own rights and best interests by making requests, asking for information, and generally expressing your needs.
Responsiveness:	The degree to which you are aware of and sensitive to the needs of others.
Willingness to communicate:	An individual's tendency to invite or avoid communication with others.
Communication apprehension:	The fear or anxiety associated with either real or anticipated communication with other people.
Shyness:	The behavioral tendency not to talk or interact with other people.

Learning about the role your own personality plays in your self-concept can provide clarity about your perceptions of other people. We tend to evaluate our own behavior positively, while we apply more rigid expectations to others. This is especially true if we are dealing with someone who is a personality type opposite to our own. For example, an Extrovert may tend to find an Introvert

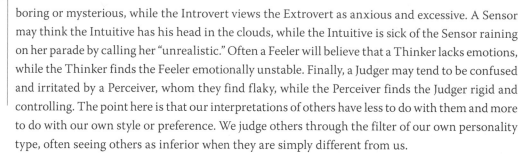

boring or mysterious, while the Introvert views the Extrovert as anxious and excessive. A Sensor may think the Intuitive has his head in the clouds, while the Intuitive is sick of the Sensor raining on her parade by calling her "unrealistic." Often a Feeler will believe that a Thinker lacks emotions, while the Thinker finds the Feeler emotionally unstable. Finally, a Judger may tend to be confused and irritated by a Perceiver, whom they find flaky, while the Perceiver finds the Judger rigid and controlling. The point here is that our interpretations of others have less to do with them and more to do with our own style or preference. We judge others through the filter of our own personality type, often seeing others as inferior when they are simply different from us.

There are several personality assessments that individuals can take to learn more about themselves. Researchers and theorists continue to develop these assessments for use in such contexts as couple and family therapy, business and organizational consulting, and individual analysis. If you choose to learn more about yourself through personality assessments, keep in mind that many of these measures are not considered scientific because they were not derived using the scientific method. Furthermore, they are not falsifiable, meaning they cannot be *disproved*, which is required for a concept to be considered a scientific theory. In addition, any assessment where an individual determines his or her own results is prone to a *social desirability bias*, meaning the respondent answers the questions based on who they would *like* to be, not who they are. Lastly, when taking any assessment, be aware of the *confirmation bias*, which is the tendency to find it valid because you are only paying attention to the parts of it that are true and ignoring the parts that are inaccurate (a tendency that occurs frequently when reading ones horoscope!).

HOW SELF-CONCEPT AFFECTS COMMUNICATION WITH OTHERS

As emphasized throughout this chapter, self-concept has a major impact on our interpersonal communication. In any interaction with another person we are constantly reacting to who we think we are (self-concept), who we think they think we are (looking glass self), and who we think they are (perception, filtered through your own personality, of course!). We attempt to manage these multiple identities through impression management, which comes in the form of self-monitoring and face work.

IMPRESSION MANAGEMENT

Impression management is our attempt to control how others see us.[137] We do this by controlling what we say and do, constantly assessing the impression we are making, and adjusting accordingly. Individuals vary in the degree to which they manage their own behavior in order to control the impression they give.

SELF-MONITORING

Trying to control your impressions is referred to as **self-monitoring**,[138] and each person has a tendency toward more or less monitoring. High self-monitors are constantly taking the situational temperature and adjusting their behavior by controlling what they say and do. Low self-monitors are less preoccupied with what others think of them, and therefore they are more likely to offend or surprise others. Self-monitoring can correlate with introversion and extroversion: often extroversion is characterized by expressing feelings out loud before giving them thought, which is low self-monitoring; in contrast introversion is characterized by thinking things through before expressing them, which is one form of high self-monitoring. As with communication apprehension, self-monitoring is more prevalent in certain contexts such as first dates, interviews, or any situation that is highly uncertain or intimidating.

FACEWORK

One way we manage impressions is through facework. **Facework** is the use of communication to maintain a certain image of yourself and others.[139] We attempt to maintain positive face by avoiding embarrassment and acting in a socially appropriate way. In addition to managing our own impressions, we also try to help others manage their impressions by supporting or reinforcing their "face." Using facework to help others maintain a positive self-concept is very common in many Asian cultures, and preventing "loss of face" is a goal that drives many of the social customs typical of these societies. In fact, many Asian languages have words that emphasize the importance of facework in social relationships. For example, in Chinese, the term "mianzi" represents social perceptions of a person's prestige, and losing face of this kind is considered a loss of authority. The word "lian" represents confidence in a person's moral character, and losing face of this kind results in a loss of trust.[140]

Identity Management

The chapter discusses how much of our communication is affected by the impression we'd like others to have of us. Although this tendency is natural, it can sometimes lead to inauthentic communication, or messages that communicate who you want to be, rather than who you really are. View your own social media profile and, as honestly as possible, identify your own impression management strategies using the following table:

What I Wrote/Posted	The Impression I Wanted to Make
1.	
2.	
3.	
4.	
5.	

THE MEDIATED SELF

What is the purpose of displaying our Facebook Friends for the world to see? Researchers believe that it may have to do with impression management. By showing others how many friends we have, we are often trying to say something about ourselves. But is there any connection between how we "friend" others online and in real-life?

Current research offers at least two competing hypotheses to explain how we utilize online communication for our social needs. The **social enhancement hypothesis** suggests that people who are more popular offline augment their popularity by increasing it on social media platforms. In contrast, the **social compensation hypothesis** claims that users attempt to increase their online popularity to compensate for inadequate offline popularity. Findings show that our usage depends on our pre-existing personalities and communication styles. People who are more extroverted and who have higher self-esteem support the social enhancement hypothesis, being more popular both offline and online. Another subset of users who are less popular offline support the social compensation hypotheses—they are more introverted, have lower self-esteem, and therefore strive more to look popular online.

When it comes to our perception of others, it turns out we tend to be suspicious about online popularity. One study found that when Facebook users have more than 300 friends, viewers start to rate them as desperate or socially undesirable. In this study, published in the Journal of

Computer-Mediated Communication, college students rated the social attractiveness of individuals from looking at their Facebook profiles. Researchers controlled for all variables so that the profiles were identical except for the number of friends—either 102, 302, 502, 702, or 902. There seemed to be a distinct difference in the ratings, depending on the number of friends each profiler listed. The number with the best results was 302, and social appeal started to decrease as the number went up from there. People with "too many friends" were not considered more socially skilled, more interesting, or even more popular. In fact, they were considered very uncool.

IMPROVING COMMUNICATION USING OTHER ORIENTATION

This chapter was dedicated to helping you understand how your self-concept affects the way you relate to others. While an understanding of the self is essential for successful relationships, there is a time and place for self-analysis. In general, when we interact with other people it is helpful to take the focus *off* ourselves. In Chapter 1 you learned about **other-oriented communication**, which is communication that is thoughtful about the needs, goals, and desires of the other person. Other orientation is a skill that requires you to take the focus off yourself, and instead think about the other person in the conversation so that you are a better listener and a more authentic communicator.

To practice other orientation, try to replace common self-oriented (egocentric) behaviors with other-oriented behaviors. Self-oriented communicators think about what they are planning to say while the other person is speaking to make sure they sound and look good, or to make sure they are right. Instead, try to listen to the details of what the other person is saying rather than planning your response. Self-oriented listeners also tend to judge the statements of the person with whom they are interacting. Instead, try your best to reserve your judgment, knowing that you can always evaluate the conversation later. The most common error of self-oriented communicators is giving unsolicited advice or opinions. Before you advise, consider what the other person is seeking; does he or she need "help" or is he or she just trying to vent or chat? Finally, try to avoid using the other person's story as a platform for your own story, otherwise known as stage-hogging. Say you can relate if it's true, share your brief example, then ask the person to continue.

INTERPERSONAL SKILLS ACROSS CONTEXTS

Social Networking: It's All about You

Social scientists are concerned about the widespread narcissism that characterizes today's generation of young adults. One explanation for the attitudes of the so-called "iGeneration" is the growing popularity of socializing methods that focus on self-promotion instead of relationship development. Social networking tools such as Facebook encourage communication between interpersonal partners to be public, creating "stage" relationship behavior as opposed to private relationship behavior. Facebook allows viewers to comment on and approve or disapprove of wall posts between two people, so that users receive attention when they choose to post their interpersonal communication publicly. Interactions between two people then become multi-purpose: Purpose one is to send a message to the recipient, and purpose two is to send a message about oneself to the public viewers. Identity management often becomes the primary goal, replacing the goal of relationship maintenance with the recipient of the message.

Next time you are about to post something on the public "wall" of a friend's social networking page, stop and evaluate your goal. Are you attempting to make an interpersonal connection, or make an impression?

As you learned in this chapter, the self-concept is complex and multifaceted. In reading about self-esteem, self-fulfilling prophecies, and the six identities you've learned that what we think about ourselves and others has an enormous impact on how we communicate. Equally as important as your individual identity is your group identity, also known as "social identity." Social identity is a component of your self that manifests through your group memberships, and greatly impacts all of your social relationships. The focus of the next chapter will be the various groups to which you belong and the effect of these group memberships on your interpersonal communication.

CHAPTER SUMMARY

This chapter explained what is meant by your self-concept. The uniquely human trait of self-awareness was described, including objective, subjective, and symbolic self-awareness. The development of the self-concept was analyzed to help you better understand where your identity comes from and how it is perpetuated. The looking glass self was described as the image of yourself you see reflected in others' interpretations of you. This image creates a perpetual cycle of self-fulfilling prophecies whereby we tend to confirm what it expected of us. You also learned that we derive our concepts of ourselves through social comparison to our reference groups, during which we decide whether we are the same or different, and better or worse than others to whom we can realistically compare ourselves. From this process we derive self-esteem, or an evaluation of ourselves.

The ways in which we express ourselves include the material, social, and spiritual selves, which comprise our attitudes, values, and beliefs. Personality was introduced as your reaction to your environment (including people and information), which is fairly stable across time and contexts. We explored several personality types to give you a better understanding of how different personalities perceive each other. Finally, you learned how the self-concept affects communication with others through impression management, self-monitoring and facework. The chapter concluded with suggestions for how to take the focus off yourself by practicing other-oriented communication.

CHAPTER ACTIVITIES

TEST YOUR UNDERSTANDING

True or False

_____ 1. When it comes to self-esteem, more is always better.

_____ 2. Self-esteem is an evaluation of personal value, which includes perceptions of such traits as your skills, abilities, talents, and appearance relative to others.

_____ 3. One study found that gamers who created an avatar that reflected their ideal self engaged in more interactivity online with other players than those who created a replica avatar mirroring their actual self.

Multiple Choice: Circle the best answer choice.

1. What are the three kinds of self-awareness?

    A. Subjective self-awareness, objective self-awareness, and symbolic self-awareness

    B. Comparative self-awareness, subjective self-awareness, and biased self-awareness

    C. Objective self-awareness, decisional self-awareness, and biased self-awareness

    D. None of the above

    E. All of the above

2. To reduce egocentric communication and increase other-orientation, you should try to do all of the following EXCEPT

    A. Plan your message while the other person is speaking.

    B. Listen to the details of what the other person is saying.

    C. Reserve your judgments and evaluations for when you are alone.

    D. Consider what the other person is seeking, (confirmation, support, agreement, etc.).

    E. You should do all of the above.

3. Which of the following statements are TRUE?

    A. Researchers find that the same personality traits generally exist across most cultures in the world.

    B. Personality is culture-specific, meaning certain personality traits probably don't exist everywhere.

    C. It is impossible to test which personality traits exist in different places.

    D. Personality traits have important survivalist functions, which is why the same traits exist across the globe.

    E. Both A and D are true.

**Answers are listed at the end of this section before the references.

Short Answer

1. Define self-concept and self-esteem.

    _____

    _____

    _____

    _____

    _____

    _____

    _____

    _____

    _____

    _____

    _____

    _____

2. Identify factors that shape the development and maintenance of the self-concept.

    _____

    _____

    _____

    _____

    _____

    _____

    _____

    _____

    _____

    _____

    _____

    _____

3. Describe the ways we identify and communicate the self.

    _____

    _____

    _____

    _____

    _____

    _____

    _____

    _____

    _____

    _____

    _____

    _____

    _____

4. Explain the characteristics that make up the personality and how these affect perceptions of others.

    _____

    _____

    _____

    _____

    _____

    _____

    _____

    _____

    _____

    _____

    _____

    _____

5. Explain how the self-concept affects interpersonal relationships with others.

_____

_____

_____

_____

_____

_____

_____

_____

_____

_____

_____

_____

_____

_____

_____

_____

_____

_____

_____

_____

_____

_____

_____

IN-CLASS ACTIVITY
Self-Concept

Write three brief descriptions of each of the following:

Your mood	Your appearance

Your social traits	Your talents or lack thereof

Your intellectual capacity	Your strong beliefs

Your social roles	Miscellaneous

From the twenty-four descriptions, list the ten most "important" to your identity:

SKILL PRACTICE: OTHER ORIENTATION

What Is the Goal of Other Orientation?

As you've learned in this chapter, we tend to be preoccupied with impression management in our conversations with others. In Chapter 1 you learned about other-oriented communication, which is communication that is thoughtful about the needs, goals, and desires of the other person. Other orientation is a skill that requires you to take the focus off yourself, and instead think about the other person in the conversation. The goal is to be a better listener and a more authentic communicator.

How Do You Do It?

Next time you find yourself in an interpersonal conversation, try to replace the self-oriented behaviors on the "Don't" list with the other-oriented behaviors on the "Do" list below:

Don't (self-oriented)	Do (other-oriented)
1. Think about what you are planning to say.	1. Listen to the details of what the other person is saying.
2. Judge the other person's statements.	2. Reserve your judgments and evaluations for when you are alone.
3. Give unsolicited advice or opinions.	3. Consider what the other person is seeking, (confirmation, support, agreement, etc.)
4. Use the other person's story as a platform for your own story (stage-hogging).	4. Say you can relate if that's true, and if you explain your similar situation make it very brief, and then ask him/her to continue.

Write out a dialogue that demonstrates your use of this skill. Include in parentheses what you were inclined to do (from the "Don't" list above), then write what you did/said instead that shows use of the skill:

_____

_____

_____

_____

_____

_____

_____

_____

_____

HOMEWORK ACTIVITY

PERSONALITY ASSESSMENT

Take the personality assessment found at:

www.humanmetrics.com (click the link that says "Jung Typology Test")

Below list your four-letter type and the percentages. What did you learn about yourself? Are your findings consistent with what you know about yourself? Did you learn anything that was surprising or unexpected?

_____

_____

_____

_____

_____

_____

_____

_____

_____

_____

_____

_____

_____

_____

Answers to True/False and Multiple Choice

1. False

2. True

3. True

1. A

2. A

3. E

REFERENCES

[110]Beaman, A.L., Klentz, B., Diener, E., & Svanum, S. (1979). Self-awareness and transgression in children: Two field studies. *Journal of Personality and Social Psychology, 37*, 1835–1846.

[111]Barnlund, D. (1968). *Interpersonal communication: Survey and studies*, New York: Houghton-Mifflin, Co.

[112]Steele, C. & Aronson, J. (1995). Stereotype threat and the intellectual test performance of African Americans. *Journal of Personality and Social Psychology, 69*(5), 797–811.

[113]From: http://www.janeelliott.com

[114]Osborne, J.W. (2007). Linking sterotype threat and anxiety. *Educational Psychology, 27*(1), 135–154.

[115]Blumer, H. (1969). *Symbolic interactionism: Perspective and method*. Berkeley: University of California Press. See also Mead, G. H. (1967). *Mind, self, & society: From the standpoint of a Social behaviorist*. (C.W. Morris, Ed). Chicago: University of Chicago Press.

[116]Cooley, C.H. (1902). *Human nature and the social order*. New York: Charles Scribner's Sons.

[117]McIntyre, L. (2006).*The practical skeptic core concepts in sociology*. New York: McGraw Hill.

[118]Yeung, K., and Martin, J.L. (2003). The looking glass self: An empirical test and elaboration. *Social Forces 81.3*, 843–879.

[119]Rosenthal, R. & Jacobson, L. (1992). *Pygmalion in the classroom. Expanded edition.* New York: Irvington.

[120]Merton, R.K. (1968). *Social theory and social structure*. New York: Free Press.

[121]Festinger, L. (1954). A theory of social comparison processes. *Human Relations, 7*(2), 117–140.

[122]Suls, J., Martin, R., & Wheeler, L. (2002). Social comparison: Why, with whom and with what effect? *Current Directions in Psychological Science, 11*(5), 159–163.

[123]Ibid.

[124]James, W. (1983). *The principles of psychology*. Cambridge, MA: Harvard University Press. (Original work published 1890).

[125]Robins, R.W., Trzesniewski, K.H., Tracy, J.L., Gosling, S.D., & Potter, J. (2002). Global self-esteem across the life span. *Psychology and Aging, 17*(3), 423–434.

[126]Jin, S.A. (2009). Avatars mirroring the actual self versus projecting the ideal self: The effects of self-priming on interactivity and immersion in an exergame, Wii Fit. *Cyberphychology Behavior, 12*(6), 761–765.

[127]Defined as early as in Homer's *Odyssey*.

[128]Sedikides, C., Rudich, E.A., Gregg, A.P., Kumashiro, M., & Rusbult, C. (2004). Are normal narcissists psychologically healthy? Self-esteem matters. *Journal of Personality and Social Psychology, 87*, 400–416.

[129]Twenge, J.M. & Campbell, W.K. (2003). Isn't it fun to get the respect that we're going to deserve? Narcissism, social rejection, and aggression. *Personality and Social Psychology Bulletin, 29*(2), 261–272.

[130]James, W. (1983). *The principles of psychology*. Cambridge, MA: Harvard University Press. (Original work published 1890).

[131]Myers, I.B. (1980). *Gifts differing: Understanding personality type*. Palo Alto, CA: Davies-Black Publishing.

[132]Jung, C.G., & Hull, R.F.C. (1991). *Psychological types* (a revised ed.). London: Routlege.

[133]Rieman, R., Angleitner, A., & Strelau, J. (1997). Genetic and environmental influences on personality: A study of twins reared together using self- and peer-report NEO-FFI scales. *Journal of Personality, 65*, 449–75.

[134]Goldberg, L. (1981). Language and individual differences: The search for universals in personality lexicons. In *Review of Personality and Social Psychology*, by L. Wheeler (ed.), 141–61. Beverly Hills, CA: Sage.

[135]McCrae, R.R., & Costa, P.T. Jr. (1997). Personality trait structure as a human universal. *American Psychologist, 52*, 509–16.

[136]McCroskey, J.C. (1976a). The effects of communication apprehension on nonverbal behavior. *Communication Quarterly, 24*, 39–44.

[137]Goffman, E. (1959). *The presentation of self in everyday life*. Garden City, New York: Doubleday.

[138]Snyder, M. (1974). Self-monitoring of expressive behaviour. *Journal of Personality and Social Psychology 30*, 526–537.

[139]Goffman, E. (1955). On face-work: An analysis of ritual elements of social interaction. *Psychiatry: Journal for the Study of Interpersonal Processes. 18*(3), 213–231.

[140]Ho, D.Y. (1976). On the concept of face. *American Journal of Sociology, 81*(4), 867–84.

Social Identity and Interpersonal Communication

"Very little in our language or culture encourages looking at others as parts of ourselves."
—Patricia Williams

Learning Objectives

After studying this chapter, you should be able to:

1. Compare and contrast the concepts of schemata, worldview and paradigm.
2. Define social identity and describe how it contributes to the self-concept.
3. Describe the impact of culture, gender, and age on social identity and communication.
4. Explain how social identity affects our perception of and communication with ingroup and outgroup members.
5. Identify ways to improve interpersonal communication with outgroup members.

Who are "your people"? When you think of that question is it your friends that come to mind? Your family? Your race? You've already learned how the self-concept is developed through human interactions when we engage in social comparisons and see ourselves through the eyes of others. In addition, you learned how your self-concept manifests as your material, spiritual, and social selves because of your attitudes, values, and beliefs as discussed in the last chapter. This chapter focuses on another vitally important component to your communication: your group memberships. The groups to which you belong have a strong impact on what you believe about the world around you, or your "worldview."

The way you answer the question "who are your people" depends on the context in which you find yourself. First, this chapter will explain how your social identity shifts and changes depending on the situation you are in. Then, the various group memberships to which you belong will be compared and contrasted for a better understanding of not only yourself, but also others around you. Finally, this chapter will conclude with some suggestions for how to curtail your natural tendency toward using your own perspective as the framework by which you perceive and judge others. The goal of this chapter is to help you better understand where your perceptions come from, for the ultimate goal of increasing shared meaning and effective communication in your interpersonal relationships.

WORLDVIEW

Imagine the crayons you used as a child. If someone were to ask you what kind of container crayons come in, you would say "a box." Faster than you can say "box" your mind has already created an image of a Crayola crayon box (this is the *thought* that is associated with the *referent* c-r-a-y-o-n b-o-x, as you may recall from a previous chapter). The immediate image of the crayon box that is stored in your brain is one of an infinite number of ideas you have about the world around you, which collectively combine to form schemata (the plural of schema), or building blocks of knowledge in your brain. Thus, **schemata** are the webs of interconnected ideas and knowledge that you learn from experiencing the world.[141]

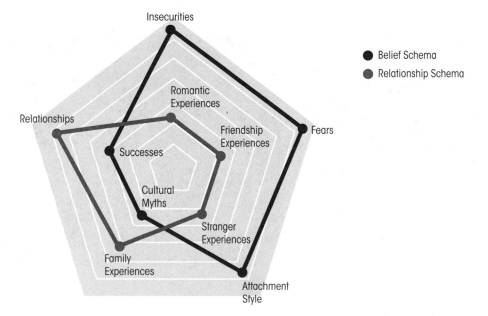

Figure 5.0. The brain is composed of overlapping schemata. This chart highlights a relationship schema and a belief schema.

Every time you learn something new, it gets evaluated in terms of its relationship to other things you know, and then it gets appropriately stored in your mind, near other similar concepts that make it easily accessible and understandable. When you were a child and someone handed you the green crayon, you knew just where to put it in the box: by the other green crayons, in order of dark

to light. Just as colors are organized in a crayon box, information is organized in your brain. As you grow and mature, this web of related concepts forms an elaborate understanding of the world around you. This overall understanding of the world creates filters through which you eventually view all new life experiences, and these filters combine to form your "worldview." **Worldview** is derived from the German word *Weltanschauung*, meaning to "look onto the world." Your worldview is the framework through which you interpret the world, including everyone you meet and everything that happens to you.

Worldviews are often shared by groups of people because their life experiences are composed of similar geography, climate, economy, religion, social systems, and language. Thus, anyone who was raised in a similar environment to you has a shared idea of what a crayon box looks like. Yet, in another country crayons do not come in a box, and in other places they do not know what crayons *are*. But for you, the idea of a crayon box is so concrete, so certain, that it is Truth.

The best way to understand your worldview is to be faced with worldviews that are in conflict with your own. Religion is an example of a worldview that can differ among groups of people in the same society and culture. You and I can coexist in the same country, at the same time in history, with the same general guidelines for the way the world operates (such as the laws of physics), but we can still disagree on who created humankind, who is the prophet or messenger of this creator, and how we should worship and express our faith. Consequently our beliefs about what is true, real, and right overlap in some ways, but not in others. Although worldviews differ from region to region and from person to person, there are some values that appear in nearly every culture around the world, such as the "Golden Rule." However, our worldviews tend to clash more than they overlap. When communicating with another person we often assume that he or she sees the world in the same way as us, when in reality we may be coming from different schools of thought. This presents a special challenge for achieving shared meaning and communicating effectively.

To exemplify the strength of worldview, consider the cultural differences between India and the U.S. when it comes to perceptions of social status. The United States was founded upon the concept of equal opportunity for all people, as stated in the constitution, "with liberty and justice for all."[142] Many people would argue about whether or not equal opportunity is a reality in the United States. However, India's history includes the development of a more clearly defined system of social stratification, known as the caste system. Although this system was technically outlawed in 1950, experts argue that it still plays a major role in Indian society.[143] According to the laws of this system (which some suggest is based on ancient Hindu scripture[144]), the caste into which one is born determines the kind of work he or she can do, ranging from government jobs to "blue collar" jobs, to sanitation jobs. One's caste can also determine whom he or she marries, and with whom he or she can socialize. A group known as The Untouchables (referred to by Mahatma Gandhi as "Harijans") represent the lowest caste, and are generally considered by this system to be sub-human; members of other castes therefore ignore people born into the Untouchables caste. Although it is no longer legal to discriminate based on this system, a person's caste is indicated by his or her last name, which makes this system difficult to abolish. The caste system therefore remains a fundamental belief in the worldview of many members of Indian society.

PARADIGMS

As demonstrated by the Golden Rule, there are certain components of our worldview that we share with most other people. When a common way of understanding and organizing reality is collectively agreed upon by a society to such a degree that it is unquestioned, it is called a **paradigm**.[145] If someone asked you whether the law of gravity is true, you would likely say "Of course it is," and there are not many people on this planet that would disagree. The law of gravity is part of our paradigm; it is a shared belief that we use to understand the nature of the world around us.

We tend to have enormous confidence that our paradigms are real. Part of this certainty comes from the fact that there is no way of identifying the misconceptions of our current paradigm while we are in it. The only true way to point out a paradigm is by looking back in history once we have progressed beyond the thought system that was taken for granted during its time. To demonstrate this point let's think back to a time when people believed that all the planets, including the sun, rotated around the earth. So convinced were they, in fact, that it wasn't worth contemplating or discussing, because it was just an assumed and obvious truth. They were absolutely and completely convinced that the earth was the center of the universe. Eventually, however, scientists learned new information that allowed for a paradigm shift. A **paradigm shift** is what occurs when what was formerly considered an ultimate truth is questioned, doubted, or disproved, causing a society to undergo some fundamental change.[146] Another example of a paradigm shift is what occurred when scientists discovered bacteria. Before bacteria were discovered people believed that babies became sick from too much affection. Obviously, the more babies were touched the more likely they were to get passed a disease or infection, but before we understood the transmission of bacteria, the touching itself was blamed for the illnesses.

Although we live in a certain time and place, and therefore we share a collective paradigm about what is true, occasionally even our paradigms conflict. An example of a unique paradigm that exists within a subset of our population is the Flat Earth Society. Believe it or not there is a group of people who still believe that the world is flat (you can find them online by searching "Flat Earth Society"). Although you share a larger societal paradigm with this group, and we may share particular aspects of our worldviews like religion and other philosophies about life, their unique paradigm includes the idea that the world is flat.

To better understand worldview and paradigms, consider this tale, adapted from the book *Illusions*, by Richard Bach:

> Once there lived a village of creatures along the bottom of a river. The current of the river swept silently over them all throughout their days. Each creature clung tightly to the twigs and rocks of the river bottom, for clinging was what they had been taught to survive. One day a creature said, "I am tired of clinging. Though I cannot see ahead, I trust that the current knows where it is going. I am going to let go, and let it take me where it will." The other creatures laughed and called him a fool. They said, "Let go, and that current you worship will take hold of you and smash you against the rocks!" But he did not heed their fearful warnings. Taking a deep breath, the creature let go. He was not smashed against the rocks, he was lifted into the current and swept downstream. Upon seeing him let go and float past, a stranger

cried, "See a miracle! A Messiah! But the creature said, "I am no Messiah, no more than you are. The river conspires to lift and free us, and yet we insist on clinging. If you let go you too will see that our purpose is the unknowing, the adventure." But they insisted on calling him Savior, all the while continuing clinging to the bottom of the river. Once he drifted past they were left to their clinging, making legends of a Savior.

What shared "truths" do we have in our current paradigm that will be disproved in the future through a paradigm shift? What ideas in your own personal worldview will change as you learn and grow? Chances are, we can't even articulate these shifts because we are *just so certain* that what we believe is true. If this is the case, what happens when we try to achieve *shared meaning* with people who have worldviews that are in conflict with our own? This is a complicated question that has perplexed humankind for as long as we've existed. To begin to understand this complex issue requires that we examine our own group memberships and how they affect the way we perceive and communicate with others.

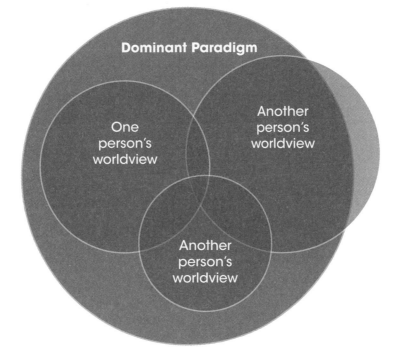

Figure 5.1. Multiple worldviews can exist within the dominant paradigm. The worldviews of individuals and even cultures can overlap, and parts of some worldviews do not fall within the dominant paradigm.

SOCIAL IDENTITY

Social identity is the part of your self-concept that is derived from your group memberships. Our memberships in various social groups affect the way we communicate with people who belong to our groups and also how we communicate with people who don't belong to our groups. Theories of **intergroup communication** strive to explain the behavior that goes on between people any

time those individuals are focused on their group memberships as opposed to their unique individual personalities. A group can be anything from a gender group or cultural group, all the way to a sports team. If the definition of a group is so wide-ranging, you can imagine that each person has multiple group memberships at any given time. For example, imagine a man named Ted who

belongs to the following groups: he is a man, he is a Harley rider, he is a Dodger fan, he is a democrat, and he is a returning adult student at the local community college. Each and every one of these group memberships may affect how he communicates with other people. The interesting thing about group membership is that it lies entirely in one's *perception* of belonging to a group at any given time. When you speak to one person you may be aware of one of your

group memberships, and when you speak to another person that group membership may not matter. Thus, purely **interpersonal interaction** occurs when the communication between two or more individuals is *fully* determined by their interpersonal relationship and individual characteristics, and not driven by the social groups or categories to which they respectively belong. In these situations a perceiver uses information about the other individual's personality, unique characteristics, and patterns of personal behavior to make evaluations and judgments. Interactions with your best friend are therefore considered interpersonal. In contrast, **intergroup interactions** are those where the communication is driven by each person's respective memberships in various social groups or categories, and not much affected by the unique personal relationship between the people involved. Intergroup communication, therefore, might occur between two fans of different teams at a football game, or two people of different political parties at a political rally.

SALIENCE

What determines whether we perceive another person as a representation of their "group" or as an individual human being? Why is our gender or cultural group important in one interaction but not important in another? This is where the idea of salience becomes helpful. You learned in a previous chapter that **salience** means "relative importance." Part of our identity is created from a comparison to others based on group memberships that are *salient* in the particular *context* in which we find ourselves making social comparisons. In different contexts we pay attention to different variables, or *accentuate* certain differences. For example, at a singles mixer or local bar, gender is a very important group membership because it is salient. However, at a medical conference, gender is not salient, but instead group memberships such as brain surgeon, general practitioner, or pediatrician are salient. Furthermore, when having a conversation with an old friend about what you did together as children, your friend's race, political affiliation, or other group memberships are simply not salient, which makes this interaction *interpersonal* instead of *intergroup*. The next section of this chapter is dedicated to explaining three different group memberships that may be salient in some of your interactions with others. By examining these group memberships, you will get closer to understanding your social identity and your worldview, which will help explain some particular barriers to shared meaning with other people.

Review! Intergroup Concepts	
Social identity:	The part of your self-concept that is derived from your group memberships.
Interpersonal interactions:	Interactions in which the communication between two individuals is fully determined by their interpersonal relationship and individual characteristics, and not driven by the social groups or categories to which they respectively belong.
Intergroup interactions:	Interactions in which communication is driven by each person's respective memberships in various social groups or categories, and not much affected by the unique personal relationships between the people involved.
Salience:	Relative importance of any particular group membership, based on the context in which it is being considered.

CULTURAL GROUPS

One of the primary group memberships that shape our worldview is culture. But what is culture? There are three common ways we refer to someone's cultural background. **Race** is based on the genetically transmitted physical characteristics of a group of people who are classified together.[147] There has been much debate on how to classify race, as indicated by the ever-changing  categories of race found on surveys such as the U.S. Census. Part of the debate centers around how to distinguish race from **ethnicity**, which is a social classification based on a variety of factors that are shared by a group of people who also share a common geographic origin or location. However, in this chapter our focus is on **culture**, which is a *learned* system of knowledge, behaviors, attitudes, beliefs, values, and norms that are shared by a group of people. Culture, therefore, includes codes of manners and etiquette, norms for behavior, dress, language, religion, rituals, laws, and systems of belief.[148] A **co-culture** is a distinct cultural group within a larger culture. Although the word "sub-culture" used to be popular, currently most groups prefer the term "co-culture" because it indicates equal importance between the dominant culture and the other culture. For example, Mexican Americans are Americans who have a Mexican co-culture.

Over time, one of two co-cultures often becomes dominant, or they mix to form a hybrid culture through **enculturation**, which is the process of communicating a group's culture from one generation to the next. Often the transmission of one culture to another can be seen through **cultural elements**, or things that represent aspects of a culture such as music, art, food, and social institutions such as schools or governments. For example, an Asian American raised by her Chinese grandmother may consider herself an American girl, although she has learned to cook Chinese food from her grandmother and her house contains various artifacts from China. Furthermore,

in her communication with others she may consciously or subconsciously use patterns of communication typical of her grandmother's dominant culture.

Cultural elements are also transmitted through **acculturation**, the process through which an individual acquires new approaches, beliefs, and values by coming into contact with other cultures to which they otherwise have no relation. Texans have become known for their Tex-Mex food, which was only possible through contact with their Mexican neighbors. Communicatively each group adopts words from the other culture, and this language adoption can result in shared values. Many Mexican Americans speak Spanglish, adding English words into their Spanish dialect to describe things that have no direct translation in their native tongue. This natural occurrence stems from the need to integrate into one's social environment. However, maintaining ties to one's culture of origin is equally important: research indicates that Spanish-speaking Mexican Americans report significantly fewer problems with social adjustment than non-Spanish-speaking Mexican Americans.[149]

Through both enculturation and acculturation, each cultural group is infused with characteristics of other cultures. However, there are some cultural characteristics that are subtler than artifacts such as food, clothing, and music. These cannot be worn, consumed, or listened to, and often operate on a level that is very hard to identify. It is important to identify these subtle cultural differences because they may explain why you might feel like you communicate so differently from another person, even though you have things in common. Most importantly, learning about these cultural differences helps us understand our own worldview.

BUILDING CULTURAL COMPETENCE

Culture or Personality?

By now you may be wondering how the concept of individual personality fits into cultural values. Within each culture there are varieties of different people, so naturally you will find group-oriented people in individualistic societies, as well as self-centered people in collectivistic societies. The terms "individualism" and "collectivism" are used to describe traits and behaviors at the cultural level, but when these traits and behaviors are not culturally-based, but instead speak to the nature of  the individual within the culture, the corresponding terms are "idiocentrism" and "allocentrism."[150] Idiocentric individuals emphasize self-reliance, competition, uniqueness, hedonism, and emotional distance from their social groups. In contrast, allocentric individuals emphasize interdependence, sociability, and family/group integrity. Allocentrics focus on the needs and wishes of their ingroup members, and they feel closer in their relationships to their ingroup members.[151]

All cultures contain idiocentrics and allocentrics, but in different proportions.[152] Researchers estimate that about 60% of people in collectivist cultures are allocentrics, and about 60% of people in individualist cultures

are idiocentrics, so over half of the people in each culture have personalities that correlate with the dominant cultural value. Interestingly, the allocentrics in individualist cultures are more likely than the idiocentrics to join groups such as gangs, communes, and unions, while the idiocentrics in collectivist cultures are more likely than the allocentrics to feel the desire to break free from their culture to escape its suppression of their individuality.

CULTURAL VALUES

One important part of cultural group membership is shared **cultural values**, which are what a given group of people values or appreciates. According to Geert Hofstede,[153] cultural values tend to range on five dimensions: comfort with uncertainty, degree of power distance, individual or group orientation, gender orientation, and concept of time.

High versus Low Uncertainty Avoidance

The first value dimension on which cultures can range is their level of comfort with uncertainty, known as **uncertainty avoidance**. Cultures that have low uncertainty avoidance have a higher tolerance for uncertainty and therefore tend to have looser social rules and more relaxed expectations of others. For example, in a low uncertainty avoidance culture such as the U.S., some professors like being addressed by their first name while others prefer being called Dr. Smith, Ms. Smith, or Professor Smith. Students learn what to call their professors by trial and error, or by asking. Other cultures have high uncertainty avoidance, which means they generally have a greater need for certainty and therefore have more rigid rules of conduct and higher levels of formality. In a high uncertainty avoidance culture such as Japan, a person of elevated status such as a professor or boss is always called by their title, unless he or she specifically invites you to call them otherwise. As with all cultural values, uncertainty avoidance usually stems from the history and demographics of a culture. Cultures that fear uncertainty generally have a homogenous population, meaning that the people are similar in background, appearance, and even beliefs, whereas cultures that have low uncertainty avoidance are those accustomed to a wide variety of different people.

High versus Low Power Distance

Often related to comfort with uncertainty are ideas about social power. The way in which a culture approaches status and power differences between its members can distinguish one culture's values from another. **Power distance** refers to the distance on the social hierarchy that separates people who have different roles in society. In cultures with **high power distance** there is a larger social "distance" between people with different levels of power, which is evidenced by multiple verbal and nonverbal forms of respect for people of higher relative status. One website advising Americans on how to conduct business abroad suggests that when meeting a business associate in South Korea "it is important to emphasize your title so that the correct authority, status, and rank are established."[154] Usually cultures with high power distance have **centralized power**, which means that power is in the hands of a small number of people. Other examples of high power distance cultures include Russia, India, and Saudi Arabia. In **low power distance** cultures there tends to be a smaller "distance" between people with different levels of social power, shown by relatively fewer verbal and nonverbal forms of respect for people of high-status roles. Australia is an example of a low power distance culture, evidenced by the attitude that no one is better than

anyone else. When taking a taxi, people in Australia are encouraged to sit in the front seat of the cab to avoid seeming "superior" to the driver. Other countries low in power distance include the United States and Canada.

Individualism versus Collectivism

In a culture where **individualism** is valued, personal goals and achievement are a priority, and it is often acceptable to pursue individual goals at the expense of other people. Therefore, individualistic cultures measure a person's worth by his or her ability to excel and accomplish things. Furthermore, individual-istic cultures value uniqueness because it shows independence, whether demonstrated through personality, personal taste, clothes or musical preferences. The laws in individualistic  cultures focus on protecting personal choices, the right to pursue one's dreams, and freedom of expression. Western European countries tend to be highly individualistic, but the United States ranks highest on individualism compared to all other countries in the world.

In contrast, a culture that does not prioritize individualism is considered **collectivistic**. In col-lectivistic cultures conformity is viewed positively, and one is expected to sacrifice personal de-sires and aspirations if necessary for the good of the group. Laws that center around the rights of the family or the common good of the society are typical, and there are many rules that provide stability and order. Collectivism is best exemplified by the popular Japanese phrase "Deru kugi wa utareru," which translates to "The nail that sticks up gets hammered down." Many Eastern cultures are collectivistic, including China, Japan, and Korea.

Long-Term versus Short-Term Time Orientation

Time orientation refers to the importance a culture places on the future versus the past and the present. In **long-term oriented** societies the future is the focus, therefore thrift and perseverance are valued. **Short-term oriented** societies focus on the past and the present through respect for tradition, fulfilling social obligations, and protecting one's "face," or sense of self.

Another way to differentiate between cultures by examining their concepts of time is by compar-ing whether they are monochronic or polychronic.[155] **Monochronic** cultures view time as limited. These cultures believe that time is tangible, meaning it can be "wasted" and "spent," as indicated by phrases such as "time is money." Monochronic cultures also view time as linear, meaning that it moves forward and has a clear past, present, and future. Germany, Switzerland, and the U.S. are examples of monochronic cultures.

Polychronic cultures view time as cyclical and plentiful. People from polychronic cultures do not run their lives by the clock (which means they may tend to be late, according to people from monochronic cultures!). Saudi Arabians, Mexicans, and Native Americans tend to operate in a polychronic time orientation. You should note that individuals within the same culture also tend to vary in their time orientations. Even within the United States, some individuals are less rigid about time, as demonstrated by their tendency to be spontaneous and to be less concerned with

punctuality, whereas other individuals tend to be more time-conscious, demonstrated by their motivation to stick to a schedule, to meet deadlines, and to plan for the future.

Masculine versus Feminine Orientation

Another important cultural value that accentuates our cultural differences is the degree to which our culture operates according to a masculine or feminine orientation. In **feminine cultures** priorities include the family, personal relationships, and the quality of life. Living takes priority over working, so sometimes these cultures have more flexible work schedules and longer vacations (Italians have an average of 42 days of vacation annually, compared to an average of 13 days for U.S. citizens![156]). Feminine cultures believe conflicts should be solved through negotiation rather than competition, and they often believe that men and women hold equally important positions in society. According to Hofstede's research, Sweden is the most feminine culture in comparison to others. Other feminine cultures include Thailand, Korea, and Spain.

In contrast, **masculine cultures** prioritize achievement, success, and material possessions. In a culture with a masculine orientation it is more acceptable to resolve conflicts through aggressive means, and women and men tend to have unequal roles in society. Examples of masculine cultures include the U.S., Germany, and Ireland. See *Fresh from the Lab* for a sample of countries and their scores on each of Hofstede's value dimensions (the countries that have the highest and lowest scores of those listed on each dimension are underlined).

Review! Dimensions of Culture		
High Uncertainty Avoidance	⟷	Low Uncertainty Avoidance
High Power Distance	⟷	Low Power Distance
Individualism	⟷	Collectivism
Long-Term Orientation	⟷	Short-Term Orientation
Feminine Orientation	⟷	Masculine Orientation

FRESH FROM THE LAB: COMMUNICATION RESEARCHERS AT WORK

Hofstede's Value Dimensions Across the World[157]

Country	Power Distance	Individualism	Uncert. Avoid.	Masculinity	Long-Term
Australia	36	90	51	61	31
Brazil	69	38	76	49	65
Canada	39	80	48	52	23
Germany	35	67	65	66	31
Great Britain	35	89	35	66	25
Hong Kong	68	25	29	57	96

Country	Power Distance	Individualism	Uncert. Avoid.	Masculinity	Long-Term
India	77	48	40	56	61
Japan	54	46	92	95	80
Netherlands	38	80	53	14	44
New Zealand	22	79	49	58	30
Philippines	94	32	44	64	19
Singapore	74	20	8	48	48
South Korea	60	18	85	39	75
Sweden	31	71	29	5	33
Taiwan	58	17	69	45	87
Thailand	64	20	64	34	56
USA	40	91	46	62	29
West Africa	77	20	54	46	16

SKILL BUILDING EXERCISE

Identifying Cultural Values

Read each of the following scenarios and identify which cultural values may be affecting each communicator's message.

A businessman in culture X asks his female colleague to step out of the room while the final negotiations are made.
The cultural value that may explain this behavior is _____ .

A teacher in culture X praises the work of three students, each who turned in the exact same paper with only their own name on it.
The cultural value that may explain this behavior is _____ .

A person in culture X needs to know exactly how many dinner guests are vegetarian so that there are enough quantities of each kind of food.
The cultural value that may explain this behavior is _____ .

A student in culture X raises his hand and tells the professor she has defined a theory inaccurately.
The cultural value that may explain this behavior is _____ .

A businesswoman in culture X is told that she needs to be less assertive during her presentations.
The cultural value that may explain this behavior is _____ .

A person in culture X cannot say exactly what time she is coming over, only that she will stop by. The cultural value that may explain this behavior is _____ .

GENDER GROUPS

We discussed how different cultures have different gender orientations, some being masculine oriented and others feminine oriented. Regardless of the culture you live in, you belong to a social category that is determined by your own gender identity and expression. **Gender** refers to psychological and emotional characteristics that cause people to feel and/or express themselves as masculine, feminine, or non-binary. Gender can be differentiated from sex, which is determined by your biological sex organs; your sex does not necessarily determine your gender identity or gender expression. Thanks to the increasing visibility and expression of gender non-conforming people, gender categories have expanded far beyond our initial concept of gender as binary (that is, either masculine or feminine). Categories such as non-binary, agender, androgynous, and gender fluid describe an array of gender identities and gender expressions. At the time this text was published, Facebook offered seventy-one gender descriptions to choose from when creating a profile. Unfortunately, social science research has a lot of catching up to do, since most research publications still refer to gender in binary terms.

female	male	bigender	neutrois	genderless
androgyne	demiboy	demigirl	intergender	third gender
genderqueer	epicene	poligender	transgender	transgender
femme	butch	transvesti	bigender	bigender
demiagender	allagender	demiagender	genderfluid	genderfluid

The primary difference researchers identify between masculine and feminine approaches to communication is that people who are classified as feminine communicators tend to communicate for relational development and those classified as masculine communicators tend to communicate to demonstrate status or to get things accomplished. As you can imagine, these two opposing views of the purpose of communication significantly affect our interactions with each other.

Overcoming Heterosexism and Cissexism

Lesbian, gay, bisexual, transgender, and queer (LGBTQ) folks have received increasing attention over the past few years for standing up and demanding the same rights afforded to their straight and cisgender counterparts. Whether the issue is adoption, bathroom choice, or pronoun usage, nationwide media coverage of LGBTQ issues and challenges is helping our society wake up to the fact that binary perspectives on gender and sexuality are outdated. Many straight and cisgender people strive to be allies to LGBTQ folks but aren't sure exactly what to do or how to communicate with people who don't match their binary understanding of gender or sexual orientation. If you are a person who wants to better understand the complexities of gender and sexual orientation, activist and educator Sam Killermann has got you covered. Sam's webpage, itspronouncedmetrosexual.com, includes an arsenal of educational tools for individuals as well as organizations striving for equity. His "Comprehensive List of LGBTQ+ Vocabulary Definitions" is particularly helpful for anyone who wants to start with the basics.

AGE GROUPS

Age is an important group to consider when reflecting on your social identity and worldview. One way to better understand the worldview of people from different age groups, and consequently their communication patterns, is to view them in terms of generations. According to generation experts Neil Howe and William Strauss, a **generation** is a group including all people born in a limited span of consecutive years, whose length approximates the span of a phase of life (approximately 22 years) and whose boundaries are fixed by location in history.[158] Your generation of origin has important implications for how you see the world, your relationships with others, and consequently your interpersonal communication. This section will cover five generations: the Matures, the Baby Boomers, Generation X, Generation Y, and Generation Z.

The Matures include people born between 1900 and 1946. This group lived in a difficult historical context, which included the stock market crash and the subsequent Great Depression, as well as the bombing of Pearl Harbor that started World War II, and the atomic bombing of Hiroshima that ended the war. As a result of this generation's upbringing, they tend to value control and self-sacrifice, respect for authority, family and community involvement, security and planning for the future. This generation also tends to believe in standard options as opposed to customizing. The Matures are characterized by their extreme dislike for wasteful behavior, and they tend to distrust technology, which should come as no surprise from a generation who witnessed the obliteration caused by the atomic bomb. You can imagine that the worldview of this generation greatly affects their expectations for others, and therefore how they communicate interpersonally. People of this generation may come across as untrusting and cynical if you are from a different generation.

Baby Boomers were born between the end of WWII in 1946 and 1964. During their childhood and adult life, members of this group experienced such optimistic events as the Civil Rights March, Martin Luther King Jr.'s "I Have a Dream" speech, and the moon landing. They also witnessed The Cold War, the Cuban Missile Crisis, John F. Kennedy's and Martin Luther King Jr.'s assassinations, and the war in Vietnam. This group is known to have characteristics such as optimism, a strong work ethic, responsibility, and a good attitude. Having experienced a time in history where optimism and activism were associated with youth, this group has been known to be sensitive about getting older, and may be responsible for the phrase "50 is the new 40." Each of these traits is likely to manifest in their communication patterns with others. Boomers are known to value openness and friendliness in their communication.

The next generation, known as *Generation X*, includes those born between 1965 and 1982. This group of individuals is characterized by witnessing events such as the Watergate scandal, the Challenger explosion, the fall of the Berlin Wall, and Desert Storm. Gen Xers are known for valuing skepticism, independence, and freedom. The "grunge" movement that occurred during this generation was symbolized by simple and basic clothing such as flannel t-shirts and loose jeans, demonstrating a dislike for superficiality and the desire to be raw and authentic as part of their worldview.[159] Therefore, when communicating this group appreciates directness and authenticity, and tries to avoid "hype."

Generation Y, also called the Millennials, includes those born between 1982 and the late 1990s. Members of this group are digital natives, as opposed to digital immigrants, meaning they were born into a society where the computer was an everyday part of life. Other events that shape the worldview of this generation include the Clinton-Lewinsky scandal, the mass shooting at Columbine High School, the Oklahoma City bombing and the terrorist attack on the World Trade Center in New York City on September 11, 2001. This group often tends to value hope, determinism, the latest technology, activism (especially environmental), and…their parents. Yes, it's true that this generation is known for being closer to their parents than any former generation, which will certainly affect their interpersonal relationships both now and in the future.

Generation Z is the most recently born generation of people, which is why the birth dates that define this generation are still uncertain. Researchers estimate that people born in the late 1990s up to the present day will comprise Generation Z, but even the name of this generation is still up for debate. Other names considered include iGeneration and Net Gen, amongst many others. The characteristics that define this new generation are also yet to be determined, but we do know some experiences they will have in common. Members of this new generation will have extreme connectivity through social media, multiple outlets for self-expression and unparalleled choices. They will be more diverse than any previous generation, many of them possessing multicultural identities and having social circles that include a wide range of ethnicities, religions, and sexual orientations. Only time will tell which real characteristics are possessed by this up-and-coming generation. Since their name is still being determined, what label would you assign this generation given your experience with them?

MINDFUL MEDIATED COMMUNICATION

Is Twitter the New Universal Language?

Intercultural enthusiasts have long sought a universal language that could help us overcome the barrier that often exists between people across the globe. The approach in the past was focused on creating a new language that everyone in the world could use. However, advancements in technology have made the necessity of an entirely new language obsolete. Now, with the click of a button on Twitter, you can communicate your thoughts and desires in any language, thanks to apps like Twinslator, Tweetrans, and Twanslate, which translate your tweets into other languages. You can also select the globe icon next to another person's tweet to translate it into your native language.

Twitter creates a virtual global community by allowing for communication between people who would otherwise be unable to understand each other (as witnessed when Egyptians created record-breaking worldwide awareness and support via Twitter during the January 2011 uprising). Some Tweeters are so fascinated by this new opportunity for communication that they are following the tweets of random strangers in other countries, just to get a glimpse of another world. Since user connections are asymmetric, a person can follow another person's tweet even without engaging him or her interpersonally. However, those studying the phenomenon find that shared interests such as video games, sports, art/entertainment, and politics tend to break down cultural barriers that exist otherwise. When you add a shared language to shared interests, real relationships blossom.

While Twitter opens up opportunities for communication that were not available to past generations, it is not a panacea for intercultural or intergroup conflict. Many users promote stereotypes and instigate conflict with divisive language and opinions. Like most social media, Twitters allows people greater access to each other, but does not change who they are.

GROUP MEMBERSHIPS AND INTERPERSONAL COMMUNICATION

INGROUPS AND OUTGROUPS

Social identity theory[160] suggests that one's social identity is that part of an individual's self-concept derived from his or her membership in a social group combined with the *emotional significance* attached to that membership. The theory is founded on the idea that the groups with whom we associate, or **ingroups,** have an enormous impact on our identity and self-esteem. As explained by the theory's authors, Tajfel and Turner, "Social groups or categories and the membership of them are associated with positive or negative value connotations."[161] Thus, people not only psychologically categorize themselves and others into social groups, but they have a need for their membership in these groups to be considered positive. One way for you to have positive feelings about your group is to make sure your group compares in a favorable light to other groups, known

as **outgroups**. This comparison, called **positive distinctiveness**, helps bolster "group-esteem," which is important for your individual self-esteem. For example, to be an authentic Dodger fan, you not only have to love the Dodgers, but you have to hate the Giants!

Interestingly, the need for positive distinctiveness results in subconscious pressure to exaggerate differences between groups. How can I have positive group-esteem if my group is not significantly *distinct* and *better* than your group? Even seemingly meaningless differences between people can provide the necessary evidence we need to see our group as distinct from, and better than, other groups. The phenomenon is best explained by the **minimal group paradigm**, which suggests that even a random categorization of people into two or more distinct groups can produce ingroup favoritism and outgroup discrimination.

This theory asserts that the variables upon which we base the distinction between groups can be completely arbitrary, to such an extent that the mere awareness of being put in one group rather than another group is enough to make us engage in discrimination of the outgroup and favoritism of the ingroup.[162]

Several research studies have been conducted to demonstrate the minimal group paradigm. You may have heard of the Prisoner's Dilemma, a game where each of two players must choose, without knowing the other's choice, between cooperating with each other and trying to take advantage of each other. One research team asked subjects to play the game, but first informed them whether they would be playing against someone of their own or different race. People who played against their own race were significantly more cooperative.[163] Another research study showed that when people were told the person they were playing against had a similar personality profile as them, they also were more cooperative.[164] Finally, another research team showed that when divided according to preference for certain artists, subjects showed significant ingroup favoritism and outgroup discrimination when asked to give rewards to members of either group in the form of points or money.[165] But finally, and most important to demonstrating the minimal group paradigm, in the same study subjects showed these biases even when they were aware that they were divided randomly. That is, they knew their group membership was not based on any similarity they had with their groups' members, and they still "preferred" their group.

Thus, the mere act of being categorized into a group is enough to develop a social identity based on this group membership, and to behave in ways that show a preference for your group members over another group's members. According to social identity theory, to maintain positive distinctiveness we are motivated to make psychological distinctions between groups of people, even if the basis for categorization is arbitrary and meaningless.

COMMUNICATING SOCIAL IDENTITY

There are also some more subtle effects of group membership on communication. **Communication accommodation theory** suggests that people adapt to their verbal and nonverbal styles to seem either similar or dissimilar to the person with whom they are interacting.[166] If you consider the person with whom you are communicating to be an "ingroup" member, you will engage in **convergence**, which occurs when we accommodate to be similar to the verbal and nonverbal style of the person with whom we are interacting in order to emphasize our similarities. In contrast, if you are communicating with someone who you would prefer to not be associated with, and whom you consider to be an "outgroup" member, you are likely to engage in **divergence**, which occurs when you differentiate yourself verbally and nonverbally from the person with whom you are interacting. Imagine how you speak with a group of your friends. Each of you uses similar slang and even vocal tones to convey that you are similar. If you switch contexts and start

communicating with your grandmother, chances are you will reduce your slang and converge to a more conservative form of speech out of respect and care for her. However, if you are in a situation where you want to make it clear that someone is old and outdated (perhaps you are talking to someone you believe is an untrustworthy, curmudgeon politician), you will actually increase the amount of slang you use, hoping to subtly point out your differences by diverging from that person's style.

Even subtler than communicative convergence and divergence is our tendency to frame our language in a way that reveals our hidden or subconscious preferences for our own ingroups (i.e., our own gender, race, social class). Researchers find that our level of abstraction, or degree to which our language is descriptive, communicates subconscious negative feelings about people who are different than us. This tendency, called **linguistic intergroup bias**, occurs when positive behavior displayed by an ingroup member is described in relatively abstract terms, whereas the same behavior shown by an outgroup member is described in relatively concrete terms. For example, if an ingroup member gives money to a homeless person, we are likely to describe her behavior using a general disposition adjective, such as "Sue is a *generous* person." If an outgroup member (someone with whom we would prefer not to associate ourselves) gives the same homeless person some money, we are likely to describe her behavior using a descriptive action verb such as "Sue *gave* away money." The same ingroup preferences are revealed when we describe undesirable behaviors.[167] If an ingroup member strikes someone, we are likely to describe the behavior using a concrete descriptive action verb, such as "John *hit* the bartender." In contrast, if the person we are describing is an outgroup member, we are more likely to use general disposition adjectives such as "John was *violent*." These selective language choices are so subtle and subconscious that when asked, people being studied report that there were no differences in the way they described ingroup versus outgroup members' behavior. We tend to believe we are less biased than we are, but our language reveals the truth about our preferences.

BEHAVIOR TOWARD INGROUP AND OUTGROUP MEMBERS

Although these differences seem purely semantic and relatively harmless, they are the foundations for intergroup problems such as prejudice and discrimination, especially in the forms of racism, sexism, and ageism. As soon as we identify our ingroups and outgroups, several processes occur to maintain these boundaries. The **outgroup homogeneity effect**[168] makes us perceive outgroup members as more similar to each other than they really are, while we allow for our own ingroups to be composed of a wide spectrum of unique individuals. From the belief that outgroup members are "all the same," we develop **stereotypes**, which are beliefs about a person based solely on the fact that they belong to a certain group. Stereotypes are usually inflexible, all encompassing categories, and are often negative.[169]

WATCH AND LEARN

View a TED Talk on interpersonal perception by typing this into your browser: TED Talk the danger of a single story.

Two phenomena that stem from oversimplifying outgroups are prejudice and discrimination. **Prejudice** is a judgment or opinion of someone formed before you know all of the facts or background of that person. In turn, prejudice often manifests behaviorally in the form of **discrimination,** which is unfair or inappropriate treatment of other people based on their group membership.

In his book *The Nature of Prejudice*, Gordon Allport suggests that what starts out as seemingly harmless behavior toward an outgroup easily evolves into dangerous territory, a process that can be seen in the Jewish Holocaust and other historical genocides. He outlines the following stages of prejudice commonly seen in history:[170]

Scale 1, Antilocution:

The majority group freely makes jokes about the minority group, and speaks in terms of negative stereotypes and negative images (also known as hate speech). This behavior is commonly seen as harmless by the offenders, but it sets the stage for more severe prejudice. Telling sexist jokes is an example of behavior that signifies this stage.

Scale 2, Avoidance:

People in a minority group are actively avoided by members of the majority group. Isolation causes harm to the minority group. An example of this stage is shown by the segregation laws that existed up until the 1960s in the United States of America.

Scale 3, Discrimination:

The minority group is discriminated against by being denied opportunities and services. The goal is to keep the minority group in its place by preventing them from achieving goals, such as getting an education and/or employment. An example of this stage is shown in Australia, where members of indigenous groups were denied the right to vote or own property until 1967.

Scale 4, Physical Attack:

The majority group violently attacks individuals or groups belonging to or associated with the minority, resulting in property damage or physical harm. This stage is exemplified by "gay bashing," such as that which took the life of Matthew Shepard in 1998.

Scale 5, Extermination:

The majority group seeks extermination of the minority group. They actively attempt to eliminate the entire group of people. The Jewish Holocaust and the genocide of the Tutsi people in Rwanda are both examples of this stage.

INTERPERSONAL COMMUNICATION FOR SOCIAL CHANGE

Unpacking Privilege

Students in an Economics class are having a discussion about poverty and the wealth gap between Black and White Americans, when one student raises his hand and says, "Why does everything have to be about race? My ancestors came here from Ireland and believe me, they struggled. My grandfather worked three jobs just to put food on the table, and my dad grew up poor. I'm the first person in my family to go to college, and it's all because of my own perseverance and the work ethic taught to me by my grandpa and my dad. I'm so sick of people pulling the 'race card' and thinking they have it worse than everyone else just because their ancestors were slaves. That was 100 years ago, it's time to get over it."

When people are asked to describe themselves, very few White folks mention their race while people who belong to other racial categories usually do. Why is this? Researchers who study identity, race, and ethnicity suspect that it comes from the fact that White is often considered the default race. Normalizing Whiteness and considering anything else "different" contributes to a phenomenon known as White Privilege. White Privilege gained a lot of media attention when a Princeton University student went on a tirade as a response to a teacher's request that White students "check their privilege."

White Privilege is an elusive phenomenon because you can't see it if you have it. Researcher Peggy McIntosh developed a checklist for White people to help shine a spotlight on the various privileges they experience due to their race. Here is a small sample of items adapted from the White Privilege Checklist[171] (you can find the complete original list by searching it online):

- I can go shopping alone, pretty well assured that I will not be followed or harassed.

- I can be in the company of people of my same race most of the time.

- I can turn on the television or open to the front page of the paper and see people of my race widely represented in positive roles.

- I do not have to educate my children about systemic racism for their own daily physical protection.

- I am never asked to speak for all the people of my racial group.

- I can be pretty sure that if I ask to talk to the "person in charge," I will be facing a person of my race.

- I can earn a prestigious position without having my co-workers on the job suspect that I got it because of my race.

- When a product is labeled "flesh" color it matches the color of my skin.

Learning more about White Privilege can help us understand the shape-shifting nature of racism that allows it to continue right under our noses. The following table lists various forms of racism in both interpersonal and institutional contexts, ranging from obvious and overt forms to those that are more subtle and covert:

	Interpersonal	Institutional
Overt	Race-based violence	More frequent police stops for People of Color/racial profiling
↓	Racist slurs, epithets, or jokes	Mostly White main characters and authors in all forms of media, and/or constant depiction of racial stereotypes
↓	Displaying or insisting on "free speech" for the display of racist symbols, such as mascots or flags	Official celebrations of and monuments dedicated to known racists; erasure from history of contributions made by People of Color
↓	Staring at, commenting on, or touching the hair or skin of People of Color	Greater likelihood of conviction for a crime and longer prison sentences for People of Color
↓	Questioning the lived experience reported by targets of racism, or requiring visual/tangible evidence of racism	Poorer quality of schools in neighborhoods inhabited mostly by People of Color
↓	Denial of White Privilege, claims of reverse racism, or responding with examples of your own hardships with "similar" problems, such as sexism	Higher rates of school expulsion for Children of Color starting in preschool, i.e., the "school-to-prison pipeline"
Covert	Color blindness/"I don't see race" claims	Greater likelihood of Whites inheriting wealth and land, i.e. perpetuation of wealth gap with no reparations

If you happen to be White, this information can be hard to accept because it may create feelings of guilt that generate defensiveness. One way to tackle this internal discomfort is to learn more. Try searching these resources online to learn more about your own privilege and how it may manifest in your interpersonal interactions:

Webpage: "Examples of Racial Microaggressions" from the University of Minnesota

Article: "White Privilege: Unpacking the Invisible Knapsack" by Peggy McIntosh

Documentary: *White Like Me* by Tim Wise

Blog Post: "What I Told My White Friend When He Asked For My Black Opinion On White Privilege" by Lori Lakin Hutcherson

1. What is your initial reaction when you hear the term "White Privilege"?

2. Do you think readers who are White react differently to this information than do People of Color?

3. Can you think of any other items to add to the White Privilege Checklist, i.e., things White folks don't have to think or worry about that People of Color do?

4. Would you be comfortable sharing this information with someone you felt was unaware of his or her privilege? What factors would determine whether or not it would be appropriate/effective to share?

METHODS FOR REDUCING INTERGROUP BIASES

We are so accustomed to our own worldview that we tend to be **egocentric**, meaning that we believe that our perceptions, beliefs, and methods are correct and superior to those of others. When these beliefs lead us to view other *cultures* only from our own cultural frame of reference it is referred to as **ethnocentrism**. According to experts in critical thinking, the tendency to judge others from our own worldview manifests in several detrimental ways:[172]

- **Egocentric oversimplification** is the natural tendency to ignore the complexities of the world in favor of overly simplistic explanations if consideration of those complexities would require us to change our belief system.

- **Egocentric memory**, also called selective memory, is the natural tendency to "forget" evidence that does not support our current way of thinking and to "remember" evidence and information that supports what we already believe.

- **Egocentric myopia**, also known as polarizing, is the natural tendency to think in absolutes, or black and white, within one's narrow point of view.

- **Egocentric infallibility** is the natural tendency to think that our beliefs are true simply because we believe them.

- **Egocentric righteousness** is the natural tendency to feel superior due to our confidence that we know the Truth.

- **Egocentric hypocrisy** is the natural tendency to ignore glaring inconsistencies between what we claim to believe and the actual beliefs indicated by our behaviors, otherwise known as a "double standard."

- **Egocentric blindness**, also called the confirmation bias, is the natural tendency not to notice facts or evidence that contradicts our favored beliefs or values.

To understand these cognitive tricks, imagine a scenario where you encounter an Arab American classmate named Khalid in your Religious Studies class. If you don't get to know him interpersonally, it is likely that your interactions are intergroup, meaning that your perceptions of him stem largely from his group membership. As you observe him commenting in class over the span of the semester, you may be inclined to engage in any of the following tendencies described above.

For example, you may employ *egocentric oversimplification* by assuming that because Khalid is Arab, he must be a practicing Muslim. You may support this assumption with *egocentric memory*, recalling some positive comments he made about the Muslim religion in class, but forgetting that he pointed out equally positive traits of the other religions discussed. You may also be inclined to engage in *egocentric myopia*, assuming that because he is Muslim and you are, for example, Christian, that you have entirely different sets of beliefs. Furthermore, the tendency toward *egocentric infallibility* naturally makes you certain that your religious perspective is the "right one," and your *egocentric righteousness* leads you to the conclusion that Khalid's beliefs come from "brainwashing" or ignorance, rather than being a part of his worldview, which is equally as subjective as yours. All the while you are likely engaging in *egocentric hypocrisy*, ignoring that your negative judgment of Khalid violates your own values. Finally, there is a good chance that your *egocentric blindness* is preventing you from noticing that he tends to treat you much more kindly than you treat him.

Understanding our human tendency to subtly judge others' behaviors in ways that elevate our personal and group esteem is essential to developing self-awareness. Ideally, as you learn these concepts you will increase your ability to view others as individuals rather than representations of their group. This ability depends on several skills, each of which is an integral part of communication competence.

First, **decentering** is the cognitive process in which you take into account another person's thoughts, feelings, values, background, and perspective. Once we imagine the circumstances that lead an individual to think and behave the way he or she does, we can start to see things in an entirely different way.

To practice decentering, imagine a person that you really dislike. Force yourself to make reasonable explanations for this person's behavior based on the characteristics of his or her life. Even though these explanations may not excuse the behavior, see if it changes how you feel.

Ask yourself:

- How was this person raised and by whom?

- What is this person's set of beliefs and values that were socially learned from his or her environment?

- What must this person think in order to behave this way?

- How must this person feel?

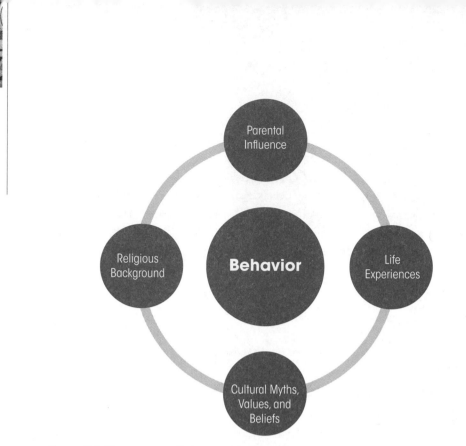

Figure 5.2. There are multiple considerations to take into account when evaluating or interpreting the behavior of another person.

Even deeper than considering where another person is coming from is imagining yourself in his or her shoes. **Empathy** occurs when you experience the emotional reaction that is similar to the reaction being experienced by another person. Empathy can be differentiated from **sympathy**, which is compassion or acknowledgment that someone may be feeling bad. For example, if someone tells you about a personal tragedy and you imagine how badly he or she must feel, this is sympathy. In contrast, if you imagine yourself in the very same situation, you are experiencing empathy.

To practice empathy:

1. **Listen** for the "feeling" (connotative) dimension of the message, rather than the information (denotative) dimension of the message.

2. **Imagine** yourself experiencing the exact same thing as the person you are listening to or thinking about.

3. **Experience** the feelings that arise as you imagine yourself in his or her situation.

4. **Share** with the other person the feelings you have when imagining yourself having his or her exact same experience.

One way to differentiate egocentric thinking from empathetic thinking is to reflect on The Golden Rule. This rule, as you learned previously, is present in almost all worldviews, and asks that you do unto others as you would have done to you. Consider instead using the upgraded Platinum Rule, which suggests that you do unto others as *they* would have done to them. To distinguish

these two approaches, imagine the situation when an individual from a low-context country such as the U.S. is trying to establish a friendship with someone from a high-context country, such as Korea. As the individuals get to know each other the American may believe that honesty is the key to intimacy, therefore explicitly stating her opinion all the time, and hoping for the same level of straightforwardness from her new friend. This behavior does not take into consideration what the friend would have done to *her*. To employ the Platinum Rule you must consider the worldview of the other, and imagine how he or she would prefer to communicate. This small difference in approach could have powerful implications for your interpersonal relationships.

Review! Methods for Reducing Intergroup Biases

Be aware of **egocentrism**, the belief that your perceptions, beliefs, and methods are correct and superior to those of others.

Avoid **ethnocentrism**, the tendency to view other cultures only from your own cultural frame of reference.

Apply **decentering** by taking into account the other person's thoughts, feelings, values, background, and perspective.

Experience **empathy** by imagining yourself going through the other person's situation.

Apply the **Platinum Rule**, which suggests that you behave toward others in the way that they would prefer, not necessarily how you would prefer.

WATCH AND LEARN

View a TED Talk on worldview by typing this into your browser: TED Talk fifty shades of gay.

CHAPTER SUMMARY

This chapter deconstructed the concept of worldview in order to better understand the filters through which you view all of your life experiences. Social identity was explained as the part of your self-concept that is salient in any given interaction with another person. To try and understand which social groups may impact your social identity, the chapter outlined three particularly important group memberships: gender, age, and culture.

The main categories of cultural values include high/low uncertainty avoidance, high/low power distance, individualism/collectivism, long term/short term orientation, and masculine/feminine orientation. Furthermore, you learned that the terms low context and high context communication describe the degree to which a culture relies on explicit and direct communication or implicit and subtle communication. Gender groups were the next social groups that were shown to affect communication. Finally, age groups were categorized by generation to help you understand some life experiences that may impact communication norms of people from different generations including the Matures, the Baby Boomers, Generation X, the Millennials, and Generation Z.

This chapter concluded with how group memberships affect interpersonal communication. "Group-esteem," also known as positive distinctiveness, was explained as the driving force behind the minimal group paradigm in which we tend to favor our own group even if that membership is random. Ways in which this preference is communicated include communication convergence or divergence and linguistic intergroup biases. Finally, methods for more positive intergroup communication were suggested in order to improve your own relationships using this new knowledge.

CHAPTER ACTIVITIES

TEST YOUR UNDERSTANDING

True or False

____1. Our cultural understanding of where people fit on the social hierarchy and therefore how we should communicate with them is called power distance.

____2. Interactions that are based on the group memberships of the participants instead of their individual personalities are called interpersonal interactions.

____3. Allocentric individuals emphasize distance from their social groups, whereas idiocentrics focus on the needs and wishes of their ingroup members.

Multiple Choice: Circle the best answer choice.

1. Cultural values are made up of five dimensions: comfort with uncertainty, power distance, individual or collective orientation, masculine/feminine orientation and

    A. Enculturation

    B. Time orientation

    C. Centralized power

    D. Degree of equality

    E. None of the above

2. The steps for feeling and expressing empathy are:

    A. Imagine, tell, listen

    B. Think, feel, then think again

    C. Look, listen, speak

    D. Listen, imagine, experience, share

    E. None of the above are correct

3. Which characteristics do experts expect members of Generation Z to possess?

    A. They will be closer to their parents than any other generation

    B. They will value skepticism, independence, and freedom

    C. They will have diverse social circles composed of people from a variety of ethnicities, religions, and sexual orientations

    D. They will value punctuality

    E. None of the answers are correct

**Answers are listed at the end of this section before the references.

Short Answer

1. Compare and contrast the concepts of schemata, worldview and paradigm.

_____

_____

_____

_____

_____

_____

_____

_____

_____

_____

_____

2. Define social identity and describe how it contributes to the self-concept.

_____

_____

_____

_____

_____

_____

_____

_____

_____

_____

_____

_____

_____

_____

3. Describe the impact of culture, gender, and age on social identity and communication.

_____

_____

_____

_____

_____

_____

_____

_____

_____

_____

_____

_____

4. Explain how social identity affects our perception of and communication with ingroup and outgroup members.

_____

_____

_____

_____

_____

_____

_____

_____

_____

_____

_____

_____

5. Describe the suggested ways to improve interpersonal communication with outgroup members.

_____

_____

_____

_____

_____

_____

_____

_____

_____

_____

_____

_____

_____

_____

_____

_____

_____

_____

_____

_____

_____

_____

_____

IN-CLASS ACTIVITY

Co-Culture Tree

Similar to a "family tree," make a diagram that shows all your various group memberships and their relationships to one another. Start with the most general part of your identity as the base of the tree, then work up, allowing the other identities to branch off from one another.

SKILL PRACTICE: EMPATHY

What Is the Goal of Feeling and Expressing Empathy?

Feeling empathy for others is an essential part of being human. However, we rarely seek to feel empathetic it situations where it does not arise naturally. Training yourself to experience and express empathy will make you a better listener and a better communicator.

How Do You Do It?

As you are listening to another person share their thoughts or experience with you, do the following. Come back later and fill in your results.

1. Listen:

   Listen for the "feeling" (connotative) dimension of the message, rather than the information (denotative) dimension of the message.

   What did you hear?

   _____

   _____

   _____

   _____

   _____

   _____

2. Imagine:

   Create an image of yourself experiencing the exact same thing as the person you are listening to.

   What did this image look like?

   _____

   _____

   _____

   _____

   _____

   _____

3. Experience:

Allow your body to experience the feelings that arise as you imagine yourself in his or her situation.

What did you feel?

_____

_____

_____

_____

_____

_____

_____

_____

_____

4. Share:

Explain to the other person the feelings you have when imagining yourself in his or her exact same experience.

What did you say?

_____

_____

_____

_____

_____

_____

_____

_____

_____

_____

HOMEWORK ACTIVITY

HIDDEN BIASES

Search "Harvard Project Implicit." Follow the steps to take one of the many tests of hidden biases.

1. What were your results?

   _____

   _____

   _____

2. Do you believe your results? Why or why not?

   _____

   _____

   _____

   _____

   _____

   _____

   _____

   _____

   _____

   _____

Answers to True/False and Multiple Choice

1. True

2. False

3. False

1. B

2. D

3. C

REFERENCES

[141]Anderson, R.C. (1984b). Some reflections on the acquisition of knowledge. *Educational Researcher, 13*, 5–10.

[142]U.S. Constitution.

[143]Bayly, S. (1999). *Caste, society and politics in India from the eighteenth century to the modern age.* England: Cambridge University Press.

[144]Mascaro, J. (1962) *Bhagavad gita* (translated). London: Penguin Books.

[145]Kuhn, T.S. (1962). *The structure of scientific revolutions.* Chicago: University of Chicago Press.

[146]Ibid.

[147]Bernier, F.A. (1684). New division of the earth, translated by T. Bendyphe in "Memoirs read before the Anthropological Society of London" in *Journal des sçavans, 1*, 360–64.

[148]Jary, D. & Jary, J. (2000). *The Harper Collins Dictionary of Sociology* (3rd ed.) (p. 101). Glasgow: Harper Collins.

[149]Griffith, J. (1983). Relationship between acculturation and psychological impairment in adult Mexican Americans. *Hispanic Journal of Behavioral Sciences, 5*(4), 431–459.

[150]Triandis, H.C., Leung K., Villareal, M. & Clack, F.L. (1985). Allocentric versus idiocentric tenden cies: Convergent and discriminant validation. *Journal of Research on Personality, 19*, 395–415.

[151]Cross, S.E., Bacon P., & Morris, M. (2000). The relational-interdependent self-construal and relationships. *Journal of Personality and Social Psychology, 78*, 791–98.

[152]Triandis, H.C., Carnevale. P., Gelfand, M., Robert, C., & Wasti, A. (2001). Culture, personality and deception. *International Journal of Cross-Cultural Management, 1*, 73–90.

[153]Hofstede, G. (2001). *Culture's consequences: Comparing values, behaviors, institutions, and organizations across nations* (2nd ed.). Newbury Park, CA: Sage.

[154]From http://www.communicaid.com/south-korea-business-culture.asp

[155]Hall, J.A., & Knapp, M.L. (1992). *Nonverbal communication in human interaction* (3rd ed.). New York: Holt Rinehart and Winston, Inc.

[156]As cited in a survey by the World Tourism Organization.

[157]Hofstede, G. (1994). Management scientists are human. *Management Science, 40*(1), 4–13.

[158]Howe, N. & Strauss, W. (1992). *Generations: The history of America's future, 1584 to 2069.* New York: Quill.

[159]Oblinger, D.G. & Oblinger, J.L. (2005). *Educating the Net Generation.* Boulder, CO: Educause.

[160]Tajfel, H. (1970). Experiments in intergroup discrimination. *Scientific American, 223*, 96–102.

[161]Tajfel, H. & Turner, J.C. (1979). An integrative theory of intergroup conflict. In W.G. Austion & S. Worchel (Eds.), The social psychology of intergroup relations (p. 101). Monterey, CA: Brooks/Cole.

[162]Turner, J.C. (1999). Some current issues in research on social identity and self-categorization theory. In N. Ellemers, R. Spears and B. Doosje (Eds.), *Social identity: Context, commitment, content,* 9. Oxford: Blackwell.

[163]Wilson W., Kayatani M. (1968). Intergroup attitudes and strategies in games between opponents of the same or of a different race. *Journal of Personality and Social Psychology, 9*, 24–30.

[164]Dion, K.L. (1973). Cohesiveness as a determinant of ingroup-outgroup bias. *Journal of Personality and Social Psychology, 28*(2), 163–171.

[165]Brewer, M.B., & Silver, M. (1978). Ingroup bias as a function of task characteristics. *European Journal of Social Psychology, 8*, 393–400.

[166]Giles, H. (1973). Accent mobility: A model and some data. *Anthropological Linguistica, 15*, 87–105.

[167]Maass, A., Salvi, D., Arcuri, L., & Semin, G. R. (1989). Language use in intergroup context. *Journal of Personality and Social Psychology, 57*, 981–993.

[168]Quattrone, G. A., & Jones, E. E. (1980). The perception of variability within ingroups and outgroups: Implications for the law of small numbers. *Journal of Personality and Social Psychology, 38*, 141–152.

[169]Lippmann, W. (1922). *Public Opinion.* New York: The Free Press.

[170]Allport, G. (1954). *The Nature of Prejudice.* Boston: Beacon Press.

[171]McIntosh, P. (July/August, 1989). *Peace and Freedom Magazine,* 10–12.

[172]Paul, R. & Elder, L. (2004). *The thinker's guide to the nature and functions of critical and creative thinking.* Dillon Beach, CA: The Foundation for Critical Thinking.

Interpersonal Perception

"A stereotype is the lazy person's way of engaging the other."
—Michael Eric Dyson

Learning Objectives

After studying this chapter, you should be able to:

1. *Define perception and interpersonal perception.*
2. *Identify and explain the stages of interpersonal perception.*
3. *Understand how individuals develop and maintain impressions.*
4. *Identify the factors that distort the accuracy of interpersonal perception.*
5. *Apply perception checking to improve interpersonal perception.*

Has anyone ever "rubbed you the wrong way?" As you meet new people, inevitably, some make good impressions and others make bad ones. Some of the impressions you form are neither good nor bad, but mere interpretations or assumptions about other people. But where do these impressions come from? The simple answer is "observations." However, your observations are not as clear-cut as they seem. You've already learned that there is no such thing as objective, factual observations when it comes to perceiving other people and forming impressions. This chapter will expose you to various cognitive tendencies that cause interpersonal perception and impression formation to be a very un-exact science. First, you will learn about the four stages of perception and the "cognitive tricks" that occur in each stage. You will then learn about some additional barriers that complicate the perception process. Finally you will be given some methods for increasing your own perceptual accuracy and thereby improving shared meaning in your interpersonal relationships.

WHAT IS PERCEPTION?

As we go through the day trying to achieve our goals, make decisions, and interact with others, we are constantly engaging in perception. **Perception** is the process of experiencing the world around you and making sense out of what you experience. The process of perception is involved in every action, in every moment. We perceive the weather and decide what to wear, we perceive the strange sound coming from under the hood of the car and wonder whether we should pull over. Most relevant to our topic at hand, however, is the fact that we constantly perceive other *human beings*. Whereas perception is the process of experiencing *all* things with your senses, **interpersonal perception** is the process of observing and interpreting the behaviors of *other people*.

The process by which we interpret the behavior of other people is more complicated than it first seems. There are three specific stages that occur during this process, and they are taken for granted because of the speed at which they happen. We usually perceive with our senses, and then communicate our interpretations without much awareness of the stages that led us there. Each of these stages will be discussed so that you can have a better understanding of where your interpretations come from.

STAGE 1: SELECTING

The first stage in the perception process occurs when you choose certain stimuli in the environment to which you direct your attention. This "choice" can be conscious or unconscious. **Passive perception** occurs simply because our senses are in operation. For example, I notice that it is cold not because I decide to pay attention to the weather, but because my body responds and signals to me that it regrets my not having brought a jacket. In an interpersonal context, passive perception includes any information you notice without any real effort. Sometimes you don't even notice that you noticed! Has anyone ever asked you a question about someone you just met, for example, "What was he wearing," and you know the answer even though you weren't aware that you noticed until you were asked?

Active perception occurs when we are motivated to pay attention to particular information. Imagine yourself in a conversation with an ex-girlfriend or ex-boyfriend for whom you still have feelings. You are paying *extra special* attention to certain details of the interaction, for example, how close to you he or she chooses to stand, his or her "tone," whether he or she mentions any new names, etc. If you have experienced such a situation, you are aware of how much effort it takes. In reality, we simply cannot be paying attention at this level at all times; it takes too much cognitive (mental) energy. Therefore, during the selection stage, we attempt to reduce and simplify the data we receive so as to not exhaust ourselves paying attention. We desire so much simplicity, in fact, that humans are referred to as "cognitive misers" by Walter Lippman in his book Public Opinion.[173] By this, Lippman means that we are motivated to use the least possible effort when thinking. This desire to keep things simple results in two specific tendencies that hinder us from gathering information accurately: selective perception and the confirmation bias.

What determines whether you actively or passively perceive information? As you learned in a previous chapter, different details have varying salience, or immediate importance, depending

upon the context. If you are in a potentially threatening situation, such as an altercation with an aggressive individual, you may fail to notice what the person is wearing while you instead focus on how quickly he moves toward you. We approach most situations from a survivalist perspective, subconsciously asking ourselves, "What is the least amount of information I need at this moment to achieve my specific goals in this context?"

PERCEPTUAL BIASES IN SELECTING

Selective Perception

Selective perception occurs when we direct our attention to specific details and consequently ignore other pieces of information.[174] If you are on a second date with someone you really like, that person may mention several "red flags" that you conveniently ignore. Instead you pay special attention to the positive attributes displayed. The play-by-play you share with your friends later on may sound something like this:

> Our date was perfect. We were talking, and he says to me: "I love pizza."
>
> And, well, you KNOW how much I ALSO love pizza! So I said:
>
> "No way! I LOVE pizza too!"
>
> It's just amazing how much we have in common, you know? Like, we *really* relate.

When your friends ask what toppings Prince Charming likes on his pizza, you reply, "Oh meatballs or something, I don't remember." They are sadly forced to point out, "But, aren't you a vegetarian?"

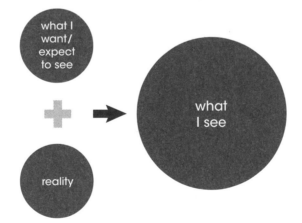

Figure 6.0. What we actually see is a combination of what is really there and what we want and expect to see.

Confirmation Bias

Part of selective perception occurs because you have pre-conceived ideas of what you expect or hope to perceive. When you conclude what you already set out to find, you are engaging in the

confirmation bias,[175] where you attend to information that confirms what you already believe, and therefore manage to find all the evidence you needed to support your expectations. Author Byron Katie says it well when she concludes, "The mind will find all the proof it ever needs to support its beliefs."[176]

MINDFUL MEDIATED COMMUNICATION

RateMyProfessor.com and the Self-Fulfilling Prophecy

If you recently logged on to RateMyProfessor.com to get the inside scoop on your teachers before the first day of class, be warned that it may affect your grade.

Looking at online ratings of services and products is a popular method by which consumers make choices. Known as "computer-mediated word of mouth communication," online dialogues and postings give people a chance to see what others are saying before they make a purchase.

Students often rely on computer-mediated word of mouth through sites such as RateMyProfessor.com, where their peers' evaluations of teachers help them in their process of course selection. However, recent research shows some unexpected consequences of viewing computer-mediated word of mouth sites before you enter into the classroom. Students who received positive computer-mediated word of mouth about a course or instructor demonstrated better learning in that course throughout the span of the semester than did students who received no information or negative computer-mediated word of mouth. Controlling for all other variables (such as the actual quality of the course and the students' grades) showed that student performance varied only because of their positive or negative expectations for their experience in the course, provided by RateMyProfessor.com.[177]

These findings show that entering into the classroom with a pre-conceived notion of your professor can trigger the "halo effect" or the "horn effect," which can have a great impact on learning outcomes. Experts suggest that students avoid professor rating sights and just plan to do their very best in each course so that they don't impose the confirmation bias on their experience, and suffer because of it.

Review! Ways We Select Information	
Active perception:	Observations that occur when we are motivated to select particular information.
Passive perception:	Observations that occur simply because our senses are in operation.
Selective perception:	Observations that occur when we direct our attention to specific details and consequently ignore other pieces of information.
Confirmation bias:	A perceptual tendency where you attend to information that confirms what you already believe, and therefore manage to find all the evidence you need to support your expectations.

STAGE 2: ORGANIZING

In the organizing stage of perception, the brain begins to organize the information that has been selected into understandable and efficient patterns that allow us to easily understand what we have observed. In the same way that we do not like to expend unnecessary amounts of energy paying attention to small details, we also do not like to spend a whole lot of time making sense of the information we have received. Thus, the way we organize data tends to be quick and imperfect, and does not always accurately represent reality.

One outcome of the organizing stage is impression formation. **Impressions** are collections of perceptions about others that we maintain and use to interpret their behaviors. We vary in the way we each form impressions of others. People who are considered **cognitively complex** do not categorize others easily or quickly. They consider more variables when categorizing others, and generally pay attention to *more stimuli* from the selection stage of perceiving. On the contrary, **cognitively simple** individuals have very few categories for understanding others. They tend to see the world in extremes, or in black and white. As a result they categorize people quickly and easily and rarely question the accuracy of their categorization. Your cognitive complexity determines how much you rely on your  schemata (the pre-existing knowledge in your mind) to organize information. In addition to the limitations of your cognitive complexity, there are several other perceptual problems that make the organization stage a harder puzzle than it seems.

PERCEPTUAL BIASES IN ORGANIZING

Punctuation

Punctuation is how we make sense out of stimuli by grouping and dividing information into time segments with beginnings and ends.[178] Punctuation is a particularly interesting phenomenon in the study of romantic couples that have an ongoing issue about which they argue regularly. Take, for example, the running conflict between a husband and wife about cleaning out the garage. If you ask the wife who started the conflict she says, "He did." Her version of the story is that she kindly requested that he clean the garage. He refused to do it, so she asked him a second time. She became increasingly annoyed as he continued to refuse her request, which became more and more evident by her tone. If you ask the husband who is responsible for the conflict he says, "It's her fault." He then reports that she constantly asks him to clean the garage in a nagging and insistent tone, which makes him want to reject her request. You can see in this example that the wife punctuated the argument at the husband's initial refusal, while the husband punctuated the argument more recently when her tone became increasingly negative. You may have also noticed from this example that we each tend to punctuate events in a self-serving way.

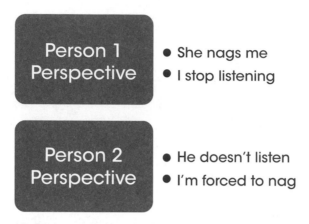

| Person 1 Perspective | • She nags me
• I stop listening |

| Person 2 Perspective | • He doesn't listen
• I'm forced to nag |

Figure 6.1. Each person punctuates the same issue in a different way.

Superimposing

Another trend in how we organize the data we receive from our observations is that we tend to superimpose. **Superimposing** is filling in information that is not there based on our assumptions. Consider the following set of numbers:

567 56 3308

252 3435

Both sets of numbers probably resemble something with which you are already familiar. It's likely that you immediately thought of the first set as a social security number and the second set as a phone number. Although this information is not there, you have superimposed it based on information that is already in your head derived from your life experience. When it comes to forming impressions of people, we do the same thing.

Clustering

Implicit personality theory[179] explains how we each have preconceived ideas about personality traits that come as a "package deal." In other words, once we learn a few details about someone, we infer other traits that are clustered with the traits we observe. For example, if you learn that someone is an artist, you might also assume that she is creative, a deep thinker, or even flaky, depending on your experience with "artist types." We maintain and use these  cumulative impressions to interpret all subsequent behavior from this person. So, if you invite your new artist friend to an event, you might assume she'll be late or won't show up, simply because you have clustered other traits with the little you already know about her personality. We often use another person's profession to "cluster" their personality. Have you ever heard someone say "Don't date an accountant if you want any excitement in your life," or "Well, what do you expect from an engineer?"

Review! Characteristics of Organization	
Impressions:	Collections of perceptions about others that we maintain and use to interpret their behaviors.
Cognitive complexity:	A term used to describe people who do not categorize others as easily or quickly as most people.
Cognitive simplicity:	A term used to describe individuals who have very few categories for understanding others and thus tend to see the world in extremes.
Punctuation:	How we make sense out of stimuli by grouping and dividing information into time segments with beginnings and ends.
Superimposing:	Filling in information that is not there based on our assumptions.
Clustering:	The tendency to use a small set of traits to make inferences about other traits that a person may possess.

STAGE 3: INTERPRETING

During the interpreting stage of perception we assign meaning to what we just observed and organized. Similar to what happens in the selection and organization stages, our interpretations are based on several principles of sense making.

Attribution theory[180] suggests that in trying to understand the world around us, we attempt to explain people's motives for their actions. The explanation we make is called an **attribution**. Attribution making includes two processes: determining the cause of someone's behavior and making a judgment about the behavior based on the cause. Attribution theory explains several dimensions of sense making.[181] There are three ways in which we analyze and attribute for a person's behavior, which include an assessment of the locus of control, the stability, and the controllability of his or her behavior.

First, the *locus of control* dimension determines the degree to which the behavior is caused by internal attributes of the actor or by external circumstances. When making an *internal* attribution, the perceiver assumes that the cause of the behavior is due to the personality characteristics of the actor, while attributing the behavior to *external* causes assumes that the behavior does not reflect the actor's personality, ability, or disposition, but instead is caused by the circumstance or situation.

Next, a perceiver assesses the *stability* of the cause, or the degree to which the cause is a stable characteristic of the actor that is consistent over time. Attributing a *stable* cause assumes that the behavior is a typical behavior of the actor that occurs across situations. In contrast, attributing an *unstable* cause assumes that the behavior was uncharacteristic of the person, and probably situation-specific.

Finally, the *controllability* dimension regards the extent of control or choice the actor had over the behavior or event: it was either within the actor's control and therefore was a conscious choice, or it was outside of his or her control, and therefore can be attributed to bad luck or other factors.

It should be clear by now that our attributions are not always based on reality, but rather on various principles of cognitive processing. To exemplify these three dimensions of causality and just how subjective they can be, consider a situation where your friend is late for dinner. If you choose to see the situation in the worst possible light, you would conclude that the lateness was caused by the lazy personality of your friend (locus of control = internal), she is always late (stability = stable), and she had a conscious choice about whether or not to be late (controllability = controllable). However, if you choose to see the situation in the most positive light, you could conclude that the lateness was caused by traffic (locus of control = external), that she is rarely late (stability = unstable), and that of course she did not have a conscious choice about whether or not she was late (controllability = uncontrollable). Each of these different interpretations will have an enormous impact on how you communicate with your friend once she arrives.

MINDFUL MEDIATED COMMUNICATION

Social Media and Sense-Making of the Isla Vista Murders

Tragedy struck the seaside university town of Isla Vista, Santa Barbara, on May 23, 2014, when a young resident committed a mass murder leaving seven people dead, and the community grief stricken and shocked. Amongst the disbelief, rage, and overwhelming sadness, a plethora of explanations for the massacre erupted on social media and in the press. As you learned about in this chapter, our own psyche demands that we make sense of others' behaviors, using a process called attribution-making. In a tragic situation like this one, the attributions people make reveal the influence our pre-formulated schema, or frameworks for thinking, have on how we interpret behaviors. Here are a few examples:

— People against gun control claimed that the Isla Vista murders could have been prevented if more citizens had guns because they could have shot the killer before his rampage continued.

— Those who support gun control insisted that if guns were not readily available then tragedies like this couldn't occur.

— Social justice advocates concluded that our culture's objectification of women and misogynistic value system were to blame, since the killer stated that he was seeking revenge on women who had rejected him.

— In response, there was a deluge of comments about women's insensitivities to men and their contribution to male rage.

These explanations are not only oversimplifications, but they serve as tools to further divide us into the ingroups and outgroups we invent because of our innate need for social identity (see Chapter 5). Viewing a tragedy from the biased lens of your ingroup prevents an interpersonal approach to outgroup members causing you to view them only as representations of their group instead of as individuals, which ultimately deters communities from healing and restoring peace.

When we channel our frustrations at inexplicable human behavior into hatred for an outgroup that we errone-ously hold responsible (whether it's the NRA, feminists, or social media users), our way of thinking becomes no better than the deluded Isla Vista assailant who blamed women and Asians for his rage. We all possess a human mind that is prone to fallacies in thinking, but resisting the instinct to simplify, categorize, and com-municate in hateful ways is what separates us from him.

PERCEPTUAL BIASES IN INTERPRETING

We tend to engage in several **heuristics**, or mental shortcuts, that prevent us from correctly in-terpreting information.

Oversimplification

The first mistake we tend to make in interpreting behavior is oversimplification. Oversimplifying means that you are always following the **principle of parsimony**, which states that the simplest explanation is usually the correct one. However, this is not always the case. Humans are complex creatures. Emotions, motivations, and interactions are complicated, and sometimes the simplest explanation, or attribution, is not the most accurate one.

Over Generalizing

Over generalizing occurs when we treat small amounts of information as if they were highly rep-resentative. Taking one specific instance and generalizing it to represent all situations is not only inaccurate reasoning, but it can be harmful. If you have ever seen someone witness a behavior from someone representing a particular ethnic group, followed by the comment "All _____ (fill in ethnic group) are _____ (bad drivers, lazy, sexist, etc.)," then you have witnessed over generalizing.

We often over generalize based on our pre-determined judgment of whether someone is likeable. The **halo effect**[182] involves attributing a variety of positive attributes to someone we like without confirming the existence of these qualities. If we like someone we assume that their behaviors are consistent with that image, so we make positive explanations for even the worst behaviors. Most professors can verify this tendency from first hand experience. If a student who has made a positive impression on the professor all semester arrives to class 20 minutes late, the professor will tend to make an explanation that maintains her positive impression of that person (e.g., he must have been studying and forgot to check the time). The opposite can also occur: the **horn effect** involves at-tributing a variety of negative qualities to people simply because we do *not* like them. Again, if a different student is late, one who has been nothing but trouble since the first day of class, the professor will attribute *that* student's lateness to an irresponsible nature.

The Fundamental Attribution Error

As we interpret our world, we have a natural, innate drive toward self-preservation. Part of our social needs require that we maintain a posi-tive self-image so that we can move confidently through life. A positive self-image includes a positive and stable self-concept, which leads to positive self-esteem. Unfortunately, our need to feel good about our-selves is sometimes derived from feeling bad about others. Hence, one tendency that lends to our positive self-image is blaming, or assuming

that others have control when negative things occur. One form of blaming is represented by the **fundamental attribution error**, or the tendency to underestimate the situational causes for others' negative behavior and instead blame the person. Imagine the situation when you are waiting behind another driver to make a right turn onto a new street, and he isn't moving even though there is no oncoming traffic. You may mutter, "Go, you idiot!" or even honk your horn, only to find that he is waiting for a pedestrian to cross. Your immediate reaction, that there is something wrong with him rather than an external circumstance preventing him from moving, is the fundamental attribution error at play.

Self-Serving Bias

Hand in hand with this error is the tendency to avoid responsibility for our own shortcomings. The **self-serving bias**[183] occurs when we believe that when things go right it is due to things within our control, rather than partially caused by others or by the circumstance. If you receive an A on an exam you rarely chalk it up to luck, but instead assume it is because of all the hard work you did. Of course part of the self-serving bias also includes the assumption that when things go wrong, it was out of your control. When you do poorly on an exam, you may tend to critique the instructor or test questions, rather than blame yourself for not studying the correct material or for cramming at the last minute.

Consider the following fable, which exists in many cultures and languages across the world:

> A farmer had only one horse on which to depend, and one day the beloved horse ran away.
> The neighbors came to console him saying, "What a terrible tragedy!"
> "What makes you think so?" asked the farmer.
> A month later the horse returned and the farmer's son was so excited he mounted the horse to go for a ride when he was thrown from the saddle, permanently disabling his right leg.
> The neighbors came to console him saying, "What a terrible tragedy!"
> "What makes you think so?" asked the farmer.
> That year there was a terrible war and all young men were being drafted to fight, all of them dying on the battlegrounds. The farmer's son was spared the draft because of his bad leg. The neighbors came to congratulate him saying, "How wonderful!"
> "What makes you think so?" asked the farmer...

What does this tell us about the "interpreting" stage of perception?

INTERPERSONAL COMMUNICATION FOR SOCIAL CHANGE

What Is Implicit Bias, and Why Does It Matter?

Other than being the buzz phrase of the year, **"implicit bias"** is an inclination in judgement and/or behavior that occurs at a subconscious level. Unlike explicit biases which we express as attitudes and opinions, implicit biases usually operate without our knowing we have them. In 1998 researchers

Greenwald, McGhee, and Schwartz developed a test called the Implicit Association Test (IAT) that aimed to bring these biases to light. Even though the IAT has been around for decades, it has gained recent attention because of its ability to help explain the increasingly publicized epidemic of police shootings of unarmed or innocent civilians.

The IAT asks respondents to match images of people with descriptor words at a fast pace using their computer keyboard. The test reveals that, in general, people demonstrate a significant delay in their ability to match positive words with people who are targets of negative stereotypes in our culture. The original version of the IAT only examined response rates between positive and negative words and Black and White faces, but the test has evolved to include measurements of response biases for weight, age, disability, sexuality, and many other categories through which we judge others. You can take any number of these tests by searching Harvard University Project Implicit.

The IAT can help us learn more about subconscious biases that affect our attitudes and behavior toward others, thereby impacting our interpersonal relationships. Researchers have also become interested in using the IAT to learn more about split-second judgements that may have more serious consequences than just relational outcomes. Researchers developed the Shoot/No Shoot Test to see if police officers display race-based implicit biases against targets that are either holding a cell phone, a wallet, or a gun in a computer simulated police altercation. Results of their research show a significantly higher likelihood that officers will shoot a Black man holding a wallet or a cell phone than a White man holding a gun.[184]

Thankfully, few of us will have the opportunity to determine the outcome of another person's life based on our split-second judgments about his or her character and intentions. However, learning more about the nature of our biased judgements and reactions to others in interpersonal settings can help us extend our communication knowledge to become more informed citizens, policy makers, and agents of social change.

Reflection

1. Are you willing to go online and take the Implicit Association Test? Why or why not?

2. Which of your own biases would you be most interested in testing (e.g., gender, race, weight, age, religion)?

3. What do you think are the most common criticisms of this test? Search "Project Implicit FAQs" to find out.

4. Once you become aware of an implicit bias, what are some steps you could take to reduce it?

Review! Errors in Interpretation	
Attribution:	The explanation we make for peoples' behavior.
Oversimplification:	Assuming that the simplest explanation is the correct one.
Over generalizing:	Treating small amounts of information as if they were highly representative.
Fundamental attribution error:	Underestimating the situational causes for others' negative behavior and instead blaming the person.
Self-serving bias:	Believing that when things go right, we controlled them.

STAGE 4: REMEMBERING

The final stage of perception involves recalling what you observed. This is an especially important stage because your memory of past interactions with others has a great impact on how you choose to communicate with them in the present. If you remember that someone has behaved badly in the past (or rather, you made a negative attribution for something he or she did), your verbal and nonverbal behaviors may be cold, suspicious, or apathetic. In contrast, if someone has behaved well in the past (or rather, you made a positive attribution for something he or she did), you are warm, open, and friendly.

THE PERCEPTUAL BIAS OF REMEMBERING: SELECTIVE RECALL

If you've ever had a friend who reunited with an old flame despite the fact that their relationship was horribly dysfunctional, you have witnessed one of the major phenomena that influence our perceptions in the remembering stage. **Selective recall**, also called egocentric memory, occurs when we remember things we want to remember and forget or repress things that are unpleasant, uncomfortable, or unimportant to us. Your own memory of people's actions, words, and intentions are certainly influenced by this principle. Researchers consistently find that we selectively recall events from our relationships in a way that helps us maintain the impressions we already have. If we are satisfied in our relationships we tend to remember things in a positive light, whereas if we are dissatisfied we tend to remember negative things more easily.

FRESH FROM THE LAB: COMMUNICATION RESEARCHERS AT WORK

The Green-Eyed Monster

One of the most powerful and most undesirable emotions is jealousy, which is why communication theorists love to study it. Most people report having felt jealousy, some more often and more extreme than others. Jealousy manifests as cognitive (thoughts), emotional (feelings), and sometimes behavioral (actions) reactions to your perception that another person is threatening the status or your relationship.[185]

While some feelings of jealousy are based on real observations of threat-provoking behavior (for example, someone openly flirting with your partner), many times jealousy arises from misperception. Relationship experts offer this list of do's and don'ts for effectively dealing with jealousy:

Don'ts:

1. Don't become a sleuth. People who sneak around checking texts and email report feeling demeaned and embarrassed afterward.

2. Don't ruminate. Going over your jealousy over and over again in your mind only feeds the fire. Furthermore, your imagination invokes real feelings that cause stress, even if they aren't based on real events.

3. Don't become passive aggressive. Your partner will not respond well to subtle attempts for power. If you have an issue with his or her behavior, address it.

Do's:

If you are experiencing jealousy, it may be a good time to practice perception checking.

1. Explain to your partner what you observed or thought you observed.

2. Explain to your partner your emotional reaction to this.

3. Ask your partner to help you understand what's going on.

If your partner gives a reasonable explanation that you are willing to accept, do your part by attempting to curb your jealousy. If the explanation is not acceptable to you, practice assertiveness by stating what you need and asking what he or she needs in order for you both to feel comfortable with the situation.

The perception process occurs instantly, at a speed that makes each stage indecipherable to the perceiver. It only takes a matter of seconds for perceivers to select, organize, and interpret information. It is from this quick internal process of perception that our communication is born. Once we think we understand what we perceive, we then react, we comment, we share our perceptions with others—we *communicate.* Communicating our perceptions is one way in which our thoughts are solidified. As we verbally express what we think, we make a stronger commitment to those thoughts. Over time, these thoughts no longer feel like perceptions, but instead they are our reality. The more we engage in the process of interpersonal perception, the more information we gather from which to make our process easier and quicker, because, after all, we are lazy thinkers. We develop theories upon which to base our judgments, and we operate as if these theories are facts. As the cycle of perception continues our impressions are solidified, and they color all of our subsequent perceptions; we end up selecting stimuli based on the interpretations we've made previously, thereby creating a reality consistent with our past experience and our expectations.

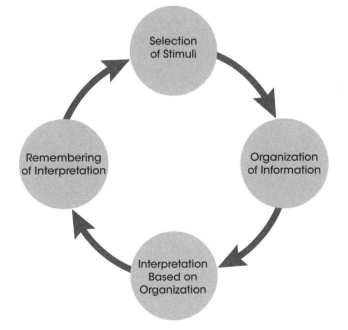

Figure 6.2. The cycle of perception.

Review! Stages of Perception	
Selection stage:	The stage of perception in which the perceiver selects the stimuli to which he or she will pay attention.
Organization stage:	The stage of perception in which the perceiver's mind organizes the information selected into easily understood clusters and categories, usually based on pre-existing information already in the brain.
Interpretation stage:	The stage of perception in which the perceiver makes sense of the information that has been selected and organized.
Remembering stage:	The stage of perception in which the perceiver recalls the information according to the way that it was selected, organized, and interpreted.

SKILL BUILDING EXERCISE

Perspective-Taking

For each of the following scenarios, describe how the behavior could be perceived positively, then describe how the behavior could be perceived negatively.

1. You see a man pick up a female hitchhiker.

    Positive interpretation:

    _____

    Negative interpretation:

    _____

2. You watch a woman buy a drink for a man with a wedding ring.

    Positive interpretation:

    _____

    Negative interpretation:

    _____

3. A teacher invites a student in his office and closes the door.

    Positive interpretation:

    _____

    Negative interpretation:

    _____

4. A person charged of a crime refuses to comment to the press.

    Positive interpretation:

    _____

    Negative interpretation:

    _____

5. A child stands in silence while being bullied by a peer.

    Positive interpretation:

    _____

    Negative interpretation:

    _____

IMPROVING YOUR PERCEPTION SKILLS

At this point you might feel overwhelmed with all the factors working against you as you try to perceive your world accurately in order to communicate more effectively with others. However, there are some simple things you can do to get closer to perceptual accuracy. Most of these habits, once practiced, will be easy to implement into your communication repertoire. As with all new skills, they will at first feel awkward and artificial; but if you are persistent, the benefits of these skills will far outweigh the effort it takes to practice them. Below, each skill is listed according to the stage where it should be exercised.

SELECTING STAGE: PAY GREATER ATTENTION

The first simple technique starts at the moment you are faced with choosing stimuli to which you will pay attention. We usually do this without thinking much about it. As mentioned at the beginning of this chapter, most of what we perceive happens passively unless we have a particular need forcing us to pay special attention. Instead of letting your brain subconsciously choose what data you will process and what data you will ignore, train yourself to pay greater attention at all times. Try this by taking the time to notice your environment, as if you might be quizzed on the information at any time. When you interact with others, force yourself to notice their nonverbal behavior, and listen to every part of their verbal message. Consciously attending to the input you receive is the first step in overcoming perceptual barriers.

Part of paying attention to as many details as possible includes noticing any patterns in the way you tend to see certain situations or certain people. Identify when and where you are likely to stereotype, if you impose the halo or horn effect, and whether you tend to select only negative or only positive information when presented with the facts. Hopefully you have considered these things as you've been reading this chapter. If it is too hard for you to assess your own tendencies, ask someone who knows you well if they can give you feedback based on their experience watching how you select information.

ORGANIZING STAGE: DEVELOP COGNITIVE COMPLEXITY

One way to improve your perceptual accuracy in interpersonal relationships is to remind yourself that people are complex. Think twice when you are tempted to organize people and their actions into quick and simple pre-formulated categories. Furthermore, when someone else seems to be making unreasonable attributions, try to understand why. Gather as much knowledge about the circumstance and the person as possible so that you can effectively understand how they organize the details they perceive. Are they cognitively simple? Are they using stereotypes to organize their information? If so, remember that these are natural tendencies to which no one is immune.

INTERPRETING STAGE: CHECK YOUR PERCEPTIONS

Once we decode another person's words or behavior we usually assume that our interpretation is correct. We then tend to act based on these interpretations, and therefore start a cycle of misunderstanding that is difficult to repair. One way to avoid unnecessary confusion is to get in the habit of perception checking.

Perception checking is perhaps the most useful skill to employ when seeking accuracy in your perceptions and shared meaning with those around you. Perception checking involves taking a good look at the interpretations you have made about a person or situation, and assessing whether or not your interpretation is faulty. **Indirect perception checking** involves seeking additional information through observation to either confirm or refute your interpretations. **Direct perception checking** involves asking straight out if your interpretations are correct. Both are equally useful depending on the situation in which you find yourself needing to do a perception check.

Direct perception checking involves three important steps:

1. Identify the perception.
2. Reconsider the accuracy of your interpretation and consider alternative explanations.
3. Ask the other person for clarification.

Here is one example:

Identify: My perception is that my boyfriend does not love me as much as I love him, because he doesn't say, "I love you" very often.

Reconsider: What are the other possible explanations for his behavior?
He might not have been raised in a family where these words come easily.
He might not be confident that his love will be returned.
He might think it is more important to show it than say it.

Ask: "I want to understand why it is that you don't tell me you love me as often as I tell you. Is it because (list possible reasons), or is there some other explanation?"

Again, applying these skills will take practice, but it is well worth the effort. Try it for one week and see how you do. One common result from perception checking is that the receiver will often be grateful that you checked instead of making assumptions and jumping to conclusions. If you are really lucky, the other person might follow your example and start checking his or her own perceptions. However, as mentioned in the opening chapter this is not a reasonable expectation. The most you can do is 100% of your 50% of the relationship, and doing this much will likely produce noticeably better results than continuing your current habits.

SKILL BUILDING EXERCISE

Perception Checking Practice

For each of the following scenarios, write out what you would say to check your perception instead of making assumptions.

A friend will not return a phone call, and on your fifth try you finally reach him or her.

_____

_____

_____

You have asked out the same person three times and keep being told that he or she wants to go out with you but is really busy.

_____

_____

_____

You find a text on your significant other's phone from your best friend. It's a meaningless message, but you weren't aware that they were in communication.

_____

_____

_____

You notice that your significant other erased the browser history on his or her computer.

_____

_____

_____

BUILDING CULTURAL COMPETENCE: EAST MEETS WEST

Applying Age-Old Concepts to Modern Relationships

Most people are familiar with the popular word uttered by American yogis and laypeople alike: "Namaste." People who attempt to engender a holistic, centered lifestyle have probably whispered the term at the end of a yoga session, scribbled it on holiday cards, or even included the sentiment within an email auto signature. Used most often as a greeting and departure between strangers or acquaintances, perhaps the greatest application of this well-known concept is being missed.

It turns out that this Eastern idea, derived from Sanskrit and common to both Hindi and Nepali languages, is not as foreign as we may think. Relationship researchers and scholars here in the West are undivided in their advice regarding the application of Namaste to our closest interpersonal relationships, only on this continent it goes by a different name: mindfulness (from Chapter 1). Researchers and practitioners in cognitive sciences equate mindfulness with an open awareness to the present experience, without the mental flooding of interpretation, blame, and attachment. This definition of mindfulness stems from ancient Buddhist practices of non-attachment, but parallels the Hindi sentiment of Namaste, which can be translated as:

> The Divine in me recognizes and honors the Divine in you.
> I greet that place where you and I are one.

In laymen's terms, what Eastern philosophers and Western relationship scholars are both advising is an abandonment of the perception that we are separate, or that one of our points of view is more valid than the other. Mindfulness, in essence, requires giving up the need to be right, to win, and to blame. It requires present engagement without any attempt to satisfy our ego by inflating ourselves through pointing a finger at others.

Studies show that this advice is far more than new age self-help; the implications of these practices (or lack thereof) are serious not only for relational health, but for emotional and physical well-being. Research consistently reveals that people who see things only from their own perspective and tend to blame others are more likely to experience dysphoric symptoms such as depression and general feelings of discontent.[186]

CHAPTER SUMMARY

This chapter outlined the process of interpersonal perception so that you can better understand your own tendencies and overcome perceptual barriers to shared meaning. First, interpersonal perception was defined as the process of making sense of people and their behavior. Next, the stages of perception were each described: selecting, organizing, interpreting, and remembering.

In the selecting stage, people tend to engage in selective perception and the confirmation bias, both of which depend upon the salience of the information one is receiving from others. Next, in the organizing stage, several errors in organization were described including punctuation, super-imposing, and clustering. In the interpreting stage common errors included oversimplifying, over generalizing, the fundamental attribution error and the self-serving bias. Finally, selective recall affects the remembering stage, perpetuating the cycle of self-fulfilling perceptions. The chapter concluded with suggestions for ways to improve your perception skills in each stage. In the selecting stage this requires paying greater attention, in the organizing stage this means developing cognitive complexity, and in the interpreting stage this requires the new skill of checking your perceptions.

CHAPTER ACTIVITIES

TEST YOUR UNDERSTANDING

True or False

_____ 1. Impressions usually are difficult to form, and take a long time to generate.

_____ 2. The fundamental attribution error is when one underestimates the situational causes and circumstances affecting someone's negative behavior, and instead blames the person.

_____ 3. Research consistently reveals that people who see things only from their own perspective and tend to blame others are more likely to experience dysphoric symptoms such as depression and general feelings of discontent.

Multiple Choice: Circle the best answer choice.

1. What are the four stages of perception, and in what order do they occur?

   A. Perceiving, selecting, interpreting, remembering

   B. Acquiring, organizing, remembering, applying

   C. Selecting, organizing, interpreting, remembering

   D. Perceiving, interpreting, remembering, applying

   E. None of the above are correct

2. The steps for perception checking include all of the following except:

   A. Describe the behavior in question.

   B. Explain your interpretation of the behavior.

   C. Ask if your interpretation is correct.

   D. Try to compromise.

   E. All of the above are steps in perception checking.

3. People who make clear and quick judgments and tend to have limited categories for classifying people and behavior are considered:

   A. Cognitively complex

   B. Cognitively simple

   C. Cognitively slow

   D. Cognitively mindful

   E. Cognitively accurate

**Answers are listed at the end of this section before the references.

Short Answer

1. Define perception and interpersonal perception.

_____

_____

_____

_____

_____

_____

_____

_____

_____

_____

_____

2. Identify and explain the three stages of interpersonal perception.

_____

_____

_____

_____

_____

_____

_____

_____

_____

_____

_____

3.   Explain how individuals develop and maintain impressions.

_____

_____

_____

_____

_____

_____

_____

_____

_____

_____

_____

_____

_____

4.   Identify the factors that distort the accuracy of interpersonal perception.

_____

_____

_____

_____

_____

_____

_____

_____

_____

_____

_____

_____

_____

5. Describe the strategies one can apply for improving interpersonal perception.

_____

_____

_____

_____

_____

_____

_____

_____

_____

_____

_____

_____

_____

_____

_____

_____

_____

_____

_____

_____

_____

_____

_____

_____

IN-CLASS ACTIVITY

Interpersonal Perception

By yourself, take a walk across campus, or take a seat somewhere close to the classroom. Make sure you are by yourself, not with others in this class.

Actively observe the behavior of at least a few people or groups of people that seems different than how you would behave (this could include what they are wearing, what they are saying, how they are speaking, walking, eating, or anything else).

Write down the behaviors and your interpretation of the behaviors here:

_____

_____

_____

_____

_____

_____

_____

_____

_____

_____

_____

_____

_____

_____

_____

Return to class and share your observations.

SKILL PRACTICE: PERCEPTION CHECKING

What Is the Goal of Perception Checking?

The goal of perception checking is to reduce the tendency to make assumptions and instead check if your interpretations are correct or incorrect.

How Do You Do It?

1. Describe the behavior in question, without evaluating it.

   Example:
   "I noticed that you don't call me as often as I call you."

   Describe:

   _____

   _____

   _____

2. Explain your own interpretation and consider possible alternative interpretations.

   Example:
   "My assumption is that you aren't that committed to our relationship. But I realize another possibility is that you aren't a phone person."

   Explain:

   _____

   _____

   _____

3. Ask if you are correct or if there is another explanation.

   Example:
   "Is it true that you are not that interested in this relationship, or do you just not like talking on the phone? Or is it something else?"

   Ask:

   _____

   _____

   _____

HOMEWORK ACTIVITY

PERCEPTION-CHECKING

Any behavior observed by two different people is interpreted in two different ways:

- The meaning given to it by the person who *does* the action.

- The meaning given to it by the person who *observes* the action.

Over the next 24 hours, when you notice yourself making an evaluation of someone's behavior STOP and do the following:

1. DESCRIBE: What did you see and hear? Be as literal as possible (She hung up the phone without saying goodbye versus She abruptly hung up on me).

   _____

   _____

   _____

   _____

2. YOUR INTERPRETATION: List your interpretations and emotional reactions to the situation.

   _____

   _____

   _____

   _____

3. THEIR POSSIBLE INTERPRETATIONS: Imagine what possible interpretations the other person might have. Use indirect perception checking and ask someone else what his or her interpretations might be. Or use direct perception checking and ask the person directly.

   _____

   _____

   _____

   _____

4. EVALUATION: Evaluate the behavior again, this time using your new information.

   _____

   _____

   _____

   _____

Answers to True/False and Multiple Choice

1. False

2. True

3. True

1. C

2. D

3. B

REFERENCES

[173]Lippman, W. (1922). *Public Opinion*. New York: Macmillan.

[174]Hastorf, A. H. & Cantril, H. (1954). They saw a game: A case study. *Journal of Abnormal and Social Psychology, 49,* 129–134.

[175]Wason, P.C. (1960). On the failure to eliminate hypotheses in a conceptual task. *Quarterly Journal of Experimental Psychology, 12,* 129–140.

[176]Katie, B. (May 14, 2007). Mind and SuperMind series. Marjorie Luke Theater, Santa Barbara, CA.

[177]Edwards, A., Edward, C., Shaver, C., Oaks, M. (2009). Computer-mediated word-of-mouth communication on RateMyProfessors.com: Expectancy effects on student cognitive and behavioral learning. *Journal of Computer Mediated Communication, 14,* 368–392.

[178]Watzlawick, P., Beavin, J., & Jackson, D. (1967). *Pragmatics of human communication.* W. W. Norton: New York.

[179]Wishner, J. (1960). Reanalysis of 'Impressions of People.' *Psychological Review, 67,* 96–112.

[180]Heider, F. (1958). *The psychology of interpersonal relations.* New York: Wiley.

[181]Weiner, B. (1980). *Human Motivation.* New York: Holt, Rinehart and Winston.

[182]Kelly, G.A. (1955). *The psychology of personal constructs (Vols. 1 and 2).* New York: Norton.

[183]Jones, E.E., & Nisbett, R.E. (1971). *The actor and the observer: Divergent perceptions of the causes of behavior.* New York: General Learning Press.

[184]Correll, J., Park, B., Judd, C.M., & Wittenbrink, B. (2002). The police officer's dilemma: Using ethnicity to disambiguate potentially threatening individuals. *Journal of Personality and Social Psychology, 83*(6), 1314–1329.

[185]Sharpsteen, D.J., & Kirkpatrick, L.A. (1997). Romantic jealousy and adult romantic attachment. *Journal of Personality and Social Psychology, 72,* 627–640.

[186]Schrovers, M., Kraaij, V. & Garnefsji, N. (2007). Goal disturbance, cognitive coping strategies, and psychological adjustment to different types of stressful life events. *Personality and Individual Differences, 43,* 413–423.

SECTION 3

Relationship
Paths

CHAPTER 7

Relational Development

"Love is divine only and difficult always. If you think it is easy you are a fool."

—Toni Morrison

Learning Objectives

After studying this chapter, you should be able to:

1. *Explain what factors attract people to each other.*

2. *Identify the communication that occurs in each stage of relational development.*

3. *Understand the ways in which individuals reduce uncertainty when developing relationships.*

4. *Understand the role of self-disclosure in the development of intimacy.*

5. *Describe the natural tensions that occur as a relationship becomes more integrated.*

6. *Apply effective strategies for managing dialectical tensions.*

Do you believe that "opposites attract," or is it the case that "birds of a feather flock together"? Do you have a "type" that you like? No doubt you frequently discuss these ideas with your friends, bouncing theories off each other to help you figure out what on earth you're doing when it comes to starting and ending intimate relationships. Although interpersonal attraction and relational development are not exact sciences, communication researchers have found that there are some similar stages through which most relationships travel. Starting from the moment of attraction, this chapter will outline each of the stages of relational escalation, focusing on some specific communication theories that become relevant in each stage. Although some of the information here is directed specifically at romantic relationships, friendships seem to travel similar paths when it comes to developing intimacy. As you read this chapter, think about your own friendship or romantic relationship experiences and decide whether your behavior fits into the stages described. Before we address the stages of developing relationships, it is important (and fun) to learn a little bit about what attracts us to others in the first place. What topic could possibly be more appealing?

INTERPERSONAL ATTRACTION

PHYSICAL ATTRACTION

Researchers have identified several specific reasons that we become attracted to other human beings. The first reason is obvious: physical attraction. Although we would like to believe that other things are more important than physical traits, physical attractiveness does indeed play a large role in our initiation of a relationship with another person, even a friend. American culture places a high value upon how much a person weighs, the style of our hair, and the clothes we wear. These things all get entered into the complicated formula of physical attraction.

Physical attraction is a widely studied phenomenon in many fields, including sociology, psychology, biology, and communication. For example, Hatfield and colleagues[187] randomly matched 752 incoming freshmen students for blind dates to a dance at their university. Students rated their partner's physical attractiveness and their desire to see him or her again. Surprisingly, *only* physical attractiveness predicted the desire to go on another date with the person, while intelligence, sincerity, and sensitivity had no effect!

Although physical attractiveness loses its importance as a relationship progresses, it usually has to be there in some form for a relationship to start, especially a romantic one. Keep in mind, however, that physical attractiveness is in the eye of the beholder: there is no one model for what everyone finds attractive. We tend to be attracted to people who appear to have a similar level of attractiveness as ourselves, and furthermore, if you believe others think a person is attractive, you'll also be more likely to evaluate that person as attractive.

PROPINQUITY

In addition to these considerations, there are several other factors that have been found to increase attraction. *Propinquity*, also called proximity, is physical or geographical accessibility. The rule of propinquity states that people are simply more attracted to others who are geographically or physically closer to them. Thus, you are more likely to be attracted to a person in your class than a person you see walking down

the street, and you are more likely to be attracted to a person from your school than someone who is from a school that is far away. Researchers found that when children were asked who their friends were they tended to report being friends with children whose last name started with the same letter as theirs in the alphabet. It turns out that this was the case because teachers had arranged their seating charts by last name, so students whose last names began with the same letters sat closest to each other in class, therefore becoming friends.[188]

EXPOSURE

Similarly, the more we see someone, the higher we rate his or her attractiveness. This tendency is explained by the **mere exposure hypothesis**, which states that the more exposure we have to

a stimulus, the more positively we evaluate it. In one study supporting this hypothesis, infants smiled more at the faces of strangers to which they were repeatedly exposed.[189] You can see this phenomenon occurring in the mass media: the more we are exposed to popular stars, the more attractive they become to us.

REINFORCEMENT

Reinforcement is another reason we become attracted to others. We are conditioned to like people who validate and support our pre-conceived notions of the world and how it works. We generally like to spend time with those people who reinforce our values, beliefs, and attitudes. This explains why people join groups simply to spend more time with larger numbers of people who are just like them. One researcher paired students at the beginning of the year to see who stayed friends the longest, finding that dyads that were paired based on attitude similarity were more likely to be friends at the end of the year.[190]

While people tend to be attracted to and end up with partners that are similar to them, they still seem to claim that they are attracted to dissimilar others. One study found that nearly 86 percent of participants claimed to want someone who had their opposite traits. However, when asked to list their own traits and then list the traits they'd like in an ideal partner, it turns out that they want someone similar to themselves, especially when it comes to personality. In support of these natural inclinations, research shows that a similar personality can be more important than attitudes, values, and even religion when it comes to maintaining a happy relationship.[191]

APPROACHABILITY

Lastly, we tend to feel attracted to people who we think are approachable. When it comes to romantic relationships, approachability is often communicated through nonverbal body movements, referred to as **quasi-courtship behaviors**.[192] Quasi-courtship behaviors usually occur in four phases that show increasing readiness to engage in an interaction with another. In stage one, people demonstrate confident behaviors to show *courtship readiness*. Animals and mammals of all kinds exude confidence to seduce their potential mates. For example, peacocks show courtship readiness by spreading their feathers to capture the attention of the opposite sex. The second stage of readiness involves *preening* behaviors, or manipulations of our appearance such as combing our hair with our hands, applying makeup, straightening the tie, and double-checking our appearance in the mirror. In stage three we demonstrate *positional cues*, which means that we use our positioning and body orientation to be seen and noticed by others. Finally, in the fourth stage we

give more *direct appeals to invitation*, including close proximity to the target, exposed skin, and eye contact to signal desire, availability, and interest.

Not only do we communicate interpersonal interest with our nonverbal behavior, but we can also communicate disinterest. Liking is communicated by nonverbal cues of open body and arm position, forward lean, and more relaxed posture.[193] People are also considered approachable, or "warm" when

they face their communication partners directly, smile, make direct eye contact, don't fidget, and make fewer unnecessary hand movements. In contrast, "cold" behaviors include less eye contact and smiling, more fidgeting, and turning away from the other. To exemplify these behaviors, think about the last time you were speaking to someone with whom you no longer wanted to interact. You probably avoided warm behaviors so that you could escape!

Review

Review! Reasons for Attraction	
Physical attractiveness:	We are attracted to people whose physical characteristics are appealing, such as body type, hair, or personal style.
Propinquity:	People are attracted to others who are geographically or physically closer to them.
Mere exposure:	The more exposure we have to someone the more positively we evaluate his or her attractiveness.
Reinforcement:	We are conditioned to like people who validate and support our pre-conceived attitudes, beliefs, and values.
Approachability:	We are attracted to those who send messages of being approachable.

REDUCING UNCERTAINTY

For many people, initiating contact with desirable others is quite awkward, even when the other is just a potential new friend. In order to make the entire process a little easier we engage in strategies to reduce our uncertainty about the person with whom we are interacting, or with whom we intend to interact. Uncertainty reduction theory gives us insight into the predictable ways in which we go about learning information about strangers, especially those who are about to become non-strangers.

Uncertainty reduction theory[194] suggests that a primary motivation for most of our interactions is to reduce uncertainty about the world around us. We constantly move about our environment asking questions, both internally and externally, in order to gather information and feel secure. There are four specific situations that provoke us to pay even greater attention than we normally do. First, if someone piques your *interest*, you are motivated to learn more information about him or her. In addition, we are especially motivated to seek information to reduce uncertainty about a person who behaves in a way that is *deviant* or unexpected. For example, if you see someone wearing a costume, you are curious about why he or she is doing so. Furthermore, we are motivated to reduce our uncertainty if the other person can *reward or punish* us in some way. It behooves us to glean certain information about this person so that we can obtain the rewards he or she can offer, and avoid the punishments. For example, you may be curious about what makes your professor tick because she can either pass or fail you in her class. Lastly, we try to reduce uncertainty by gathering information if we anticipate *repeated interaction* with the person. If you plan to see someone again, it is a wise investment of your time to understand him or her. We tend to be less interested and curious about people we know will never cross our paths again. Charles Berger and

Richard Calabrese, the founders of uncertainty reduction theory (URT), present several additional axioms, or "truths," about how we reduce uncertainty. The fact that each of these axioms can be tested and can be disproved is what makes URT a scientific theory. Think about whether these are true for you, based on your interpersonal experiences:

Axiom 1:

Strangers enter an interaction with high levels of uncertainty about the other, but <u>uncertainty decreases as they interact</u>. Also, as u<u>ncertainty decreases, talking increases.</u>

Axiom 2:

As <u>nonverbal communication increases</u>, <u>uncertainty levels decrease, </u>and vice versa.

Axiom 3:

High levels of uncertainty result in strangers asking more questions of the other. As uncertainty decreases, so does question-asking.

Axiom 4:

People are less likely to share intimate information when high levels of uncertainty exist. Low levels of uncertainty result in more sharing and emotional intimacy.

Axiom 5:

High levels of uncertainty lead to more reciprocity in question-asking. As uncertainty decreases, so does the need for equality in asking or answering questions.

Axiom 6:

Uncertainty is decreased when we believe someone is similar to us. Perceptions of dissimilarity will produce higher levels of uncertainty.

Axiom 7:

An increase in uncertainty will lead to a decrease in liking. A decrease in uncertainty will lead to an increase in liking.

Review

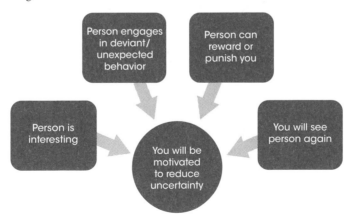

Figure 7.0. There are several factors that determine whether we are motivated to reduce our uncertainty about certain individuals.

FRESH FROM THE LAB: COMMUNICATION RESEARCHERS AT WORK

Self-Disclosure of Sexually Transmitted Infections: Still Taboo After All These Years

People seeking a career in health services may be interested to know that there's a brand new job available. The job requires that you make phone calls to past sexual partners of people who have been diagnosed with a sexually transmitted infection (STI), to prevent the infection from becoming an epidemic. You won't be surprised to learn that job candidates aren't beating down the door for this one. The job was created because certain STIs, including gonorrhea, are on the rise and reaching epidemic proportions, and experts say that poor interpersonal communication is to blame.[195] People tend not to discuss their sexual histories before engaging in intercourse, and they also fail to contact past partners who may have been exposed, once they learn that they are infected.

Why are we willing to be sexually intimate with each other but so afraid to communicate openly about our sexual behavior? One study attempted to find out, revealing that both men and women tend to avoid communicating about their sexual past due to four main concerns:

- The belief that the past should be kept in the past. People simply don't want to taint the newness and excitement of a budding relationship with their baggage.

- Identity issues. People are concerned that revealing details about their sexual behavior may invoke judgment or dislike from their partner.

- Perceived threats to their relationships. Disclosing sexual history may create tension, conflict, or breakup.

- Emotionally upsetting feelings. People may not want to revisit hurtful events or situations, they may become upset by a partner's reaction, or they simply can't bear the emotional difficulty of these kinds of conversations.

As we attempt to gather information and therefore reduce our uncertainty, we utilize three specific strategies for information acquisition. We can choose *passive observation*, which includes gathering information by simply watching. Many times you'll notice someone who strikes your fancy, but you proceed to observe him or her for quite some time before you interact. You might also pursue *active observation*, which includes directly asking others about the target person. Finally, you may initiate *direct interaction*, which involves asking the target direct questions to learn more about him or her.

A DEVELOPMENTAL MODEL OF RELATIONSHIPS

Interpersonal communication between two people often depends on where they are in the progression of their relationship. We don't expect two new friends to communicate in the same way as two life-long friends, nor is it reasonable to think that people on a first date would communicate like a married couple. According to developmental models of interpersonal relationships, movement through relationships can be described as occurring in stages that are identifiable based on the verbal and nonverbal communication that occurs between the two people in the relationship. **Relational escalation** is the process of moving through these stages toward interpersonal intimacy.

The process of relational escalation will be described in this chapter in five stages. In contrast, relational de-escalation is the process of relational deterioration, which will be described in an upcoming chapter. Knapp's staircase model of relationship stages depicts the stages of relational escalation and de-escalation as steps going up toward intimacy and down away from intimacy.[196]

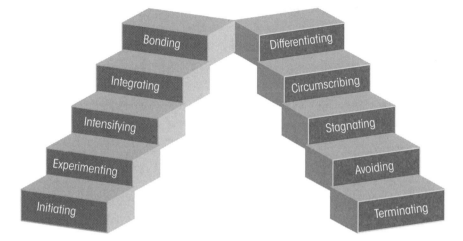

Figure 7.1. Knapp's staircase model of relational escalation and de-escalation.

The staircase model is descriptive, not prescriptive, meaning that it describes what happens in relationships, not what you should do. Although you can behave in certain ways to move your relationship toward or away from intimacy, the model of relational stages does not tell you how to do this. Furthermore, the model simplifies the complex process of relationships in order to study it. This means that it is not 100% accurate for every relationship, and there are definitely exceptions to the stages outlined by the model.

Although it is most often used to describe romantic relationships, you'll find that it is also descriptive and useful for understanding the stages of friendships, as well. Another assumption of the model is that although relationships can skip stages, they are most likely to jump immediately up or to the opposite side. Thus, relationships either increase in intimacy, or they start down the path toward de-escalation; relationships very seldom revert back to a former stage without the movement being considered de-escalation.

People can spend a long or short amount of time in any stage, and each relationship is different. Many people "date" or "see each other" for up to a year or more before they consider themselves an integrated couple; equally, many troubled marriages stagnate in one stage of de-escalation for years before they divorce. Another important assumption of this model is that any given relationship can really only be in one stage at a time. This rule can be confusing because sometimes it seems like one person is moving ahead more quickly than the other; however, if one person is holding back from escalating the relationship, then the relationship stays in that stage. Similarly, if one person is moving toward breakup, the relationship is in de-escalation whether the other person believes it or not. Now that you understand the assumptions of the model, let's look at the stages of escalation.

INITIATING STAGE

Once we've decided we are attracted to someone and we've reduced enough uncertainty to know the risks, the next step is to approach the "target" (although this term may evoke images of hunter and prey, this is simply the term researchers use when examining relational initiation). When we begin to actually interact with the object of our desires, we have officially entered the initiating stage. The **initiating stage** is characterized by verbal introductions. Interaction in this stage is typically scripted, meaning both people adhere to social norms for introductory conversations, sticking to safe and superficial topics. Both individuals are presenting a "public self" to the other person, meaning that there is little vulnerability or depth of self-disclosure. The relationship could remain at this stage if neither person shares other information, if the impression either person forms of the other is not favorable, or if the circumstances aren't right for progressing. Many of our "relationships" stop at this stage and the other person remains an acquaintance, or we never see him or her again. However, if you want to continue getting to know the person with whom you are interacting, then the next stage ensues. Often times if two people are immediately and mutually interested in one another they spend very little time in the initiating stage; in fact, it could be a matter of seconds or minutes. Imagine the last time you "hit it off" with someone in either a platonic or romantic way. If you connected instantly, chances are you immediately started making inquiries that are typical of the next stage: experimenting.

Review

Review! Strategies for Reducing Uncertainty	
Passive observation:	Gathering information by simply watching.
Active observation:	Directly asking others about the target person.
Direct interaction:	Asking the target about him or herself directly.

EXPERIMENTING STAGE

The bridge between the initiating stage and the **experimenting stage** occurs when scripted introductions become more like real conversation. Many times you only need to spend a few seconds or minutes engaging with someone before you realize that you need to escape. Other times, you may have planned to engage in polite chitchat and then learned information that sparked your interest in the other person. In the experimenting stage both people desire to know more, and increasingly personal, information about the other person in order to assess whether continuing the interaction is a worthy investment of each person's time.

The experimenting stage is characterized by some specific nonverbal indicators, including little physical contact and non-intimate distance. Those communicating are still relatively uncomfortable so they don't touch or show affection at the start of the experimenting stage. There is limited time spent together because each person is still deciding if they would like to pursue a relationship with the other.

There are also unique verbal indicators of the experimenting stage. At first this stage may have the tone of an interview. However, as the stage progresses communication becomes easier and less awkward. The verbal communication in this stage is characterized by some **self-disclosure** by each person, which is the process of revealing personal information to the other for the purpose of developing intimacy and understanding. Researchers find that when we are becoming more intimate, our ability to disclose personal information and open ourselves to others makes us more attractive. In contrast, people who do not disclose and share openly with others in the experimenting stage are perceived as less attractive.[197]

To be considered self-disclosure, the information exchanged has to fit three qualifications: 1) the information must be directly and intentionally revealed, 2) it must be personal and private, and 3) it must be information the other person would not know if they had not been told. Of course, self-disclosure can be about either positive or negative information, and can vary in its level of intensity and importance to the relationship.[198] Self-disclosure in the experimenting stage starts with more scripted topics, such as "What's your major," or "What high school did you go to?" As the relationship progresses through this stage, the topics usually increase in depth.

Research on computer-mediated communication (CMC) presents some interesting findings about the effect of the communication medium on self-disclosure. Internet users are more likely to self-disclose intimate information through the Internet, rather than face-to-face. Especially for adolescents, the more they use the Internet, the more they self-disclose. Interestingly this online disclosure appears to enhance the quality of both their face-to-face and online friendships, allowing for greater development of intimacy that may not occur in face-to-face settings because of shyness, anxiety, or insecurity.[199]

Social penetration theory offers a model to show how self-disclosure in this stage and every stage thereafter varies in both intensity and range of topics.

Social Penetration Theory

Social penetration theory[200] states that as a relationship develops, the partners share more aspects of the self through an exchange of information, feelings, and activities. *Breadth* is the array or variety of topics that are shared, while *depth* is the amount of information shared about each topic. The two can be examined together in the form of a model that gives a visual depiction of the self-disclosure in any given relationship. Imagine that the model is like an onion; if you were to cut the onion into quarters, these pieces would represent the topics of self-disclosure, or the breadth, while the layer of each piece would represent the depth of the disclosure on that topic. In most interpersonal relationships topics of discussion (breadth) might include money, religion, politics, family and friends, work, the relationship itself, and future plans, among other things. When a relationship first starts there is a lot of ground to cover at the superficial levels of each of these topics. For example conversations that occur during a newly budding relationship might include how many siblings each person has, what each person does on the weekends, where their parents live, and what kinds of pets they have. As intimacy develops over time, dyads tend to go into greater depth on each topic. A well-established pair knows, for example, the history of each of their parents' divorce, they have learned about the other person's dreams and fears, and they know all about how the other person spends money.

View a TED Talk on self-disclosure and intimacy by typing this into your browser: TED Talk the power of vulnerability.

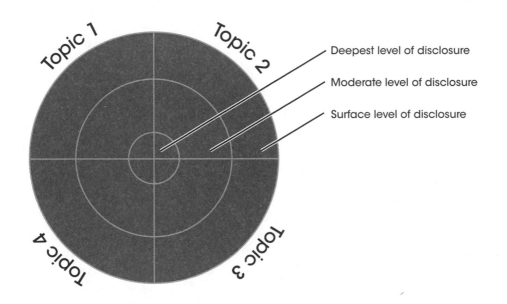

Figure 7.2. Social penetration model of self-disclosure.

To give a visual representation of the breadth and depth of disclosure in any given relationship one can color in the pieces of the onion to show the level of intimacy in that relationship. Thus, in a non-intimate relationship the outer areas of the onion are filled in, but the inner areas remain untouched. In an intimate relationship, the inside of the onion is filled in, but many of the outside layers remain untouched because they have already shared that information or because it gets taken for granted when they are operating at a deeper level. Think of your closest, most intimate relationship. Have you asked that person recently about their favorite color? Chances are you don't talk much about topics like this anymore, but you did when you first met.

A dyad in which either person does not desire an increase in intimacy can stay in the experimenting stage for a long time. Examples of relationships that may remain in the experimenting phase include casual dating relationships that never seem to move past relatively superficial interactions, or friendships with people in class who you get to know slowly but never develop a real friendship with outside of class. The amount and type of self-disclosure paves the way between the experimenting stage and the next stage. If both people desire for the relationship to progress toward even greater intimacy, the intensifying stage ensues.

SKILL BUILDING EXERCISE

Self-Disclosure and Relational Development

At what stage of a relationship do you believe it is expected that each person would reveal the following pieces of personal information?

Choose from the following stages: Initiating, Experimenting, Intensifying, Integrating, Bonding

Income/Savings   Appropriate Stage: _____

Number of previous sexual partners   Appropriate Stage: _____

Past illegal activity or trouble with law   Appropriate Stage: _____

Any childhood trauma   Appropriate Stage: _____

An eating disorder   Appropriate Stage: _____

A current or past addiction   Appropriate Stage: _____

Religious beliefs   Appropriate Stage: _____

Past relational transgressions   Appropriate Stage: _____

Phobias   Appropriate Stage: _____

Medical history   Appropriate Stage: _____

Family secrets/problems   Appropriate Stage: _____

Review! Self-Disclosure Concepts	
Self-disclosure:	The process of revealing personal information to the other for the purpose of developing intimacy and understanding. Self-disclosure only includes information that is 1) directly and intentionally revealed, 2) personal and private, and 3) would not otherwise be known.
Social penetration theory:	The theory that states that as a relationship develops, the partners share more aspects of the self through an exchange of information, feelings, and activities.
Depth:	The amount of information shared about each topic.
Breadth:	The array or variety of topics that are shared.

INTENSIFYING STAGE

The **intensifying stage** is characterized by the mutual understanding that the relationship is important and significant to both members. Members of the dyad are no longer in "interviewing" mode (although they will continue to self-disclose and to gather information throughout the entire relationship). In addition, there is a new set of nonverbal behaviors that evolve as the dyad becomes increasingly comfortable, including changes in touch, distance, and body orientation.

Haptics, or touching behaviors, often signal a movement from the experimenting stage to the intensifying stage. People in the intensifying stage tend to touch each other more often than they did in the previous stages. Some couples touch each other more during this stage than they ever will again! Other people take longer to engage in regular touch and may use it in later stages. For each individual the amount of touch we need, tolerate, receive, and initiate depends upon many factors. The amount and kind of touching you receive in your family has a major impact on how you touch others in relationships. In addition, your cultural norms affect your attitude about touch.[201]

Proxemics, or distance, is another indicator of increased intimacy. As you already learned in an earlier chapter, personal space is the zone most often used for conversation, ranging from one and one-half to four feet apart. Most of our conversations with family and friends occur in this zone.[202] In the intensifying stage dyads comfortably move between personal and intimate space, which is the zone of space most often used for close interactions (ranging from zero to one and one-half feet apart). Finally, kinesics, or body movements also demonstrate an increase in intimacy. Two people in the intensifying stage are likely to copycat each other's nonverbal behaviors by engaging in **interactional synchrony**, where they relate by mirroring the posture or other bodily movements of the other.[203]

In addition to engaging in more risky self-disclosure, there are other indicators of the intensifying stage. In this stage each person starts to depend on the other for self-confirmation and support. Dyads will spend more time together in this stage, and increase the variety of activities they share together. Language between the individuals becomes personalized with unique words, pet names, and inside jokes. The dyad becomes accustomed to using "we," even when they are not together, to describe their lives, events, and activities. You can usually tell when one of your friends has entered the intensifying stage of his or her new relationship because you start hearing the "we" word a lot! Conversations in this stage begin to include **metacommunication**, or communication about the way the couple communicates. After an argument the dyad may talk not just about why they fought, but how they fought. Either person may comment on the listening habits of the other, or point out whether the way they speak to each other is satisfying or dissatisfying.

In romantic relationships especially, this stage usually includes a "relationship talk" where one or both people express verbally what the relationship means and what expectations they have. In relationships that are expected to continue, disclosures such as "I've never felt this way about

someone" or "I want this relationship to work" are characteristic of this stage. One verbal trademark of the intensifying stage for romantic relationships may be that very big moment when one or both people say, "I love you." This can be a pivotal moment because if the feelings are mutual it solidifies the relationship. However, once one person has revealed these feelings it might put pressure on the other person if he or she does not share the same sentiment. The mutuality of these feelings can make the difference between staying in the intensifying stage, moving to the next stage, or entering into a stage of de-escalation.

Styles of Intimacy

Often people's expectations for how love should "look" will determine how they feel about a relationship and their willingness to intensify. In romantic relationships there are different degrees of "intensity" in the intensifying stage depending on the preferred love style of each partner. Studies find that love style correlates with the way we approach others to show interest in the initiating stage, and the strategies we use to propel relationships through the stages of increasing intimacy.[204] Your love style may also impact how you deal with conflict in intimate relationships.[205] Your notion of love depends on past experiences, your upbringing and parental models, and popular culture influences such as movies and television.

Identifying your own love style can be helpful to understanding why you find some romantic relationships desirable, and others lukewarm. Love styles that seem to have passion in the driver's seat are Eros, Mania, and Ludus. The style **Eros** is characterized by a passionate physical and emotional love. This style is based on attraction and enjoyment, and it is the stereotype of romantic love depicted in the media. Research indicates that the Eros style leads to more satisfying relationships for both men and women than any other style.[206] **Mania** is a highly volatile love verging on obsession, which is usually fueled by low self-esteem. Experts warn against limiting your notion of love to the Mania style unless you are prepared for a relationship that feels like an emotional roller coaster. Couples whose relationship is based on a Mania style of love usually have high levels of conflict and instability. **Ludus** is a style of love that is played as a game or sport; this is the "conquest" approach to love. Ludus lovers are easily bored and often feel the need to move on to new conquests. Those with a Ludus style typically use avoidance, withdrawal, and denial strategies during conflict.[207] Long-term, satisfying relationships for both men and women are characterized by the presence of Eros and the absence of both Mania and Ludus.[208]

Other styles of love can still include emotional involvement, but passion and emotion do not drive the entire relationship. **Storge** is an affectionate love that slowly develops from friendship and is based on similarity, shared interests, and feeling understood. Experts recommend that couples that intend to last nurture this style of love in their relationships. **Pragma** is a love style characterized by rationality and good decision-making; pragmatic love is practical, and thus dictated by the head, not the heart. Finally, **Agape** is selfless altruistic love such as the love a mother feels for a child; this style involves the role of care taking and nurturing. This style often utilizes integrative and compromising conflict styles because of a strong focus on other-orientation.[209]

Review! Love Styles	
Eros:	A love style characterized by a passionate physical and emotional love.
Mania:	A highly volatile love verging on obsession, which is fueled by low self-esteem.
Ludus:	A style of love that is played as a game, sport, or conquest.
Storge:	An affectionate love that slowly develops from friendship and is based on similarity, shared interests, and feeling understood.
Pragma:	A love style characterized by rationality and good decision-making; pragmatic love is practical, and thus dictated by the head, not the heart.
Agape:	Selfless, altruistic love such as the love a mother feels for a child; this style is spiritual and care-taking in nature.

BUILDING CULTURAL COMPETENCE

Linguistic Relativity Meets Knapp's Staircase Model

Knapp's staircase model of relationship escalation and de-escalation describes the common experiences we all encounter when coming together and breaking apart. Linguistic relativity, on the other hand, questions whether our unique cultural words for different experiences cause us to "feel" them differently. Examine the list of words below used by different cultures to describe their experiences of the relational stages and decide whether we experience things differently, or if they just have more elaborate words to describe the complex experiences of falling in love.[210]

In the Initiating Stage, Japanese use the term *koi no yokan* to describe the feeling, when you first meet someone, that the two of you will end up in love. This concept differs from "love at first sight," because it is not about initial attraction or feelings of love, only the sense that in the future there will be a love relationship. In Tierra del Fuego, speakers of the indigenous language Yagan, use the term *mamihlapinatapei* to describe a meaningful look between two people who would like to initiate an interaction, but are both reluctant to start.

In the Experimenting Stage, the Chinese word *yuanfen* describes a relationship driven by destiny. In contrast to the U.S. concepts of choice that dictate this stage, this Chinese term emphasizes the important concept of predetermination, which is the driving force of all life encounters.

In the Intensifying Stage, Brazilians use the Portuguese word *cafuné* to describe the act of running your fingers through someone's hair in loving way. While Americans engage in this behavior, we don't have an exact term for it.

In the Bonding Stage, the romantic Arabic sentiment *ya'aburnee* literally means, "You bury me." It's an expression of the hope to die before one's beloved, because it would be impossible to go on living without him or her.

See the Building Cultural Competence section of Chapter 8 for culturally relative words that describe the other side of Knapp's staircase: The stages of breakup!

INTEGRATING STAGE

The intensifying stage can include a lot of time spent with each other during which the relationship becomes increasingly important to both people. At some point spending time together naturally evolves into an integration of both individuals' social lives. In the **integrating stage** the dyad is clearly a social unit. Each person has a clearer definition of their roles than they did before, and these roles become more public. It is not unlikely that this stage would include an integration of each other's social circles, and perhaps time spent with each other's families. Consequently, there are increased obligations to the relationship and the partner in this stage, such as attending social events together.

Nonverbal indicators of the integrating stage include even more synchronization of nonverbal behaviors: both individuals may start to dress, talk, and even look and sound alike. The dyad shares a great deal of physical contact, and spends more time together than they do in any other relationship. In addition, the couple may symbolize their integration through artifacts such as shared clothes, pets, money, trinkets, or even signing a lease together.

Verbal behaviors during the integrating stage include a free flow of information and self-disclosure. Both partners rely on each other to confirm and validate their self-concepts. The partners share an understanding of one another's language and nonverbal cues, and therefore they can use fewer words to communicate effectively.

BONDING STAGE

The **bonding stage** is characterized by a social commitment and/or ritual that signifies the intention to continue the relationship indefinitely. Although marriage is the most common type of bonding ritual in romantic relationships, this stage can also be signified by buying a home together, having a child, or deciding to live together "permanently." The significance of these rituals depends, of course, on the meaning of  the ritual to each person; the ritual itself does not determine the bonding stage. One couple may not want to ever get married, but they plan to be together forever and decide to have children to seal their bond. Another couple may not have enough money for a wedding and a house, so they buy the house and may decide to get married later, if ever. Friendships can also reach the bonding stage, which can come in the form of a verbal agreement to be friends forever, or even through childhood rituals such as making friendship bracelets or becoming "blood brothers."

Review! Knapp's Stages of Relational Escalation	
Initiating stage:	Includes approaching another and making verbal introductions.
Experimenting stage:	Seeking information through conversation and interaction to determine if either part would like to develop the relationship.
Intensifying stage:	Characterized by the mutual understanding that this relationship is becoming increasingly significant.
Integrating stage:	Each person has a clearer definition of their roles and obligations, and these roles become more public.
Bonding stage:	Characterized by a symbolic commitment and/or ritual that signifies the intention to continue the relationship indefinitely.

INTERPERSONAL COMMUNICATION FOR SOCIAL CHANGE

Intergroup Empathy Bias

Our ability to relate to each other is what causes our relationships to grow and deepen. What does it mean, then, when researchers find that we are less likely to have empathy for outgroup members than for ingroup members? This phenomenon, known as the **intergroup empathy bias**[211] helps explain why relational development with outgroup members is so rare. The fact that we tend to empathize less with outgroup members right from the outset creates a barrier to the development of meaningful relationships between highly dissimilar people.

The perceptual bias that causes us to be less empathetic toward outgroup members has consequences that span far beyond our interpersonal relationships. When we see or hear about the suffering of people in geographically far away places, especially those who don't look like us, we are less likely to experience empathy and therefore less compelled to do anything about it. Furthermore, even when the people suffering are our own neighbors or community members, we have little empathy for them as long as we've been convinced that they are outgroup members.

Researchers found that there was, in fact, one way to reduce the intergroup empathy bias, which is to weaken the perception of the entitativity of each group. Entitativity means "groupness," or the degree to which a group is really a group and not just a collection of highly individual people. If we are able to see members of our group *and* other groups as individuals who just happen to be lumped together based on a common trait, our degree of empathy for members of both groups is equally high.

Reflection

1. Think of an outgroup that is *as dissimilar as possible* to your own ingroup (whether that difference is based on religion, political party, or any other identities that are strong for you).

2. Think of a real situation where someone from the outgroup you listed above was suffering. Is it difficult to generate empathy?

3. How challenging would it be for you to develop deep and meaningful relationships with people you consider outgroup members? What would be the costs and benefits?

4. Can you think of any other people for whom you have limited or lower empathy because they belong to an outgroup, such as a different race, sexual orientation, religious belief system, etc.? Be as honest as possible.

A DIALECTICAL MODEL OF RELATIONSHIPS

Another way we can view relationship processes is by taking a dialectical perspective. **Relational dialectics theory**[212] suggests that as partners increase their intimacy it becomes more important to be aware of and manage the naturally occurring tensions in the relationship. Because the relationship is composed of two unique individuals, each person's needs may contrast with the others' at any given time as needs change from day to day, week to week, and month to month. Furthermore, sometimes our own needs are in conflict. For example, we want to spend enough time with our relationship partner, but we also want to see our friends regularly. The way a couple deals with these tensions can determine whether the relationship lasts or deteriorates. These tensions come in the form of three sets of contrasting needs: autonomy versus connection, privacy versus transparency, and novelty versus predictability.

AUTONOMY-CONNECTION

As social creatures, we all have the need to connect to others. However, each individual also has the need to be independent and autonomous in his or her own life. The need for personal *autonomy* and the need for *connection* with the other are often in competition causing a tension in the relationship. At any given time, one of these needs can dominate, and it is likely that the dominant need at that moment may be different for each person in the dyad. For example, if a wife is overwhelmed by family obligations, she may react by seeking independence in all areas of her life, including her relationship. This need may come just at the same time that her partner is feeling especially lonely, and desires connection. These tensions ebb and flow over time. Sometimes both parties' needs meet at the same place on the spectrum, while other times they find themselves on opposite ends.

Autonomy   Connection

Figure 7.3. There is a constant tension between the needs for autonomy and connection in any interpersonal relationship.

PRIVACY-TRANSPARENCY

In addition, the need for *transparency* can conflict with the need for *privacy* for each individual in the relationship at a different time. It feels good to tell other people about ourselves in the form of self-disclosure, but sometimes we enjoy keeping part of ourselves private, even in a bonded relationship. For example, imagine the situation where you are in a long-term committed friendship with someone. If you begin a new friendship with someone else, you may enjoy having secrets with this new person that you do not share with the other friend, yet the old friend may desire that you share everything. When relationship partners have different needs on this dimension a relational tension is created over how much privacy or transparency is desirable.

Privacy   Transparency

Figure 7.4. There is a constant tension between the needs for privacy and transparency in any interpersonal relationship.

MINDFUL MEDIATED COMMUNICATION

Improved Parental Invasion of Privacy

Between email, social media, and texting, it seems that Mom and Dad have more ways of violating their children's privacy than ever. However, it turns out that despite the increase in channels where parents can "meddle" (cell phone, computer, etc.) parents intrusive behavior is getting better, not worse.[213]

One team sought to discover how frequently and in what ways do parents invade their children's privacy either at home or away at college. Contrary to expectations, an increase in communication technology does not necessarily mean an increase in parents' invasiveness. In fact, compared to a similar study conducted almost ten years earlier, parent intrusion is now at an all-time low. One explanation for this finding is that communication technologies provide more ways for children to communicate not only with their peers, but with their parents as well. Nowadays, when children are away at college they are able to keep in closer contact with parents than they were in the past via mediated channels such as Facetime and texting. More regular communication seems to alleviate the kinds of fears that cause parents to invade their children's privacy in the first place. Another explanation is that parent-child relationships are changing, so what may have been considered an intrusion in the past, is now acceptable. Adolescents and young adults in modern times report feeling closer to their parents than they did in previous decades, and therefore seem not to mind sharing more

private information than would have been shared by members of past generations. So, while parent "meddling" will never go away completely, it does seem to mostly be a problem of the past.

NOVELTY-PREDICTABILITY

Finally, in order to feel secure, everyone needs structure and stability in a relationship. We feel most comfortable when our roles are clear, and we have routines and habits. However, a relationship in which nothing new or different occurs can quickly become boring. The struggle to have interesting *novelty* in a relationship while maintaining a feeling of stable *predictability* is the basis for this tension. A typical example is that which occurs when couples get into habitual patterns regarding how they spend their weekends. At some point one person may feel like they need to "mix it up" and do something risky, fun, or unique. This feeling may arise just at the time that the other partner was feeling grateful for the predictability and safety that comes at the end of a difficult week. Again, members of the relationship may feel either of these needs more strongly at any given time, and their needs may not be mutual or compatible all the time.

Figure 7.5. There is a constant tension between the needs for novelty and predictability in any interpersonal relationship.

STRATEGIES FOR MANAGING DIALECTICAL TENSIONS

Experts find that people have one of several reactions to dialectical tensions that occur in a relationship.[214] Sometimes people choose to *deny* that the tension exists, which is considered one of the least effective methods for dealing with it. *Disorientation* is another reaction, whereby one or both members of the dyad are overwhelmed by the challenge of managing the tension. Disorientation often occurs when one or both people realize that the seamless interactions of the honeymoon phase are over and the relationship may actually require work in order to remain satisfying.

If a dyad chooses to actively address the tension, they may opt for the *selection* strategy, which means that instead of trying to balance between the two needs, they choose the one that they feel is the most important. For example, if a couple feels like they struggle between transparency and privacy, they may make an agreement to always reveal everything to each other.

Other strategies require compromising. Using *alternation*, a dyad will switch between the two dialectics. A couple may address their tension between predictability and novelty by deciding to maintain a predictable life, except for twice a year when they go on an exotic vacation with no itinerary. *Segmentation* is another compromising choice for managing tensions. This strategy requires that a dyad compartmentalize the dialectics, sticking to one end of the spectrum in some situations and moving to the opposite end in other situations. For example, a couple can agree to be completely open regarding their opinions about other people, except when it comes to family

members; both people agree that they are not allowed to share personal opinions, especially criticism of the other person's family. *Moderation* is the strategy of moving away from either side of the spectrum and trying to find a middle ground. Two friends may decide to live together but not to take classes together in order to moderate the autonomy-connection tension.

The final methods for dealing with dialectical tensions require a change in perspective. *Reframing* involves viewing the tension in a different way: not as a struggle but as differences that balance out the personalities of each individual in the dyad. A "clingy" partner may learn the beauty of alone time from his independent partner; whereas his partner learns that time together can include silence or simply sharing space instead of always "doing" something together. Finally, *reaffirmation* is a strategy that allows dyads to acknowledge the tension as a natural part of a relationship and simply allow for it without feeling like it threatens their bond. Each person must reassure the other that the relationship is intact despite this difference in needs.

Dialectical tensions will occur throughout the stages of relational escalation and de-escalation, and the strategy you choose to manage them depends on the situation. These tensions can break a relationship before it escalates to the next stage, or if managed properly they can propel it into greater intimacy.

Review! Methods for Managing Dialectical Tensions	
Denial:	Refusing to admit that there is a tension.
Disorientation:	Becoming overwhelmed by and hopeless about the tension.
Selection:	Choosing one end of the dialectic to focus on.
Alternation:	Alternating between two ends of the dialectic at different times.
Segmentation:	Choosing the approach depending on the situation.
Moderation:	Finding a middle ground between the two tensions.
Reframing:	Choosing to view the tension as an opportunity for growth.
Reaffirmation:	Allowing the tension to exist and not threaten the relationship.

CHAPTER SUMMARY

This chapter walked you through the process of relational initiation and development starting from where all relationships begin: attraction. The reasons for interpersonal attraction and types of human attraction were discussed. The processes by which we reduce uncertainty about others were explained, including the axioms of uncertainty reduction theory. You were then introduced to a developmental model of relationships, which describes the verbal and nonverbal behaviors that change as intimacy develops.

The initiating stage is the first interaction. Once the "interview" begins, the experimenting stage has started. Within the experimenting stage social penetration theory was described as a useful tool by which to analyze our interactions in terms of the breadth and depth of self-disclosure occurring in the relationship. Next, the intensifying stage was described, where intimacy styles begin to affect both people. The integrating stage includes an intertwining of daily life, and finally the bonding stage signifies a mutual agreement to commit to the relationship indefinitely.

Lastly, you learned about a dialectical perspective on relationships, which explains the natural tensions between autonomy and connection, predictability and novelty, and privacy and transparency. The next chapter will focus on particular relationship challenges that may push the relationship toward breakup, covering each stage of relational de-escalation.

CHAPTER ACTIVITIES

TEST YOUR UNDERSTANDING

True or False

____1. Uncertainty reduction theory suggests that a primary motivation for interacting with others is to reduce uncertainty about our environment.

____2. The relational dialectic that is at play when one person wants more excitement is called privacy-transparency.

____3. Each culture seems to have unique terms and phrases for relationship experiences, some of which have no translation in other languages.

Multiple Choice: Circle the best answer choice.

1. Styles of love that include emotional involvement, but where the passion does not drive the entire relationship are:

   A. Storge, Pragma, and Agape

   B. Eros, Mania, and Ludus

   C. Mania, Eros, and Agape

   D. Storge, Eros, and Agape

   E. None of the above are correct

2. Strategies for managing dialectical tensions include all of the following, except:

   A. Selection

   B. Alternation

   C. Segmentation

   D. Moderation

   E. Escalation

3. Which is NOT true of the stages of relational escalation:

   A. The stages tend to occur in order.

   B. People can spend a long or short amount of time in any stage.

   C. Not all relationships are meant to go through to the bonding stage.

   D. People tend to skip around to the stages they are most comfortable with.

   E. All of the above are true.

**Answers are listed at the end of this section before the references.

Short Answer

1. Explain the nature of interpersonal attraction and types of attraction.

   _____

   _____

   _____

   _____

   _____

   _____

   _____

   _____

   _____

   _____

   _____

   _____

2. Identify the stages of coming together and the communication behaviors that are typical of each stage.

   _____

   _____

   _____

   _____

   _____

   _____

   _____

   _____

   _____

   _____

   _____

3. List the ways in which individuals reduce uncertainty when developing relationships.

_____

_____

_____

_____

_____

_____

_____

_____

_____

_____

_____

_____

4. Describe the role of self-disclosure in the development of intimacy.

_____

_____

_____

_____

_____

_____

_____

_____

_____

_____

_____

_____

_____

5. Describe the natural tensions that occur as a relationship becomes more integrated.

_____

_____

_____

_____

_____

_____

_____

_____

_____

_____

_____

_____

_____

_____

_____

_____

_____

_____

_____

_____

_____

_____

_____

_____

_____

IN-CLASS ACTIVITY

Relational Initiation

How do you show someone you are interested in him or her? What do you do verbally and nonverbally?

_____

_____

_____

_____

_____

_____

What are your "deal breakers"? What questions do you try to get answers to in the experimenting stage to evaluate whether you want to progress?

_____

_____

_____

_____

_____

_____

_____

_____

What are your own "deficits"? That is, what information about yourself might you try to avoid in order to give yourself a fair chance with a new person? How honest is the experimenting stage of relational development?

_____

_____

_____

_____

_____

_____

_____

SKILL PRACTICE: MANAGING DIALECTICAL TENSIONS

What Is the Goal of Managing Dialectical Tensions?

The goal of managing dialectical tensions is to maintain a relationship that both people want to be in, despite their different needs.

How Do You Do It?

Try any of the following methods to see what works for both people:

Use Selection: Choose one end of the dialectic to focus on.
Example: If one person's need for connection is a priority in order for the relationship to survive, focus on meeting this need.

Use Alternation: Switch between two ends of the dialectic at different times to meet each person's needs.
Example: If one person needs time apart and the other needs closeness, spend one weekend apart each month.

Use Segmentation: Compartmentalize the dialectics, sticking to one end for certain situations and another end for other situations.
Example: If one person needs complete openness about interactions with ex-boyfriends or girlfriends, agree to be completely open about this topic but agree to maintain privacy about other topics.

Use Moderation: Find a middle ground between the two tensions.
Example: If one person needs predictability but the other does not like to be home every night for dinner, agree to eat dinner together on certain nights, and other nights make last minute plans or eat separately.

Use Reframing or Affirmation: Choose to view the tension as an opportunity for change and growth, and allow the tension to exist while affirming that it does not threaten the relationship.
Example: Reframing and Affirmation require regular conversations about the tensions so that they are not taboo topics.

Select a relationship where one of these methods might useful for managing a dialectical tension. Write out how you would suggest this method to the person with whom you experience this dialectical tension. First explain what you perceive the problem to be, then suggest a method from above.

_____

_____

_____

_____

_____

HOMEWORK ACTIVITY

MANAGING DIALECTICAL TENSIONS

Try to identify a relationship in your life where there exists a struggle between each person's need for either autonomy or connection, transparency or privacy, novelty or predictability.

Explain how this dialectical tension affects the relationship, then determine which strategy suggested in this chapter may be an effective method for managing the tension.

_____

_____

_____

_____

_____

_____

_____

_____

_____

_____

_____

_____

_____

_____

Answers to True/False and Multiple Choice

1. True

2. False

3. True

1. A

2. E

3. D

REFERENCES

[187]Hatfield, E., & Sprecher, S. (1986). *Mirror, mirror...The importance of looks in everyday life*. Albany, NY: State University of New York Press.

[188]Byrne, D., & Buehler, J. A. (1955). A note on the influence of propinquity upon acquaintanceship. *Journal of Applied Social Psychology, 51*, 147–148.

[189]Brooks-Gunn, J., & Lewis, M. (1981). Infant social perception: Responses to pictures of parents and strangers. *Developmental Psychology, 17*, 647–649.

[190]Newcomb, T. (1961). *The acquaintance process*. New York: Holt, Rinehart and Winston, Inc.

[191]Dijkstra , P. (2008). Do people know what they want: A similar or complementary partner? *Evolutonary Psychology, 6*(4), 595–602.

[192]Scheflen, A.E. (1965). Quasi-courtship behavior in psychotherapy. *Psychiatry 28*, 245–257.

[193]Mehrabian, A. (1972). *Nonverbal communication*. Chicago, Illinois: Aldine-Atherton.

[194]Berger, C.R., Calabrese, R.J. (1975). Some exploration in initial interaction and beyond: toward a developmental theory of communication. *Human Communication Research, 1*, 99–112.

[195]Anderson, M., Kunkel, A. & Dennis, M.R. (2011). "Let's (not) talk about that": Bridging the past sexual experiences. *Journal of Sex Research, 48*(4), 381–391.

[196]Knapp, M.L. (1984). *Interpersonal communication and human relationships*. Boston, MA: Allyn & Bacon.

[197]Montgomery, B. (1986). Interpersonal attraction as a function of open communication and gender. *Communication Research Reports, 3*(1), 140–145.

[198]Derlega, V.J., Metts, S., Petronio, S., & Margulis, S.T. (1993). *Self-disclosure*. Newbury Park, CA: Sage.

[199]Valkenburg, P., & Peter, J. (2009). The effects of instant messaging on the quality of adolescents' existing friendships: a longitudinal study. *Journal of Communication, 59*(1), 79–97.

[200]Altman, I., & Taylor, D. (1973). *Social penetration: The development of interpersonal relationships*. New York: Holt, Rinehart and Winston.

[201]Anderson. P.A. & Leibowitz, K. (1978). The development and nature of the construct touch avoidance. *Journal of Nonverbal Behavior, 3*(2).

[202]Hall, E.T. (1963). A system for the notation of proxemic behavior. American *Anthropologist, 65*, 1003–1026.

[203]Gatewood, J.B. & Rosenwein, R. (1981). Interactional synchrony: Genuine or spurious? A critique of recent research. *Journal of Nonverbal Behavior, 6*(1), 12–29.

[204]LeVine, T.R., Stryzewski, A., & Park, H.S. (2006). Love styles and communication in relationships: Partner preferences, initiation, and intensification. *Communication Quarterly, 54*, 465–486.

[205]Richardson, D.R., Hammock, G.S., Lubben, T., & Mickler, S. (1989). The relationship between love attitudes and conflict responses. *Journal of Social and Clinical Psychology, 8*, 430–441.

[206]Hendrick, S.S., Hendrick, C., & Adler, N,L. (1988). Romantic relationships: Love, satisfaction, and staying together. *Journal of Personality and Social Psychology, 54*, 980–988.

[207]Richardson et al. (1988).

[208]Ibid.

[209]Ibid.

[210]Haag, P. (November 18, 2011). The top 10 relationship words that aren't translatable into English. *Big Think*. Retrieved June 21, 2011 from http://bigthink.com/marriage-30/the-top-10-relationship-words-that-arent-translatable-into-english?page=all

[211]Meyer, M.L., Masten, C.L., Ma, Y., Wang, C., Shi, Z., Eisenberger, N.I, & Han, S. (2014). Their pain gives us pleasure: How intergroup dynamics shape empathic failures and counter-empathic responses. *Journal of Experimental Social Psychology, 55*, 110–125.

[212]Baxter, L.A. (1988). A dialectical perspective on communication strategies in relationship development. In S. Duch (Ed.), *Handbook of personal relationships: Theory, research and interventions*. New York: John Wiley & Sons.

[213]Ledbetter, A.M., Heiss, S., Sibal, K., Lev, E., Battle-Fisher, M., & Shubert, N. (2010). Parental invasive and children's defensive behaviors at home and away at college: Mediated communication and privacy boundary management. *Communication Studies, 61*(2), 184–204.

[214]Baxter, L.A. & Montgomery, B.M. (1998). A guide to dialectical approaches to studying personal relationships. In B.M. Montgomery and L.A. Baxter (Eds.) *Dialectical approaches to studying personal relationships*. New York: Erlbaum.

Relational De-Escalation

"In every crisis there is a message. Crises are nature's way of forcing change—breaking down old structures, shaking loose negative habits so that something new and better can take their place."

—Susan L. Taylor

Learning Objectives

After studying this chapter, you should be able to:

1. *Identify various challenges that create relational hardships.*

2. *Explain the two different models of relational de-escalation and the communication behaviors that are typical in each stage of these models.*

3. *Describe the types of breakups.*

4. *Summarize the communication strategies people use when terminating a relationship.*

5. *Explain the variables that help determine how each individual tends to respond to relationship challenges.*

If we were realistic about the likelihood of our relationships ending, we probably wouldn't invest in them at the level that we do. It is a simple and well-proven reality of life that many, if not most, relationships end. Think about all of the interpersonal relationships you've had throughout your life. It's likely that you've had 50–100 or more, and unlikely that you have maintained all of them due to the natural changes that occur over the lifespan. Even the relationships we vow to maintain sometimes end. Recent studies report that nearly one-third of all marriages fail within the first 5 years[215] and between one-half and two-thirds will end in divorce.[216]

The fact that relationships end is not necessarily a bad thing. Not all relationships are meant to endure. Many relationships are only satisfying and healthy for a period of time, after which continuing them is not in the best interest of either party. Carrying on in a relationship where the costs

are extremely high and there is no foreseeable potential for things to change can cause a great deal of suffering to both people. However, many relationships go on too long before they end simply because many people fear the pain and stress that comes with breaking up.

"Should I stay or should I go?" is a common thought of either relational partner that can occur in any stage of relational escalation, and at any point during a committed relationship. What are the situations, behaviors, or events that cause one formerly committed partner to question whether the relationship should continue? For some people, cheating is a "deal breaker," that is, the costs of anger, humiliation, and deception significantly outweigh the rewards of being in the relationship. Other people weigh "benefits" such as money, social status, or identity confirmation in their formula for determining whether a relationship is worth it. Relationship costs and rewards are relative concepts, meaning each individual pays greater attention and gives more weight to different variables. You may not even know what your "deal breakers" are until they happen in your relationship.

There are several categories of communication behaviors that provoke the "stay or go" decision-making process, including relational violence, hurtful communication, and deception. This chapter will explain these challenges and trace what happens when a relationship begins to deteriorate and eventually terminates. You will also learn about some personal variables that help determine how each individual reacts to relational difficulties. The goal of this chapter is for you to understand the often-confusing process of relational deterioration, ultimately gaining a greater understanding of your own communication patterns that emerge when relational hardships occur.

RELATIONAL TRANSGRESSIONS

Throughout the lifespan of any interpersonal relationship both people should expect that events and situations will occur that threaten the health and stability of the relationship. There are as many types of relationship problems as there are types of people in relationships. However, there are several types of communication behaviors that are especially problematic. This section will define some of these behaviors and discuss the impact they have on an interpersonal relationship.

Relational transgressions are violations of implicit or explicit rules between people in relationships. Transgressions vary in their severity and impact on relationships, and can include an extremely wide range of behaviors such as emotional involvement with others, flirting, breaking a promise, or continued attachment or communication with former partners.[217] Many transgressions are based on a violation of *implicit* rules, or unspoken agreements about what is expected from each person in the relationship. For example, partners may have unspoken expectations about whether they engage in profanity and name-calling during a fight. When these unstated rules are broken, it can cause surprise, anger, and hurt. Other transgressions result from either person breaking an *explicit*, or verbally stated, rule such as agreements about monogamy or honesty. These types of failures are usually even more detrimental to the future of the relationship, and usually result in feelings of anger and betrayal.

The more severe the transgression, the more difficult it is for victims to forgive their partners and engage in constructive relational repair.[218] Sexual betrayal, known as infidelity, is ranked as the most

hurtful transgression, and the most unlikely to be forgiven. Other common relational transgressions include violence, hurtful communication, and deception, each of which will be covered next.

INTIMATE PARTNER VIOLENCE

If you don't think violence is an important issue to discuss when it comes to interpersonal communication, here are some facts to gain your attention:[219]

■ In the United States, researchers estimate that 40% to 70% of female murder victims were killed by their husbands or boyfriends.

■ Nearly 25% of women have been raped and/or physically assaulted by an intimate partner at some point in their lives.

Intimate partner violence (IPV) is abuse that occurs between people in a close relationship.[220] IPV includes four types of behavior, including the following:

■ *Physical abuse,* which is when a person hurts or tries to hurt a partner by hitting, kicking, burning, or other physical force.

■ *Sexual abuse*, which occurs when one partner forces the other to take part in a sex act when the partner does not consent.

■ *Threats of physical or sexual abuse*, which include the use of words, gestures, weapons, or other means to communicate the intent to cause harm.

■ *Emotional abuse*, which involves threatening a partner or his or her possessions or loved ones, or harming a partner's sense of self-worth, such as stalking, name-calling, intimidation, or not letting a partner see friends and family.

Intimate partner violence received media attention when the press got a hold of police photographs showing pop star Rihanna after she was abused by her boyfriend, Chris Brown. Rihanna's decision to forgive her partner created a mob of critics, and great concern amongst scholars who study intimate partner violence.

Intimate partner violence occurs across all populations, regardless of social and economic status, religion, or culture. However, there are several groups where it is especially prevalent. Young women, especially those considered below the poverty line are affected more than any other group. Although both men and women experience intimate partner violence, women are two to three times more likely to report that they were pushed, grabbed or shoved by an intimate partner, and seven to fourteen times more likely to report being beat up, choked, or tied down by an intimate partner. Specific cultural groups are also more prone to this particular type of violence. American Indian/Alaska Natives report more violent victimization than do people of other racial backgrounds, and Hispanic women are more likely than non-Hispanic women to report instances of rape by a relational partner.

In addition to some socio-economic, gender, and cultural factors that contribute to IPV, recent research points to several relational factors that put people at greater risk, including relational

conflict and instability, male dominance or beliefs in strict gender roles, desire for power and control in relationships, and emotional dependence and insecurity.[221]

You may believe that the above statistics are not relevant to your relationship, but intimate relational violence is more common than most people realize, and can take many forms. If you have ever made an intentional jab at your partner to damage his or her self-esteem, or even thrown something toward your partner during a conflict, this is considered relational violence, even though you may have justified it because it occurred "in the heat of the moment." Relational violence is often tolerated because it becomes a part of the relationship climate over time, so it is often hard to evaluate objectively from within the relationship. Outsiders to the relationship often seem less tolerant of the behavior, even when the people in the relationship excuse it away. These excuses usually focus on making sense of the abusive behavior by explaining why it occurred. One study found that women were less likely to take legal action in response to partner violence if their partner was an alcoholic, because it makes it easier to excuse the behavior.[222] Whether or not you believe you have been a victim or perpetrator of intimate relational violence, it is an important behavior to watch for in your communication patterns.

WATCH AND LEARN

View a TED Talk on intimate partner violence by typing this into your browser: TED Talk why domestic violence victims don't leave.

HURTFUL COMMUNICATION

Probably more common than physical violence is emotionally hurtful communication. Hurtful communication is a complicated concept because it is often the receiver who defines the communication as hurtful. Senders and receivers can disagree about the intentions, motivations, and the appropriateness of a message. Directly hurtful messages, such as insults and attacks, are often easy to identify, but subtle hurtful communication, such as back-handed compliments or "constructive criticism," can be confusing because it is unclear whether the intention is malicious or benign. Often someone is intending to be forthright, but even honesty can be hurtful (hence the term "brutal honesty"). Research shows that intentions are everything when it comes to honesty. If a message was accidentally hurtful, and the speaker's goal was simply to be honest, the ramifications of the message are often less severe. However, if the receiver interprets that the sender may be intending to invoke hurt feelings, the ramifications are negative.[223]

The degree to which hurtful messages affect us also depends on the nature of the relationship. Research indicates that people are more hurt by messages from family members than by non-family members and that romantic relationships are more damaged by hurtful communication than any other kind of relationship.[224]

Depending on the communication style of the receiver, there are several general categories of reactions people tend to give when their communication partner delivers a hurtful message.[225] Three

reactions that are particularly common include invulnerable, acquiescent, or active responses. **Invulnerable responses** are indirect, such as ignoring the message, laughing, or being silent. **Acquiescent responses**, such as crying, conceding, or apologizing can be considered either direct or indirect. **Active verbal responses** are verbal and direct, which can include counterattacks, self-defense statements, sarcastic statements, and demands for explanations. Most responses tend to be either non-assertive or aggressive, thus preventing the issue from being resolved and leading to built-up resentment or gradual deterioration of self-esteem.

Figure 8.0. Responses to hurtful communication.

Nonetheless, hurtful communication does not always have to signify the decline or end of a relationship. Managing our communication effectively can lead to a better and stronger relationship in the end.[226] The ability to be assertive and communicate openly can make the difference between hurtful messages being fatal versus being constructive to the relationship.

INTERPERSONAL COMMUNICATION FOR SOCIAL CHANGE

Microaggressions: Not So "Micro" Afterall

Stranger: "You have such a stunning face. Where are you from?"

Maggie "I'm from Santa Barbara."

Stranger: "No, I mean where are you originally from?"

Maggie: "I was born here, in Santa Barbara."

Stranger: "I mean, where are your parents from?"

Maggie: "They were both born in Fresno."

Stranger: "Well, your grandparents, then, what country are they from?"

Maggie: "My grandma is also from Fresno. My grandfather was born in Indonesia."

Stranger: "I knew it! I just love your exotic look. Just stunning."

Microaggressions are unwelcome comments or insulting behaviors directed at members of marginalized groups, such as women, People of Color, and LGBTQ folks, among others. They can be subtle, such as being overlooked or ignored in a service situation, or not-so-subtle, such as being the target of a joke or being treated according to a stereotype. When members of majority groups excuse and minimize the impacts of these kinds of comments and behaviors this is also considered a microaggression.

People who belong to majority or dominant groups often underestimate not only the number of microaggressions marginalized people experience on a daily basis, but also the degree to which the buildup of these acts affect their overall well-being. Microaggressions are not only annoying and disruptive, but often remind the target about the history of trauma and violence experienced by members of their group. Recent research shows that microaggressions can cause depression, hopelessness, and anxiety, ultimately affecting life outcomes.[227]

Here is a small sample of microaggressions:

- Asking to touch a Person of Color's hair

- Determining that certain communication styles, accents, or dialects are incorrect or improper

- Expecting or demanding that girls or women act "ladylike"

- Appointing gender to negatively evaluate a behavior such as, "you run like a girl"

- Using the word "lifestyle" to describe someone's sexual orientation or gender identity

- Using someone's sexual orientation as an insult (for example, "that's so gay")

- Asking an adoptive parent about his or her child's "real" mother or "real" father

Educator Derald Wing Sue suggests that we create awareness about microaggressions by calling them out.[228] Activist Brittany Packnett couldn't agree more—she started the hashtag #BlackWomenAtWork in response to two highly publicized incidents of microaggressions directed at Congresswoman Maxine Waters and White House reporter April Ryan in March of 2017. What ensued was a social media deluge of Black women listing their own stories about daily microaggressions, followed by the hashtag #BlackWomenAtWork. Search the story, or learn more at The Microaggression Project: www.microaggressions.com.

Reflection

1. Have you ever been the target of a microaggression? Which group membership of yours was the microaggression based on? How did it make you feel?

2. Do you think you've ever unintentionally committed a microaggression? When, and to whom?

3. If you catch yourself committing a microaggression, what do you think is the best way to address it?

4. If you overheard someone else committing a microaggression, do you feel like it would be appropriate to say something? Why or why not? For ideas search: "How to be an ally to someone experiencing microaggressions."

DECEPTION

Would you call yourself a liar? Probably not. As human beings, we have complex attitudes toward deception. Most people consider honesty a virtue, and believe that they are honest people. However, those same people may not believe that *other* people are entirely trustworthy and honest. The

truth is: everyone lies. Whether it is a white lie to spare someone's feelings, an exaggeration to make your partner jealous, or leaving out details that might get you in trouble, we all lie. We often tend to justify our own lies and we don't really believe that they speak poorly of our character and moral code, yet we tend to find the lies of others unacceptable. There are several types of deception, and each varies in level of acceptability depending on the nature of the relationship, the issue around which the deception occurred, and the perception of the person who was deceived.

Deception by Omission

Deception by omission, often called concealment, involves intentionally holding back some of the information another person has requested or that you are expected to share. Sometimes information is left out to intentionally mislead the listener, while other times it is just an oversight. If you fail to tell a new dating partner that you are divorced, this is deception by omission. It would be normal to reveal this information within the first few dates, so its omission seems intentionally misleading. Thus, failing to share information that you know you should provide to another because of the expectations of that particular relationship is considered deception. For example, if you are in a serious committed romantic relationship you may have implicit or explicit rules about spending time with former partners. By not telling your partner about your lunch with an ex, you are deceiving him or her because it is expected that you would share this information. Omitting information is not always considered as malicious as fabricating information, but the outcome may have an equally severe impact on the relationship depending on the intentions of the deceiver and the perceptions of the receiver.

Deception by Commission

Deception by commission is the intentional presentation of false information. Fabricated information can come in several forms. **Bold-faced lies** are outright falsifications of information intended to deceive the receiver. For example, if you tell your friend in the situation above that you played in a band, when you in fact have never played music with others, you are committing a bold-faced lie. **White lies** are a category of bold-faced lies, but they are typically benign because they only deviate from the truth in a minor or inconsequential way. If a friend asks to borrow your iPod and you tell him that you can't find it instead of revealing that you don't want to lend it out, you are committing a white lie. White lies are often used to spare someone's feelings or to save face. In addition, white lies are often used when making excuses for imperfect behavior. If you are late to work because you slept in but you tell your boss you had car trouble, this is a white lie because it is used to save face for yourself—you wouldn't get fired either way, but you are trying to avoid embarrassment or a pointless lecture. When revealed, bold-faced lies tend to be considered a more severe violation and are less forgivable than exaggerations.

Exaggeration, also known as embellishing, is used when you make a smaller or bigger claim than what is true. If you are getting to know a new friend who is skilled at several instruments, you might mention that you "love playing the piano," when in fact you played as a child but are out of practice.

Each individual has his or her own reasons for engaging in relational deception. Some deception stems from *altruism*, or a concern for other people that overrides concern for oneself. Thus, even if deception goes against your personal values, lying to another person to prevent him or her from getting hurt may be altruistic. If you happen to see your friend's ex out with a new and incredibly attractive date, you may omit this information from your next conversation simply to avoid unnecessary pain to your friend. Altruistic lying is often considered acceptable behavior in collectivistic cultures because it is intended to save face. In this sense, certain lying behaviors are common and expected in cultures where social rules and obligations dictate behavior.[229]

In contrast, *self-serving goals* are motivated by the desire for personal gain or to avoid unfavorable consequences, which can include gaining resources or avoiding harm or loss of resources. The resources we are trying to protect can be emotional, such as approval or support of another. For example, you may lie to avoid being embarrassed. Resources can also be material such as use of the car, an allowance, or gifts. In this case you might have lied about your grades to receive a reward from your parents. Finally, resources can be physical, which can include affection, sex, or even physical safety in the case where punishment may come in the form of abuse, as discussed in the section on intimate relational violence. If you know your partner tends toward verbal or physical abuse, you may hide certain details of your life that he or she would disapprove of in order to protect yourself.

Review! Types of Deception	
Deception by omission:	Often called concealment, this type of lying involves intentionally holding back some of the information another person has requested or that you are expected to share.
Deception by commission:	The intentional presentation of false information.
Bold-faced lies:	Outright falsifications of information intended to deceive the receiver.
White lies:	A type of bold-faced lie that only deviates from the truth in a minor or inconsequential way.
Exaggeration:	Also known as embellishing, this is a type of deception used when one makes a smaller or bigger claim than what is true.

MINDFUL MEDIATED COMMUNICATION

What Happens in VR Stays in VR?

As many people already know, Second Life is a virtual world that became available on the Internet in 2003 (secondlife.com). Internet users become "residents" of this virtual world by downloading a program that allows them to create an entirely new identity, in the form of an "avatar." In Second Life members communicate with other members via their avatars, and can engage a wide range of pseudo real-life activities such as shopping, going out, meeting others, dating, buying property, and selling goods. Users claim that the things that makes Second Life more interesting than "first life" (real life, that is), is the fantasy component that allows for such activities as flying, teleporting, and…infidelity.

Amy Taylor and David Pollard met in an online chat room, and soon developed an off-line romance. Because of their common interest in the virtual reality game Second Life, they decided to compliment their real life relationship with a Second Life romance between their avatars, Laura Skye and David Barmy.

The relationship hit a wall when one day Amy walked in on David sitting at the computer watching his avatar having relations with a prostitute. Although Amy was hurt by the transgression of David's avatar, she eventually forgave David and the two married in 2005. They also decided to have Skye and Barmy marry each other in Second Life, for good measure.

All was well in both real and virtual life, until Amy noticed David's avatar engaging in an overly friendly new relationship with another woman in Second Life. Devastated by yet another episode of Barmy's infidelity against Skye, Amy filed for divorce from David…in real life.

The opportunity to develop second selves is of particular interest to communication scholars. Two main questions being asked by current research are:

1. Do people create a "second life" because they are somehow unhappy with their real life? If so, does having a second life seem to help these problems? Why would users choose to develop a second life instead of making necessary changes to their real life?

2. Do individuals' behavioral and ethical standards change when they are using an avatar? If so, what does this suggest?

Think about your own responses to these questions. If you know someone who enjoys gaming or virtual reality, see if you can seek some answers.

RESPONDING TO TRANSGRESSIONS

Before you decide how to respond to a relational transgression, there are several steps to take to ensure clarity. First, it must be determined that a transgression has actually occurred. Then, it must be clarified that both parties agreed to and understood the rule that was violated. You may also want to ask yourself if the rule was reasonable for the context of this specific relationship.

Once it is certain that a transgression has been made, the person who feels transgressed usually makes a reproach. A **reproach** is a message that one person's expectations have been violated. When asked to explain a relational transgression the offender will usually respond with an **account**.

There are three main ways in which people usually express an account.[230] **Justifications** occur when there is no denial of having committed the transgression on the part of the offender, and he or she attempts to explain why the behavior is good, sensible, or permissible. Apologies and excuses seem to be the most acceptable types of accounts.[231] **Excuses** occur when the offender admits the act was bad, but includes that it was caused or influenced by an external source. **Apologies** occur when there is an acknowledgment of wrongdoing and the person accepts responsibility for the action. Using an apology increases the likelihood that the hurt partner will forgive the deviant behavior. Most importantly, the sincerity with which the apology is made adds to the probability of the hurt partner forgiving the guilty one. We can usually detect insincere apologies, and these attempts may worsen the situation. If the account is expressed sincerely rather than defensively, it is more likely to be accepted.[232]

Once an account has been received, the offended person must decide whether they find the account acceptable. Interpersonal accounts are not automatically accepted. One may offer an account for his or her behavior that others disagree with or dismiss. If the offended individual accepts the offender's account as evidence of the behavior being unintentional and justifiable, then blame is less likely. However, if the perceiver does not interpret the account as reducing the intentionality and responsibility of the actor, then blame will ensue.[233] Once the offended person has determined the causes and effects of the transgression, he or she must decide whether the issue is resolved. When the violation is not resolved, the offended party may harbor resentment, retaliate, or detach from the relationship, which could lead to relational deterioration and eventual breakup.

Considering the prevalence of mediated communication, transgressions that occur online are of special interest to researchers. In one study, researchers noticed some interesting trends when examining online reactions to offensive posts. "Offensive" posts were first categorized into seven groups: (1) incorrect or novice use of technology; (2) bandwidth piggery; (3) violation of Usenet conventions; (4) violation of newsgroup conventions; (5) ethical violations; (6) inappropriate language; and (7) factual errors.[234] By analyzing five newsgroup postings, these researchers examined the patterns of communication regarding wrongdoings online.[235] They found that the particular type of offence set the stage for the type of reaction. In addition, there were gender differences between the reactions. Males who made an offensive post responded to critics with more sarcastic behavior, whereas females tended to use more humor and wit. Females were also more likely to mitigate. They admitted errors, provided excuses or justified their behavior, while males often denied wrongdoing.

Review! Types of Relationship Challenges	
Relational transgressions:	Violations of implicit or explicit rules between people in relationships, including but not limited to intimate partner violence, hurtful communication, and deception.
Intimate partner violence:	Any destructive behaviors aimed at emotionally, psychologically, or physically hurting another person, including physical abuse, aggressiveness, and threats.
Hurtful communication:	Communication that causes emotional pain to the receiver.
Deception:	Communication that is not truthful, ranging from exaggeration to bold-faced lies.

SKILL BUILDING EXERCISE

Responding to Relational Transgressions

This chapter explains how there are many variables that determine how each person reacts to a relational transgression. For each situation described below, read each type of account the offender might make: A) justification, B) apology, or C) excuse, and consider how each account might affect your reaction to the transgression, and why.

1. Your significant other receives a text from an ex saying, "Thanks for coffee." You weren't aware that a coffee date had occurred and when you confront him/her, he/she says:

    a. "I don't know why you are so upset. You would have done the same thing."
        Your reaction to this account: _____

    b. "I'm really sorry. I know it was the wrong thing to do. I should have thought about it before I did it."
        Your reaction to this account: _____

    c. "I knew you wouldn't like me doing that. But what else was I supposed to do, considering the situation?"
        Your reaction to this account: _____

2. Your dad reads an open piece of personal mail addressed to you. When you find out he says:

    a. "I don't know why you are so upset. You would have done the same thing."
        Your reaction to this account: _____

    b. "I'm really sorry. I know it was the wrong thing to do. I should have thought about it before I did it."
        Your reaction to this account: _____

    c. "I knew you wouldn't like me doing that. But what else was I supposed to do, considering the situation?"
        Your reaction to this account: _____

3. You overhear your best friend sharing a secret you told her with another friend. When you ask her about it she says:

   a. "I don't know why you are so upset. You would have done the same thing."
      Your reaction to this account: _____

   b. "I'm really sorry. I know it was the wrong thing to do. I should have thought about it before I did it."
      Your reaction to this account: _____

   c. "I knew you wouldn't like me doing that. But what else was I supposed to do, considering the situation?"
      Your reaction to this account: _____

4. Your friend blows off plans with you for a last minute date with someone he/she really likes. When you call to explain that you are angry, your friend says:

   a. "I don't know why you are so upset. You would have done the same thing."
      Your reaction to this account: _____

   b. "I'm really sorry. I know it was the wrong thing to do. I should have thought about it before I did it."
      Your reaction to this account: _____

   c. "I knew you wouldn't like me doing that. But what else was I supposed to do, considering the situation?"
      Your reaction to this account: _____

DECIDING TO TERMINATE A RELATIONSHIP

SOCIAL EXCHANGE THEORY

As a dyad navigates the sometimes-turbulent waters of the relationship, both people constantly evaluate the relationship in terms of its costs and rewards. **Social exchange theory** posits that people seek the greatest rewards and the least amount of costs when it comes to relationships.[236] According to social exchange theory, there are predictable ways in which we tend to evaluate our relationships. As two people progress toward greater intimacy, both parties make decisions about the immediate, forecasted, and cumulative rewards and costs of staying together.

Immediate rewards and costs are those that occur in a relationship at the present moment in time. Rewards of this type include the day-to-day enjoyment of the other person's company, whereas costs might include the inability to have enough time alone to do the things one enjoys in solitude.

Forecasted rewards and costs are those that are based on projection or prediction. Rewards of this type involve expectations for future circumstances with this person and the life you envision together if the relationship endures.

Finally, *cumulative rewards and costs* represent the total rewards and costs that we have accrued during the duration of the relationship. These types of rewards and costs are based on all relational events that have occurred up until this moment in time.

Rewards and costs can also be evaluated in terms of their intensity. In other words, some rewards are "worth" the costs. Similarly, the ratio of positive to negative experiences is important. Most people are willing to endure many costs if there are twice as many rewards. Our perception of how many costs and rewards are reasonable has to do with our *expected costs and rewards*, which are the expectations we hold based on ideas we've formed about how rewarding a relationship *should* be, especially relative to the costs of the relationship. Some people believe that relationships are naturally a struggle, and this expectation dictates their level of satisfaction with the relationship's costs and rewards. Other people believe that relationships should always be fun and that having to work too hard is a sign of a troubled relationship. In one study, participants described a hurtful behavior performed by their partner and were asked to recall their reaction. When respondents evaluated the hurtful event as a highly negative behavior that strongly violated their expectations, *and* they judged their partner as contributing to an unrewarding relationship overall, then they were more likely to report breaking up with him or her.[237]

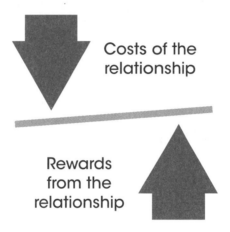

Figure 8.1. The costs and rewards of any relationship are weighed to determine its value and longevity.

Although social exchange theory provides a useful tool for explaining why some relationships end, there are several criticisms of this theory.[238] The most important criticism to consider is that the theory assumes that human interaction is an entirely rational process, viewing relationships similar to economic exchanges. People often stay in relationships when the costs outweigh the rewards, which defies the "logic" of the theory.

However, it is usually the case that relational de-escalation starts to occur if one or both people want a better balance of costs and rewards.[239] Research indicates that once we have determined that a relationship falls below our expectations, we tend to move fairly quickly toward terminating it. This happens even more rapidly if we believe that there are opportunities to develop a different relationship with someone else that might satisfy all of our expectations.

Review! Types of Rewards and Costs in Relationships	
Immediate rewards and costs:	Rewards and costs that occur in a relationship at the present moment in time.
Forecasted rewards and costs:	Rewards and costs that are based on projection or prediction of future events.
Cumulative rewards and costs:	The total rewards and costs that we have accrued during the duration of the relationship.
Expected rewards and costs:	The expectations we hold about how rewarding a relationship *should* be.

INTERPERSONAL SKILLS ACROSS CONTEXTS

How Family Members React to Coming Out

The stages of relational de-escalation can occur in any type of relationship, whether romantic, platonic, or even familial. One commonly cited impetus for a decline in the family relationship is when one family member "comes out," and reveals a sexual orientation that some family members may find unfavorable. The research on coming out suggests that there is no one right way to come out that will guarantee a warm reception from all family members. However, there are some family characteristics that may help individuals predict the reaction they will get. Parental values and characteristics associated with homophobia were found to be good predictors of how the disclosure impacted the relationship, but even parents who initially reacted negatively to their child coming out became more accepting over time.[240]

One study found that attachment bonds between the child and parent in the younger years were one of the best predictors of the adult child's willingness to disclose and the parent's reaction to the disclosure of homosexuality. Respondents who perceived their mother as accepting in childhood were more likely to come out to her, and parents who were more accepting and independence-encouraging in childhood were reported to react more positively to their child's later disclosure of sexual orientation. These parents encouraged exploration while allowing for the safe haven necessary to facilitate a secure attachment style. Overbearing or over-controlling parents did not react well to the disclosure.[241] Research on computer-mediated communication shows that the increasing prevalence of anonymous outlets for safe coming out, such as chat rooms and online interest groups, may allow for the self-acceptance that ultimately leads adults to come out to their family members, whether those family members accept it or not.[242]

"COSTS" THAT LEAD TO TERMINATION

When people are asked why they broke up, the "costs" of the relationship that ultimately made it an unrewarding pursuit usually fall into one of three types. *Faults* are the most commonly reported cause of breakup, which are problems with personality traits or behaviors that one partner finds in the other. *Unwillingness to compromise* is another reported reason for breakup, which include failing

to put enough effort into the relationship, a noticeable decrease in effort toward the relationship, or failure to make concessions and sacrifices for the good of the relationship. *Feeling constrained* is another cited reason, which reflects one partner's desire to be free from the commitments and constraints of a relationship. There may be more than one reason a relationship ends. For romantic relationships loss of interest, decreased attraction, or conflicting values can combine with the other costs in the relationship that ultimately provoke a breakup.

Similar to romantic relationships, friends are also able to cite specific reasons why their relationship terminated. In friendships these reasons usually include unreasonable jealousy, criticism, breaking trust, not helping in a time of need, and lack of confiding. Other typical reasons friendships end include physical separation and replacing old friends with new ones as either person's needs change over time.

Whether it is your choice or someone else's, ending an important relationship is never easy. One way to better manage the emotions and behaviors associated with breakups is to understand *why* they happen, as we've been studying thus far. Another way to feel acceptance and closure about your own relationship endings is to understand *how* they happen, which will be covered in the upcoming section.

STRATEGIES FOR RELATIONAL TERMINATION

Because relationships and the people in them are so unique, there are a variety of different types of breakups and breakup strategies.[243] In **bilateral dissolutions**, both parties are predisposed to ending the relationship and simply need to go over the details. However, because of the potentially incompatible desires and needs each person seeks in a relationship, the decision to end is not always mutual. In **unilateral dissolutions**, only one person desires the breakup. In these cases, the person who wants to end the relationship uses specific strategies, which can be direct or indirect. Indirect strategies are most often used for less intimate relationships, whereas direct strategies are most often used for intimate relationships with a high degree of closeness. When strategies are examined in terms of mutuality of choice and level of directness, there are four combinations: unilateral/indirect, bilateral/indirect, unilateral/direct, and bilateral/direct.

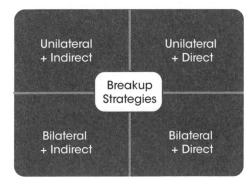

Figure 8.2. Types of breakup strategies.

Indirect, unilateral termination strategies (meaning non-mutual and not stated) are very popular. From people who report their breakup strategies, 76% reported using these. In order of popularity, the withdrawal strategy takes first place. *Withdrawal* involves reducing the amount of contact and interaction without any explanation. Next likely, the *pseudo-de-escalation* strategy occurs when one partner claims that he or she wants to redefine the relationship at a lower level of intimacy, but in reality, he or she wants to end the relationship. This strategy has the lowest likelihood of partner acceptance, probably because it is confusing. Finally, *cost escalation* is an attempt to increase the costs associated with the relationship in order to lead the other person to terminating it. For example, someone may start to intentionally violate relationship rules such as staying out too late, flirting with others, or engaging in hurtful communication toward the partner so that he or she decides to leave the relationship.

Direct, unilateral strategies (meaning stated, and non-mutual) are the most likely to be accepted by the other partner, and 24% of people who have broken up claim to have used these strategies. Of all direct unilateral strategies, the *fait accompli* is by far the most widely used, which is a direct statement that the relationship is over, with no attempt to discuss it. The alternative is the *state of the relationship talk*, whereby the problems are discussed, but the decision is still made to breakup.

Direct, bilateral strategies (meaning stated and mutual) include *attributional conflict*, in which the couple argues not about whether to end, but about why the relationship is ending. Also in this category is the *negotiated farewell*, which is simply a mutual agreement to end without conflict or aggression.

Indirect bilateral strategies (meaning mutual but unstated) include *fading away*, or allowing the relationship to slowly de-escalate. This often occurs through *incrementalism*, which is the process by which conflicts and problems continue to accumulate in the relationship until they reach a critical mass that leads to the breakup, or until the relationship becomes intolerable or too costly.

Sudden death is an abrupt and unplanned ending caused by a single transgression, such as deception or infidelity, or a rapid change of feelings of either partner. In these cases, the relationship does not end in phases, but terminates immediately. Other breakups take steps toward dissolution whereby they de-escalate over time. **Relational de-escalation** is the movement that occurs when a relationship decreases in intimacy. Because each stage in a relationship has unique communication qualities, we assess which stage of the breakup the dyad is experiencing by examining the verbal and nonverbal communication occurring between members of the pair. Next, a popular model for understanding communication patterns in the stages of relational de-escalation will be outlined.

BUILDING CULTURAL COMPETENCE

Culturally Relative Words for Disengagement

In Chapter 7 you learned about culture-specific words used to describe feelings and behaviors from the stages of relational escalation. Now consider these non-English terms for experiences from the stages of breaking up. Can you relate to any of these, or, as suggested by linguistic relativity, are these experiences unique to the speakers of the language in which they are uttered?[244]

Relational transgressions in the Bantu language come in degrees. The term *ilunga* describes a person who is willing to forgive abusive behavior once, may tolerate it a second time, but will never forgive it a third time. This concept is different from the "three strikes, you're out" sports analogy used in English, because it suggests increasing annoyance and intolerance that climaxes to into being unacceptable.

Once a relationship has ended (or never gotten off the ground), Portuguese speakers use the word *saudade* to describe the feeling of longing for a love that is lost or impossible.

The French leave room for revisiting past relationships with the term *retrouvailles,* which describes the happiness experienced when two people who have not seen each other in a long time finally meet again.

It appears that there is one common sentiment you can use to breakup in any language you choose: adios, sayonara, ciao, or just plain goodbye—they all say it clearly!

KNAPP'S MODEL OF RELATIONAL DE-ESCALATION

One of the most well known descriptions of how relationships de-escalate comes from Knapp's staircase model introduced in the previous chapter when you learned about relational escalation. The journey down the other side of the staircase occurs in five stages: differentiating, circumscribing, stagnating, avoiding, and terminating.[245]

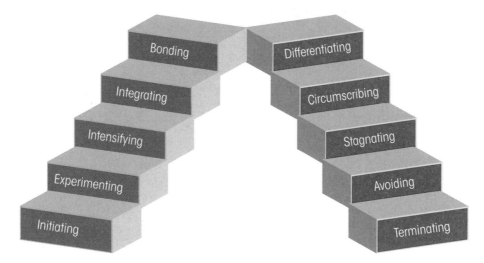

Figure 8.3. Knapp's staircase model.

DIFFERENTIATING

In the **differentiating stage** partners start to prefer autonomy over connection. Members of the couple tend to start to define their lives more as individuals and less as a couple. They reduce descriptions of their lives as "we" and begin to describe events, attitudes, and beliefs in terms of "me." Here each individual decreases their dependence upon the other for self-confirmation and validation. Often times they will focus on each other's characteristics that provide evidence for how they see the world differently, and complain about their differences internally, to each other, or to others.

CIRCUMSCRIBING

In the **circumscribing stage**, information exchange decreases in both breadth and depth. Couples stick to "safe" topics that will not allow old conflicts to re-surface, and generally don't dive deeply into their conversations with each other. Often times this stage involves an avoidance of friends or family members who may exacerbate already existing conflicts. However, couples in this stage can still fool others into believing that they are happy by enacting their social roles as a couple, but engaging in limited intimacy when alone with each other.

STAGNATING

The **stagnating stage** is characterized by scripted communication occurring in predictable and habitual patterns. Dyads in this stage are "going through the motions" of a partnership with little emotional involvement. Nonverbal communication can be cold, distant, and awkward. Both members "don't bother" voicing judgments or bringing up conflict topics because they feel that they can predict how it is going to go. At this stage there are several options; the relationship can continue to stagnate for a long time, the individuals can repair or revitalize it, they can redefine it, or it can continue de-escalating. Many types of relationships, including marriages, can stagnate for years or even for a lifetime. If the relationship continues to de-escalate it enters into the avoiding stage.

AVOIDING

In the **avoiding stage** the couple engages in fewer interactions and there is an increase of physical, emotional, and psychological distance. This stage can be infused with excuses for not seeing each other and avoidance strategies. Either party may manipulate the environment to spend the least amount of time possible with the other. There is no effort to repair or revitalize, and the couple is no longer actively working on the relationship.

TERMINATING

When a couple has entered the **termination stage** there is an overt decision to eliminate further interaction as a couple. As mentioned previously, a relationship can enter the termination stage instantly, when a relational transgression results in the "sudden death" of the relationship caused by a specific behavior or circumstance. In other relationships couples go through months or even years of dialogue and discussion about how to end. Some people try to council each other through the breakup, resulting in hours of heartbreaking conversations about why the relationship must end. The terminating stage can take many forms that signify the relationship is over. At some point, the division of property, resources, and social networks ensues, and the couple is officially considered "broken up."

Review! Knapp's Stages of Relational De-Escalation	
Differentiating stage:	Partners start to prefer autonomy over connection, and start to define their lives more as individuals and less as a couple.
Circumscribing stage:	Information exchange decreases in both breadth and depth.
Stagnating stage:	Communication is scripted, occurring in predictable and habitual patterns.
Avoiding stage:	The couple engages in fewer interactions and there is an increase of physical, emotional, and psychological distance.
Terminating stage:	There is an overt decision to eliminate further interaction as a couple.

DUCK'S DE-ESCALATION PHASES

We can learn even more about how relationships break up by examining another perspective on the typical phases that a relationship goes through on the way out. Relationship theorist Steven Duck describes relational dissolution as a communication process that starts with the individual, then involves the partner, and subsequently involves the social network.[246]

INTRA-PSYCHIC PHASE

In the **intra-psychic phase**, one partner reaches a threshold of dissatisfaction and starts to focus on the other's problematic personality traits and negative behaviors in order to gather evidence that will ultimately justify withdrawing from the relationship. This phase usually occurs during the *differentiating stage* of relational de-escalation described above. Couples in the intra-psychic phase of relational de-escalation usually have a "brooding focus on the relationship and on the partner."[247] Duck emphasizes how in this phase there is a major perceptual shift. For example, someone who was once "exciting" may now be seen as "dangerously unpredictable," or a partner who was "attractively reliable" is now considered "boring." Thus, the same characteristics of the partner are observed, but the labels shift from positive to negative.[248]

DYADIC PHASE

The couple then enters into the **dyadic phase**, where one or both person's internal contemplations about the relationship turn into an actual confrontation. If one partner does not agree with the problems or issues, the other might have to justify his or her thoughts and feelings about ending the relationship. At this stage, issues may be raised that cause either partner to re-evaluate the costs of the relationship and the costs that

would be associated with the breakup. If this process results in the feeling that it would be more costly to end the relationship than to work on it, the couple may choose to revitalize the relationship rather than end it.

SOCIAL PHASE

In the **social phase**, members of the dyad begin to inform the members of their social circle that things are not going well. Here each person has to justify his or her feelings about the relationship to the social group. Included in the social phase are attempts at preserving social ties that involve both members of the relationship, and possibly winning friends or family members over to "your side."

GRAVE-DRESSING PHASE

As the relationship ends, this leads directly to the **grave-dressing phase**, where one or both partners create the "tombstone" of the relationship, telling how and why it ended and making summarizing statements about it. Much of the grave-dressing phase is internal, which involves re-analyzing information to gain closure on the cause of the breakup. This process can also include conversations with others whereby the end of the relationship is justified, explained, or re-analyzed. Of course, the story each partner tells him or herself and others is often biased in a self-enhancing way in order to keep the self-concept and self-esteem intact.

Intra-Psychic Phase

Dyadic Phase

Social Phase

Grave-Dressing Phase

Figure 8.4. Duck's phases of relational de-escalation.

Review! Duck's Phases of Relational De-Escalation	
Intra-psychic phase:	One partner reaches a threshold of dissatisfaction and starts to focus on the other's problematic personality traits and negative behaviors.
Dyadic phase:	There is a move from one or both partners' internal contemplations about the relationship to an actual confrontation about the issues.
Social phase:	There is an agreement to end the relationship and both partners begin to inform the members of their social circle.
Grave-dressing phase:	One or both partners create the "tombstone" of the relationship, telling how and why it ended and making summarizing statements about it.

VARIABLES THAT DETERMINE HOW WE RESPOND TO RELATIONAL HARDSHIPS

As you may already know, people are prone to create and maintain patterns in their relationship behavior. While reading this chapter it may have occurred to you that you "tend" to have certain kinds of breakups, or you are usually playing a particular role in the de-escalation and termination of either your friendships or romantic relationships. If this is the case, and even if it is not, it can be extremely beneficial to understand our personal characteristics that help determine how we act and react in relationships.

In a previous chapter you learned the difference between allocentric and idiocentric personalities and how these traits can affect the way you relate to people in your social groups. Allocentric individuals are focused on maintaining the harmony of relationships and the functioning of the group, whereas idiocentric individuals are more focused on their own personal happiness. When it comes to interpersonal relationship challenges, research indicates that allocentrics and idiocentrics many handle problems differently. Idiocentrism was related to a focus on self-actualization, which correlated with less love for the partner and less caring for the needs of the partner. In fact, some researchers conclude that idiocentrism may be a factor in the high divorce rate of individualist countries.[249] This is just one example of how our personal disposition determines how we react to the people and events around us. There are innumerable other personal traits and characteristics that impact the way each person handles relationship challenges. This chapter will conclude with an analysis of the most important factors, including attachment style, relational expectations and cognitive emotion regulation.

ATTACHMENT STYLE

From interactions as infants with their caregivers, individuals develop models for relationships that persist in their adult interactions. These models act as perceptual filters that affect how rela-

tional information is processed.[250] Two individuals with different upbringings will form very different notions of relationships from their experiences with parental figures. Thus, once they reach adulthood, each individual will experience and process the *same* information in *different* ways. For example, one person may find himself becoming especially anxious and clingy when he perceives that his significant other might leave him, while another person reacts by withdrawing or detaching.

Attachment theory suggests that your relationship with your primary caregiver as a child shapes the relationships you have with your significant others as an adult. The theory attempts to predict how *particular* types of childhood attachments to care-givers affect the role each of us take in adult relationships, especially romantic ones.

Bartholomew and Horowitz attempt to explain attachment by analyzing how we see ourselves in our relationships (positively or negatively) and how we see others (positively or negatively).[251] Each

person tends to fall into one of four possible combinations of self/other perceptions, resulting in four categories of attachment. This four-style model of attachment was used to create the simple but useful Attachment Style Questionnaire, which asks respondents to select the style that is *most* typical in his or her relationships:

1. It is relatively easy for me to become emotionally close to others. I am comfortable depending on others and having others depend on me. I don't worry about being alone or having others not accept me.

2. I am comfortable without close emotional relationships. It is very important to me to feel independent and self-sufficient, and I prefer not to depend on others or have others depend on me.

3. I want to be completely emotionally intimate with others, but I often find that others are reluctant to get as close as I would like. I am uncomfortable being without close relationships, but I sometimes worry that others don't value me as much as I value them.

4. I am somewhat uncomfortable getting close to others. I want emotionally close relationships, but I find it difficult to trust others completely, or to depend on them. I sometimes worry that I will be hurt if I allow myself to become too close to others.

Secure Attachment Style

The statement in the first item demonstrates a positive view of the self and a positive view of others, resulting in a **secure attachment style**. This style usually results from a history of warm and responsive interactions with parents, and consequently relationship partners. Secure individuals tend to have positive views of themselves, their partners, and their relationships. They often report greater satisfaction and adjustment in their relationships than people with other styles, and they feel comfortable both with intimacy and with independence, seeking to balance both in their relationships. People with secure attachment styles are generally less anxious about relational hardships because they believe they can work through difficulties with their partner. Mikulincer and Shaver describe this phenomenon, writing, "People with a strong sense of having a secure base tend to appraise threatening events optimistically and believe in their capacity to deal effectively with these events."[252]

Dismissive-Avoidant Attachment Style

The second item above indicates a positive view of the self and a negative view of others, resulting in a **dismissive-avoidant attachment style**. People who have this attachment style desire a high level of independence and tend to seek less intimacy with relationship partners, which often appears as an attempt to avoid attachment altogether. They view themselves as self-sufficient and invulnerable to feelings associated with being closely attached to others, and often deny needing close relationships at all. They tend to be defensive because they view relational partners less positively than they view themselves. Dismissive-avoidant styles tend to suppress and hide their feelings, and they tend to deal with rejection by distancing themselves from the sources of rejection. This habit will greatly influence the way they deal with any relational hardship. This style often results in an attitude of "This relationship is more trouble than it's worth."

Anxious-Preoccupied Attachment Style

The third item of the Attachment Style Questionnaire represents a negative view of the self and a positive view of others, which manifests in an **anxious-preoccupied attachment style**. People with this style of attachment seek high levels of intimacy, approval, and responsiveness from their partners, which often results in over-dependency. They have less positive views about themselves than secure styles, which includes doubt of their worth as a partner and self-blame for their partner's lack of responsiveness. They have less positive views about their partners; they do not trust in people's good intentions. Finally, anxious-preoccupied styles may experience high levels of emotional expressiveness, worry, and impulsiveness in their relationships, which make them tend to overreact to relationship challenges and suffer from higher levels of concern and worry than the other styles. This style may react to relationship difficulties by clinging or being overly concerned that the relationship will end and trying to prevent that from happening.

Fearful-Avoidant Attachment Style

The last style indicates a negative view of the self and negative view of others, which creates a **fearful-avoidant attachment style.** This style expresses mixed feelings about close relationships: They desire to have emotionally close relationships, but they tend to feel uncomfortable with emotional closeness. They tend to have negative views about themselves and their partners, and commonly view themselves as unworthy of responsiveness from their partners. This individual often will not trust the intentions of their partners, and therefore seeks less intimacy from the partner, frequently suppressing and hiding their own feelings. This style may tend to react to relationship hardships with an attitude of "I knew I would end up getting hurt."

Attachment styles are related to relational difficulties because they determine how each person perceives threatening or undesirable behavior from others, and thus the impact of such behavior on the relationship. People with secure attachment styles are less likely to filter incoming information through insecurities and often exercise greater cognitive complexity when making attributions for negative behavior.[253] In other words, *new* information and evidence is more likely to be evaluated in their judgments about others, rather than basing judgments strictly on their negative expectations. One theorist summarizes it this way: "Securely attached persons do not seem to be motivated to maintain self-esteem by distorting self-views or perceptions of others under stressful contexts. Rather they tend to seek the support of significant others who seem to function as pillars of their positive models of self."[254]

People with fearful-avoidant or anxious-preoccupied attachment styles are more likely to have low self-esteem, and therefore need to positively distort themselves and negatively distort others, resulting in a trend of negative attributions for others' behavior. Consequently, people with insecure attachment styles (fearful-avoidants, anxious-preoccupieds, and dismissive-avoidants) tend to report more negative attributions for their partners' behavior than do people with secure attachment styles.[255] One study shows that in intimate contexts, respondents with secure styles rated messages as more truthful, whereas fearful-avoidant and dismissive-avoidant respondents were relatively likely to perceive the same messages as deceptive.[256]

Attachment styles can even impact our use of communication technologies. People with secure attachment styles tend to use mediated channels such phone calls and texting on a regular basis to maintain their relationships, while dismissive-avoidant and fearful-avoidant styles tend to avoid calling their significant others.[257] Studies on relationships created in virtual realities such as Second Life show that our attachment styles carry across contexts. Even with virtual romantic partners most people exhibit the same attachment style as they do in their "real life" romantic relationships.[258] Even behind the façade of an avatar, we cannot escape our preconceived notions about our role in relationships.

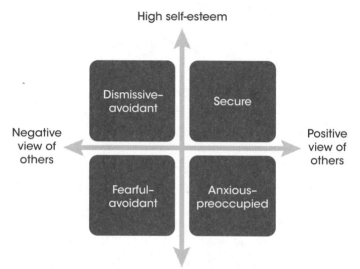

Figure 8.5. Attachment styles are related to how we see ourselves and how we see others.

The Effect of Relational Satisfaction on Perceptions of Transgressions

You may have wondered how some couples seem to bounce back from hardships that would destroy another couple. In relationships, attributions are used to explain the behaviors of either partner as well as the reasons for unexpected relational transgressions or hardships. Attribution theory acknowledges the importance of perceptual differences in individuals' view of reality, and how these subjective perceptions influence communication with others. Ultimately, one's "experience" of a situation based on his or her own perceptual filters has a much greater effect on relationships than the actual "objective" reality of the situation.[259] We can observe the way people process their relational hardships by examining the attributions they make for what happened. Remember the halo effect: we attribute positive qualities to people simply because we like them. Consistent with this idea, researchers find that people in healthy and happy relationships make partner-enhancing attributions for negative relationship events, but when the relationship starts to decline, the effect goes away or even reverses.[260] What this means is that satisfied couples are more likely to generate relationship enhancing, or adaptive attributions, whereby negative events are interpreted as being caused by external, unstable and

specific causes; in other words, in satisfied couples negative events are less likely to be viewed as controllable, intentional, or as the responsibility of the partner.[261]

Happy couples are also more likely to see positive events as global, or as a typical behavior of the partner.[262] In contrast, distressed or unhappy couples most often make distress-maintaining interpretations, such that negative events are viewed as caused by internal and stable characteristics of the partner and are globalized with statements such as "He always does that." Additionally, in unhappy couples when one partner behaves in a negative way that person is viewed as being in control and responsible for the act.[263] Even worse, in dissatisfied couples each person is less likely to give credit to the other for positive behaviors; they will attribute positive behaviors to external sources that had nothing to do with the partner's kindness or good intentions.

EXPECTATIONS

Attachment styles are linked to expectations. What we learn about relationships from our infancy determines what we expect in future relationships. There are numerous studies that demonstrate how expectations affect the way information is processed. Researchers confirm what you already learned in the chapter on perception:

> People often seek out and attend to information that is consistent with their expectations; they resist data that contradict their beliefs, and they bias their memories of events or circumstances to fit with their current perceptions and expectations.[264]

Studies consistently find that people often ignore information that contradicts their beliefs.[265] In addition, people will develop rationalizations to support their desired beliefs and have selective memory for beliefs such that events that confirm their pre-existing beliefs are better remembered than events that contradict their beliefs.[266]

One theory that helps explain how expectations shape perception is **expectancy violation theory**.[267] This theory suggests that people develop expectations about the verbal and nonverbal communication of others, and when these expectations are violated it causes attention to become hyper-focused on the communicator and the relationship. More importantly, the *direction* of the violation affects the impact it has on the perceiver. Behaviors that are better than those expected constitute *positive violations*; behaviors that are worse than expected result in *negative violations*; behaviors that are consistent with expectations often go unnoticed. Thus, an individual's reaction to relational failures and transgressions has much to do with the set of expectations they have of their partner. If they expect the partner to behave badly, the behavior may go unnoticed or have little impact. However, if the bad behavior is an extreme violation of what was expected, it could have enormous repercussions. Afifi and Metts found that there are nine types of expectancy violations commonly found in close relationships. Identify whether or not any of these have occurred in your relationships.[268]

Violations that can be positive or negative:

- *Support* or *confirmation* is an act that provides support in a time of need or crisis, such as attending to a friend who is ill. It is a violation when a partner provides more or less support than what is expected.

- *Relationship intensification* communicates a desire to escalate commitment, for example when one person chooses to say "I love you." When one partner tries to escalate the relationship unexpectedly it can create a violation.

- *Gestures of inclusion* show an unexpected interest in including the partner in special activities or social circles. Inviting the partner to spend a holiday with family is an example of this violation.

- *Uncharacteristic relational behavior* is unexpected action that is not consistent with the partner's perception of the norms of the relationship. This violation can be exemplified when one member of the dyad suddenly expects that a friendship become romantic.

- *Acts of devotion* are unexpected gestures that imply meaningfulness of the relationship. An example is giving a gift for no reason. This type of violation is usually positive, but can be negative if the receiver considers it inappropriate.

Violations that are usually negative:

- *Acts of disregard* show that the partner is unimportant. Failing to show up for a date or forgetting a birthday fall under this category. This type of violation is usually negative.

- *A criticism or accusation* is a critical statement toward the receiver, accusing the individual of an offense. These are violations because they are accusations that are unexpected or considered unreasonable.

- *Relational de-escalation* communicates a desire to de-intensify the relationship, such as an expression of the need to spend more time apart. When one partner does so unexpectedly it is usually a negative violation.

- *Relational transgressions* are violations of the implicit or explicit rules of the relationship, such as disloyalty, cheating, or lying.

GENETIC SET POINT AND RELATIONAL EVENTS

Researchers use the term "**genetic set point**" to refer to our tendency to come back to a relatively set state of happiness or satisfaction, regardless of positive or negative events that should dramatically affect us. That is, we each have a certain individual baseline for happiness that remains relatively stable throughout our lives, and positive or negative events may temporarily cause a shift toward extreme happiness or unhappiness, but ultimately we return to our "typical" level of satisfaction. Our attributional style and our personality combine to form our expectations, and these expectations somehow always land us right back where we started, ala the self-fulfilling prophecy. If you are a person with a relatively high happiness set point, negative **relational events** will not have an enduring and damaging impact. In contrast, if you have a relatively low happiness set point (meaning, you tend to be unhappy or dissatisfied much of the time), negative relational events will only further solidify this disposition.

COGNITIVE EMOTION REGULATION

We know from research on cognition that the way we perceive an event determines how we react to the event, and that our perceptions are habitual. This means that each person tends to view unpleasant or difficult situations according to their own patterns, which are developed over time. A few patterns that have a particularly strong influence on how we perceive relational hardships are self-blame, rumination, and catastrophizing. People who self-blame tend to see negative experiences and events as being caused by them, even when they may be coincidental or random. People who engage in rumination constantly think back about the negative experience or situation instead of thinking about the present moment. Finally, individuals who catastrophize events emphasize the horribleness of what happened. Researchers Garnefski and Kraaij developed a measure of individual styles for responding to stressful events based on these variables called the Cognitive Emotion Regulation Questionnaire (CERQ), which you can find in the next skill building box.

A beneficial cognitive habit that can counteract tendencies to self-blame, catastrophize, and ruminate is called **positive reappraisal**. Positive reappraisal is the process of perceiving negative experiences as opportunities for personal growth and development.[269] Researchers, theorists and clinicians suggest that negative thought patterns can be reduced by replacing them with patterns of positive reappraisal, which include seeing the benefits of even difficult situations, and choosing to learn from negative experiences. When you notice that your thoughts sound or feel like self-blame, ruminating, or catastrophizing, try and replace them with these positive reappraisals:[270]

- I think I can learn something new from this situation.

- I think I can become a stronger person as a result of what happened.

- I think that the situation also has its positive sides.

Over time, it is possible to retrain your brain to use positive reappraisals instead of its negative counterparts. When you are able to effectively manage your emotions surrounding an event, your intrapersonal and interpersonal communication will change for the better.

SKILL BUILDING EXERCISE

Assessing Your Cognitive Emotion Regulation

On a scale of 1–5 rate the accuracy of each of these statements, using the following scale:

1 = never   2 = sometimes   3 = about half the time   4 = usually   5 = always

When there is a difficult situation or event in one of my important relationships:[271]

1. I feel that I am the one to blame.	1	2	3	4	5
2. I often revisit my feelings about what happened.	1	2	3	4	5
3. I often feel like what I've experienced is worse than what others have experienced.	1	2	3	4	5

4. I feel responsible for the negative situation or event.   1   2   3   4   5

5. I would describe myself as preoccupied with what
    happened.   1   2   3   4   5

6. I keep thinking about how terrible it was.   1   2   3   4   5

7. I think about how it reflects my own mistakes.   1   2   3   4   5

8. I am constantly seeking to understand why I feel the
    way I do about this experience.   1   2   3   4   5

9. I believe it's probably the worst thing that could
    happen to a person.   1   2   3   4   5

10. I assume that the cause is something about
    me personally.   1   2   3   4   5

11. I tend to dwell upon the negative feelings that
    came from the experience.   1   2   3   4   5

12. I often think about how horrible this situation has been. 1   2   3   4   5

Add your score from items 1, 4, 7, and 10 _____

   This is your self-blame score. A score over 10 indicates a tendency to self-blame.

Add your score from items 2, 5, 8, and 11 _____

   This is your rumination score. A score over 10 indicates a tendency to ruminate.

Add your score from items 3, 6, 9, and 12 _____

   This is your catastrophizing score. A score over 10 indicates a tendency to catastrophize.

Learning about relational transgressions and relational de-escalation can be enlightening, allowing you to realize that the thoughts and stages you may have endured during a breakup are perfectly natural. However, if you are in a relationship that you would like to keep, it can be depressing to think about the possible end that may lie ahead. So how should a dyad that wants to avoid de-escalation manage the natural tensions

and conflicts that will occur throughout the relationship without breaking up? The key, of course, is communication.

People often assume that once a formalized commitment has been made, the relationship no longer needs work. This myth is the cause of many unhappy endings to relationships that at one time seemed intact. Every relationship, no matter what stage it is in, needs regular maintenance. The first sign of relationship doom is when one or both people refuse to work on the relationship or believe that good relationships shouldn't require "work." Thus, the remaining chapters will address some specific skills that both people should learn and practice regularly in order to sustain a satisfying and healthy interpersonal relationship.

CHAPTER SUMMARY

This chapter began with an overview of several particularly problematic communication issues in relationships, defined as relational transgressions: intimate partner violence, hurtful communication, and deception. It was emphasized that each individual deals with relationship challenges in different ways, and whether or not the difficulty will end the relationship depends on the choices each partner makes.

The reasons we decide to stay together or separate were outlined according to the assumptions of social exchange theory, which set the stage for a discussion about strategies for relational breakup. Each stage of de-escalation was described, including the differentiating, circumscribing, stagnating, avoiding, and terminating stages of Knapp's model of relational de-escalation, and the intra-psychic, dyadic, social, and grave-dressing phases from Duck's model of interaction. This chapter concluded by highlighting some of the personal variables that affect how we each react to relational challenges, including attachment style, expectations, and cognitive emotion regulation.

CHAPTER ACTIVITIES

TEST YOUR UNDERSTANDING

True or False

____ 1. An exaggeration is the same as a bold-faced lie.

____ 2. A bilateral breakup is when both people want to end the relationship.

____ 3. If you feel that your safety is at risk, you should break up over the phone or through a letter or email.

Multiple Choice: Circle the best answer choice.

1. John and Steve were close friends in high school. Now they go to college on different sides of the country and are making new friends. If their friendship dissolves, the process is:

    A. Withdrawal

    B. Fading away

    C. Fait accompli

    D. Incrementalism

    E. None of the above

2. Which of the following is true of relational transgressions?

    A. People react in the same way to relational transgressions.

    B. Flirting is not a relational transgression.

    C. The way you manage a transgression may have to do with your attachment style.

    D. Transgressions occur more in the U.S. than anywhere else.

    E. All of the above are true.

3. The stages of relational de-escalation include all of the following EXCEPT:

    A. Differentiating

    B. Circumscribing

    C. Stagnating

    D. Denial

    E. Termination

**Answers are listed at the end of this section before the references.

Short Answer

1. Identify some typical challenges that create relational hardships.

   _____

   _____

   _____

   _____

   _____

   _____

   _____

   _____

   _____

   _____

   _____

2. Identify the stages of coming apart and the communication behaviors that are typical of each stage.

   _____

   _____

   _____

   _____

   _____

   _____

   _____

   _____

   _____

   _____

   _____

3. Explain the various types of breakups.

_____

_____

_____

_____

_____

_____

_____

_____

_____

_____

_____

4. Summarize the communication strategies people use when terminating a relationship.

_____

_____

_____

_____

_____

_____

_____

_____

_____

_____

_____

5. Explain the variables that help determine how each individual tends to respond to relationship challenges.

_____

_____

_____

_____

_____

_____

IN-CLASS ACTIVITY

Breaking Up

What do you think is the most effective strategy for ending a relationship with a romantic partner? List at least three breakups you have experienced yourself, or have heard about from a friend. Describe whether the breakup was unilateral or bilateral, and direct or indirect. List the strategy from this chapter that each person used.

_____

_____

_____

_____

_____

_____

_____

What is the best strategy for ending a friendship? What strategies have you used or observed in the past?

_____

_____

_____

_____

_____

_____

SKILL PRACTICE: BREAKING UP WITH DIGNITY

What Is the Goal of Using an Effective Breakup Strategy?

Not all relationships are meant to last. However, the strategy you use to break up with a relational partner may help determine how long it takes him or her to heal. While a few certain situations call for evasive communication, it is almost always better to use direct and clear communication when breaking up with another person. Not doing so may create emotional confusion, unclear boundaries, and could drag out the painful experience for both people.

How Do You Do It?

1. **Decide** that the breakup is the best choice. Write down your thoughts about your choice and/or talk it over with a friend, in case you need to remind yourself later of why you make the decision.

2. **Ask** your relational partner to meet you somewhere from which you are able to leave. Do not have him or her come to your house where an awkward situation will be created once the conversation is over. Meeting someone on his or her own "territory" may make the process easier. Do not attempt a breakup in public.

3. **Don't wait** to break the news. Tell the person why you asked to meet, and explain why you have come to this decision.

4. If the other person is upset, make sure to **show concern** for his or her feelings, but do not get involved in lengthy soothing. Doing so only strengthens your role in the "relationship," which no longer exists. Comforting the other can cause confusion and may even cause you to change your mind. Instead suggest someone he or she could visit or call.

5. If the other person resists the breakup, it is your choice how long you negotiate and reason with him or her. Sometimes talking through the relationship problems can help both people heal, but other times it is a slippery slope toward getting back together. If you are certain that you want to break up, do not get persuaded into giving it another try simply because you feel guilty. You will only prolong the inevitable breakup and cause the other person more pain.

   Most people on the receiving end of a breakup appreciate a face-to-face conversation. However, if you feel that your safety is at risk, break up over the phone or through a letter or email. Once you have stated that you no longer wish to be in a relationship with a person, it is your right to discontinue communication with him or her. If the other person insists on contacting you further, explain that you need some space. If they still persist and you feel threatened, contact the police.

Once you complete this breakup, write a dialogue of what happened, focusing on your use of the communication skills listed above:

_____

_____

_____

_____

_____

_____

_____

_____

_____

_____

_____

_____

_____

_____

_____

_____

_____

_____

_____

_____

_____

_____

_____

_____

_____

HOMEWORK ACTIVITY

ATTACHMENT STYLE

Google search "What Attachment Type are You?" Follow the first link and complete the embedded Attachment Style Test to assess your attachment style.

1. What were your results?

   Avoidance of Closeness = 4/100

2. Were you surprised by your results? Why or why not?

   Yes, they are very low. Although I answered the questions as accuratley as possible I feel like I am an averagely open person, while the results make it seem like I am incredibly open.

3. How can you use this information?

   I can use it to help me have a clearer image of how I form relationships w/ people. My results seemed pretty positive so I will try e continue whatever im doing.

Answers to True/False and Multiple Choice

1. False

2. True

3. True

1. B

2. C

3. D

REFERENCES

[215]National Center for Health Statistics. (1991). Advance report of final marriage statistics, 1988 (Monthly Vital Statistics Report 39). Hyattsville, MD: Public HealthService.

[216]Cherlin, A. (1992). *Marriage, divorce, and remarriage.* Cambridge, MA: Harvard University Press.

[217]Waldron, V.R. & Kelley, D.L. (2005). Forgiving communication as a response to relational transgressions. *Journal of Social and Personal Relationships, 22,* 6, 723–742.

[218]Bachman, G.F., Guerrero, L.K. (2006). Forgiveness, apology, and communicative responses to hurtful events. *Communication Reports, 19*(1), 45–56.

[219]Center for Disease Control Website: Understanding Intimate Partner Violence Fact Sheet. Retrieved June 4, 2008 from http://www.cdc.gov/ncipc/dvp/ipv_factsheet.pdf

[220]Ibid.

[221]Ibid.

[222]Kaiz, J. & Arias, I. (2001). Women's attributions for hypothetical dating violence: Effects of partner alcohol use and violence severity. *Journal of Applied Social Psychology, 31*(7), 1458–1473.

[223]Zhang, S., & Stafford, L. (2009). Relational Ramifications of Honest but Hurtful Evaluative Messages in Close Relationships. *Western Journal of Communication, 73*(4), 481–501.

[224]Miller, C.W. & Roloff, M.E. (2005). Gender and willingness to confront hurtful messages from romantic partners. *Communication Quarterly, 53,* 323–337.

[225]Vangelisti, A.L. & Crumley, L.P. (1998). Reactions to messages that hurt: The influence of relational contexts, *Communication Monographs, 65,* 173–196.

[226]Waldron, V.R. & Kelley, D.L. (2005). Forgiving communication as a response to relational transgressions. *Journal of Social and Personal Relationships 22,* 6, 723–742.

[227]Nadal, K. L., Griffin, K.E., Wong, Y., Hamit, S., & Rasmus, M. (2014). Racial microaggressions and mental health: Counseling clients of color. *Journal of Counseling and Development 92*(1), 57–66.

[228]Sue, D.W. (2010). *Microaggressions in Everyday Society.* New York: Wiley.

[229]Triandis, H.C. (2001). Individualism-collectivism and personality. *Journal of Personal Relationships, 69,* 907–924.

[230]Potter, J. & Wetherill, M. (1987). *Discourse and Social Psychology.* London: Sage. Ross, L. (1977).

[231]Ibid.

[232]Scott, M.B. & Lyman, S.M. (1968). Accounts. *American Sociological Review, 33,* 46–62.

[233]Shaver, K.G., & Drown, D. (1986). On causality, responsibility, and self-blame: A theoretical note. *Journal of Personality and Social Psychology, 4,* 697–702.

[234]McLaughlin, M., Osborne, K. & Smith, C. (1995). Standards of conduct on Usenet. In S. Jones (Ed), *Cybersociety,* 90–111. CA: Sage.

[235]Smith, C., McLaughlin, M. & Osborne, K. (1997). Conduct control on Usenet. *Journal of Computer-Mediated Communication, 2*(4), 1–11.

[236]Thibault, J.W., & Kelley, H.H. (1952). *The social psychology of groups.* New York: John Wiley & Sons.

[237]Bachman, G.F. & Guerrero, L.K. (2006). Relational quality and communicative responses following hurtful events in dating relationships: An expectancy violations analysis. *Journal of Social and Personal Relationships, 23*(6), 943–963.

[238]Miller, K. (2005). *Communication theories.* New York: McGraw Hill.

[239]Thibault, J.W., & Kelley, H.H. (1952). *The social psychology of groups.* New York: John Wiley & Sons.

[240]Cramer, D.W., Roach, A.J. (1988). Coming out to mom and dad: A study of gay males and their relationships with their parents. *Journal of Homosexuality, 15,* 79–91.

[241]Carnelley, K.B., Hepper, E.G., Hicks, C. & Turner, W. (2011). Perceived parental reactions to coming out, attachment, and romantic relationship views. *Attachment & Human Development, 13,* 217–236.

[242]McKenna, K & Bargh, J.A. (1998). Coming out in the age of the Internet: Identity "demarginalization" through virtual group participation. *Journal of Personality and Social Psychology, 75,* 681–694.

[243]Baxter, L. (1985). Accomplishing relationship disengagement. In S. Duck & D. Perlman (Eds.), *Understanding personal relationships: An interdisciplinary approach*. London: Academic Press, 243–65.

[244]Haag, P. (November 18, 2011). The top 10 relationship words that aren't translatable into English. Big Think. Retrieved June 21, 2011 from http://bigthink.com/marriarge-30/the-top-10-relationship-words-that-arent-translatable-into-english?page=all.

[245]Knapp, M.L. (1984). *Interpersonal communication and human relationships*. Boston, MA: Allyn & Bacon.

[246]Duck, S.W. (1982). A topography of relationship disengagement and dissolution. In S. W. Duck (Ed.), *Personal relationships 4: Dissolving personal relationships*. London: Academic Press.

[247]Duck, S. (1998). *Human relationships*. London: Sage, p. 88.

[248]Ibid, p. 90.

[249]Dion, K.K. & Dion, K.L. (1996). Cultural perspectives on romantic love. *Journal of Personal Relationships, 3*, 5–17.

[250]Vangelisti, A.L. (2002). Interpersonal processes in romantic relationships. In M. L. Knapp & J.A. Daly (Eds.), *Handbook of Interpersonal Communication*, (643–679). Thousand Oaks, CA: Sage.

[251]Bartholomew, K. & Horowitz, L.M. (1991). Attachment styles among young adults: A test of a four-category model. *Journal of Personality and Social Psychology, 61*, 226–244.

[252]Mikulincer, M. & Shaver, P.R. (2001). Attachment theory and intergroup bias: Evidence that priming the secure base schema attenuates negative reactions to out-groups. *Journal of Personality and Social Psychology, 81*, 99.

[253]Mikulincer, M. (1997). Adult attachment style and information processing: Individual differences in curiosity and cognitive closure. *Journal of Personality and Social Psychology, 72*, 1217–1230.

[254]Ibid, p. 12.

[255]Sumer, N. (2002). The impact of mental models of attachments on partner and self-attributions and relationship satisfaction. *Dissertation Abstracts International: Section B: The Sciences & Engineering, 57*, American Psychological Association.

[256]Cole, T., Leets, L., Bradac, J.J. (2002). Deceptive message processing: The role of attachment style and verbal intimacy markers in deceptive message judgments. *Communication Studies, 53*, 74–89.

[257]Borae, J. & Pena, J. (2010). Mobile communication in romantic relationships: Mobile phone use, relational uncertainty, love, commitment, and attachment styles. *Communication Reports, 23*(1), 39–51.

[258]Schönbrodt, F.D., Asendorpf, J.A. (2011). Attachment dynamics in a virtual world. *Journal of Personality, 80*, 429–463.

[259]Bradbury, T.N. & Fincham, F.D. (1991). A contextual model for advancing the study of marital interaction. In G.J.O. Fletcher, F.D. Fincham (Eds.), *Cognition in close relationships* (127–147). Hillsdale, NJ, England: Lawrence Erlbaum Associates, Inc.

[260]Fletcher, G.L.O., & Fincham, F.D. (1991). Attribution processes in close relationships. In G. Fletcher & F. Fincham (Eds.), *Cognition in close relationships* (7–36). Hillsdale, NJ: Erlbaum.

[261]Jacobson, N.S., McDonald, D.W., Follette, W.C., & Berley, R.A. (1985). Attribution processes in distressed and nondistressed married couples. *Cognitive Therapy and Research, 9*, 35–50.

[262]Karney, B.R., Bradbury, T.N., Fincham, F.D. & Sullivan, K.T. (1994). The role of negative affectivity in the association between attributions and marital satisfaction. *Journal of Personality and Social Psychology, 66*, 413–424.

[263]Fincham, F.D., Beach, S.R., & Nelson, G. (1987). Attributional processes in distressed and non-distressed couples: 3. Causal and responsibility attributions for spouse behavior. *Cognitive Therapy and Research, 11*, 71–86.

[264]Vangelisti, A.L. (2002). *Interpersonal processes in romantic relationships*. In M.L. Knapp & J.A. Daly (Eds.), *Handbook of Interpersonal Communication*, (651) Thousand Oaks, CA: Sage.

[265]Miller, R.S. (1997). Inattentive and contented: Relationship commitment and attention to alternatives. *Journal of Personality and Social Psychology, 73*, 758–766.

[266]Murray, S.L., & Holmes, J.G. (1993). Seeing virtues in faults: Negativity and the transformation of interpersonal narratives in close relationships. *Journal of Personality and Social Psychology, 65*, 707–722.

[267]Burgoon, J.K. (1978). A communication model of personal space violation: Explication and an initial test. *Human Communication Research, 4*, 129–142.

[268] Afifi, W. A. & Metts, S. (1998). Characteristics and consequences of expectation violations in close relationships. *Journal of Social and Personal Relationships, 15*, 365–392.

[269] Garnefski, N. & Kraaij, V. (2006). Cognitive emotion regulation questionnaire—development of a short 18-item version (CERQ-short). *Personality and Individual Differences, 41*, 1045–1053.

[270] Ibid.

[271] This assessment is a nonscientific adaptation of the Cognitive Emotion Regulation Questionnaire.

SECTION 4

Relational
Maintenance

CHAPTER 9

Managing Interpersonal Conflict

"Challenges make you discover things about yourself
that you never really knew."
—Cicely Tyson

Learning Objectives

After studying this chapter, you should be able to:

1. Understand typical myths that shape our beliefs about conflict.

2. Identify what makes a conflict constructive versus destructive.

3. Summarize the types and stages of conflict.

4. Understand your own and other conflict styles.

5. Identify the effect your emotions have on how you handle conflict.

6. Apply conflict management strategies to work through emotions and increase the likelihood of constructive conflict.

The 2016 U.S. Presidential Election and its ongoing aftermath highlight one of the most contentious political divides in American history. Folks on both sides continue to engage in impassioned conflict about the important issues that divide us, such as gun regulation, women's reproductive rights, immigrant rights, and much more. With no resolution in sight, most Americans report feeling exhausted by the state of our Union.

Even though our national debate represents an *intergroup* conflict, it trickles down into our interpersonal interactions. Whether in your home, at family gatherings, amongst friends or at work, our political attitudes and beliefs can create enormous interpersonal conflict. Many Americans report dreading family gatherings now more than ever, and some have even cited the 2016 election as the impetus for their divorce.

These conflicts, however challenging, are opportunities to better understand the nature of human conflict and explore ideas for managing it. Even when agreement is impossible, effective communication can go a long way in preserving important relationships.

This chapter will cover typical myths of conflict that you may have learned and explain why they may be causing problems in your approach to conflict. In addition, you will uncover your own style of conflict and learn how to better engage with others in interpersonal conflict situations. Finally, the important role of emotions in conflict will be explained, and some strategies for dealing effectively with emotions will be presented. The goal of this chapter is to make conflict less intimidating, and to help you realize that effective communication during conflict can pave the road to even greater relationship satisfaction.

WHAT IS CONFLICT?

When is the last time you had a conflict? It may be hard to identify, because we don't always know what qualifies as a conflict. Some people use synonymous terms such as a fight, a disagreement, or an argument to describe conflict situations. All of these are conflicts, but conflicts can take many other forms—some obvious and others not so clear. **Interpersonal conflict** is a struggle that occurs when two *interdependent* people have seemingly incompatible goals or needs. When two people are **interdependent,** what each person does, says, and feels affects the other person. Because each person's actions affect the other, two interdependent people often find situations where either their needs are incompatible, or there are too few resources to accomplish each person's individual goals. A simple example of the first situation of incompatible goals is deciding where to go for lunch. If I want to eat Mexican food but my friend wants Italian food, then our needs are incompatible. To exemplify the second type of conflict, limited resources, imagine a situation where one spouse wants a new car, but the other wants to take a vacation. If the couple only has enough money in their bank account for one or the other, there are simply not enough resources for both people to have their needs met. This information on types of conflict is probably intuitive; it makes good sense to you. But what are some other things you think you know about conflict, and are you right?

CONFLICT MYTHS

There are several "myths" about conflict that we learn from our social environment, which includes our parents, siblings, and friends. Through their own behavior these people teach us what conflict means and how it should be handled. However, the information we learn is not always correct and sometimes it is flat out wrong. Before learning how to deal with conflict in a constructive way, we must first dispel some of the myths we've learned growing up.

Myth 1: Conflict Can Always Be Avoided

The first myth, that *conflict can always be avoided*, creates an environment where one or both people never feel quite comfortable being themselves. To avoid conflict altogether would mean to set aside our own needs any time they are not entirely consistent with those of another person.

This myth is especially problematic if only one person in the dyad believes it is true. Chances are that the person who believes conflict can be avoided is also the one who will be sacrificing his or her own needs on a regular basis. Individuals who are afraid to say what they want and need in a relationship can easily be taken for granted. Additionally, failing to voice your needs can stunt the development of intimacy in a relationship. As discussed in a previous chapter, the only way to develop true intimacy is through self-disclosure, which includes being honest even when your thoughts, needs, and ideas conflict with another person's.

Myth 2: Conflict Arises from Misunderstanding

The next myth, that *conflict arises from misunderstanding*, only takes into consideration a few types of conflicts. Although some conflict is based purely on lack of correct information and understanding, many conflicts occur because of real differences between people. You and I can talk all day long clarifying our perspectives, and at the end of the day I might still disagree with you. As complex human beings, it is likely that we are not going to see eye to eye on many issues and that our unique needs will be incompatible. In many of these cases there is no solution to these incompatibilities, which leads to the next myth.

Myth 3: Conflict Can Always Be Resolved

The belief that *conflict can always be resolved* is a common myth shared by many. This myth is especially dangerous because it sets the relationship up for failure. Not all disagreements can be resolved by being more clear, listening harder, or taking a different perspective. Once you have tried all of the methods for resolving a conflict, the issues may still exist as a problem area in your relationship. Relationship experts suggest that most interpersonal conflict is *not ever* resolved, but rather managed. Again, this suggests that the conflict issue itself is not as important as how you handle it. Often times agreeing to disagree can be the best tool for moving through an issue and keeping the relationship intact.

Myth 4: Conflict Is a Sign of a Troubled Relationship

The last and most important myth to dispel is that *conflict is always a sign of a poor or troubled interpersonal relationship*. Because conflict often makes people in a relationship feel uncomfortable, we tend to associate conflict with unhappiness. The truth is that the only way to have both people's needs met is to have a little conflict; relationships with no conflict are problematic because someone is usually less satisfied than he or she could be. Relationship researcher John Gottman has found in his studies that couples that do not fight at all are more likely to end up divorced than couples that fight often but constructively.[272] In sum, it's not how often you fight, but how you fight that determines whether or not your relationship is healthy.

So how *do* you fight? First let's deconstruct the types of conflicts you may encounter and the stages that occur in these conflicts, and then we will take a look at your conflict behaviors and see if they can be improved.

Family Communication and Conflict Schema

Koerner and Fitzpatrick's general theory of family communication is based on family communication schemas, which are "knowledge structures that represent the external world of the family and provide a basis for interpreting what other family members say and do."[273] Like other schemas, family communication schemas are built from experiences in the family, and solidify over time as expectations and norms for communication. The Family Communication Environment Instrument (FCEI) is a tool that considers both marital and parent-child communication, and identifies three dimensions that summarize individuals' schema for family communication.[274]

The first dimension, expressiveness, represents the degree of conversation orientation. For example, are all family members, including children, encouraged to express their thoughts and feelings openly? The second dimension, structural traditionalism assesses the level of conventionalism in the beliefs about marriage roles and child conformity. This dimension asks whether parent and child roles are rigid and traditional, or flexible. Finally, the conflict avoidance dimensions seeks to understand whether or not family members avoid conflict. Do members suppress unpleasant topics or avoid conflict by enforcing conformity?

Examining these "norms" for behavior in one's family of origin can give enormous insight into our own family communication schema. Once we grow up and have families of our own, we take our family communication schema into these new families, for better or for worse. A great deal of marital conflict can occur between two individuals operating from contrasting family communication schema. Differing norms for family communication can also cause major problems with blended families, or the combination of families that can occur when divorced parents marry new partners. The more you examine the communication expectations from your own family of origin, the better prepared you will be to negotiate these norms and develop new habits to pass along.

Review! Conflict Myths	
Myth 1:	Conflict can always be avoided.
Myth 2:	Conflict arises from misunderstanding.
Myth 3:	Conflict can always be resolved.
Myth 4:	Conflict is a sign of a troubled interpersonal relationship.

WHAT DOES CONFLICT LOOK LIKE?

Conflict can take many forms and follow many different paths. In order to better diagnose the conflicts you have in your interpersonal relationships, the type of conflict with which you are dealing must be identified. It also helps to know the typical stages of conflict. Knowing this information will help you apply the appropriate tools to manage each unique type of conflict.

TYPES OF CONFLICT

Pseudo Conflict

Pseudo conflict is conflict triggered by miscommunication or misunderstanding. It occurs when we understand a different meaning from a message than that which was intended. You can see examples of pseudo conflict by watching sitcoms on TV. Usually what makes an episode funny is the audience's awareness of the misunderstanding between two or more characters, and we watch as they run around in confusion trying to solve what, in the end, is not a real conflict at all but rather an innocent misunderstanding. These conflicts are the easiest to manage because they can be resolved with clear communication and listening skills. However, often times what starts out as a pseudo conflict ends up evolving into one of the other types of conflict. Thus, pseudo conflict can still cause relational damage even once the issue has been clarified if constructive conflict skills are not used while working it out.

Simple Conflict

Simple conflict stems from differences in ideas, definitions, perceptions, or goals. When two people have clearly stated their own needs and perspectives and there is an obvious clash between them, a simple conflict ensues. This type of conflict can be managed in several ways that will be discussed later on in this chapter.

Ego Conflict

When two people are in conflict because neither will let go of their personal position, this can result in an **ego conflict**. Ego conflicts often include personal attacks from one or both people, which put the other person on the defensive. These conflicts usually follow an entangled pattern of attack-defense, and often times both people cannot even recall the original issue that started the conflict. Ego conflicts can emerge out of either a pseudo conflict or a simple conflict, which is why it is important to manage these two types of conflicts the best you can before they become personal. The best way to avoid ego conflicts is to eliminate personal attacks and criticisms during conflict, and refuse to respond negatively when you are attacked. Dyads often benefit from creating conflict "rules" that allow them to stop the pattern of using unhealthy conflict strategies such as personal attacks. For example, if one person directs a personal insult at the other, the offended individual should call a "time out" to signify that he or she feels like they have just been personally attacked. Unless one person stops the cycle of attack-defense, it can slowly deteriorate the entire relationship.

Scholars across communication and health fields are becoming increasingly interested in the effects of **rumination**, which often occurs with people who perceive all conflicts as ego conflicts. Rumination is the continual thinking about an unpleasant event after it has occurred, such as an argument with another person, which distracts people from focusing on the present moment. One type of ruminating is called "imagined interactions" (or, IIs), whereby the ruminator imagines how the event could have gone differently, with him or her saying exactly the right thing. Some IIs are even hurtful or abusive, where the ruminator imagines "getting back at" the person who has angered him or her. While most of us can admit that we've experienced these kinds of thoughts, research suggests that people who take conflicts personally are even more likely to engage in rumination

and especially imagined interactions. Experts note that taking conflict personally tends to be a trait, which is an enduring personal characteristic, as opposed to a state, which is a temporary way of being that is not constant. People who possess the trait of taking conflict personally (TCP) are bigger ruminators than those who do not possess the trait.[275]

We all know the harmful effects of negative thoughts, and rumination by negative imagined interactions is a particularly harmful kind of intrapersonal communication. Despite allowing temporary feelings of vengeance, creating imagined interactions actually cause us to "relive" the conflict. By doing so our bodies experience the feelings associated with the conflict, which creates almost as much internal stress as it would if we were having an actual conflict with the other person.

Imagined interactions are not a healthy or effective way to deal with the real problem. If you would characterize yourself as a "ruminator," try examining your own feelings about conflict. Do you feel like conflicts are often your own fault? Are there conflict behaviors of yours that you could work on in order to have better conflict outcomes and less rumination? This may help you to stop wasting time thinking about what's already happened, and start focusing on what you can do differently right now.

Review! Types of Conflict	
Pseudo conflict:	Conflict triggered by miscommunication or misunderstanding.
Simple conflict:	Conflict that stems from differences in ideas, definitions, perceptions, or goals.
Ego conflict:	Conflict that continues because neither person will let go of their personal position.

STAGES OF CONFLICT

Although each conflict is unique, conflicts usually go through several common and predictable stages. These stages do not necessarily occur in a linear fashion, but they do show how we can distinguish the different parts of a conflict.[276]

In the **latent conflict stage**, one or both people become aware that there are important differences between members of the dyad. The differences can include different relationship expectations, conflicting perceptions, incompatible goals, or different values. From these perceived differences comes **conflict emergence**, or frustration awareness, where at least one person becomes aware that the differences in the relationship are causing increased internal turmoil and dissatisfaction.

During **conflict escalation**, or active conflict, one or both people make their frustrations explicit to the other. These expressions can take many forms; they can occur verbally in a straightforward manner, or they can be communicated nonverbally. Of course, frustrations can also be expressed calmly or aggressively.

During the **stalemate stage** both parties are stuck in their perspectives and attitudes. Conflicts can stay in this stage over long periods of time, especially if the individuals do not have the skills to de-escalate the conflict. Eventually, one or both people attempt to push the conflict into the **de-escalation stage,** where emotions calm down and each person is willing to negotiate to resolve the conflict. In the **dispute settlement** stage one or both individuals try to either manage or resolve the conflict entirely by suggesting approaches or solutions.

A conflict is usually not entirely over, however, just because it has been managed or resolved. In the **post-conflict stage,** or aftermath, each person assesses how the conflict has affected the overall dynamic, and tries to get the relationship back on track. Again, although these stages may not occur in sequence every time, it is still likely that this pattern sounds familiar to you based on conflicts you've experienced in your interpersonal relationships.

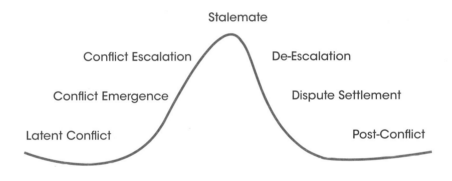

Figure 9.0. The stages of a conflict.

As you probably know, a conflict can go south in any one of these stages and quickly turn from a simple disagreement to a destructive conflict. What measures can be taken to manage conflict so that it doesn't get out of control? First, you need to be able to distinguish between constructive and destructive conflict, then you must become aware of your own conflict style in order to learn new tools by which to manage your interpersonal conflicts.

APPROACHES TO CONFLICT

How you choose to engage in a disagreement or argument entirely determines the outcome of the conflict. You may want to read that sentence again. What this means is that there are very few conflict issues that can make or break a relationship. Rather, *communication during and after conflict is what makes or breaks a relationship.* This perspective may contrast with your previous understanding of conflict, and may be why conflict situations can seem scary or difficult. Learning skills for constructive conflict takes control away from the conflict *issue* and gives control to the people managing the conflict.

CONSTRUCTIVE VERSUS DESTRUCTIVE CONFLICT

Conflict is considered **constructive** if it ultimately helps build new insights into the relationship and establishes new patterns of communication.[277] In this sense, the conflict was good for the relationship. If after a conflict both people feel understood by each other and closer to one another, the conflict was constructive. In fact, many people report feeling much closer to each other after a constructive conflict than they did before the conflict.[278] Getting issues out into the open often feels liberating for both people, and airing differences when they arise can lead to a more satisfying relationship in the long run.

There are many benefits to constructive conflict in interpersonal relationships.[279] Engaging in conflict puts a spotlight on problems that need to be solved; until a problem is addressed it can negatively influence every aspect of the relationship. If both people are generally satisfied but could imagine being happier, conflict clarifies what needs to be changed in order for a relationship to reach its maximum potential. When a conflict arises, it makes clear what is important to you and your partner, therefore helping you learn about each other in new ways. Perhaps most important, the ability to constructively manage conflict increases both parties' confidence that they can handle relationship challenges effectively, and makes conflict issues less threatening in the future. Lastly, conflict prevents relationships from becoming stagnant by keeping them interesting. A relationship between two people who never disagree about anything can't keep either person excited for very long!

The benefits of conflict can easily be outweighed by the damage caused if conflict is handled destructively. **Destructive conflict** dismantles rather than strengthens a relationship.[280] You can usually assess whether a conflict was destructive by assessing how each person feels after the conflict is over. If the individuals who experience the conflict feel like there may have been irreparable damage done, they are disappointed by the other, or they are having second thoughts about the relationship, chances are the conflict was destructive. Because few people ever learn effective conflict skills, destructive conflict tends to be the norm.

Current research on the impact of parent conflict on children highlights the fact that conflict is not inherently bad. Decades ago, parents were taught "Do not fight in front of the children." Along with many other conflict myths, this once has since been invalidated. In fact, contemporary scholars and therapists now argue that *avoiding* parent conflict in front of children is potentially harmful. Even when we attempt to hide conflict, parents engage in about eight conflicts per day ranging from bickering to shouting, and children witness almost half of these.[281] Leading expert in child development E. Mark Cummings suggests that children are exceptionally sensitive to conflict: Even when parents fight away from children the kids can detect the conflict, they are just fuzzy about the details. However, the effects of parental fighting are not what you might expect. Children who witness parents fighting without constructive communication or conflict resolution show increased aggression and antisocial behavior at school, but those who witness conflict that does not escalate or include insults and is resolved with affection actually display improved social behavior at school (as rated by their teachers). Witnessing a constructive argument equips children with the skills of positive negotiation, compromise, and fairness. It also helps them learn that conflict is not bad and does not necessarily harm relationships.

Review! Constructive versus Destructive Conflict	
Constructive conflict:	Helps build new insights into the relationship and establishes new patterns of communication.
Destructive conflict:	Dismantles rather than strengthens a relationship.

You can often predict whether your conflicts will be constructive or destructive by taking a look at the way you tend to approach your partner in a conflict, which is known as your conflict style. Certain styles contribute to constructive conflict, while other styles facilitate destructive conflict. Next we'll examine the different conflict styles so that you can diagnose your own style and consider whether there are better options.

CONFLICT STYLE

Each of us typically gravitates toward our preferred conflict style when faced with an interpersonal challenge. **Conflict style** is the learned and consistent pattern or approach we use to manage disagreements with others. We learn styles of conflict from our parents very early in life, and we tend to stick to our learned style unless we choose to learn additional skills. Becoming skilled in conflict management requires that you learn to adapt your style to fit the circumstance. Keep in mind that there is no one best style for managing conflict. The choice of which style to use depends on how much energy you want to invest in the conflict, the amount of time you have, the quality and importance of the relationship, and the relative power roles in the dynamic. Conflict styles are characterized by two considerations: concern for others and concern for self.[282] These dimensions result in five conflict management styles.

Avoidance

An avoidant conflict style results from a low concern for others and a low concern for self. **Avoidance** involves "managing" conflict by trying to work around it, never addressing it directly. Reasons for avoiding conflict can include not having the mental or physical energy to deal with it, not wanting to hurt another person's feelings, being unable to assert one's own rights, or feeling concerned that the relationship cannot withstand the conflict.

Sometimes avoiding a conflict is a useful approach because it can allow time for each person to step back from the issue, emotionally cool down, and gain a different perspective. Often after stepping away, a conflict will not seem quite as important as it did before. Avoiding conflict has several disadvantages, however. By rejecting someone else's attempt to deal with the conflict you may send the message that the other person or the relationship is not important to you. In addition, if you avoid the conflict forever it will never get addressed, which may prevent the relationship from reaching its full potential. More importantly, you will never become skilled at conflict management if you consistently refuse to engage in conflict. Because of these outcomes, conflict avoidance is often viewed as a "lose-lose" approach.

Accommodation

Accommodation involves managing conflict by giving in to the demands of others, often at the expense of meeting your own needs. This style comes from a high concern for others, but a low concern for the self. Those who tend to use an accommodating style often do so because they fear rejection, they seek approval, or they simply want to avoid "drama." Because of this, accommodating is considered **non-assertive**. Non-assertive communication is that which aims to address others' needs only, usually by sacrificing your own needs. Non-assertive behavior often occurs when people want to avoid conflict or are afraid of being disliked when their needs conflict with another person's. For example if you and your colleague both have the opportunity to move into the new corner office and you decide just to give it to her because you want to seem nice or don't want to seem demanding, then you are behaving non-assertively.

However, in some situations people realize that the other person's needs take priority over their own and their overall care and concern for the other leads them to accommodate. There are several advantages to using the accommodation style that don't require non-assertiveness. First, it can be an authentic way to show helpfulness and concern for another. In addition, you may want to accommodate when you were wrong about something or you've realized that your needs are unreasonable. However, accommodating can have equal disadvantages. Sometimes accommodating can be a quick solution to a larger problem that could re-emerge. In these cases, accommodating creates a "pseudo solution" which only delays having to deal with the issue. It is also possible that when other people recognize a non-assertive accommodator they may learn to take advantage of the person. Thus, if you accommodate regularly, especially if you are the only one who does it, this is considered a "win-lose" approach.

Competition

Competition is managing conflict by seeking to win, often at the expense of the other person involved. This is also a "win-lose" approach because it evolves from a low concern for others and a high concern for self. People who compete tend to blame others rather than taking responsibility for their share of the conflict and working collaboratively for a satisfying resolution. A competitive conflict style usually includes the use of aggressiveness. **Aggressiveness** is expressing one's own needs while denying the needs and rights of others. Direct aggressiveness usually includes a strong verbal component, often in the form of threats, demands, or attacks. For example, if during a conflict your boyfriend or girlfriend chooses to yell and scream at you without letting you get a word in, that person is denying your need to defend and express yourself.

As with all styles, competition can be useful and appropriate under certain circumstances. In situations where you truly believe that your perspective is correct, and compromising would violate your values or harm others, then you should compete to win. However, this does not mean that aggressiveness is in order. You can aim to win a disagreement without violating another person's rights to speak and be listened to. Even if you feel certain of your position, considering the other's perspective is always valuable.

Passive Aggressiveness

Passive aggressiveness is another aggressive conflict style. Passive aggressiveness is characterized by verbal or nonverbal behaviors intended to subtly "punish" the other, to make him or her feel bad, guilty, or confused. If your best friend forgets your birthday you may react with passive aggressiveness by not answering her calls for a week just to elicit a reaction. Even though passive aggressiveness may not involve shouting or demanding, it is still a style that denies the other person their rights, and it is therefore aggressive. People who are passive aggressive will never state directly that they are upset or angry but will instead show their feelings through indirect behaviors. A passive aggressive person will never confront the other person directly so that the conflict can be addressed.

Compromise

Compromise is managing conflict by attempting to find a middle ground, which stems from a high concern for both the self and the other. Although compromise has a positive ring to it, if both parties compromise then each has to give up part of what they desired, therefore this approach is considered "lose/win" or "win/lose" because each person loses something.

Compromise is useful if the issue is relatively unimportant, if a quick and satisfying resolution can be reached this way, if it helps maintain equality in the relationship, or if it saves face for one or both people. However, compromise can be problematic if either person feels like they are sacrificing more, or if neither person is entirely satisfied with the outcome but would rather compromise than work harder for a mutually beneficial solution.

Collaboration

Collaboration is managing conflict by using a creative and thoughtful approach to achieve the most positive solution for both people involved. To visualize collaboration, imagine two people sitting across from each other at a table passing an issue back and forth. Now imagine if one person came around so that both people were sitting side by side, together looking at the issue on the table. Using a collaborative style requires that the conflict be approached as a problem or set of problems that the team is going to solve together. This is considered a "win-win approach" because both people can get exactly what they wanted, and sometimes even more. Because this approach puts both people on the same side, collaboration can build cohesion and commitment.

To master the art of compromise and especially collaboration, one must learn to practice assertiveness. **Assertiveness** is communication that expresses your own needs while also considering the needs of the other. Explaining to your roommate that you find it stressful to come home to a dirty apartment at the end of the day and asking what each of you can do to create a mutually desirable living space is an example of assertiveness. People who use assertiveness believe that both individuals can get their needs met, and they do not fear disclosing what their own needs are.

Sometimes being assertive is easier said than done. There are many reasons why people choose other approaches, including the way they were raised and what they were taught about dealing with others. Non-assertiveness is typical of relationships where one or both people fear "rocking the boat," or where one or both people believe that addressing others' needs first is the "good" thing to do. Aggressiveness is usually used when people do not feel heard or validated, and believe that force is the only way to make others listen to their needs. Thus, both aggressiveness and non-assertiveness stem from the same fear: that your own needs are not likely to get met. People who use aggressiveness are overcompensating because they don't believe their needs will get met without force; people who use non-assertiveness are acquiescing because they figure their needs probably will get overlooked anyway.

WATCH AND LEARN

View a TED Talk on conflict management by typing this into your browser: TED Talk from no to yes.

Figure 9.1. Conflict styles.

Review! Approaches to Conflict	
Assertiveness:	Communication that expresses your own needs while also considering the needs of the other.
Aggressiveness:	Communication behavior aimed at expressing one's own needs while denying the needs and rights of others.
Non-assertiveness:	Communication that aims to address others' needs only, possibly at the risk of your own.

INTERPERSONAL COMMUNICATION FOR SOCIAL CHANGE

A Win-Lose Approach to Criminal Justice

Kendra: "I just don't see why African Americans are being so divisive. Can't we agree that All Lives Matter and not make everything about race?"

Quick facts:[283]

- About 14 million White Americans and 2.6 million Black Americans report using illicit drugs, meaning five times as many Whites are using drugs.

- Black Americans are sent to prison for drug offenses at ten times the rate of White Americans.

- Black Americans represent 12% of the total population of drug users, but they represent 38% of those arrested for drug offenses, and they represent 59% of those in state prison for a drug offense.

- Black Americans serve virtually as much time in prison for a drug offense such as possession (58.7 months) as Whites do for a violent offense such as rape or assault (61.7 months).

- Black Americans are incarcerated at nearly six times the rate of Whites, even though the rates of illegal activity by their race is no higher than that of Whites.

Why is so little being done about these blatant inequalities in the treatment of Black and White Americans by our criminal justice system? Experts point to a variety of reasons, one being our ingrained perception of scarcity. **Scarcity** is an economic model that causes us to believe that there are only a limited number of

resources to go around.[284] This means one group can only win at another group's expense, an approach described in this chapter as win-lose.

The problem with the scarcity model is that it has very little basis in reality. Social scientists have been scratching their heads for a long time about the human tendency to compete for resources even when there is no clear evidence that resources are limited. You already learned about the

Minimal Group Paradigm in an earlier chapter, which shows that mere division of people into arbitrary groups is enough to cause them to start competing. You also read about Positive Distinctiveness, the concept that our "group esteem" is higher when we can prove that we are superior to a particular outgroup. Yet there is another aspect of this line of research which is even more disturbing: When given the choice to help only our own group, or to help our group *and* an outgroup (at no additional cost to us), we choose to help only our group about 85% of the time.[285]

Social justice groups trying to raise awareness about faulty intergroup thinking have been spreading the message on T-shirts, posters, and via social media, explaining, *"Equal rights for others does not mean fewer rights for you. It's not pie."* While this mantra makes a valid point, other groups believe that more direct action is required if we expect social change. For information on specific solutions to racial disparities in our criminal justice system search "Innocence Project," "Sentencing Project," and "The Justice Project."

Reflection

1. Do you believe that win-win outcomes are always possible in interpersonal conflict?

2. Can you think of any intergroup conflicts across the globe where a win-win outcome seems impossible or unlikely?

3. If someone tried to tell you that more People of Color are in prison because they commit more crimes, how would you respond?

4. What careers should students who are interested in solving problems like these pursue?

THE CHALLENGES OF MEDIATED INTERPERSONAL CONFLICT

If you've ever posted a snide comment on a blog, shot back a nasty reply to a text or forwarded an embarrassing email, you know that it's easier to behave badly when the recipient of your message isn't right in front of you. The words we choose during mediated conflict can have a great impact on how the struggle unfolds.

Mediated communication in the form of texting, chatting, email, and blogging has changed the nature of interpersonal conflict. Some of the characteristics of mediated communication that you learned about already are especially problematic when it comes to conflict situations:

DELAY

When communication through a mediated channel such as email or text message, you can take as long as you want to craft your message or retort. This takes away from the spontaneous nature of conflict because each person can edit their messages until they are satisfied. Although it seems like this would give those in conflict more time to construct less damaging messages, it can have the reverse effect by allowing otherwise inarticulate communicators to create "better" insults and jabs. Another issue caused by the delay of mediated communication is that the recipient does not always receive the message right when it was sent. By the time he or she reads the message, its sender may have changed how he or she feels by either thinking it through, sleeping on it, or gathering additional information.

DISINHIBITION

People in conflict often transmit messages without considering their consequences, a phenomenon known as disinhibition. Research shows that people are even more likely to be disinhibited when using mediated channels because they cannot see the reaction of the person on the receiving end of the message. We often demonize the person with whom we are in conflict, and having them in front of us can break this spell and show us they are human. Without seeing the other, we tend to underestimate the severity of our messages or the impact they have on the emotions of the receiver.

PERMANENCE

The fact that emails and text messages come in the form of written "transcripts" creates several problems. First, people in the heat of an argument can forward or show others the conflict dialogue. Sometimes this can help those fighting to seek the perspective of an objective third person, however most often the paper trail is used to embarrass or derogate each other by involving unintended recipients. Furthermore, once the conflict has been smoothed over, evidence of the harsh words that were said is left lingering in an email inbox or text thread. Revisiting old conflict messages can stir up emotions that make it hard to get over what happened.

Experts in the field recommend that if you find yourself involved in a destructive conflict through mediated channels, stop the spiral of negativity and ask the other if they can meet with you face to face. Although mediated conflict may feel "easier" at the time, it may create more lasting damage to the relationship.

MINDFUL MEDIATED COMMUNICATION:

Troll Patrol

Trolling is defined as making intentionally offensive or provocative online posts with the goal of upsetting a specific person or group of people. Often a troll wishes to elicit an angry response so that he or she can continue to engage with and upset others. It makes sense, then, that trolling is becoming the new favorite pastime of people with insecurity issues and related bullying tendencies. Two unique characteristics of the communication between a troll and his or her target are that (1) most times the troll doesn't even believe his or her own statements but simply uses them to enjoy getting a reaction, and (2) most times it takes a while for the target to recognize that they are entertaining a troll instead of having a real debate based on each person's actual thoughts and feelings.

Even though trolls are just insecure bullies hiding behind a screen, their words can hurt no matter how false. The sooner we can recognize a troll the more likely we are to be able to protect ourselves from any emotional or mental harm caused by their behavior. The best way to strip a troll of his power is to not respond, or to let others know that there is a troll in the conversation. Calling out a troll may elicit further provocation, but resist the temptation to engage any further or risk handing him back his power. You really can't win an argument with a troll because he or she just wants to continue arguing.

Writer and entertainer Lindy West decided to confront her troll, and learned that the lion on the other side of cyberspace is often really just a mouse. Google her story by searching "What happened when I confronted my cruellest troll."

Interpersonal relationships where both parties regularly practice assertiveness and approach conflict using a compromising or collaborative style usually create an environment where both people feel safe expressing their needs. Sounds great, doesn't it? So why is it so hard for otherwise reasonable and mature people to learn and practice these skills? In a word, the answer is…emotions. When there is a threat of our own needs being violated we tend to feel unsafe, and this feeling causes emotional trigger reactions. Often times the immediate goals of preserving our own self-esteem, being right, "showing" the other person they are wrong, or getting what we want, override the ultimate goal of engaging in a productive and constructive conflict and avoiding damage to the relationship. Thus, the remainder of this chapter will focus on understanding your own emotions as a critical component to managing conflict.

EMOTIONS AND CONFLICT

The main reason conflicts spiral out of control is because we are flooded with emotions that make it difficult to make sound behavioral choices. Once people calm down and return to a more relaxed emotional state, they are often regretful about how they behaved during a conflict. **Emotional contagion theory**[286] points out that emotional expression is contagious; people can "catch" emotions just by observing each other's emotional expressions. When viewed this way it makes perfect sense how tit-for-tat personal attacks and other negative

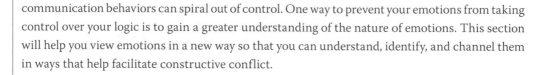

communication behaviors can spiral out of control. One way to prevent your emotions from taking control over your logic is to gain a greater understanding of the nature of emotions. This section will help you view emotions in a new way so that you can understand, identify, and channel them in ways that help facilitate constructive conflict.

WHERE DO EMOTIONS COME FROM?

Emotions are simply reactions based on social constructions.[287] This means that emotions are not based on a concrete reality, but instead are reactions to people, situations, and events, determined by social rules for what we expect and roles we expect ourselves and others to play. To figure out this seemingly complicated idea, ask yourself the following question: What are some behaviors of others that "make" you mad? Sad? Frustrated? For example, you may get mad when someone cuts you off on the freeway. You may get sad when your best friend doesn't compliment your new haircut. Finally, you may get frustrated when your partner is late for a special event. You are mad, sad, or frustrated because you were hoping for a different behavior. But how do you know how that person was "supposed" to act? **Norms** are ideas held by most members of the society about what is appropriate and expected behavior. You know what would have been the "normal" behavior because you have learned it through socialization. **Socialization** is the acquisition of the norms of your culture through experience with its members. Thus, negative emotions come from a deviation of what we believe is good, appropriate, and right behavior, ideas that only exist because they were taught to us. Without these teachings, we would not have a natural emotional reaction to a behavior because we wouldn't expect its alternative. Thus, emotions are not caused by an event itself, but instead they are reactions based on *expectations*. This helps us understand why in some cultures being late is not an offense, but in others it is taken personally and can cause major conflict.

Each field of study takes a different approach to understanding emotions. These approaches are not mutually exclusive, meaning one does not necessarily contradict another. Each of these perspectives can work together to help us understand the nature of our own emotions. The biological explanation for emotions suggests that emotions are physiological reactions that help ensure survival.[288] For example, the feeling of fear drives blood into large muscles, making it easier to run. Experiencing surprise triggers the eyebrows to rise, allowing the eyes to widen their view and gather more information about an uncertain environment. Anger primes the body for action, giving a surge of energy that will allow it to fight off the offending party. These feelings provoke physical reactions that allow us to react to our environment in a way that will help us remain safe.

Although this perspective may be helpful in understanding the origins of human emotions, the psychological perspective on emotions may be particularly helpful in learning not only how to understand our emotions, but how to manage them. This approach assumes, in short, that events or people do not cause us to experience emotions, but rather our thoughts about events and people cause our emotions. Through the process of perception, as described in an earlier chapter, we pick out details that support a preconceived idea that we have. Through this selective perception we confirm an idea about a person or situation, and we experience a corresponding emotional reaction, when in reality the emotion is the result of our thoughts about what is real, not necessarily what is real. One philosopher describes this phenomenon, explaining that emotions are the body's reaction

to the mind: "The thought creates an emotion. By dwelling mentally on the situation, event, or person that is the perceived cause of the emotion, the thought feeds energy to the emotion, which in turn energizes the thought pattern, and so on."[289]

If you subscribe to this perspective, you realize that you can control your emotions by better understanding your thoughts. One study reports that women who were unhappy in their relationships experienced measurable increases in blood pressure just from thinking about past fights they had had with their husbands.[290] Can you conjure up a thought in your mind right now that causes you to experience a strong emotion? Now how can you think differently about that thought to change the emotion? Playing with your emotions this way can allow you to realize that emotions do not control you, but rather you control your emotions with your thoughts.

BUILDING CULTURAL COMPETENCE

There's No Southern Comfort in a Southern Conflict

Comparisons between 110 nations over 70 years on rates of various violent crimes such as homicide, rape, and criminal assault show that the U.S. is relatively high when compared with other industrialized nations. Researchers believe that one reason for the elevated number of incidents is our tendency for a more aggressive and direct conflict style. One study found that "U.S. respondents were more likely than respondents of other nations to suggest aggressive solutions to interpersonal conflicts,"[291] which may ultimately lead to greater incidents of criminal violence. A team of researchers wondered if some states were more prone to aggression than others, so they set up an experiment where respondents were bumped by a stranger then called a profane name. Respondents from southern states reacted more aggressively than any other respondents, causing the scholars to conclude that people from southern U.S. states tend to be more dominant and aggressive than those residing in other parts of the country. However, the researchers' explanation for the violent reactions of southern folks is somewhat flattering: They suggest that rules for politeness are stricter in these states, and therefore it's a greater violation of common courtesy when a stranger behaves rudely.

THE EFFECT OF EMOTIONS

One way to make sure emotions do not drive us toward destructive communication behavior is to recognize them early. There are six *primary emotions* that are experienced universally by all human beings, and these are sadness, anger, disgust, happiness, fear, and surprise.[292] Combinations of the primary emotions are referred to as *secondary emotions*.[293] These secondary emotions can be especially confusing because it is often hard to distinguish which primary emotions are present when an emotional rainfall occurs. For example, we often lash out at others, engaging in behavior that may be perceived as anger, when in reality we are feeling insecure, unappreciated, jealous, or inferior.

Usually the first sign that we are emotionally unstable is a feeling of anger, frustration, fear, or even sadness that sweeps over us. In addition, we may experience physiological changes such as increased heart rate, increased sweating, or dilated pupils.[294] Usually these feelings manifest

through nonverbal reactions such as facial expressions, kinesics, proxemics, and vocalics. Don't forget, these nonverbal expressions of emotion are contagious, meaning that by this point the negative spiral is well on its way. Verbal expressions of feelings usually come next, which is where destructive communication behaviors emerge such as personal attacks, insults, or defensiveness.

An important thing to try and remember is that emotions have an enormous impact on cognitive interpretations. This means that once we have a feeling, all other stimuli are interpreted through the lens of that feeling. For example, if you are arguing because you are feeling jealous about your partner's behavior toward another person, the interpretation of your partner's entire subsequent communication has to go through the filter of jealously that already exists. As such, emotions make it difficult to achieve shared meaning because they color reality in an often "unrealistic" way. Once you feel a strong emotion, it is unlikely that you and your partner are perceiving things the same way.

FRESH FROM THE LAB: COMMUNICATION RESEARCHERS AT WORK

Battle of the Sexes

As you've already learned, conflict causes emotional, psycho-logical, and physiological reactions in the brain and body of the people in the argument. Over the past few decades researchers have been especially interested in knowing if there are gender differences in these reactions. Contrary to what you might ex-pect, we've learned that during conflict, men tend to experience greater physiological arousal than women, which comes in the form of increased heart rate and blood pressure, among other

©Hayden-McNeil, LLC

things. The reason for this difference is made clear by relationship researcher John Gottman, who explains it from an evolutionary perspective in an interview:

"Men have a lot of trouble when they reach a state of vigilance, when they think there's real danger, they have a lot of trouble calming down. And there's probably an evolutionary history to that because it functioned very well for our hominid ancestors, anthropologists think. For men to stay physiologically aroused and vigilant is conducive to cooperative hunting and protecting the tribe, which was a role that males had very early in our evolutionary history. Whereas women had the opposite sort of role, in terms of survival of the species, those women reproduced more effectively who had the milk-let-down reflex, which only happens when oxytocin is secreted in the brain, it only happens when women—as any woman knows who's been breast-feeding, you have to be able to calm down and relax. But oxytocin is also the hormone of affiliation. So women have developed this sort of social order, caring for one another, helping one another, and affiliating, that also al-lows them to really calm down and have the milk-let-down reflex. And so—it's one of nature's jokes. Women can calm down, men can't."[295]

So how can we help manage this gender inequality when it comes to emotional reactivity to conflict? Gottman suggests that the answer lies mostly in the hands of women. He states, "It's women who matter here, because we find that 80% of the time women are the ones in our culture who raise issues, and they raise them harshly in an unhappy relationship and more gently in a happy relationship."[296] Gottman asserts that when women

use critical, negative, or accusatory verbal and nonverbal behaviors when bringing up a conflict issue, they set the stage for destructive conflict.[297] Once the man's physiological arousal sets in, it's very hard to reverse. Although it sounds unfair to put responsibility on the women for starting arguments more gently, it may be a small price to pay for preventing a destructive conflict that both people regret.

FALLACIES IN THINKING

There are several patterns in thinking that can debilitate one's ability to perceive the situation clearly, resulting in emotional distress. These potentially destructive thoughts are presented here as fallacies, or errors in reasoning, that may cause you to have an emotional reaction. The first is the *fallacy of perfection*. This is the idea that you can or should be able to handle everything. If you tend not to want to apply collaborative methods with another individual because you feel like you should be able to work it out yourself, you are probably committing the fallacy of perfection.

The *fallacy of approval* is the belief that every person must approve of you. You are exhibiting this fallacy when you behave non-assertively: you are clearly showing that your need to be liked and to not rock the boat override getting your own needs met. The *fallacy of should* suggests that everything should be a certain way, and if things do not go the desired way this causes great emotional anxiety. For example, if you grew up learning that conflict is bad, chances are you feel like something is terribly wrong when you have an interpersonal conflict, when in truth conflict is not always a sign of relational distress, but relational strength. In addition, many people commit the *fallacy of overgeneralization*, which is applying words such as "never" or "always" that show sweeping conclusions about a person or situation. Over generalizing is an attempt to gain control by summarizing the meaning of things, however, these summaries usually reflect the current emotional state rather than the overall state of the relationship.

The last three fallacies reflect problems with personal accountability. The *fallacy of causation* occurs when you believe that someone else *causes* your emotions, when in fact we choose how we react to the behaviors of others. On the flip side, this fallacy can manifest as one person taking too much responsibility for causing reactions in others. If you feel like you are solely responsible for someone's pain, anger, anxiety, or grief, you are giving yourself too much credit and not allowing for their ability to choose their attitude about and reaction to a situation. The *fallacy of helplessness* is the belief that forces outside of ourselves are responsible for all that happens to us, good or bad. This is the belief that we really have no control over our lives and therefore we are unmotivated to be proactive in our relationships. Finally, the *fallacy of catastrophic expectations* is the certainty that the worst possible outcome is that which will likely occur. Consider this the "Eeyore" effect (from *Winnie the Pooh*). According to the principles of the self-fulfilling prophecy discussed in an earlier chapter, people who impose a rain cloud over their lives are likely to have their worst fears confirmed.

Recognizing and overcoming fallacious thinking is one way to prevent your emotions from controlling your conflicts and learning to manage them more effectively. When you are experiencing an overpowering emotion, try to take a quick inventory of the fallacies and see if one of these

is causing an unreasonable reaction. There are several additional steps you can take to manage emotions and make your conflicts more constructive, which will be covered in the last section.

SKILL BUILDING EXERCISE

Identifying Fallacies in Thinking

For each situation described, list the fallacy that may be contributing to the thoughts and emotions being expressed.

I hate how I feel after visiting your parents' house. I know your mom and dad like me but your sister looks at me like I'm worthless. It makes me feel like a total loser.

Fallacy: _____

I know our relationship is doomed. We met online, so there's no way it could work out.

Fallacy: _____

Your friends make me nervous. They bring out the worst in me, that's why I act rude sometimes.

Fallacy: _____

You are too good for me and we both know it. Since you're eventually going to leave me why should I bend over backwards to try to make you happy?

Fallacy: _____

I'm not going to talk to my parents about my breakup because they will feel sorry for me. I need to figure out how to deal with this on my own.

Fallacy: _____

How could you arrive late for our very first date? This is not the way it's supposed to go.

Fallacy: _____

Now list the fallacy that you commit most often in your interpersonal relationships. How could you think differently in order not to experience the unnecessary negative emotions that result from the fallacy?

Fallacy: _____

MANAGING EMOTIONS, MANAGING CONFLICT

Table the Issue

As you've learned, when we are emotionally charged we experience physical changes that affect what we think and say, such as elevated adrenaline flow and heart rate. Knowing this, when you experience intense emotions you have a choice to make: you can decide to express your feelings at that very moment, or you can decide to wait. Sometimes when our needs are violated we feel like we need to take immediate control by expressing ourselves. If you instead acknowledge that your mind and body are having a reaction, decide to let it go for a while (an hour or even a day), and promise yourself to re-evaluate it later, you can prevent the common errors of bad timing and bad delivery. This method is called "tabling" the issue. Rest assured that if your concern is valid it will not go away. The chances of actually getting your needs met are much greater if you approach the issue calmly after some thought because your relational partner is much less likely to want to meet your needs if he or she is feeling attacked.

Evaluate Your Own Expectations and Needs

One of the advantages to tabling your immediate needs is that you can evaluate their origins and meaning and really get to the bottom of why you are feeling the way you are. You can often save your relationship hours of destructive conflict by analyzing the problem yourself before you approach your partner with it. While you are alone, figure out how you feel and why. Think back on all the information you've learned so far and recognize your own attachment style, your own level of self-esteem, and your own set of expectations for others' behaviors. Keep in mind that these expectations derive from your own identity, which can include your culture, gender, age, and your personality as discussed in an earlier chapter. Ask yourself whether your expectations are realistic for the person with whom you are upset or angry. Are your feelings arising from your own insecurities or attachments? While emotions *are* real, they are not always *based on reality*. Consider whether your own selective perception may be causing you to experience certain emotions. While you have the opportunity, plan your message by trying out a few ways of saying how you feel. Writing your thoughts down or bouncing ideas off someone else can be helpful.

Pick a Mutually Acceptable Time and Place to Reconvene

Once you have decided to address the issue after emotions have settled, select a mutually acceptable time and place when you can be certain both you and your relational partner are in a state of mind to deal with the problem effectively. Often times we think that if someone is unwilling to deal with our immediate needs right now, then they must not care enough. Instead, recognize that some people need to go away from the conflict in order to calm down and approach it effectively, and therefore demanding that they deal with you right then and there will only make them pull away even more. If one partner is having a hard time accepting that the other person needs to deal with this conflict at a later time, be specific about when you plan to re-address the issue with him or her.

Establish a Positive Tone

Once you and your relational partner get together, take the time to establish a positive emotional climate before you dive into the problem. This step is perhaps the most important for avoiding the spiral of negativity. In fact, starting a conflict discussion in a negative tone or using harsh words is considered one of the greatest predictors of divorce.[298] Show open and supportive nonverbal behaviors such as smiling, using humor, touching, or positioning yourself toward the other person.

Describe How the Conflict Emerged

Once you've shown that you "come in peace," describe the events from which the conflict arose and ask your partner to contribute to your understanding of the latent conflict stage, the time that either of you felt like a problem was emerging. When your relational partner is speaking, give your full attention to him or her and check your understanding by summarizing and asking questions. Make sure both of you avoid **gunny sacking**, or bringing up old problems and issues from the past. If your partner tries to bring up old issues ask permission to table that issue until the current one is resolved. Focusing on the issues at hand can be tricky, but will avoid the type of conflict where you can't remember the original issue you were fighting about!

That's a lot to remember! Try to keep in mind the following six steps to make it easier. You may even consider posting these steps somewhere visible so you can access them when you aren't thinking clearly:

1. *Recognize* when emotions are heightened by being aware of physiological reactions such as increased heart rate, or feelings of anger or overwhelming sadness.

2. If emotions are too intense to communicate constructively, ask your partner's permission *to go away from the conflict.* Be specific about when you plan to re-address it (in 10 minutes, after dinner, tomorrow, when I get home from work, etc.), and make sure you agree on a mutually acceptable time and place to reconvene.

3. *Get a clear understanding* of what your real feelings are. Assess your own insecurities and issues and go through the fallacies to see if you are making unfair or untrue assumptions.

4. Consider writing down your thoughts or talking to someone else. *Decide* on what needs of yours are not getting met and plan a way to articulate them.

5. "Come in peace." Establish a *positive emotional climate* before you re-address the conflict through humor, touch, or other positive nonverbal behaviors.

6. *Apply collaboration*, if possible, by deciding together to attack the issue instead of each other. Explain each person's perspective on how the conflict arose, what each person's needs are and what the ideal outcome would be for both people.

Now that you've learned about your own approach to conflict and some new strategies for helping you experience more positive conflict outcomes, you can hopefully approach difficult relationship situations with greater confidence. However, your work is far from over. One of the keys to successful relationships is not only managing communication in times of trouble, but applying good communication skills during everyday normal interactions. The next chapter will suggest methods for creating an overall positive communication climate in your interpersonal relationships during both good and bad times.

CHAPTER SUMMARY

The first half of this chapter was dedicated to explaining what conflict is and dispelling some conflict myths that may affect how you approach conflict, including the myths that conflict can always be avoided, that conflict arises from misunderstanding, conflict can always be resolved, and that conflict is a sign of a troubled interpersonal relationship. Three types of conflict were outlined including pseudo conflict, simple conflict, and ego conflict. Next, the stages of conflict were explained to help you understand some common trends in conflict escalation and resolution. Constructive conflict was distinguished from destructive conflict and each of the conflict styles were described, including avoidance, accommodation, competition, compromise, and collaboration. Finally, the chapter concluded by acknowledging the powerful role of emotions in conflict. It was suggested that you avoid debilitative fallacies of thinking and utilize specific conflict management skills in order to keep your relationship intact, even when conflict arises.

CHAPTER ACTIVITIES

TEST YOUR UNDERSTANDING

True or False

_____ 1. Most dyads do not solve conflict issues; instead they manage the conflict issue.

_____ 2. Assertiveness is described as only considering the other person's needs while ignoring your own needs.

_____ 3. The U.S. has fewer incidents of violent crimes than other industrialized nations, which may be because Americans have a less aggressive conflict style than people in other countries.

Multiple Choice: Circle the best answer choice.

1. Jenny has high concern for others, but low concern for herself. She manages conflict by giving in to the demands of others, often at the expense of meeting her own needs. Her conflict style is:

    A. Compromising

    B. Accommodation

    C. Avoidance

    D. Collaboration

    E. None of the above

2. Which of the statements below are NOT true:

    A. The best way to get rid of an online troll is to ignore him.

    B. Trolls are insecure bullies.

    C. Trolls can cause emotional damage to their target even if what they say isn't true.

    D. Trolls usually mean what they say.

    E. All of the above are true.

3. Assertiveness requires that you do three things. Which of the following is NOT one of those things:

    A. Identify and express your own needs.

    B. Identify or ask about the other person's needs.

    C. Try to compromise or collaborate on a solution that meets both sets of needs.

    D. Evaluate whether the other person's needs are logical or legitimate.

    E. All of the above are requirements of assertiveness.

**Answers are listed at the end of this section before the references.

Short Answer

1. Identify what makes a conflict constructive versus destructive.

_____

_____

_____

_____

_____

_____

_____

_____

_____

_____

_____

2. Summarize the types and stages of conflict.

_____

_____

_____

_____

_____

_____

_____

_____

_____

_____

3. Describe your individual conflict style and identify that of one important person in your life.

    _____

    _____

    _____

    _____

    _____

    _____

    _____

    _____

    _____

    _____

    _____

    _____

    _____

4. Explain the effect your emotions have on how you handle conflict.

    _____

    _____

    _____

    _____

    _____

    _____

    _____

    _____

    _____

    _____

    _____

    _____

5. Explain the strategies to manage emotions and increase the likelihood of constructive conflict.

_____

_____

_____

_____

_____

_____

_____

_____

_____

_____

_____

_____

_____

_____

_____

_____

_____

_____

_____

_____

_____

_____

_____

_____

IN-CLASS ACTIVITY

Implicit Theories of Conflict

What are your "implicit theories" about conflict? Write down at least five "rules" about conflict that are prevalent in your family's interactions.

Examples

- Don't fight in front of children.

- Don't go to bed angry.

- Don't use profanity.

- Agree with Dad no matter what he says.

1. _____

2. _____

3. _____

4. _____

5. _____

Explain which of these are useful, and which ones do not serve you well:

_____

_____

_____

_____

_____

_____

_____

_____

_____

_____

_____

SKILL PRACTICE: ASSERTIVENESS

What Is the Goal of Assertiveness?

The goal of assertiveness is to clearly communicate your own needs and also attempt to meet the needs of the other person.

How Do You Do It?

Replace the focus from being entirely on your needs (aggressiveness) or entirely on the other person's needs (non-assertiveness) by:

1. **Stating** your needs without demanding (aggressiveness) or apologizing (non-assertiveness).

   Example: "It's really important to me that we invite my parents on this vacation."

2. **Asking** the other person what his/her needs are and what you can do to help meet his/her needs.

   Example: "What kind of vacation do you want?"

3. **Applying** compromise or collaboration to get both needs met.

   Example: "Let's see if we can plan a trip where we have at least a couple of days alone. We could also stay at a different hotel than my parents. How does that sound?"

Write out a dialogue where you practiced the skill of assertiveness:

_____

_____

_____

_____

_____

_____

_____

_____

_____

_____

_____

_____

_____

_____

HOMEWORK ACTIVITY

Needs Analysis

Think about the last "simple" conflict you had, meaning it was based on real differences. What were your specific needs that were not getting met? What were the other person's needs? What outcome would have satisfied you both?

_____

_____

_____

_____

_____

_____

_____

_____

_____

_____

_____

_____

_____

_____

_____

_____

Answers to True/False and Multiple Choice

1. True

2. False

3. False

1. B

2. D

3. D

REFERENCES

[272]Gottman, J.M. (1994). *What predicts divorce? The relationship between marital processes and marital outcomes.* Hillsdale, NJ: Lawrence Erlbaum Associates.

[273]Fitzpatrick, M.A. & Ritchie, L.D. (1994). Communication schemata within the family: Multiple perspectives on family interaction. *Human Communication Research, 20,* 276.

[274]Fitzpatrick, M.A. & Ritchie, L.D. (1994). Communication schemata within the family: Multiple perspectives on family interaction. *Human Communication Research, 20,* 275–301.

[275]Wallenfelsz, K.P. & Hample, D. (2010). The role of taking conflict personally in imagined interactions about conflict. *Southern Communication Journal, 75*(5), 471–487.

[276]Brahm, Eric. "Latent Conflict Stage." Beyond Intractability. Eds. Guy Burgess and Heidi Burgess. Conflict Research Consortium, University of Colorado, Boulder. Posted: September 2003 at http://www.beyondintractability.org/essay/latent_conflict/

[277]Deutsch, M. (1973). *The resolution of conflict: Constructive and destructive processes.* New Haven, CT: Yale University Press.

[278]Pietromonaco, P.R., Greenwood, D., & Barrett, L.F. (2004). Conflict in adult close relationships: An attachment perspective in W.S. Rholes & J.A. Simpson (Eds.), *Adult attachment: New directions and emerging issues.* New York: Guilford Press.

[279]Johnson, D.W. & Johnson, R.T. (1995a). *Teaching students to be peacemakers* (3rd ed.). Edina, MN: Interaction Book Company.

[280]Ibid.

[281]Cummings, E.M., Goeke-Morey, M.C., & Papp, L.M. (2003). Cildren's responses to everyday marital conflict tactics in the home. *Child Development, 74,* 1918–1929.

[282]Thomas, K.W. & Kilmann, R.H. (1974) *Thomas-Kilmann Conflict Mode Instrument.* Tuxedo, NY: Xicom.

[283]NAACP Criminal Fact Sheet: http://www.naacp.org/pages/criminal-justice-fact-sheet

[284]Murray, M. (2008). "Goods and commodities." In S.N. Durlauf & L.E.. Blume (Eds.): *The New Palgrave Dictionary of Economics* (546–548). Palgrave Macmillan.

[285]Weisel, O., & Böhm, R. (2015). "Ingroup love" and "outgroup hate" in intergroup conflict between natural groups. *Journal of Experimental Social Psychology, 60,* 110–120.

[286]McDougall, W. (1920). *The group mind.* N.Y. Knickerbocker Press.

[287]Averill, J. (1980b). A constructionist view of emotion. In R. Plutchik and H. Kellerman (Eds.), *Emotion: Theory, Research, and Experience, Vol 1.* New York: Academic Press.

[288]Darwin, C. (1965). *The expression of the emotions in man and animals.* Chicago: University of Chicago Press. (Original work published 1872).

[289]Tolle, E. (1999). *The power of now.* Novato, CA: New World Library, p. 23.

[290]Kiecolt-Glaser, J.K. & Newton, T.L. (2001) Marriage and health: His and hers. *Psychological Bulletin, 127*(4), 472–503.

[291]Nisbett, R. (1993). Violence and U.S. regional culture. *American Psychologist,* 48, 411–449.

[292]Ekman, P., Sorenson, E.R., & Friesen, W.V. (1969). Pan-cultural elements in facial displays of emotions. *Science, 164,* 86–88.

[293]Damasio, A. (1994). *Descartes''s error: Emotion, reason, and the human brain.* New York: Gosset/Putnam.

[294]Kiecolt-Glaser, J.K., Newton, T., Cacioppo, J.T., MacCallum R.C, Glaser, R., & Malarkey, W.B. (1996). Marital conflict and endocrine function: Are men really more physiologically affected than women? *Journal of Consulting and Clinical Psychology, 64*(2), 324–332.

[295]Gottman, J. (2004, May 14). Interview with Edge: The Mathematics of Love. Available at: http://www.edge.org/documents/archive/edge159.html

[296]Ibid.

[297]Carrère, S., Gottman, J.M. (1999). Predicting divorce among newlyweds from the first three minutes of a marital conflict discussion. *Family Process 38*(3), 293–301.

[298]Ibid.

CHAPTER 10

Creating Communication Climate

"If you don't like something, change it.
If you can't change it, change your attitude."
—Maya Angelou

Learning Objectives

After studying this chapter, you should be able to:

1. Identify the specific behaviors that create a negative communication climate.
2. Identify the specific behaviors that create a positive communication climate.
3. Describe the barriers to effective listening and responding.
4. Determine your own listening style, and identify other listening styles.
5. Describe the difference between disconfirming and confirming responses.
6. Apply confirming responses to improve relationship climates.

A few decades ago, a group of researchers published an article claiming that they had found the secret to predicting divorce.[299] Indeed, this team was able to predict with 94% accuracy which of the 56 couples in their study would divorce and which would stay married. Later, in 1999, some of the same researchers concluded that they only needed to watch and listen to a couple interact for *three* minutes to accurately predict whether or not they would divorce.[300] How on earth did they do it? What were they looking for in the couples' behavior that was so telling of their future together (or apart)? It turns out that we can learn about the likelihood of relational success or failure by examining specific verbal and nonverbal communication behaviors between members of a dyad both during conflict and in everyday interactions.[301]

Over the course of the past 25 years, research in interpersonal communication has uncovered several findings that can provide great insight into your own relationships, romantic or otherwise.

You learned in the last chapter that interpersonal conflict is an inevitable part of having meaning-ful relationships, and that the way a dyad manages conflict helps create the entire tone of the re-lationship. However, some of the most important interpersonal skills are not those we apply in times of trouble, but on a regular basis during the most stable times of the relationship. Regular, everyday thoughts and behaviors combine to create an underlying tone, or climate, in the relation-ship that will cause it to either dismantle or to flourish. This chapter will introduce you to several communication behaviors that are necessary for a positive climate and warn you about behaviors that create a negative climate, so that you can help determine the fate of your relationships through your own behavior.

WHAT IS COMMUNICATION CLIMATE?

CLIMATE VERSUS WEATHER

Long ago in one of your first science classes you learned the difference between weather and climate. If you recall correctly, weather is the day-to-day variability in the conditions of an area that includes such features as the temperature, rain, wind, and humidity level. Climate, on the other hand, is the overall trend of conditions in a particular area. Although the weather may vary, the climate of a particular region stays relatively stable over time; it is predictable. In the same way, relationship conditions vary each day. However, once your relationship endures certain weather patterns regularly over time, they become the climate. Therefore, in assessing relationship health it is not only necessary to take the temperature daily but to examine the overall climate. Is the general tone of the relationship supportive or defensive? Do members of the dyad feel exhausted or exhilarated?

You have probably spent time with a couple that was really hard to be around. Something about the way they related to each other just put everyone else on edge. It is likely that this indefinable discomfort had to do with the couple's relational climate. In contrast, you've probably witnessed a conflict between two people that have an otherwise stable relationship, and thought to yourself, "They'll work it out." This confidence likely came from their overall relational climate. Truth be told, we know a good climate or a bad climate when we see one. However, we often can't identify *exactly* what makes that troubled couple so bad, and specifically what makes that stable couple so good. This chapter is dedicated to making you a climate expert, whereby you can pinpoint your own and others' behaviors that are contributing to your relationship climates, and learn how to manage these behaviors for more positive interpersonal relationships.

CLIMATE KILLERS

THE FOUR HORSEMEN

At the beginning of this chapter you read that researchers believe they can predict divorce by paying attention to certain behaviors between members of a couple. Relationship researcher John Gottman refers to these communication behaviors as the Four Horsemen of the Apocalypse.[302] Although happy couples are also seen engaging in these negative behaviors, the key to their success

is that the negative behaviors are outweighed by positive behaviors. In a troubled climate, negative behaviors dominate the interactions and are not "made up for" by other positive behaviors.

Criticism

The first behavioral indicator of a troubled relational climate is overt criticism. **Criticism** is an attack on a person's character or personality. Critical statements tend to be global, meaning that they rarely refer to an incident as an isolated event, but instead target a behavior and suggest that it happens all the time. Criticisms are usually delivered with a dose of blame, suggesting that the target behavior is intentional or can be controlled. Imagine the situation of one partner forgetting to send a card to his mother-in-law on her birthday. The other partner may engage in criticism by making statements such as "You *always* forget things that are important," or "You are an *inconsiderate person*." Keep in mind that complaints differ from criticism. Complaints are reasonable statements about a person's behavior that bothers you without the character assault and the over generalizing.

Stonewalling

Stonewalling is another behavior that indicates a distressful climate when used in excess. **Stonewalling** occurs when one partner tries to talk about difficult issues, and the other refuses to engage in the discussion. This behavior has an appropriate label, as one partner feels like they are talking to a stone wall. Stonewalling can come in the form of nonverbal withdrawal or disengagement, refusal to acknowledge that there is even a problem, silence, or even getting up and walking out of the room. Stonewalling is usually a response to criticism and therefore results in what is referred to as a demand-withdrawal cycle. Once criticism starts, the stonewaller begins to disengage, which only makes the criticisms harsher, louder, and more frequent, which results in further withdrawal by the stonewaller. This is a very common pattern found in troubled relational climates, and it is very hard to break without the proper skills.

Defensiveness

Defensiveness is another detrimental communication behavior that can kill the climate. People on the defensive usually attempt to appear as the innocent victim; they deny responsibility, and make excuses for their behavior. Defensiveness can take the form of "yes, but" statements. In many situations one partner has an honest and reasonable complaint, but the defensive partner responds with a criticism of their own instead of addressing the issue. A defensive pattern might go something like this:

Susan: "You always leave your wet towel on the floor after you shower, could you hang it up?"

Gil: "Well, what about you? You said you'd clean the microwave a month ago and it's still a mess, now that's disgusting!"

Soon enough Susan's complaint turns into a criticism "I can't get through to you, you are so bullheaded!" And you know where it goes from there... Author Byron Katie says it well when she claims "Defense is the first act of war."[303]

Contempt

Contempt is the final and most harmful of the "Four Horsemen." **Contempt** is an exaggerated form of criticism intended to insult and hurt the partner. Contemptuous behavior shows intense dislike or disrespect for the other, often in the form of insults, name-calling, hostile humor, mockery, or eye rolling. Contempt is using *mean* behavior with the intention of demonstrating your dislike or disappointment in the other person. Although contempt is a quick and dirty trigger reaction to our own threatened self-esteem, it is a very serious relationship offense because it can cause emotional scarring to both partners. An example of a contemptuous statement is, "What was I thinking when I married you?" However, contempt can also be subtler. If one partner is sharing an idea or desire and the other partner rolls her eyes, this is contemptuous behavior. Although this seems harmless, it indicates that the partner does not take the other seriously, and shows general disrespect or dislike. Contempt is so damaging, in fact, that Gottman and his colleagues find that the presence of contempt by itself is enough to predict divorce between married couples.[304]

The Four Horsemen			
Criticism	Stonewalling	Defensiveness	Contempt

Figure 10.0. Gottman's Four Horsemen of the Apocalypse.

GIBB CATEGORIES

Communication theorist Jack Gibb describes communication climate in terms of two opposing sets of behaviors. Defensive behaviors are those that provoke defensiveness from the other, while supportive behaviors help facilitate a positive environment. In the defensive category, Gibb lists evaluation, control, strategy, neutrality, superiority and certainty.[305]

Evaluation

Evaluative communicators cannot explain without judging. When a person's communication includes evaluative "you" language and nonverbal behaviors such as eye-rolling, the other person has no choice but to feel defensive. The positive counterpart of evaluation is description, otherwise known as I Language, which is nonjudgmental communication that focuses on sharing the interpretations of the communicator rather than blaming the other.

Control

Control is the behavior that includes trying to inappropriately manage the person or situation by imposing a solution that both people have not worked toward together. The positive correlate to control is problem-orientation. Problem-orientation invites the other person to participate in solving the problem together.

Strategy

Strategy includes manipulating people and situations in order to get what you want. Strategic communication does not allow for an honest, dynamic interaction because it requires that the communicator constantly be thinking about his or her "next move." Gibb suggests that communicators replace strategy with spontaneity, an approach that allows for new solutions, information and perspectives to a problem or issue.

Neutrality

Neutrality is an emotionless stance that doesn't allow for perspective-taking. Neutral observers are not invested in the conversation or the other person, but instead remain "neutral," or unaffected and unattached. **Empathy**, in contrast, requires contemplation of the other person's perspective and feelings, even imagining yourself in his or her shoes.

Superiority

Superiority is another negative communication behavior that creates a defensive communication climate. People with a superiority complex speak down to others, belittling them and often exercising little patience. Showing equality rather than superiority requires that the communicator show that he or she considers the other an equally important participant through such behaviors as focused listening and asking questions.

Certainty

Finally, certainty is the firm stance that your one perspective, belief or attitude is the correct one, and there is no room for argument or negotiation. Someone who employs certainty leaves no options for problem-solving through communication because he or she will not budge. In contrast, provisionalism can include the general feeling that you are correct, but with the willingness to listen to the other person's thoughts or attitudes and adapt your perspective accordingly.

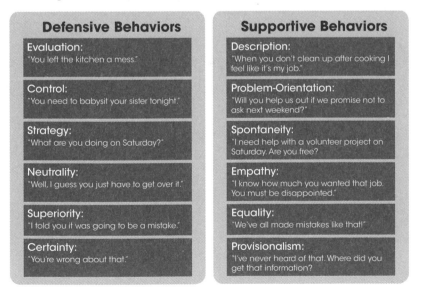

Defensive Behaviors

Evaluation:
"You left the kitchen a mess."

Control:
"You need to babysit your sister tonight."

Strategy:
"What are you doing on Saturday?"

Neutrality:
"Well, I guess you just have to get over it."

Superiority:
"I told you it was going to be a mistake."

Certainty:
"You're wrong about that."

Supportive Behaviors

Description:
"When you don't clean up after cooking I feel like it's my job."

Problem-Orientation:
"Will you help us out if we promise not to ask next weekend?"

Spontaneity:
"I need help with a volunteer project on Saturday. Are you free?"

Empathy:
"I know how much you wanted that job. You must be disappointed."

Equality:
"We've all made mistakes like that!"

Provisionalism:
"I've never heard of that. Where did you get that information?"

Figure 10.1. The Gibb categories of defensive and supportive communication behaviors.

NEGATIVE SENTIMENT OVERRIDE

When the behaviors described above dominate the communication climate, a relationship experiences what is called Negative Sentiment Override.[306] In climates with **Negative Sentiment Override**, the pair develops a negative filter through which they interpret events, and this filter tends to screen out the few positive events that exist. These skewed perceptions affect everyday interpretations of events, and may even cause the couple to "rewrite" their relationship history (See the *Fresh from the Lab* learning box for more on the importance of how couples perceive their history together).

Negative Sentiment Override is characterized by a few specific patterns that get out of control. First, conflict shows a continuous pattern of demand and withdrawal, as described above. These conflicts usually start with one partner (research indicates that it is often the female) aggressively confronting the other, using a strategy that is termed "harsh start-up." This means that the communication is aggressive rather than assertive, which includes the words and/or tone used. The confronted partner responds by withdrawing (usually the male, described above as "stonewalling"). As you'll recall from the last chapter, during conflict men tend to experience more intense physiological responses such as elevated heart rate and blood pressure, and they therefore often experience greater stress during an argument.[307] Being approached with a harsh start-up can set off a series of uncomfortable physical reactions to stress, which results in the need to withdraw in order to calm down. This pattern leads to what Gottman calls "gridlock," much like a relational traffic jam with one or both people honking their horns. Partners resolve gridlock in one of two ways, each of which affects their climate. They can disengage and enter into an apathetic, emotionless climate, usually resulting in a lengthy breakup, or they can continue a high conflict climate, which results in a faster and more dramatic de-escalation and breakup.

INTERPERSONAL SKILLS ACROSS CONTEXTS

Family Communication Climate

We learn our first lessons about communication climate from our families, and we tend to take the patterns we learn into the climates of new relationships as we grow older and detach from our families of origin. While each family has a unique climate, there are several communication patterns that are characteristic of either healthy or unhealthy dynamics. The *family strengths perspective* suggests six major qualities that distinguish healthy from unhealthy family communication climates.[308] They are:

1. A commitment to the family and to the well-being of each family member.

2. Positive communication and an ability to resolve conflict constructively.

3. Regular expressions of affection and confirmation among family members.

4. A tendency to enjoy quality time together.

5. A sense of spiritual well-being.

6. An ability to effectively manage stress and unexpected crises.

In addition to these family attributes, there are two key characteristics that distinguish resilient families from those unable to cope with conflict and stress.[309] The first attribute is called family coherence, which includes acceptance, loyalty, pride, faith, and trust, especially when coping with tension and strain. The second attribute, family hardiness, has to do with a family's strengths, sense of purpose, and commitment to learn from new and challenging experiences.

Together these eight family climate characteristics can determine the health of the family system as well as the personal well-being of its individual members.

CLIMATE SAVERS

POSITIVE SENTIMENT OVERRIDE

A consistent theme in the relationship literature is the idea that perception plays a major role in how people experience their relationships. Like anything else, the way you perceive what is happening around you entirely determines how you feel about it. Research on partner idealization shows that in happy couples, each partner has positively skewed perceptions of the other.[310] Satisfying dating and even marital relationships are characterized by "positive illusions," or idealized constructions of the partner, that allow individuals to maintain confidence and satisfaction by overlooking the often harsh "objective" realities of the relationship. In fact, in happy dyads, partners often rate their significant other more highly than they deserve (as assessed by a stranger) on dimensions of attractiveness, intelligence, and charisma. Furthermore, idealization of one's partner not only makes both people satisfied in the moment, but it has been linked to long-term relational satisfaction. If people interpret their partners' behaviors through rose-colored glasses, they are more likely to employ the "halo effect," whereby even their negative behaviors receive the most positive interpretation.[311] Researchers suggest that this tendency can perpetuate a positive communication climate, and actually minimize the likelihood of destructive conflict.[312]

The tendency to see the partner in the most positive light creates **Positive Sentiment Override**, which puts a positive filter on how couples remember past events and view new issues. Climates in which there is Positive Sentiment Override usually have "soft start-ups" to conflict, especially by the female, in which problems are brought up in a gentle and tactful way. Soothing is also a common behavior during conflict, which includes using humor and verbal or physical affection during an argument to keep overwhelming negative emotions in check. Finally, attempts to compromise are common during conflict in a climate characterized by Positive Sentiment Override. These couples avoid gridlock by trying to explore the underlying reason for the conflict and focusing on a way to meet both partners' needs.

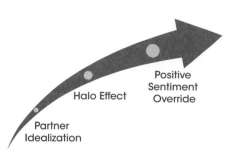

Figure 10.2. Partner idealization leads to the halo effect, which creates a climate of Positive Sentiment Override.

Telling "Our Story"

One popular measure for assessing relationship climate is the Oral History Interview (OHI). In the OHI,[313] a researcher asks the couple to tell their relationship story, including how they met, and a particular struggle they have endured together. During the telling of these relationship stories each partner's verbal and nonverbal behavior is recorded and analyzed according to whether it is positive or negative.

In the category of positive behaviors, researchers look for Fondness/Affection, We-ness, and Expansiveness. The Fondness/Affection scale rates each spouse's expressions of fondness and affection for his or her partner, and looks for expressions of pride in the other, especially in the form of complimenting. The We-ness scale reflects the degree to which each spouse uses terms during the interview that indicate unity, such as using the term "We" more than "I," and emphasizing shared beliefs, values, and goals. The Expansiveness scale measures how expressive and expansive the spouses are in the interview by looking at how each spouse responds to and expands on what his or her partner is saying.

Another set of behaviors and perceptions analyzed by the Oral History Interview take a negative form. These are Negativity and Disappointment/Disillusionment. The Negativity scale measures the extent to which spouses are critical of their partners, are vague about what attracted them to their partners, and display negative emotional expression toward their partners. The Disappointment and Disillusionment scale assesses the degree to which each member of the couple expresses depression about the relationship or an inability to articulate what makes it worthwhile.[314]

Finally, there are three subscales of the Oral History Interview that evaluate information about how the couple reports handling marital conflict. These are Glorifying the Struggle, Chaos, and Volatility. Couples who tell the story of a struggle, but emphasize the positive outcome, how it made them closer, or how it was a blessing in disguise, are "glorifying the struggle." These pairs have a better chance of staying together than those who do not. Alternatively, couples that focus on the negative outcome of a situation, fail to see anything positive about it, and seem distressed or hopeless when recounting the event, tend not to last. Couples who glorify may have endured even worse relationship tragedy than those who do not glorify, but the difference is in their perception of the hardships. Another dimension that is closely related to glorifying the struggle is the Chaos dimension. Couples who have a high rating of "Chaos" talk about their relationship as if it is not in their control or has

been negatively impacted by external forces. The Volatility scale measures the intensity of feelings toward each other. Highly volatile couples express feeling intense passion for each other, but they fight frequently and with equal intensity.[315] Clearly, the perceptual frameworks individuals have for the past shape the expectations they have for their partners and determine their own behaviors in the future. Thus, understanding how a dyad tells their relationship stories allows for predictions about what their future will be like.

FIVE TO ONE

Marital counselors have found that couples who divorce early tend to have identifiably negative emotional communication patterns, but couples that divorce later do not necessarily have negative communication but rather an *absence* of positive communication toward each other. Therefore, behaviors such as The Four Horsemen (criticism, stonewalling, defensiveness, and contempt) need not be overtly present for a climate to be negative; instead the climate might be characterized by the *absence* of positive behaviors.

Marriage researchers have boiled this down to a pretty simple calculation: they find that stable relationships have a "five to one" ratio of positive to negative interactions.[316] This means that for every one negative behavior such as criticism or contempt, there are five equally important and meaningful positive behaviors such as affection, compliments, or praise. Interestingly, they suggest that this is the bare minimum in order to just *maintain* the relationship: in couples that have a particularly satisfying relationship, positive comments and behaviors outweigh negative ones about twenty to one! Of course, relationship partners are not counting the positive and negative behaviors; they happen as a natural side effect of the positive or negative climate. Because the climate has such a powerful impact on positive or negative communication behaviors, researchers easily can add them up just by observing regular interactions.

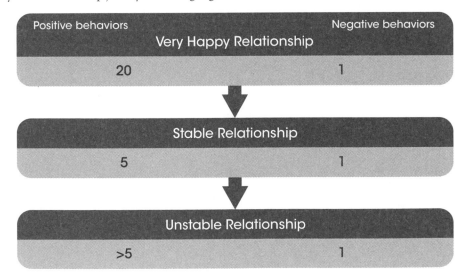

Figure 10.3. The ratio of positive to negative behaviors between individuals affects the stability of the relationship.

WATCH AND LEARN

View a TED Talk on satisfaction in romantic relationships by typing this into your browser: TED Talk the secret to desire.

MEDIATED INTERPERSONAL COMMUNICATION: CLIMATE SAVER OR KILLER?

Sometimes you probably feel like your relationships are better because of your frequent access to the Internet and/or a cell phone. However, it's worth asking whether there is such a thing as too much mediated communication. Indeed, there is a link between heavy reliance on mediated communication and conditions including depression, loneliness, and social anxiety.[317] People who spend excessive time communicating with others on the Internet may begin to experience problems at school or work and withdraw further from their offline relationships.[318] Many people who pursue exclusively online social contacts do so because they have social anxiety or low social skill to begin with. For these people, retreating further from offline relationships may diminish their already low social skills.

There are two competing hypotheses for how people use mediated communication tools for social interaction, especially social networking. The *displacement hypothesis* suggests that we tend to replace face-to-face interactions with mediated ones. On the other hand, the *increase hypothesis* argues that social media only augment our face-to-face relationships, simply adding more communication tools, allowing for a more open climate. As it turns out, most of us use mediated communication according to our personalities: people with social anxiety or shyness often use it instead of face-to-face social interaction, while those who need a lot of human contact use it to increase their social interaction.

While trying to attend to some relationships online you may be neglecting those that are primarily face-to-face. People who live in the same household such as husbands, wives, and their children, commonly complain about the excessive use of Internet and texting that detracts from their face-to-face relationships with one another. Researchers have been especially interested in determining when cyber communication crosses the bridge from normal to excessive. When it becomes excessive, it can damage the climates of face-to-face relationships. Danger signs of excessive Internet use include:

■ Failure to resist the urge to use the Internet.

■ Increase in time needed online to achieve satisfaction.

- Time of Internet use exceeds the amount anticipated or intended.

- Failure in attempts to reduce Internet use.

- Internet use results in failure to fulfill responsibilities at work, home, or school.

- Important social or recreational activities are given up or reduced.[319]

Although experts disagree about whether Internet Addiction Disorder (IAD) is a certifiable addiction, or just a symptom of another issue, they suggest several strategies for reining in excessive Internet use. Unlike other addictions such as those to drugs and alcohol, treatment for Internet addiction focuses on moderation and controlled use of the Internet rather than abstinence.[320] If you are worried about your Internet use:

- Keep track of the amount of time you spend online so you can assess whether it is too much.

- Insert planned Internet time into your daily schedule and see if you can stick to it.

- Make a list of problems in your life that may have occurred because of your time spent online.

- If you do not feel able to change your behavior on your own, seek the help of a counselor or therapist.

MINDFUL MEDIATED COMMUNICATION

Relational Climate across Contexts

Researcher Susan Wildermuth[321] cites the emergence of a new type of greeting card as a clear sign that interpersonal relationships are changing. Consider this cyber card from Blue Mountain Arts:

I can't believe you're mine,
and we met online!
Who would ever believe it's true,
I met someone as wonderful as you
And to think we met….
On the Internet.

The film Second Skin documents the lives of people who have developed interpersonal relationships with others who play Massively Multiplayer Online Role Playing Games (MMORPGs) such as World of Warcraft, EverQuest, and Second Life.

Throughout the film several interviews with participants reveal that they place enormous value upon their online gaming relationships, and many consider them more intimate and satisfying than their daily face-to-face interpersonal relationships. Andy Belford, a World of Warcraft player, met three other gamers online who he now considers his best friends. In fact, Andy packed up and moved from California to Ft. Wayne just to be closer to his new pals.

Although many of these relationships are strictly friendships, some do progress into romance. Kevin Keel, an EverQuest II player from Texas, develops an in-game relationship with Heather Cowan, who plays the game from Florida. Viewers watch their relationship progress from a first face-to-face date to their eventual cohabitation.

However, as the relationship develops intimacy it becomes clear that maintaining a satisfying relationship climate may be easier online than in person.

Viewers are also introduced to the tense relational climate that occurs between couples in which one person is a gamer and the other is not. The pregnant wife of one player displays clear concern about the role of gaming in her husband's life and his ability to be present in the "real world" once their twins are born, citing gaming as the ultimate barrier to effective listening.

You can watch a glimpse of the drama unfold by searching "Second Skin the movie" on YouTube.

LISTENING

Out of all of the interpersonal skills, listening is perhaps the most important, and ironically is the most misunderstood. In western cultures, talking is typically viewed as the indicator of whether someone is skilled in communication. Although choosing your words wisely and communicating clearly is important, *you* already *know* how you feel. So what are you really going to learn from talking? Talk show host Larry King, who has spent over 50 years interviewing over 40,000 people, says, "I never learned anything in my life while I was speaking."[322] If the goal of your interpersonal relationships is shared meaning, you are only doing half of your work by expressing *your* views. The other half lies in learning about the perspectives and feelings of the other person.

Experts from all fields, including communication, business, healthcare, and even sports, agree that listening skills are one of the most important attributes an individual can fine-tune in order to be more successful in all areas of life. Steven Covey, author of *The Seven Habits of Highly Effective People*,[323] chooses listening as one of the seven habits. He advises those who desire to be successful to "seek first to understand, then to be understood."

Author Richard Wiseman asked people who consider themselves "lucky" to participate in a research study to find out what traits these people had in common. He learned that one of the things that differentiates "lucky" people from average people were excellent listening skills. This finding explains the truism: "The better you listen, the luckier you will be." In reality, your good fortune has nothing to do with luck, but rather your ability to pay attention to your environment.

We generally think that if we can hear, we can listen. We rarely view listening as a skill, and if we do view it as a skill, we are uninformed about how to get better at it. While **hearing** is the physiological function of receiving sound, **listening** is defined as a complex process of selecting, attending to, creating meaning from, and responding to verbal and nonverbal messages. Although hearing comes naturally, listening does not. Most people are worse listeners than they realize. In fact, people who

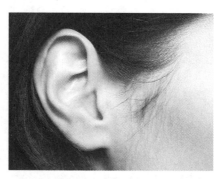

rate themselves highly on listening skills are often rated as poor listeners by their friends, family members, and co-workers. Next, you will learn some barriers that can help you understand why we are such naturally poor listeners.

BARRIERS TO EFFECTIVE LISTENING

Just as your own listening style has the potential to create relational misunderstandings, listening barriers work against you and your relational partner as well. Identifying common listening barriers will allow you to recognize these tendencies in yourself and work to overcome them.

Conversational Narcissism

The first listening barrier is **conversational narcissism**, which occurs when a self-absorbed listener focuses on his or her own personal agenda rather than listening to others. Thus, the conversational narcissist's time is spent waiting for the other to stop talking rather than just listening to what she or he has to say. Often he or she will interrupt or appear disinterested when anyone else is speaking.

Emotional Noise

Another listening barrier is **emotional noise**, which occurs when emotional arousal interferes with communication's effectiveness. Emotional noise can result from hearing certain words that may distract you, otherwise known as "trigger words." Words or phrases that act as **trigger words** are highly individual and usually come from experiences in the past that have caused these words to bother you. Trigger words often include sexist, racist, or derogatory slurs, but can also be as personal as someone's name. Perhaps your friends know better than to utter a certain person's name in front of you (for example the name of someone who hurt you) because of the emotional reaction it causes. This is an example of a trigger word that causes emotional noise.

One study of online learning showed that there appears to be a gender difference when it comes to use of and reaction to trigger words and statements made online. Male students' behavior was perceived by female students as not conducive to a harmonious communication environment. These female students identified a range of male statements including personal attacks and sexist comments. They reported that their female colleagues had never written anything controversial, but their male colleagues tended to write controversial issues and harassing statements. The study found that female students tended to react to the negative behaviors by using three main strategies: ignoring the behavior, posting responses in attempts to curb the behaviors, and withdrawal from participation.[324]

Criticizing the Speaker

In both online and face-to-face settings, **criticizing the speaker** can serve as yet another barrier to effective listening. We form quick and certain impressions of others that may prevent us from listening to their message. If we don't like the way someone speaks, how he or she looks, or where they come from, we are quick to dismiss the message, which acts as a barrier to effective listening.

Speech-Thought Differential

Another barrier to listening is having too much time. **Speech-thought differential** is the difference between how quickly you can think and how quickly someone can speak. The average person speaks at a rate of 125 words a minute, while as a listener you are able to process up to 600 or 800 words a minute.[325] Thus, when someone is speaking to you there is plenty of leftover time to have distracting thoughts and internal dialogue.

Information Overload

Another listening barrier, **information overload**, can occur when you are faced with an onslaught of information that is too intense in quality or quantity, and therefore you either miss important pieces or block out the message entirely. Research suggests that men are more likely to have difficulty attending to multiple messages, while women seem more able to shift between two or more messages at the same time.[326]

External Noise

Finally, **external noise** can prevent you from listening attentively, which is the literal noise of sounds in the environment. If you have ever tried to listen to a lecture in a class where a car alarm was going off outside, you have experienced the external noise barrier. Because we tend to select and attend to noises that are intense, external noise often competes with interpersonal messages, and usually wins.

Figure 10.4. There are several barriers through which each message must pass before it is received.

SKILL BUILDING EXERCISE

Identifying Barriers to Listening

For each of the following scenarios, identify how your own attitudes, values, and beliefs would affect the way you listen.

Example:

1. A classmate is telling you about his extensive music collection that he downloaded online for free.

    My attitude: I dislike this behavior.

    My belief: Downloading music without paying for it is stealing.

    My value: Stealing is wrong.

2. Students in your class are trying to talk the teacher into curving an exam.

    My attitude: _____

    My belief: _____

    My value: _____

3. A homeless person is trying to tell you about his troubles.

    My attitude: _____

    My belief: _____

    My value: _____

4. Your best friend is seeking advice about how to tell her boyfriend that she cheated on him.

    My attitude: _____

    My belief: _____

    My value: _____

5. Someone in your philosophy class is arguing for polygamy.

    My attitude: _____

    My belief: _____

    My value: _____

6. One of your parents wants to complain to you about your other parent's behavior.

    My attitude: _____

    My belief: _____

    My value: _____

THE LISTENING PROCESS

In order to diagnose your own listening deficiencies and improve your listening skills, you must first become familiar with the listening process, which includes five steps. The first step, **selecting**, is choosing one sound as you sort through the various sounds competing for your attention. In an earlier chapter you learned about selective perception; selective listening involves the same processes: you tend to hear that which you are looking for and miss details that do not confirm your preconceived ideas. Have you ever been in a group setting and found yourself selecting certain conversations over others? Imagine yourself seated between two conversations at a large dinner table. You may shift your focus between the two conversations. When you are in one conversation you can't hear what is going on in the other, even though it is within earshot.

Once you select certain sounds over others, you decide to pay attention to them. Therefore, the next step, **attending**, is focusing on the sound you select. You generally attend to sounds and messages that meet your needs or goals, the ones that are important to you, that stand out, or that are intense. So, chances are that at the dinner gathering mentioned above you will gravitate toward the conversation that is the most interesting to you or serves your immediate needs (perhaps there is an attractive person involved in the conversation and you are interested in getting to know him or her better, so you attend to this conversation over another one).

Understanding is the step where you assign meaning to the message. People understand best if they can relate what they are hearing to something they already know (as you may recall from our discussion in an earlier chapter regarding perceptual organization and schemata). Also, the greater the similarities between individuals, the greater the likelihood for more accurate understanding, or shared meaning. Variables we can have in common that assist shared meaning may include gender, culture, age, or personality. If you halt the listening process before the understanding step, you are not listening at all. Real understanding requires that you make sense of the information, what it means, and how it relates to you.

Remembering is recalling information, and finally, **responding** is confirming your understanding of a message. These last two steps were also mentioned in the perception chapter when we discussed how we tend to remember things that confirm the version of reality that we have already created. As we listen, information is gathered in a way that perpetuates a self-fulfilling prophecy. Then, when it is time to respond, we generally respond in a predictable way because of what we have chosen to hear and how it was understood and remembered. When two people tend to have the same argument about the same thing, each person feels like they already know what the other is going to say. They are often right because of the self-fulfilling nature of listening.

LISTENING STYLES

Each of the stages of listening is impacted by your personal listening style. **Listening styles** are your preferred ways of making sense out of the spoken messages you hear.[327] Knowing your listening style can help you better understand how to adapt to various listening situations, and knowing the listening style of your communication partner can help you adjust your style to improve shared meaning.

The first listening style is **people-oriented listening**, which tends to focus around listening to the feelings, emotions, and perspectives of others. People-oriented listeners focus on empathizing with the speaker and searching for commonalities between themselves and the person to whom they are listening. There is some evidence that people-oriented listeners tend to have Feeling and Intuitive personality types as measured by the Myers-Brigg Personality Type Indicator.[328]

Action-oriented listeners prefer information that is organized, to the point, and accurate. Action-oriented listening tends to focus on the big idea behind a message, and these types of listeners may get annoyed with lengthy and unimportant details and stories. Action-oriented listening usually correlates with a masculine communication style.[329]

Content-oriented listeners focus on facts, intricate details, and evidence in a message. They tend to reject or question messages that do not include ample evidence. These listeners tend to be skeptical and they need information to be credible and believable. Content-oriented listeners tend to focus on small details to prove inaccuracies, which means they may be considered argumentative. Researchers find a correlation between content-oriented listening and the Thinking personality type as measured by the Myers-Brigg Personality Type Indicator.[330]

Lastly, **time-oriented listeners** prefer communication be efficient. They tend to be multitaskers who have a lot to do, and they therefore do not like to "waste time" in listening situations. Time-oriented listeners value brevity and usually prefer bullet pointed information that is delivered clearly and concisely.

Each of these listening styles has both strengths and weaknesses. For example, people-oriented listeners are great at making others feel validated, respected, and heard. Action-oriented listeners excel at summarizing a message and getting the "big idea." Content-oriented listeners are good at critical thinking and playing the devil's advocate to see all angles of an issue. Finally, time-oriented listeners are great in crises when the clock is ticking or when deadlines are just around the corner.

Although each listening style has much to offer, when two people of different listening styles enter into an interpersonal exchange their styles can clash. If a people-oriented listener has a personal crisis and calls her friend who happens to be a content-oriented listener, she may not get the empathy she is seeking because the content-oriented listener will likely try to analyze or argue the details of her problem instead of empathizing with it. Similarly, a time-oriented listener may have little patience debating the validity of certain details with a content-oriented listener. For these reasons it is incredibly important to be aware of your own preferred style, as well as the styles of others. Once both people are aware they can each adapt accordingly, and hopefully meet somewhere in the middle.

Review! Listening Styles	
Action-oriented listeners:	A listening style that prefers information that is organized, to the point, and accurate.
Content-oriented listeners:	A listening style that focuses on facts, intricate details, and evidence in a message.
People-oriented listeners:	A listening style that tends to focus around listening to the feelings, emotions, and perspectives of others.
Time-oriented listeners:	A listening style that prefers communication be efficient.

FRESH FROM THE LAB: COMMUNICATION RESEARCHERS AT WORK

Responding to Bids for Connection

When the person with whom you have a relationship communicates his or her needs, you have the option of responding in several different ways. According to researcher John Gottman, the type of response you give indicates your interest, concern, and respect for the other person. Gottman emphasizes the importance of responding to particular types of needs he calls "bids for connection."[331] Bids are any attempt to create closeness between people. A bid can come in any number of forms, it can be emotional (such as giving or asking for a hug) intellectual (such as asking someone's perspective on a topic), or even humorous (such as trying to make someone laugh at your joke). Bids are both verbal and nonverbal, and can be subtle or direct.

On his webpage, Gottman offers a few sample questions to assess an individual's style of bidding for connection. To assess your own style circle your reaction to each of the following questions,[332] based on your relationship with ONE specific important person.

1. I sometimes get ignored when I need attention the most.

   Strongly Agree   Agree   Feel Neutral   Disagree   Strongly Disagree

2. This person usually doesn't have a clue as to what I am feeling.

   Strongly Agree   Agree   Feel Neutral   Disagree   Strongly Disagree

3. I often have difficulty getting a meaningful conversation going with this person.

   Strongly Agree   Agree   Feel Neutral   Disagree   Strongly Disagree

4. I get mad when I don't get the attention I need from this person.

   Strongly Agree   Agree   Feel Neutral   Disagree   Strongly Disagree

5. I often find myself becoming irritable with this person.

   Strongly Agree   Agree   Feel Neutral   Disagree   Strongly Disagree

6. I often feel irritated that this person isn't on my side.

  Strongly Agree   Agree   Feel Neutral   Disagree   Strongly Disagree

7. I have trouble getting this person to listen to me.

  Strongly Agree   Agree   Feel Neutral   Disagree   Strongly Disagree

8. I find it difficult to get this person to open up to me.

  Strongly Agree   Agree   Feel Neutral   Disagree   Strongly Disagree

9. I have trouble getting this person to talk to me.

  Strongly Agree   Agree   Feel Neutral   Disagree   Strongly Disagree

Score your answers by summing your points for each question:

Strongly disagree: 0
Disagree: 1
Neutral: 2
Agree: 3
Strongly agree: 4

Your score for questions 1–3: _____

Scores below 8 mean that you are direct in your relationship. This is great news for your relationship, because you have the ability to state clearly what you need from this person. If your score is 8 or higher, you may be too reticent in bidding. The other person in your relationship may feel as if they have to be a mind reader to understand what you need.

Your score for questions 4–6: _____

Scores below 8 mean that you are not overly forceful in expressing what you need from this person. Your relationship benefits from this quality of yours because it's easier for the other person to hear and understand what you need. If your score is 8 or higher, you may be expressing so much anger in your bidding that you are turning this person away. Maybe this is because of past frustrations, or maybe it is the way your personality is.

Your score for questions 7–9: _____

If your score is below 8, this means you have a high level of trust in your relationship. If your score is 8 or higher, this reflects a problem with the level of trust in your relationship. You may need to do more to win this person's trust. Some people accomplish this by concentrating more on responding to the other person's bids, rather than trying to get the other person to respond to you.

ACTIVE LISTENING

As described at the outset of this chapter, the listening process includes not only receiving and making sense of information, but responding to that information as well. Responses come in the form of both verbal and nonverbal behaviors, and it is often lack of response skills that can create a negative communication climate. Have you ever been listening to someone but you just weren't sure how to show that you cared or were interested? If you want to send specific response messages such as care, concern, and interest this can be accomplished by providing evidence of **active listening**, which is the conscious process of responding mentally, verbally, and nonverbally to a speaker's message. Common active listening behaviors include nodding, utterances such as "mm hm," and eye contact. However, active listening is not quite as simple as it seems. To mimic active listening many people become skilled at **pseudo listening**, whereby they show all the signs of active listening when they really aren't listening at all. Because pseudo listening is so common, it is easily detectable to the speaker and may do more harm than good. If anyone has asked you to repeat what he or she just said, that person was accusing you of pseudo listening.

Often when listeners are trying to show that they are paying attention, they select the easiest type of response: **advising**. In reality most people don't need or want advice; most advice that we could offer they have already considered or could come up with on their own. In this sense, advice can frustrate the speaker because it shows little faith that he or she can handle his or her own problems. Occasionally, advising is an appropriate response, but instead of immediately dishing out advice, consider the following options to show that you are actively listening:

- **Paraphrase** your partner's message by checking the accuracy of your understanding. Paraphrasing should include a summary of the content *and* relational component of the other's message, checking to see if you understood what they are saying *and* how they are feeling. Paraphrasing is different than *parroting*, which is using the other's words without showing any understanding of the meaning.

- *Analyze* the issue with the other person, trying to get to the bottom of it together by considering multiple perspectives.

- Get more information. *Question* the other so that you can understand him or her completely.

- Simply show *support* by expressing empathy and confirming the other person's feelings. Often people just want to know that you understand their feelings.

- Before advising, *ask* the person if he or she is seeking advice.

The words of author Henri Nouwen help summarize the power of good listening without advising:

> "When we honestly ask ourselves which person in our lives mean the most to us, we often find that it is those who, instead of giving advice, solutions, or cures, have chosen rather to share our pain and touch our wounds with a warm and tender hand. The friend who can be silent with us in a moment of despair or confusion, who can stay with us in an hour of grief and bereavement, who can tolerate not knowing, not curing, not healing and face with us the reality of our powerlessness, that is a friend who cares."[333]

Paraphrasing Practice

Imagine that you are having a conversation with someone who says the following statements. Use active listening by first paraphrasing his or her message, then asking questions for clarification.

- I hate my English professor.

_____

_____

_____

_____

- I just don't get you.

_____

_____

_____

_____

- I like my girlfriend but I just can't commit.

_____

_____

_____

_____

- I don't want to deal with any drama so let's just forget it.

_____

_____

_____

_____

- I'm thinking about a change of scenery.

_____

_____

_____

_____

AVOIDING DISCONFIRMING RESPONSES

When it comes to creating a relationship climate, avoiding the wrong behaviors is just as important as doing the right ones. Disconfirming responses cause the other to feel invalidated and misunderstood, while confirming responses show an authentic interest in the other. Let's talk about the communication behaviors that qualify as both disconfirming and confirming, so that you can identify the difference and improve relationship climates by choosing the latter.

Impervious responses fail to acknowledge an attempt by the other to communicate, and can make the other person feel awkward or embarrassed. When someone seems not to hear you even though they are within earshot, or when they clearly hear you but say nothing in return, you are receiving an impervious response.

Irrelevant responses show that the person was not listening, which is indicated when his or her response has nothing to do with what the other has said or asked. When one friend says, "Hey, we should go see that new movie together sometime" and the other responds, "What do you want for dinner?" this is an irrelevant response. Similarly, a **tangential response** acknowledges what the other person said, but instead of addressing the comment, it is used to introduce a new topic. In this case, the other friend may respond to the movie suggestion by saying, "I saw the funniest movie with my boyfriend last week." Irrelevant and tangential responses invalidate the speaker and do not address his or her need to be heard.

Interrupting responses imply that what one person has to say is more important than what the other was saying. When one person interrupts the other in midsentence to make his or her own point, the speaker is invalidated. Research on gender differences shows that women are viewed by men as frequently interrupting them. However, recent research has termed this pattern *overlapping* rather than interrupting because it tends to be confirmation of what the other was saying in the form of verbal or nonverbal agreement or empathy. Overlapping is therefore not a disconfirming response but a confirming one, as long as the intention to agree or empathize is clear.[334]

Impersonal responses are an attempt to take an objective or intellectual approach to the other person's need. For example, if you approach a friend with a problem and her response comes in the form of a philosophical mantra or religious scripture, you may feel like the advice is impersonal and generic. Impersonal responses can also come in the form of using the third person, such as "If one needed a vacation so badly, wouldn't it indicate that one may be working too hard?" This type of response makes the speaker feel inferior and patronized.

Incoherent responses are inconsistent with the accompanying nonverbal behavior. If your friend responds in favor of your idea, but he looks disappointed, he is sending a mixed message, or an incoherent response. People often send incoherent responses intentionally, when they are too afraid to disagree with the other but want to communicate their unhappiness in a subtle way. Remember, we tend to pay greater attention to nonverbal messages, so this form of communication is not as subtle as you might think.

USING CONFIRMING RESPONSES

There are four levels of verbal responses you can give someone when he or she seeks your attention and support, and each level of response increases in interest and effort. We usually rely on **acknowledgement** as a default response, which is simple recognition of the speaker's existence. When Elise tells her husband Jonathan that she's been thinking they should take a vacation together, and he simply responds by uttering "mm hm," this is acknowledgement. If communication between two people tends to follow this pattern, it sets the stage for one or both people feeling rejected or disappointed most of the time. Although it is polite to acknowledge the speaker, it doesn't take much effort or consideration.

Agreement is the second level of response, which communicates that you think the other person is right about something to which they have brought your attention. If Jonathan responds by saying, "I agree, we should take a vacation sometime soon," he is showing agreement. Although you shouldn't use an agreement response when you don't actually agree, if you do agree you should say so.

Support is the third level, which shows that you are interested in helping the other achieve his or her needs. If Jonathan responds by saying, "Well, would you like me to look into it?" he is supporting Elise's idea. Support is especially confirming because sometimes the other person is testing out a new idea and needs support in order to follow through with it. In giving a supporting response you are showing that the relationship is interdependent: your partner's ability to meet his or her needs directly affects your own satisfaction.

The final and most validating type of response is **endorsement**, or sharing the enthusiasm communicated by the other. If Jonathan responds to his wife's suggestion of a vacation by saying, "That sounds fantastic, let's get online and start making some plans" he is endorsing her need. Endorsement is the most validating response one person can give. Endorsement doesn't necessarily require complete agreement. Jonathan might say, "Honey, we agreed that we didn't have enough money for a vacation this summer, but I need a break too. What if we got out the old camping equipment and did a weekend trip instead? We could camp by the beach!" Although this response is not in complete agreement with Elise's suggestion, it shows involvement, and enthusiasm for addressing her need.

In relationships with disconfirming climates people often feel rejected, misunderstood, or ignored because one or both partners tend to do the bare minimum when attending and responding to the other. In most interactions, conversation stops at the acknowledgement level of response. In contrast, confirming climates are characterized by regular endorsement of the other person's ideas, needs, and opinions.

NONVIOLENT COMMUNICATION

Nonviolent communication (NVC) is a popular term for a type of relating to others that focuses on meeting our own and others needs through compassion and honesty. This approach, popularized by Marshall Rosenberg, suggests that by communicating empathy and compassion while attempting to get our own needs met, we can create more authentic and fulfilling relationships. An important part of the formula for nonviolent communication is honesty. According to NVC,

honest self-expression must include both clarity and compassion in expressing needs. This process includes four specific steps, which are:

1. Observing without evaluation, and without judgment or analysis.

2. Looking for the relational component of each person's communication, or the feelings behind the words.

3. Looking for each person's unmet needs being communicated. Here it is important to focus on which needs are not being met instead of whether the needs are valid or important.

4. Making a suggestion for how you both can help get the need met.

NVC has been widely applied to assist in international conflict such as the genocide in Rwanda and the conflict between Northern and Southern Ireland. It has also been used to help recovery for victims of crime, people going through divorce, and prison inmates. Although users of NVC are encouraged to follow the above steps, Rosenberg suggests that NVC can be used more casually, as long as the overall goal is maintained, which includes a focus on what ourselves and our communication partners are observing, what our underlying needs are, and what each of us would like to have happen.[335]

The key to positive communication climate is avoiding climate killers and utilizing climate savers. Now that we've come full circle in this course, hopefully you remember the value of this first skill you learned: I language. You can use it now in combination with the other skills in your new communication repertoire, such as paraphrasing, perception checking, assertiveness, and collaboration.

At the beginning of this text you were warned about trying to teach the skills you've learned to your relationship partners. People tend to feel patronized when one person in an otherwise equal interpersonal relationship takes the role of "communication guru." Although it is not recommended that you try and tell your partner how to communicate effectively, one way to share your new knowledge is through metacommunication. Remember from the first chapter that **metacommunication** is *communicating* about how you communicate. Regularly assessing the communication patterns in your relationship, what works for each person, and what needs improvement can be empowering for both people. A relationship where neither person analyzes and assesses the communication often has very little room for improvement or change. Although it can be scary to communicate about communication, this type of interaction is imperative to maintaining a healthy relationship.

Keep in mind that there is no such thing as perfecting these skills: the challenges of verbal and nonverbal communication are as unique as the individuals with whom you have relationships, and just like your relationships, they are ever-changing. Because of this, communication competence is a life-long pursuit.

INTERPERSONAL COMMUNICATION FOR SOCIAL CHANGE

From Bystander to Disruptor

As you read at the outset of this textbook, most people in the United States feel dissatisfied with the current social climate in our country. Now more than ever, Americans are forced to closely examine real differences between them and how those differences can be effectively navigated. While many groups are performing direct actions of political resistance, very few people are taking interpersonal "action" to mend our troubled relational climate.

Research shows that it is much easier to get people to *not* do something (such as not smoking), than to actually *do* something (such as flossing). This is why most people choose silence over difficult conversations, and a "do no harm" attitude instead of a "speak out against harm" approach. However, when we refuse to speak out against all of the social problems you've read about in Interpersonal Communication for Social Change, such as microaggressions, biases, and injustice, we officially become part of the problem.

The Southern Poverty Law Center (SPLC) is an organization well-known for its research aimed at fighting hate and teaching tolerance. They offer several excellent resources to help regular people understand how small changes in communication can make a major impact. One resource they offer called "Speak Up: Responding to Everyday Bigotry" suggests communication strategies for real situations in our interpersonal relationships where you may want to speak up but don't know exactly how. They present a variety of effective options for how to address hurtful and harmful communication in specific contexts such as these:

- What Can I Do among Family?

- What Can I Do about Sibling Slurs?

- What Can I Do about Joking In-Laws?

- What Can I Do about Stubborn Relatives?

- What Can I Do among Friends and Neighbors?

- What Can I Do at Work?

- What Can I Do about a Stranger's Remarks?

If you are interested in moving from being a bystander to being an agent of social climate change, take a look at the resources on their webpage, www.splcenter.org, which are guaranteed to help you improve your interpersonal relationships, and also improve our world.

Reflection

1. Which concept from Interpersonal Communication for Social Change was the most interesting to you?

2. Which concept did you disagree with or find hard to accept?

3. Have you shared this information with anyone else?

4. If you shared this information, how did others react?

CHAPTER SUMMARY

This chapter opened with a comparison of relational climate versus relational weather. Some particularly problematic communication behaviors referred to as climate killers were identified, specifically the Four Horsemen: criticism, stonewalling, defensiveness, and contempt. Suggestions for climate savers included creating a climate where there is positive sentiment override and employing the five to one rule.

The next skill suggested for creating a positive climate was listening. The difference between listening and hearing was explained, suggesting that listening is a complex skill. The barriers to effective listening were listed in order for you to identify the challenges you face when in the position of listening. Next, the stages of the listening process were covered, which include selecting, attending, understanding, recalling, and responding. Finally, the four main listening styles were highlighted, including people-oriented, action-oriented, content-oriented, and time-oriented listeners.

The remainder of this chapter focused on response skills, comparing disconfirming and confirming responses. The chapter ended with specific suggestions for responding, including paraphrasing.

CHAPTER ACTIVITIES

TEST YOUR UNDERSTANDING

True or False

_____ 1.   Insults and name-calling are a form of contempt.

_____ 2.   People-oriented listeners focus on the feelings, emotions, and perspectives of others.

_____ 3.   Communication climate is the changing day-to-day tone of the relationship. One day there can be a bad climate and the next day a good one.

Multiple Choice: Circle the best answer choice.

1.   Kim often plays the innocent victim, denying responsibility and making excuses, even when Jennifer has a reasonable complaint. Kim is taking part in which behavior?

   A.   Criticism

   B.   Stonewalling

   C.   Defensiveness

   D.   Contempt

   E.   None of the above

2.   The options for responding include:

   A.   Advising

   B.   Questioning

   C.   Analyzing

   D.   Supporting

   E.   All of the above

3.   To show that you would like to help or be involved in something your relationship partner thinks is important, you should use:

   A.   Endorsement

   B.   Agreement

   C.   Empathy

   D.   Support

   E.   None of the above

**Answers are listed at the end of this section before the references.

Short Answer

1. Identify the characteristics of a negative versus positive communication climate.

_____

_____

_____

_____

_____

_____

_____

_____

_____

_____

_____

_____

2. Describe the barriers to effective listening and responding.

_____

_____

_____

_____

_____

_____

_____

_____

_____

_____

_____

3. Describe your individual listening style and identify that of one important person in your life.

_____

_____

_____

_____

_____

_____

_____

_____

_____

_____

_____

_____

_____

4. Describe the difference between disconfirming and confirming verbal responses.

_____

_____

_____

_____

_____

_____

_____

_____

_____

_____

_____

_____

_____

_____

_____

IN-CLASS ACTIVITY

Assessing Relational Climates

Think of a relationship of yours that has an imperfect climate.

Who is the person and what is your relationship? _____

Describe the climate:

_____

_____

_____

_____

_____

_____

_____

If this is a consistent problem, what can you do to change it?

_____

_____

_____

_____

_____

_____

_____

Think of the last time you did not feel listened to.

Who was the person and what is your relationship? _____

Using the terms from this chapter, identify the specific type of listening that caused the problem:
If this is a consistent problem, what can you do to change it?

_____

_____

_____

_____

_____

SKILL PRACTICE: ACTIVE LISTENING

What Is the Goal of Active Listening?

The goal of active listening is to consciously participate in the dialogue in a meaningful way.

How Do You Do It?

1. Use **questioning** by asking for more information.

   Example: "So, how did you react when your boss said that? What do you think you are going to do?"

2. Use **analyzing** by helping the speaker look at the issue/topic in different ways.

   Example: "How do you think he/she felt? Why do you think your boss would say that?"

3. Use **supporting** by validating the concerns or needs of the speaker and showing you understand, without stage-hogging.

   Example: "I know how you feel. Going to work at a place where no one appreciates the hard work you do can be so exhausting."

4. Use **paraphrasing** by relaying back your understanding of the content and relational component of the message.

   Example: "It sounds like you felt humiliated by what your boss said in front of your co-workers."

5. **Ask** before giving advice.

   Write out a dialogue that demonstrates your use of active listening in an important interpersonal relationship.

   _____

   _____

   _____

   _____

   _____

   _____

   _____

   _____

   _____

   _____

   _____

   _____

SKILL PRACTICE: CONFIRMING RESPONSES

What Is the Goal of Giving Confirming Responses?

The goal of using confirming responses is to create a positive and safe relationship climate.

How Do You Do It?

Replace disconfirming responses (impervious, irrelevant, interrupting, impersonal, or incoherent responses) with any or all of the following:

1. Use an agreement response. If you do not agree with the entire message, highlight the part you do agree with.

   Example: "Well, I don't know if Bob's motivation is what you say it is, but I can see why you think you should not call him."

2. Use a supportive response to show that you are in support of the person's need, desire, or idea.

   Example: "I think that it's a really good idea to think about it for a day or so before you call him back."

3. Use endorsement to show that you would like to help or be involved.

   Example: "Let's go see a movie to get your mind off it."

Write out a dialogue that demonstrates your use of confirming responses in an important interpersonal relationship.

HOMEWORK ACTIVITY

Listening

Think of a current problem or dilemma you have in your life. Over the next 48 hours, tell your problem to at least three different people.

1. How many people gave you an "advising" response?

   _____

   _____

   _____

   _____

   _____

   _____

   _____

2. Try prefacing your sharing by telling the person you just need to vent and you aren't looking for advice. Does this prevent people from advising you?

   _____

   _____

   _____

   _____

   _____

   _____

   _____

3. How can you control your own urge to advise as a "default" response?

   _____

   _____

   _____

   _____

   _____

   _____

   _____

COURSE CONCLUSIONS

Try to summarize, in your own words, what you consider the most important concept you've learned about in this course and how you plan to use it to improve a specific interpersonal relationship in your life.

I believe that the most important ~~thing~~ Concept
I have learned during this Course is
~~relational Maitnence Strategies~~, the
relational Climate between people, &
how this can make or break a relationship.
~~to~~ Strategies for managing behaviors that
Contribute to my relationship Climates.

Answers to True/False and Multiple Choice

1. True

2. True

3. False

1. C

2. E

3. A

REFERENCES

[299]Buehlman, K., Gottman, J.M., & Katz, L. (1992). How a couple views their past predicts their future: Predicting divorce from an oral history interview. *Journal of Family Psychology, 5*, 295–318.

[300]Carrere, S. & Gottman, J.M. (1999). Predicting divorce among newlyweds from the first three minutes of a marital conflict discussion. *Family Process, 38*(3), 293–301.

[301]Gottman, J.M. (1993). A theory of marital dissolution and stability. *Journal of Family Psychology, 7*, 57–75.

[302]Gottman, J.M. (1994). *What predicts divorce? The relationship between marital. processes and marital outcomes.* Hillsdale, NJ: Lawrence Erlbaum Associates.

[303]Katie, B. (May 14, 2007). *Mind and SuperMind series.* Marjorie Luke Theater, Santa Barbara, CA.

[304]Gottman, J.M. (1994). *What predicts divorce? The relationship between marital. processes and marital outcomes.* Hillsdale, NJ: Lawrence Erlbaum Associates.

[305]Gibb, J.R. (2007). Defensive communication. In C. D. Mortensen (Ed.), *Communication theory (2nd ed.),* 201–212. New Brunswick, NJ: Transaction Publishers.

[306]Hawkins, M.W., Carrere, S., & Gottman, J.M. (2002). Marital sentiment override: Does it influence couples' perceptions? *Journal of Marriage and Family, 64*, 193–201.

[307]Brown P.C. & Smith T.W. (1992). Social influence, marriage, and the heart: cardiovascular consequences of interpersonal control in husbands and wives. *Health Psychology, 11*, 88–96.

[308]DeFrain, J. & Stinnett, N. (2003). Family strengths. In J. J. Ponzetti (Eds.), *International encyclopedia of marriage and family* (2nd ed., 637–642). New York: Macmillan Reference Group.

[309]Allison, S., Stacey, K., Dadds, V., Roeger, L., Wood, A., & Martin, G. (2003). What the family brings: Gathering evidence for strengths-based work. *Journal of Family Therapy, 25*, 263–284.

[310]Murray, S.L. & Holmes, J.G. (1993). Seeing virtues in faults: Negativity and the transformation of interpersonal narratives in close relationships. *Journal of Personality and Social Psychology, 65*, 707–722. See also: Murray, S.L., & Holmes, J.G. (1996). The construction of relationship realities. In G. Fletcher & J. Fitness (Eds.), *Knowledge structures in close relationships: A social psychological approach.* Mahwah, NJ: Erlbaum.

[311]Mackie, D.M. & Smith, E.R. (1998). Intergroup relations: Insights from a theoretically integrative approach. *Psychological Review, 105*, 499–529, p. 513.

[312]Murray, S.L., Holmes, J.G., & Griffin, D.W. (1996). The self-fulfilling nature of positive illusions in romantic relationships: Love is not blind but prescient. *Journal of Personality and Social Psychology, 71*, 1155–1180.

[313]Buehlman, K.T. & Gottman, J.M. (1996). The Oral History Coding System (In J. Gottman (Ed.), *What predicts divorce? The measures*, (pp. OHI1–OHI118). Hillsdale, NJ: Erlbaum.

[314]Carrere S., Buehlman K.T., Gottman J.M., Coan J.A. & Ruckstuhl L. (2000). Predicting marital stability and divorce in newlywed couples. *Journal of Family Psychology, 14*, 42–58.

[315]Gottman, J.M. & Levenson, R.W. (1992). Marital processes predictive of later dissolution: Behavior, physiology and health. *Journal of Personality and Social Psychology, 63*, 221–233.

[316]Ibid.

[317]Caplan, S.E. (2005). A social skill account of problematic Internet use. *Journal of Communication, 55*, 721–736.

[318]Ibid.

[319]Ko, C., Yen, J., Chen, C., Chen, S., & Yen, C. (2005). Proposed diagnostic criteria of Internet addiction for adolescents. *The Journal of Nervous and Mental Disease, 11*, 728–733.

[320]Young, K. (1998). *Caught in the net: How to recognize the signs of Internet addiction and a winning strategy for recovery.* New York: Wiley.

[321]Wildermuth, S.M. (2001). Love on the line: Participants' descriptions of computer-mediated close relationships. *Communication Quarterly, 49*, 90–95.

[322]http://transcripts.cnn.com/TRANSCRIPTS/0206/01/lklw.00.html

[323]Covey, S. (1989). *The seven habits of highly effective people.* New York, NY: Simon and Schuster.

[324]Meyers, W., Bennett, S., & Lysaght, P. (2004). Asynchronous communication: Strategies for equitable e-learning. In R. Atkinson, C. McBeath, D. Jonas-Dwyer & R. Phillips (Eds), *Beyond the comfort zone: Proceedings of the 21st ASCILITE Conference*, 655–662.

[325]Drullman, R. & Smoorenburg, G.F. (1997). Auditory-visual perception of compressed speech by the profoundly hearing impaired subjects. *Audiology, 36*, 165–177.

[326]Briton, N.J. & Hall, J.A. (1995). Beliefs about female and male nonverbal communication. *Sex Roles, 32,* 79–90.

[327]Barker, L.L. (1971). *Listening behavior.* Englewood Cliffs, New Jersey: Prentice Hall. See also: Watson, K.W. and Barker, L.L. (1995). *Listening styles profile.* Amsterdam: Pfeiffer & Company.

[328]Worthington, D.L. (2003). Exploring the relationship between listening style preference and personality. International. *Journal of Listening, 17*, 68–87.

[329]Villaume, W.A. & Bodie, G.D. (2007). Discovering the listener within us: The impact of trait-like personality variables and communicator styles on preferences for listening style. *International Journal of Listening, 21*(2), 102–123.

[330]Ibid.

[331]Carrere S., Buehlman K.T., Gottman J.M., Coan J.A., & Ruckstuhl L. (2000). Predicting marital stability and divorce in newlywed couples. *Journal of Family Psychology, 14,* 42–58.

[332]http://www.gottman.com/marriage/relationship_quiz/quiz2/

[333]Nouwen, H.J.M (1990) *The Road to Daybreak: A Spiritual Journey.* New York: Doubleday.

[334]Tannen, D. (1994a). *Gender and discourse.* New York: Oxford University Press. See also Tannen, D. (1994b). *Talking from 9 to 5.* New York: William Morrow and Company.

[335]Rosenberg, M. The Center for Nonviolent Communication Webpage: http://www.cnvc.org/index.htm

SECTION 5

Appendices

Understanding Interpersonal Communication Research

Every day your mind is infiltrated with statistics. If you pick up a magazine, turn on the computer, or watch TV you are bound to learn something new in the form of a tidy number, a percentage out of 100, that helps you understand the causes and effects of the world around you. Here are a few numbers you may have heard before:

- 50% of married couples will eventually divorce.

- People communicate over 90% of meaning nonverbally.

- Women over 45 are the most rapidly increasing users of social media.

Where do these numbers come from? Do you believe them? In this chapter you will learn how research is conducted. This chapter is meant to introduce you to social science research so that you can be a better consumer of the information that comes your way. This information is not typical for an introductory text because authors often assume that students trust the information given by an "expert" on the topic. However, to practice critical thinking it is extremely important to assess the credibility of the findings reported in this text and others so that you know how the information is gathered; only then can you determine for yourself whether you agree with it. If the information in this chapter intrigues you, you can take a communication research methods course to understand more about how research is conducted beyond the brief summary provided here.

HOW DO SCHOLARS STUDY INTERPERSONAL COMMUNICATION?

Interpersonal communication research has evolved drastically over the past few decades; however it is still a relatively new field compared to its sisters, psychology and sociology. The first documented research in the topic occurred as early as the 1950s, but the field really began to boom in

the 60s and 70s. Before this time, communication studies mainly focused on public speech and persuasive messages. However, the social changes that occurred in the 60s prompted a focus on personal and meaningful communication, rather than strategic and mechanized behavior. As such, scholars began to ask questions about how humans relate to each other in the contexts of their meaningful relationships. In the 80s the first professional conference in interpersonal communication was held. Soon thereafter, the reputable journals where current research is now cited were established, such as the *Journal of Nonverbal Behavior*. Over time, communication research methods have become increasingly complex and sophisticated, with a greater focus on established theory and methodological designs.

WHAT METHODS ARE USED TO STUDY HOW PEOPLE COMMUNICATE?

By now you have recognized that communication is a complex process, and because of this it can be quite difficult to study. This section will briefly summarize some popular methods for researching the complicated and perplexing topic of interpersonal communication.[336]

All the findings reported in this book come from research done by social scientists who try to answer questions about how people communicate, why they communicate the way they do, and with what effect. However, because the topic of interpersonal communication is such a popular one, it is common for people who are *not* researchers or credentialed experts of any kind to make broad claims designed to teach people about relationships. You may be familiar with some of these folks from television talk shows.

All research begins with a question. Sometimes researchers have a general question they are seeking to answer, such as, "Are there differences in the way men and women use text messaging?" Questions that have no proposed answer are called **research questions.** However, sometimes a researcher thinks she knows the answer, and would like to support her expectation with data. In this case, the researcher would create a **hypothesis**, which is a prediction about what a researcher expects to find. An example hypothesis is, "Women will use more emoticons than men in their text messages."

The method a researcher uses to answer a question depends upon the question being asked. Some questions about how people communicate can be answered by conducting a **content analysis**, which is a method of study whereby a researcher looks at communication to find certain behaviors or patterns. A content analysis is directed at answering five important questions about communication, which are: *"who (says) what (to) whom (in) what channel (with) what effect?"*[337] Researchers can analyze content through several methods. Textual analysis examines written communication, or a transcript of verbal communication. For example, if a scholar wants to find out which conflict management strategies are used by characters in television shows, he or she might examine a transcript of the show and look for particular strategies. A simple numeric count would reveal which strategies are most frequently used.[338] Observation is another method for analyzing content that occurs when a researcher watches or videotapes an interpersonal interaction and assigns codes to certain behaviors or patterns so they can be kept track of in order to make conclusions. For example, researcher John Gottman solicits couples to come to his Love Lab, where he asks them

to talk about certain controversial topics and records their conversation to find patterns in their conflict styles. Gottman's findings are reported throughout this text.[339]

A **survey**, or self-report, is when a researcher composes questions that ask respondents to report their own behavior. For example, a researcher might compose a survey or interview asking a couple how often they fight, and about what topics. Surveys are a common measure used in research, but the results may be unreliable if respondents are not reporting their own behavior honestly or accurately. We are often poor judges of our own behavior, so inaccurate survey answers are often unintentional.

Perhaps the most complex research method is the **experiment**, which is used when a researcher wants to control a situation to see how individuals react.[340] An experiment usually includes respondents (sometimes called subjects), a pre-designed context, various conditions of study including a control group, and sometimes confederates, who are people planted by the researcher to act in the experiment. For example, an experiment testing how couples deal with stress might introduce a couple (the respondents) into a situation created by the researcher (the context) where they have to play a game with a difficult third person (the confederate). There may be two conditions to which each set of respondents will be randomly assigned: Condition 1, where the difficult person is *mildly* aggressive, or Condition 2, where the difficult person is *very* aggressive. There will also be a control condition, where the confederate plays normally. The experiment also usually includes a pre-test and post-test to see if the experimental condition made any kind of difference in the respondents' behaviors, feelings, or thoughts. In our example this would include measuring the couple's level of stress before the game and afterward. Many experiments include some level of deception toward the respondents, but researchers are required to follow strict guidelines to ensure that no damage is done, including a lengthy debriefing session where they explain the purpose of the study to the respondents once they are done participating.

HOW DO COMMUNICATION SCHOLARS MAKE CONCLUSIONS?

Many studies utilize a combination of the above methods, each of which can be used to investigate the same question but in a different way. A researcher chooses a method based on how he or she wants to go about analyzing the data gathered from watching, recording, or asking about people's communication behaviors. There are two major types of analyses in the social sciences: quantitative and qualitative.

Quantitative research uses samples of people who represent the population. From this sample the researcher's conclusions are put into the form of **statistics**, which are numbers derived from the sample that are supposed to apply to the larger population. For example, if I conduct a study on 600 college-aged friends in the U.S. and I learn that 50% of these friendships ended because of lying, I can reasonably generalize my findings to say that about half of all friendships for college-aged Americans deteriorate because of lying. To make sure my conclusions are valid, I can only generalize to people who are from the same demographic breakdown (gender, culture, age, etc.) as the sample I tested; I would not be able to make conclusions for people in other countries, or about friendships of older adults. This type of analysis often assumes people are fundamentally similar and human behavior is predictable, and therefore we can find information about a sample of people and generalize it to the population that they represent.

Qualitative research analyses are more interested in explaining the reasons behind human behavior, and therefore often allow for the interpretation of the researcher to be included in the findings. This type of analysis assumes people are sometimes different, and considers how the context makes each individual episode unique. Thus, qualitative research goes into greater depth with a smaller sample; a representative sample is not necessarily required. Qualitative research is often used to perform case studies, which only examine a few people or situations. An example of qualitative methods can be found in a study where the researcher lives with ten homeless people for a month to learn more about their coping mechanisms, and then compares and contrasts their situations. The researcher does not attempt to generalize the findings to all homeless people, but comments about one group in particular, and often examines the larger social meaning of the findings. These findings are not usually quantifiable with statistics and numbers, as are quantitative research findings.

Mixed methods research incorporates both quantitative and qualitative methods and is often ideal for finding information that can be somewhat generalized, but also may depend on individual factors and contexts. The study described above would be a mixed methods study if the researcher asked all of the people she was studying to take a survey and she used those results in combination with her observations.

Although the past few decades of research have been extremely fruitful, thus far most studies have focused on traditional definitions of interpersonal relationships, with the majority of research focusing on relationships between White, upper-middle-class heterosexuals,[341] often ages 18–21 (since this age group is easily researched at colleges and universities). Future directions in research aim to investigate the many different types of relationships that exist in our changing world. Because the findings reported in this text are limited to the research that has already been conducted, they may not apply to all relationship types such as LGBTQ romantic relationships and friendships, interracial couples and friends, polygamists, Internet relationships, and any of a number of other relationship types. Although these relationship types may contain unique features, there are still many interpersonal concepts and theories that span across relationship types.

WHAT DO RESEARCHERS DO WITH THEIR RESEARCH?

When scientists get answers to their research questions or hypotheses, they are very excited. To be considered an "answer," their findings usually have to be "statistically significant," meaning that is it unlikely that the findings are due to chance. Many types of research such as case studies and qualitative analyses report findings without them being "proven" by a statistical analysis. These findings can still be useful, but you may not be able to apply them to the general public. You may run into social scientists who believe that only statistical analyses produce reliable findings, and others that believe numerical analyses cannot explain the intricacies of human behavior. Think about your own attitudes about this issue: Do you tend to trust statistics, or do you like to examine information on a case-by-case basis?

Once a study produces an answer to the questions the researchers sought to understand, the results are usually written up in the form of a paper and submitted to a peer-reviewed journal. A **journal** is an academic publication that features several articles by different people. Journals are often published annually, semi-annually, or quarterly, which is why they have a year and a volume number. A **peer-reviewed journal** is a journal that only publishes articles once they have been approved by a panel of experts on the topic. This ensures that the article is credible, comprehensive, and free of any false claims. The panel determines if the methods of data collection are valid, if the findings are accurate based on the data presented, and if it is well written enough to be published.

There are many types of publications that do not require a peer review, such as magazine articles, newspaper articles, web pages, and textbooks. These types of publications are reviewed by an editor or team who decide on the appeal and usefulness of the information to a particular audience. In general, you should assume that any information from a non peer-reviewed source is either opinion or a summary of someone else's research, neither of which are entirely reliable. This is why these sources are not acceptable to use in most academic research papers.

Most non peer-reviewed publications cite research published in peer-reviewed academic journals. For example, a textbook is a compilation of what other sources say. An article in Psychology Today will cite the latest research. However, the research was rarely conducted by the actual author of these publications, which is why they are considered "secondary sources." If you cite these works you are citing what they said someone else said. It's always best to read the original source.

WHERE CAN I FIND THE RESEARCH?

You can find academic journals in print at a college or university library, or you can access the electronic versions online through your library's website. Your college library has a paid subscription to these journals, which is why you need a username and password to access them. Below you will find a short list of just some of the many peer-reviewed academic journals where you will find research on interpersonal communication.

An Abridged List of Research Journals in the Field of Communication

American Communication Journal	*Asian Journal of Communication*
Atlantic Journal of Communication	*Australian Journal of Communication*
Canadian Journal of Communication	*Chinese Journal of Communication*
Communication & Health Outcomes	*Communication & Medicine*
Communication Education	*Communication Monographs*
Communication Quarterly	*Communication Reports*
Communication Research	*Communication Research Reports*
Communication Review	*Communication Studies*
Communication Theory	*Conflict Resolution Quarterly*
Gender & Society	*European Journal of Women's Studies*
Howard Journal of Communications	*Health Communication*

Human Communication Research	Human Communication
Interaction Studies	Human Relations
International Journal of Listening	International Journal of Conflict
Journal of Asian Pacific Communication	Journal of Applied Comm. Research
Journal of Communication & Religion	Journal of Communication
Journal of Development Communication	Journal of Conflict Resolution
Journal of Health Communication	Journal of Family Communication
Journal of International Communication	Journal of Intercultural Communication
Journal of Language, Identity & Education	Journal of Intercultural Communication Research
Journal of Memory & Language	Journal of Language & Social Psychology
Journal of Politeness Research	Journal of Marriage & Family
Language & Communication	Journal of Nonverbal Behavior
Quarterly Journal of Speech	Language & Intercultural Communication
Social Psychology Quarterly	Research on Language & Social Interaction
Southern Speech Communication Journal	Southern Communication Journal
Speech Communication	Southern Speech Journal
Studies in Communication Sciences	Speech Monographs
Sex Roles	Women's Studies in Communication
Texas Speech Communication Journal	Western Journal of Speech Communication

HOW DO I UNDERSTAND THE JOURNAL ARTICLES?

There are specific sections you will find in most academic peer-reviewed research articles in communication journals. If you read an article and it does not contain these parts, it may not be a research article from a peer-reviewed journal.

- Abstract
    - A one to two paragraph summary of the researcher's questions and findings.
- Intro/Literature Review
    - A review of all the other research that has been done on this topic.
- Methods
    - An explanation of who was studied and how they did it.
- Results
    - An analysis of the data they collected, usually in the form of statistics.
- Conclusion
    - An explanation of the statistical findings from the results section, in more "normal" language (without all the numbers).

HOW DO I CITE MY SOURCES?

If you want to write or speak about research findings, you need to cite the source of the information. In most social science courses such as this one, you are required to use the style created by the American Psychological Association (APA style) when citing sources. Please only use APA style for this class.

The APA Style Manual shows the correct APA formatting for all types of sources. You can also learn how to cite a specific kind of source by typing *Purdue Owl APA Reference List* into the search bar on your Internet browser.

Below is the APA citation format for the types of sources you'll use in the assignments for this class, which will most likely come from your school library's online database.

Article from an Online Periodical with DOI Assigned

Because online articles could change URLs over time, APA recommends that writers citing an online article provide a Digital Object Identifier (DOI) when it is available (instead of a URL). DOIs provide a stable link that is unique to the document. Many publishers will provide an article's DOI on the first page of the document. If they do not, please skip to the last example in this section for how to cite an article when a DOI is not provided.

If a DOI is provided the format looks like this:

Last name, First initial. Middle initial. (year). Article title with only first word in caps. *Journal Title in Italics with First Letters of Each Words Capitalized, volume number in italics* (issue number if available), page range. doi: list doi link.

Example (one author):

Lee, E. J. (2007). Effects of gendered language on gender stereotyping in computer-mediated communication: The moderating role of depersonalization and gender-role orientation. *Human Communication Research, 33*(2), 515–533. doi: 10.1111/j.1468-2958.2007.00310.x.

Example (two authors):

Honeycutt, J., & Dole, P. (1999). Typological differences in predicting marital happiness from oral history behaviors. *Communication Monographs, 66*(3), 276–284. doi:10.1108/03090560710821161.

Example (more than two authors):

Vangelisti, A. L., Maguire, K. C., Alexander, A. L., & Clark, G. (2007). Hurtful family events: Links with individual, relationship, and perceptual variables. *Communication Monographs, 74*(3), 357–384. doi:10.1109/MCOM.2011.5741161.

Article from an Online Periodical, Found in a Library Database

Repeat the above format but replace doi: with Retrieved from: (then the database URL).

Example:

Wooldridge, M.B., & Shapka, J. (2012). Playing with technology: Mother-toddler interaction scores lower during play with electronic toys. *Journal of Applied Developmental Psychology, 33*(5), 211–218. Retrieved from: https://web-b-ebscohost-com.libproxy.sbcc.edu

REFERENCES

[336]McLuskie, E. (2003, May). *Replacing the qualitative-quantitative distinction with the critique of ideological methodological practices.* Paper presented at a non-divisional workshop held at the meeting of the International Communication Association, San Diego, CA.

[337]Laswell, H.D.

[338]See example at http://www.allacademic.com/meta/p11921_index.html

[339]See summary at http://www.gottman.com/research/family/

[340]See example at http://www.blackwell-synergy.com/doi/abs/10.1111/j.15455300.1971.00475.x?journalCode=famp

[341]Wood, J. & Duck, S. (1995a). Off the beaten track: New frontiers in relationship research. In J. Wood & S. Duck (Eds.), *Understanding relationship processes, 6: Off the beaten track: Understudied relationships*, 1–21. Thousand Oaks, CA: Sage.

APPENDIX B

Social Science Presentations

Experienced speakers know that making a successful presentation requires more than just effective delivery. The quality of a presentation is determined long before a speaker takes the stage. The goal of this supplement is to teach you the steps to researching, organizing, and delivering an effective presentation in your communication class. Here's what you'll learn about:

- Selecting Your Topic

- Organizing Your Ideas

- Providing Good Verbal Support

- Adding Visual Support

- Delivering Your Presentation

SELECTING YOUR TOPIC

A good presentation begins with the selection and development of a good topic and the speaker's understanding of his or her goals. This section will cover the important processes of analyzing your audience, setting your general and specific goals, and developing your thesis statement.

ANALYZING THE AUDIENCE

To deliver a useful and interesting presentation, you'll need to decide not only what you'd like to speak about, but also what your audience wants to hear. Sometimes you'll be speaking to a known audience with whom you're familiar, and other times your audience will be a group of strangers. Your approach to analyzing your audience will depend on what kind of access you have to them in advance of your presentation.

Known Audiences

If you already know your audience (for example, you'll be speaking to your class at school or people at work) make sure you ask yourself:

- What is the age range, cultural background, and gender makeup of the audience?

  - While you don't want to over-accommodate based on stereotypes about any given age, gender, or culture, you should make sure your message isn't crafted only for an audience of people exactly like yourself.

- Given your experience with these people:

  - Can you deduce any information about your audience's educational level, areas of expertise, or socio-economic status?

This information will be helpful in designing a message that will reach everyone in your audience.

Unknown Audiences

Even if you haven't met your audience in advance, make sure you never feel like you're talking to complete strangers. If you'll be speaking to a group you've never met before, ask the person who scheduled your presentation to provide you with some information about your audience, including:

- What is the age range of the audience?

- What is the cultural and gender makeup of the audience?

- What are their areas of expertise or level of education?

- What is their socio-economic status (i.e., lower, middle, or upper class)?

SETTING YOUR GOALS

Now that you're closer to narrowing down your topic, it's time to get specific. Before going any further, you need to determine what type of presentation you're delivering, which is referred to as your general goal. A **general goal** is a broad indication of what you're trying to accomplish. Three general speaking goals are:

- To Inform: This is your goal if you are trying to expand the audience's knowledge.

- To Persuade: This is your goal if you are trying to change what an audience thinks or does.

- To Build Goodwill: This is your goal if you are simply trying to help people enjoy themselves.

A **specific goal** is the reaction you are seeking from the audience, therefore it's more detailed than your general goal. The clearer you are about your specific goal, the better your presentation will be. When writing out your specific goal:

- Be as specific as possible.

- Make your goal realistic.

In being specific and realistic, decide what you can expect to accomplish from a presentation like this one. Consider how long you'll be speaking and what kind of audience you're dealing with to help you figure out what you want them to take away from your presentation.

Example: My specific goal is to inform my audience about interesting research on relational dialectics and suggest how the research findings may be applied to their lives.

DEVELOPING A THESIS STATEMENT

Sometimes "thesis" feels like a dirty word. Many people have a bad association with thesis statements due to their struggles in high school and college English or writing courses. Don't fret! When it comes to speaking, the goal is to keep it simple, clear, and concise. Once you've determined your general and specific goals, writing your thesis is a breeze.

The **thesis statement** is a single statement that summarizes your message. It is derived from your specific goal, but it addresses your audience directly. Remember, presentations are different than papers: Your thesis should be short, clear, and easy to remember and repeat. So:

- Make your thesis statement one sentence.

- Keep it simple. It should be easy to say, and should not include any jargon or flowery language.

- Remember that your spoken thesis statement should use the words "I" and "you" (referring to yourself and/or your audience).

Because an audience can easily lose track of the "big picture," you will repeat the thesis several times during your presentation, namely in the introduction and conclusion, and in transitions that link your main points together. You'll learn more about this later.

Now that you've learned about analyzing your audience, setting your general and specific goals, and developing a thesis, you can start to organize your thoughts into an outline using one of the organizational patterns you'll learn about next.

ORGANIZING YOUR IDEAS

No matter how clear your information is to you, the speaker, audiences frequently suffer from information overload and/or attention-deficit when listening to a presentation for the first time. If you want your audience to comprehend and remember your message, good organization of your ideas is critical.

Think about how hard it is to concentrate on a chapter in a textbook. You may find yourself frequently reading the same thing over and over. During a presentation the audience doesn't get a chance to revisit the information so it's even harder. Furthermore, tuning out or becoming distracted is human nature. Given the fast-paced nature of information sharing during presentations, you should help out your audience by having extremely organized thoughts and frequently reminding them of where you've been and where you're going. The first step is to be clear about the main points you are making in your presentation.

CREATING MAIN POINTS

The first step in organizing your presentation is to create your **main points**. Follow these basic guidelines when designing your main points:

- Use only 3–5 main points.

- Write each main point as a statement in a complete sentence.

- Make sure that every main point is a statement in direct support of your thesis (or, "big idea").

The time limits and complexities of your information should dictate the number of main points you choose, but any more than 5 will always be too many since listeners would find it very difficult to remember more than five main points. Three is the most commonly used number of main points and memory experts suggest that people seem to remember things in threes.

CHOOSING AN ORGANIZATIONAL PATTERN

Selecting an **organizational pattern** will help you have a coherent and cohesive presentation. An organizational pattern is a pre-formulated design in which you'll place your main points. Before you pick your pattern, first determine whether your goal is to inform or persuade (it's unlikely that you'll select the third goal, to build goodwill, for a class assignment).

There is a wide range of patterns from which you can choose if your speaking goal is to inform, but the **topical pattern** is the simplest and easiest to use. The topical pattern will come in handy any time you need to deliver an informational presentation. Using this pattern requires that you "divide" your topic into three equal parts (equal in both importance and time spent on the main point).

Example:

Topic: Key Concepts in Interpersonal Communication

General Goal: To inform

Specific Goal: I want my audience to know which concepts from my interpersonal class I plan to use to change my communication.

Thesis Statement: Today I'll explain three ideas from class that I plan to use to improve my interpersonal communication competence.

Main Point 1: A theory that I will utilize to better understand my relationships is relational dialectics theory.

Main Point 2: A concept that I will remember when communicating is the Four Horsemen of the Apocalypse.

Main Point 3: A skill that I will apply to my communication is perception checking.

Another common organizational pattern for persuasive presentations is the **problem-solution pattern**. When using this pattern, the speaker explains a problem, then he or she advises how to fix it. It can take various forms, with each main point addressing a different aspect of the problem and its solution, or one main point explaining the problem and the two following main points offering two different solutions.

Example:

Topic: Applying Interpersonal Communication Skills

General Goal: To inform

Specific Goal: I want my audience to know how I intend to solve three major communication problems.

Thesis Statement: Today I'll explain three solutions to my communication challenges based on what we've learned in class this semester.

Option 1:

Main point 1
Problem: I tend to act aggressively during conflict.
Solution: I am going to use the skill of assertiveness.

Main point 2
Problem: I jump to conclusions and get angry at my boyfriend easily.
Solution: I'm going to perception check before making assumptions.

Main point 3
Problem: I pick relational partners who are emotionally unavailable.
Solution: I'm going to use what I learned about attachment styles to evaluate my match with prospective partners.

Option 2:

Main point 1
Problem: I tend to get angry at my girlfriend easily and often, and express my anger aggressively.

Main point 2
Solution 1: I will use perception checking before jumping to conclusions.

Main point 3
Solution 2: I will apply the skill of assertiveness instead of using aggression.

As you can see, the same topic can be organized in different ways. To decide which is best, you can take your thesis statement and build main points according to the options discussed above to decide which organizational pattern makes the most sense.

ADDING INTRODUCTIONS, CONCLUSIONS, AND TRANSITIONS

The introduction, conclusion, and transitions should be added to your presentation only after the body is complete (you'll need to refer to the upcoming section on Verbal Support to complete the body). As you'll see, these parts practically write themselves after you've completed the entire body section. Introductions, conclusions and transitions don't need to be long-winded; their primary goal is orienting your audience to what you're about to tell them, and then reminding them of what they've learned so that the information is understandable and easy to remember.

Planning the Introduction

A good spoken introduction is concise while still making sure to include five important parts:

1. Attention-Getter

   The first thing you say should be an **attention-getter** to pique the audience's interest. Here are some ideas for getting the audience's attention:

   - Ask a question. If you want them to answer, make sure you tell them so by saying something such as, "By a show of hands, how many people have had a relationship breakup in the past year?"

   - Tell a story, or part of a story. Keep it short and to the point, since it's just an attention-getter. Consider keeping the audience guessing about the story's outcome until your conclusion, which is called "splitting the story."

   - Present a quotation. This is a commonly used attention-getter, which may mean that it doesn't carry as much impact as other types of attention-getters. If you choose to open with a quote, make sure it's compelling or thought provoking and comes from a source that will have an impact on your audience.

   - Make a startling statement. Surprise your audience (without offending them, of course) by saying something they will want to hear more about. Consider using a surprising statistic or fact.

2. Reason to listen. After you gain their attention, tell your audience why this presentation will be useful or interesting to them in particular. This is where audience analysis is key: show that you know them by saying exactly why they will benefit from listening to your information.

3. Establish your credibility. Tell your audience why they should have faith in your information. Where did you do your research? Why are you a credible speaker on this topic?

4. Introduce your thesis. This is why your thesis is created as a statement you'll say directly to your audience. Say it here.

5. Preview your main points. In one sentence, list the statements that support your thesis, otherwise known as your main points.

Here is a sample introduction, including all five parts with spaces in between only so you can see each part:

> By a show of hands, please tell me how many of you struggle with the need for "alone time" versus the need for "together time" in a relationship? (Pause for audience response.)

> Well, you're not alone, so to speak, but by listening to my presentation you may be able to get greater clarity on this problem.

> Like many of you, I struggled with this issue in my relationship with my girlfriend, but after doing extensive research across reputable social science journals, I've learned some important things I'm going to share with you today.

The struggle between the need for connection and autonomy is a natural part of every relationship that doesn't have to cause unhappiness for either partner if managed through good communication.

The three communication tools that can be useful in managing this struggle include I Language, perception checking, and awareness of attachment style.

Planning the Conclusion

The conclusion is even simpler than the introduction, requiring only three components that will help your audience to remember your important information and have a good lasting impression of your presentation.

The parts of the conclusion are:

1. Restate your thesis. Simply state your thesis again, using slightly different words.

2. List the main points you covered in this presentation. Don't retell any details, just briefly review your main points in one sentence like you previewed them in the introduction.

3. Make a closing statement. Come full circle by returning to the theme of your attention-getter.

Here is an example of a conclusion with all three components, again separated only to show you each part:

Today I explained how the struggle between openness and connection is a naturally occurring part of most relationships that can be managed by applying good communication behaviors.

The behaviors I highlighted were I Language, perception checking, and attachment style awareness.

For those of you who raised your hand at the start of my presentation indicating that you, too, have struggled with this challenge, I hope you feel empowered with the knowledge I've provided on how to effectively manage this common issue.

Adding Transitions

Transitions are signposts that connect the segments of a presentation and serve as a "road map" to the audience. They tell the audience where you're going and where you've been. Without transitions your information can seem disjointed, and audience members actually have a harder time understanding and remembering your message. Transitions occur in several key places in a presentation so that information flows smoothly from one section to another:

1. The first transition links the introduction to the first main point of the body. After previewing the main points, transition by saying, for example, "Now let's get right into the first point..."

2 and 3. The second and third transitions occur between main points two and three, and they tell the audience what they just learned and what they are about to learn. These transitions might sound something like this: "Now that I've told you about_____, I'd like to tell you about _____."

4. Finally, the last transition links main point three to the conclusion. After you've finished the main point and are ready to conclude, try something like this: "I've covered a lot of information today..."

To reiterate, I recommend leaving the introduction, conclusion, and transitions until after you've completed the body of your presentation. To first create an excellent body of material, you'll need good verbal support.

PROVIDING GOOD VERBAL SUPPORT

Verbal support is anything that backs up the claims in a presentation. Every credible presentation must give evidence for the claims made by the speaker, because without evidence the claims are simply a matter of opinion. Contrary to popular belief, your opinion is not a form of support. Most professional and academic presentations require research to find the kind of supporting material that is convincing to an audience. In this section you'll read about some options for types of support to use, and you'll learn how to appropriately cite the sources of all your good supporting material.

TYPES OF VERBAL SUPPORT

Statistics

We are a culture of numbers, or number believers at least. Most people find statistics to be an especially compelling form of support in a presentation, as long as they are presented effectively. Statistics are simply summaries of data, usually in the form of a percentage.

Here are a few guidelines for using statistics:

- Be careful overwhelming the audience with too many figures.
- Put the numbers in an understandable context (e.g., "That means half of this class.")
- Accompany statistics with a visual aid depicting the numbers.

Narratives

Humans are storytelling creatures. We love to hear a good story almost as much as we love telling a good story. As such, narratives, or stories that demonstrate a point, can serve as an excellent form of support. Narratives can be either true or fictional. Fictional narratives can take the form of hypothetical or example stories, while true narratives can retell something that actually happened to you or someone else.

Testimony and Quotes

You can quote someone else as a form of support, as long as that person has expertise with your audience (which you might have to establish by explaining who your source is). Using quotes can be effective if the way in which someone else says something is better than you could have said it yourself. If not, it's best to paraphrase, or explain what the credible source says or believes. It's also best to paraphrase long quotes, since they can bore an audience. Testimony is a particular type of quote, whereby the person being quoted is speaking about his or her opinion or personal experience with something.

CITING YOUR SOURCES

Every time you state information that you got from another source, you must cite your source. Even an honest omission can look like plagiarism, so it's best to err on the side of over-citing rather than under-citing.

You should cite your sources in two places:

- Credit sources in alphabetical order in a "Works Cited" or "References" list at the end of your written presentation outline, and

- Credit sources as you speak by stating the source verbally either before or after you give the information.

When you cite verbally keep it short. Do not give your audience the entire APA reference, but instead give just enough information to make the source credible.

Examples:

"According to communication researcher and author Dr. John Gottman… (insert information here)…"

"The author of relational dialectics theory, Dr. Leslie Baxter, says…. (insert information here)…"

"Communication researchers from UCSD have found that…(insert information here)…"

One way to make your detailed verbal support easier to understand and remember is to complement it with visual support. Next, you'll learn about a few options for creating effective visual aids.

ADDING VISUAL SUPPORT

Presentations with **visual aids** are more interesting, easier to understand and remember, and usually make a good impression when used effectively. In contrast, poorly used visual aids interfere with all of these goals. There are a few simple guidelines to follow to enhance your presentation with visual aids.

SELECTING AND DESIGNING VISUAL AIDS

Your visual aids have a specific purpose, which is to help the audience understand what you are saying. They aren't something pretty to look at or distract your audience from poor content. As a general rule, if a visual aid doesn't directly help your audience to understand and remember a key point, don't include it.

The visual aids you choose should be large enough for all audience members to see. If you are using a program such as Microsoft PowerPoint or Prezi, the text should be large and clear. Select a simple and professional background. A dark background with light-colored text is usually easiest for the audience to see in a dimmed or dark room. Most importantly, don't overwhelm the audience with wordy slides. Remember, they are supposed to be focused on you! To avoid wordy slides follow the 6×6 rule: Make sure each slide has no more than six lines of text and no more than six words per line.

TYPES OF VISUAL AIDS

There are a wide variety of visual aids you can use, including white boards, flip charts, and objects, but here we'll focus on the type most common for academic presentations like the one you'll deliver in class. Most students will be required to use PowerPoint at some stage in their academic career. PowerPoint allows you to insert photos, charts, graphs, and even sound in your presentation. While these "bells and whistles" aren't required for an impressive speech, if you'd like to experiment with these effects you can view one of the many PowerPoint tutorials on YouTube by searching the topic that interests you. A newer program called "Prezi" also offers some creative ways to design a presentation. Again, online hands-on tutorials will be useful if you're trying to learn these programs.

Once you've covered all your bases in preparing an excellent presentation it's time to think about what happens when you're in front of the audience. The next section will help you achieve effective delivery.

PRESENTING VISUAL AIDS

Your ability to control your own visual aids will either impair or enhance your credibility to the audience. A common mistake speakers make is to pass around a handout or object during their presentation. If you put something in the audience's hands you will quickly lose control of the room, as people crumple their handouts or noisily pass something from one person to the next. If you have handouts or objects, it's best to distribute them after your conclusion.

To make sure electronics don't embarrass you, check the room and equipment ahead of time, making sure you know where the on/off and volume buttons are. Be aware of any passwords you'll need, and try to load your electronic presentation in advance. It won't help your nervousness to have a room full of people watching you while you try to upload or download something on an unfamiliar machine.

If at all possible, try to practice your complete presentation in the room where you'll deliver it.

DELIVERING YOUR PRESENTATION

In addition to the credibility established through strong verbal support and an organized outline, your behavior while "on stage" will determine whether your presentation is appealing. The three most powerful tools for delivering effectively are presence, language, and connection.

PRESENCE

The first step to having presence occurs before you even begin speaking. Once the audience sees you an impression has already been made by what you wear and how you carry yourself.

- When giving a presentation, look presentable.

  Appropriate attire is usually one step up from what you expect audience members to be wearing. If you're a student in a class, don't wear a three-piece suit! Just choose shoes instead of sandals, take off your hat, and tuck in your shirt. Consider a clean shave if you're a man, and pull your hair out of your face if you're a man or woman with long hair. Don't overdo it, just clean yourself up a little to show some professionalism.

- Speak with confidence and authority.

   Speak as if you are the expert in the room on this topic—because you are! By the time you have thoroughly researched your topic, no one in the audience should know more about your subject than you do. Convince us that you have something really compelling to share.

- Stand and move effectively.

   Stand up straight, don't fidget. If the situation allows, don't get attached to one stance, but instead use the entire stage. Consider moving strategically by walking to a different area of the stage for each main point. Your audience will pay greater attention if you move around.

LANGUAGE

- Use appropriate language.

   Since this is an academic presentation, you'll want to speak professionally rather than casually. Imagine that you are at a conference with scholars who are interested in this topic. Use audience-appropriate vocabulary, meaning that you should speak at your audience's knowledge level and define anything that may be unclear to them.

- Speak clearly.

   Enunciate so that your words are clear, and pronounce words correctly. Practice hard words in advance so that you aren't saying them out loud for the first time in front of an audience.

   Speak loudly enough so that everyone in the back can hear you.

- Avoid disfluencies.

   Disfluencies are sounds or words that have no purpose and are used to fill silent space or channel nervousness. An occasional "um" won't kill your presentation, but when "um" becomes a repetitive nervous tick it's highly distracting and can ruin your credibility. If you tend to say "um" or "like" a lot, practice in front of a friend and have her raise her hand each time you utter a disfluency. Consider writing yourself reminders on your note cards or outline that say "no LIKES!!" or "Avoid ums!!"

CONNECTION

The final tip for powerful delivery is to connect with your audience. Like most tips suggested here, there are things you can do in advance to facilitate the connection you're seeking.

- Use the extemporaneous model.

   The most disconnected style of delivery tends to be the manuscript style, which is read from a paper. A close second would be the memorized style, which is recited word for word from memory and usually includes one or more awkward moments where the presenter draws a blank and becomes embarrassed. The presentational style that tends to foster the greatest rapport with the audience is the extemporaneous style, which is a presentation that follows a

well-planned outline but sounds slightly different each time it's delivered. An extemporaneous presentation can seem spontaneous and effortless if you've created a very organized outline and rehearsed your information enough so that you truly feel like an expert with something to share. It allows the audience to feel like you are actually speaking to them as people, rather than rattling off a pre-planned script that doesn't include them at all.

- Use effective eye contact.

  Good eye contact doesn't mean staring down the people in the front row, or looking only at the person who is grading you (a common error in classroom presentations). Use what public speakers call the "sprinkler effect," whereby you let your gaze bounce around from audience member to audience member, making sure you cover the entire room. Pick a few sections of the audience and make sure you revisit each with your gaze throughout the presentation.

- Show your enthusiasm.

  Enthusiasm is contagious. An audience can't help but be attracted to a speaker who has passion, and the speaker's passion for the topic usually rubs off on them. Treat the audience like a group to which you already belong and with whom you're excited to converse and share.

TACKLING NERVOUSNESS

Nervousness is the feeling that prevents really competent people from wanting to share what they know through a live presentation. I won't offer you any advice for how to eliminate nervousness because it simply can't be eliminated. It's natural to be nervous because we care what others think about us. Our hearts race because we fear judgment and disapproval, and we all have this in common. So, first, just accept it. Plan to be nervous and know that it's normal and expected. Remember that people are usually the most nervous at the beginning of their presentations and the nervousness tends to become reduced as they get into the groove. The groove, or "zone," is what will ultimately cause you to relax and focus on the message you have to share instead of your own fears. But finally, and this is important, keep in mind that practice will significantly reduce nervousness. The more familiar you are with your presentation outline the less nervous you will be.

In this section you learned about how to utilize specific delivery skills to make your information memorable and interesting to your audience. You read about the importance of self-presentation, language, and connection with the audience. Finally, there were a few tips to help soothe the nervousness that all speakers experience.

ADDITIONAL RESOURCES

In today's world there is no shortage of resources to aid you in designing and delivering an effective presentation. A simple Google search will give you many options for online videos, tutorials, articles, websites, and books. For example, for details on every aspect of the speech-making process from topic selection to delivery, try typing "Westside Toastmasters" into your web browser, then select Education, and then Communication Techniques.

Your instructor will probably have a specific presentation outline he or she would like you to use and a grading rubric that will evaluate your competency on the different aspects of presentational speaking. On the next pages, you'll find samples of both of these items.

The fear of public speaking is shared by so many people because we all share the fear of judgment. The only way to become more comfortable with this important skill is to do it as often as possible. Use your class assignments as an opportunity to fine-tune skills that you will likely use for the rest of your life in school, business, and even your personal life. Before you know it you'll barely remember what it felt like to be an inexperienced speaker and you'll be able to share important information with others, which is the ultimate goal of why we speak and listen.

GENERAL ORAL PRESENTATION OUTLINE

I. INTRODUCTION

A. Attention-getter:

B. Thesis statement:

C. Personal credibility:

D. Audience motivation/reason to listen:

E. Preview of main points:

    1.

    2.

    3.

(Transition statement into body of speech)

II. MAIN POINT 1: STATE HERE.

A. Statement in support of this main point

    1. (Example, narrative, statistic)

    2. (Example, narrative, statistic)

B. Statement in support of this main point

    1. (Example, narrative, statistic)

    2. (Example, narrative, statistic)

(Transition into main point 2)

III. MAIN POINT 2: STATE HERE.

A. Statement in support of this main point

    1. (Example, narrative, statistic)

    2. (Example, narrative, statistic)

B. Statement in support of this main point

    1. (Example, narrative, statistic)

    2. (Example, narrative, statistic)

(Transition into main point 3)

IV. MAIN POINT 3: STATE HERE.

    A. Statement in support of this main point

        1. (Example, narrative, statistic)

        2. (Example, narrative, statistic)

    B. Statement in support of this main point

        1. (Example, narrative, statistic)

        2. (Example, narrative, statistic)

(Transition into conclusion)

V. CONCLUSION

    A. Re-state thesis statement

    B. Review of main points (list briefly, no details)

    C. Reference back to attention-getter/clincher

Works Cited (list in APA format, alphabetical order)

APPENDIX C

Expanding Your Knowledge through Service Learning

Acts of interpersonal kindness are all around us. A pedestrian offers change to a homeless woman on the street, an adult counsels a troubled adolescent, a stranger comes to the rescue of an injured biker. There are plenty of one-on-one settings and situations that bring out our innate drive to help one another.

In 1961, peace activist Anne Herbert advised citizens to "practice random acts of kindness." But this chapter talks about a different kind of activity, called **service learning,** which is not random at all but rather strategically planned. In the following pages you'll read about the nature of service learning and how it can be linked to your learning objectives for this course in interpersonal communication, or any future course you take.

DEFINING SERVICE LEARNING

A good place to begin is by distinguishing "service learning" from other giving activities. Good deeds like those described in the first paragraph of this chapter are usually classified as volunteer work or community service. Other examples of volunteer activities might include walking dogs at a local animal shelter, or reading to children at a hospital. In these models of service, it is common that one person or group of people who have resources, such as knowledge, skills, or money, share those resources with a person or group that lacks them. True service learning is different from these activities. In order for an activity to qualify as service learning is must contain five elements, which will be covered next.

CONNECTION TO A FIELD OF STUDY

Most service learning projects are connected to an academic field of study: sociology, public health, communication, biology, and so on. Because service learning requires a clear connection to

something that is already being studied, the process of deciding on a project is much different than what happens when someone picks a volunteer program to work with. Instead of being driven only by the desire to perform an act of goodwill, service learning is driven by the ability to take a topic you are already studying and find a place where you can help others while learning it in more depth.

To ensure a clear connection to course content, the lessons you hope to learn by serving should be laid out in the form of learning objectives. This means that the goals must be decided on in advance, and each person must be aware of what they are. Participants should check their progress against the original goals periodically to make sure they are staying true to their plan. This is much different from a volunteer opportunity where you come away from it feeling good, and certainly having learned something, but perhaps unable to articulate exactly what it was. Example goals for your interpersonal communication service learning project might include:

- To practice interpersonal listening and responding skills by working with abused children.

- To practice skills for reducing intergroup biases by working on a service project that involves people from another race or background.

- To practice intergenerational communication by interacting with the elderly at a retirement home.

SHARED CONTROL

Another element that distinguishes service learning is shared control between learners and the community members with whom they are working. This means that a well-intentioned student does not simply show up with a service to provide to a captive audience. Quite the opposite: the needs of a specific community are often assessed by its members, not by outsiders, which defines what types of services they would find helpful. Of course the community in need doesn't control the entire project. Service learners determine what they can and cannot provide, and work with the community to assess what projects are realistic and beneficial for everyone involved.

You can better understand the nature of shared control by revisiting our example of communication students studying intergenerational communication through their work at a retirement home. Rather than dictating their own approach, students would meet with people from the home to explore what kinds of involvement the residents would find interesting and helpful. Such a meeting might reveal that what the residents want most is not for someone to entertain them, but to have young people talk with them, and especially to listen.

This example shows how, when the community being served has an active role in the decision-making process, members learn how to identify their own challenges, assess their own needs, and determine how those needs can be met. Shared control also encourages a common goal. Individuals performing the service and those being served are equally invested in the outcome of the project. Research indicates that the effects of service projects are long lasting only when the community members can take partial credit for the results and outcomes.

RECIPROCITY

Another element that distinguishes service learning from other acts of giving is reciprocity. For a service relationship to be reciprocal, both parties must receive benefits and rewards from the interaction. This requires that each participant is a teacher and learner at one time or another in the service learning experience.

REFLECTION

Finally, service learning activities are unique because they include a way for students to reflect about lessons learned. This reflection occurs at three stages: during the actual experience, after the experience, and through continued reflection of this experience in new contexts.

During the service learning experience, experts recommend that you reflect periodically on the learning objectives set out at the beginning of the project. Each participant may be required to write a journal entry or take notes as the project moves along. These tools will help you think about what you are learning rather than simply coming away with a good feeling about the project. Furthermore, these reflections will come in handy once you are asked to analyze the experience in retrospect.

The final type of reflection occurs in the years that follow the service learning experience. Over time you will find yourself applying insights gained from this experience to your life. For example, students in the retirement home project will not only increase their theoretical knowledge of intergenerational communication, but they will take the lessons they've learned and utilize them in their relationships with important older people in their lives such as grandparents, colleagues, and co-workers.

BENEFITS OF SERVICE LEARNING

The benefits that a well conceived and executed service learning project can provide for a community are usually self-evident. However, if you're reading this chapter, you are probably a student considering a service learning experience; so let's talk about the benefits for you.

Service learning can provide a stimulating supplement to the classroom and textbook learning that has occupied most of your educational career. You'll get a chance to see how research and theories operate in the world beyond school as you try to satisfy real needs and solve real problems.

Getting involved in service learning can help you discover pursuits that you find engaging and rewarding. Studying about the importance of listening when serving seniors or foster children while sitting in a college classroom, for example, won't necessarily answer questions like "Am I good at this?", "Do I enjoy it?", or "Does it feed my soul?" But a well-designed service learning project can go a long way towards clarifying whether you want to do this sort of work in the future.

Service learning will give you a set of skills that can help you after your formal education is completed, both on the job and elsewhere. You'll learn how to solve problems creatively and work collaboratively with others through methods of negotiation and compromise. As one researcher put it, "Service learning can enhance interpersonal skills that are key in most careers—skills such as careful listening, consensus building, and leadership."

This comment highlights another benefit of service learning: It can increase your chances of finding a good job and advancing in your career. Employers value job candidates who have real-life experience with decision-making, problem solving and working with others. Most of your competitors in the job market will have similar experience: part-time jobs and possibly a few internships. Having participated in service learning projects will set you apart from the competitors by showing you have the skills and dedication to tackle challenges.

Along with other schools, elite universities recognize that service learning can help prepare students for the tough competition after graduation. The eight Ivy League schools have created the Ivy CORPS (Community Outreach and Public Service), in which students join together for the common goal of connecting service with their education.

In addition to the many personal benefits you can gain from participating in service learning projects, there are benefits to the larger society that are worth recognizing. An overall sense of increased social responsibility is a natural side-effect of stepping outside of your routine and witnessing first hand some of the challenges other people face. Service learners come out of the experience with a strengthened sense of community responsibility, and a greater understanding of our similarities with all other humans. They are often inspired to educate others about what they've learned, so the effects are exponential.

RISKS OF SERVICE LEARNING

At this point service learning probably seems like a win-win situation. However, like with most worthwhile endeavors, the potential benefits of service learning come hand in hand with several risks.

Service learners don't always get the positive experience they'd hoped for, and unmet expectations are commonly cited as one reason for their disappointment. Some student complaints include that the people they were working with had nothing for them to really do that made the student feel useful, while other students complain that they were worked too hard. Other complaints include that the project was disorganized or community members weren't particularly nice or grateful. On the flip side, the group whose needs are being served often complain that students weren't on time, weren't very helpful, weren't dependable, had no real skills to offer, or they weren't very motivated. Clearly, both parties can be disappointed by the experience, especially if a project isn't well designed and well executed.

These disappointments can be frustrating, but there is another risk that stems from these unmet expectations that is especially harmful. Having a bad experience with a community of people can actually increase negative impressions and stereotypes, leading to an even greater divide between groups.

Some 20th-century theorists believed that if two different groups were put together, then they would naturally get along. This idea, termed the **contact hypothesis**, suggests that negative stereotypes between two groups can be reduced simply by increasing interaction between the groups. However, social scientists that have tested the contact hypothesis have discovered that quite the opposite can be true. Sometimes having one group help another group can actually increase hostility,

resentment, and negative stereotypes. Sometimes experience with another group can even create stereotypes that didn't exist before!

Social identity theory helps explain why exposure to another group might create negative feelings about that group. As you learned in a previous chapter, this theory makes three important assertions: 1) we tend to put ourselves and others into categories, known as ingroups and outgroups, 2) we compare our ingroup to relative outgroups, and 3) we like our ingroup to compare favorably to relative outgroups. If this theory holds water, then putting two groups together will increase the chances of each comparing their group to the other, and each group seeking to be the "better" group. You can see this phenomenon in everyday life by looking at how quickly and naturally we make negative judgments about outgroups simply to make our ingroup look better. For example, to be a dedicated football fan you don't have to just like your favorite team, you have to despise the competing team.

One student in a business communication class learned about the contact hypothesis the hard way. James was excited when his instructor proposed a service learning project to culminate the semester: each of the students would work with an at-risk resident from the local half-way house to prepare them for job interviews by teaching them good listening, verbal, and nonverbal communication skills. He was told most of them were chronically bad speakers and listeners, so James knew he would have a lot of good advice based on what he learned in the class. However, what he thought would be a real ego boost ended up being a complete bust. The man he worked with, who was fresh out of prison, thought he had something to teach James. All he wanted to talk about was how "the school of hard knocks" will teach you more than any college class. Finally, when they got around to talking about communication skills, James was shocked to find that his subject refused to practice the skills. After two sessions together James felt like his subject was creating his own failure and there was nothing he could do to help. A week later while watching a news story on early parole James commented to his friend, "They shouldn't let those guys out early. They're all losers."

In this example the service learning experience created negative stereotypes that weren't there to begin with. James went into the experience with high hopes, only to come out of it feeling negative about people undergoing rehabilitation. Unfortunately the lessons he learned were not the ones intended by his instructor. What could have happened differently in this situation to prevent such a disappointing outcome? It's reasonable to expect some negative outcomes unless certain risks are managed throughout the experience.

MANAGING RISKS

Several precautions will reduce the risk that contact between two groups will cause more harm than good.

First, the contact must be positive. Each person should be on his or her best behavior, keeping in mind that they are representing their entire ingroup. This includes being on time, respectful, hard-working, and flexible even when things don't go your way. Not only must the contact be positive, but each group must also be convinced that the positive behavior of the other group is representative of that group as a whole. Otherwise, the do-gooders will be seen as "exceptions" and not representative of their group at all, even though the contact was good.

As an example of how we convince ourselves that likeable outgroup members must be "exceptions," consider the following real-life project: To help facilitate more cooperation and positive relationships between inner-city youth and police officers, programs were designed to have them spend quality time together in order for each group to develop positive impressions of the other. Results of these programs were mixed. In some situations the contact helped both cops and adolescents develop more positive impressions of each other, while other programs had no effect at all. After interviewing participants, researchers found that in the cases where the contact had no effect, both groups believed that the people they interacted with did not accurately represent their group. That is, the adolescents felt that the cops they hung out with were not like most cops, therefore contact with them didn't change their impression of police people in general. Similarly, even though the cops enjoyed the company of the kids, they stated that these kids weren't "typical exemplars of minority youth." In the situations where people saw the others as real representatives of their group, the positive contact was very effective in reducing negative stereotypes and fostering more positive feelings toward that group in general.

Another criterion for making sure exposure to outgroups has a positive effect is that the groups must share equal status and have balanced power. In the example above, when the contact was ineffective it was partially because the kids knew that the police officers had not only greater status, but also the ability to exert the power of their position at any time. The importance of shared control was mentioned at the outset of this section as a critical component in service learning projects. The fastest way to make one group resent the other is to have unequal power. This is why it is so important for both groups to be involved in every stage of the project from design to completion.

Finally to reduce the possibility that exposure to another group will decrease your liking of that group, both groups have to mesh to form one group. For this to happen, each participant must be cooperating to achieve the same goal. Usually if two formerly distinct groups are working toward a common goal they will start to feel like one group. Members of the new "ingroup" will naturally perceive their fellow members positively and come away from the experience feeling united. One expert describes this shift from two groups to one group writing, "collaboration involves re-acculturation or re-negotiating memberships in groups or cultures we already belong to and becoming members of other groups or cultures as well."

The famous Robber's Cave experiment conducted in 1954 shows the importance of shared goals in facilitating positive experiences between groups. These researchers sent 22 boys to the same camp, then divided them into two groups. Each group developed a strong identity, so that when they were put together they were naturally competitive, and each reported perceiving their own group as superior on all dimensions. Interactions between the groups became increasingly hostile and violent over a series of days. However, the researchers then introduced the campers to a serious problem they had to solve together: there was a problem with the camp's water supply, without which they could not survive. The problem was equally important to all of the boys, regardless of their group membership. The common goal of solving this problem dissolved the boundaries of group identities. Not only did the boys work collaboratively to solve the problem, but they did not resort back to negative group-based behavior once they had accomplished their goal. Instead they reported feeling like one group. The researchers noted that after the collaboration the boys

engaged in mixed seating as opposed to sitting only with their group, and distributed rewards, such as candy, equally between both groups.

If all the conditions described above are met, including equal power, positive interaction with representative group members, and collaboration toward a shared goal, it's likely that the experience will be a good one with a lasting effect. In order to further increase your chances of positive outcomes, there are several communication behaviors to practice, and others to avoid. The next section is dedicated to helping you understand some common communication problems and how to overcome them to maximize your service learning experience.

INTERPERSONAL COMMUNICATION SKILLS FOR SUCCESSFUL SERVICE LEARNING

The way you communicate as a service learner can make the difference between a successful experience and failure. In the following pages we'll explore both communication behaviors to avoid, and approaches that boost the odds of success.

COMMUNICATION BEHAVIORS TO AVOID

Good intentions and careful planning are important ingredients in a service learning project. But unproductive communication can override all your best efforts. Here are some communication practices you'll want to avoid while working in this new context.

Ingroup Biases

You've already learned about ingroup biases in a previous chapter. To recap, when social scientists study what happens when two different groups are put together without meeting the conditions described in the last section, the results are conclusive: people show a preference their own group and often a dislike for the other group. Researchers have called this phenomenon the minimal group paradigm, because they say only a very minimal distinction between people can cause them to formulate ingroups and outgroups. For example, in one study researchers had each member of a large group flip a coin, and they created two new groups based on heads or tails. Later, when they asked the members of the "tails" group to distribute a reward amongst all people from both groups, the "tails" chose to favor their own group by giving them more. They seem to have forgotten that their designation to one group or another was based on a minimal difference: how they flipped a coin. There was no real or significant difference between the members of each group, but being divided altered their perceptions.

You may also remember learning about the linguistic intergroup bias, which is the tendency to describe the very same behavior differently depending upon whether the person committing the behavior is an ingroup or outgroup member. When it comes to a negative behavior, such as being late, if it is committed by an outgroup member it will be described as a controllable part of their character. However, if someone from your ingroup commits the same behavior it will be described as a one-time event outside his or her control. For example, when conducting a service learning project if someone from your student group is late, you will likely describe the behavior by saying, "Kim was late." But if someone from the community group is late, you will be more likely to describe his behavior by saying, "Jose isn't a very punctual person."

The same bias occurs when describing positive behavior. For example, consider a group of students working on a service learning project with a group of high-risk teens at a youth center. Over the course of the project the students start to get frustrated with the lack of enthusiasm and motivation of the group of young people. They start to lose faith that the teens even want them there, and a clear group distinction becomes evident when the teens are caught making fun of the students who are there to help them. One morning a student is praising her colleague for staying late the evening prior, noting that she is "far too generous a person." When one of the teens points out that she also stayed late to help, the student acknowledges it by saying, "Yes, you stayed a little late last night, too. Thanks for that!" There is no mention of what this behavior says about her overall good character, instead it is treated as an isolated incident.

These selective language choices are so subtle and subconscious that when asked, people being studied report that there were no differences in the way they described ingroup versus outgroup members' behavior. We tend to believe we are less biased than we are, but our language reveals the truth about our feelings toward our "own people" and "the others." The key to avoiding biased language choices lies in changing your perception of the outgroup, which leads to our next concept, stereotyping.

Stereotyping

Another concept from this course that's important to consider in your service experience is stereotyping. Remember, we tend to perceive outgroup members as more similar to each other than they really are, while we believe that our own ingroups are composed of a wide spectrum of unique individuals, a phenomenon called the outgroup homogeneity effect. From this tendency to believe that outgroup members are "all the same," we develop stereotypes, which are beliefs about a person based solely on the fact that they belong to a certain group. Stereotypes are usually inflexible, all encompassing categories, and are often negative.

Gina, a special education major, participated in a service learning project focused on teaching cooking skills to a disabled adult. On her second day at the project her mentally disabled subject lashed out and hit her. Even though she was warned that it may happen, Gina was so stunned by the incident that she found herself flinching every time one of the other participants ran toward her, even for a hug. Here nonverbal communication toward all of the members became fearful, uninviting, and suspicious. She felt like any of the participants in the group she was working with might become violent at any moment, and she rarely felt safe amongst even the most docile members of the group for the remainder of the project. In this case, Gina assumed that membership in the group "disabled" also meant that they shared the negative characteristic of being violent.

Egocentrism

You'll recall from a previous chapter that egocentrism is a major barrier to accurate perceptions of other people. When communicating with another person we often assume that he or she sees the world in the same way as us, when in reality our "worldviews" may be quite different. Your worldview is shaped by your culture, your age, and even your gender. Experts warn, "how students view themselves in regard to their own race and their social class…becomes the lens through which

they interact with both community members and peers in the service setting."[342] Judging others according to your own worldview, or egocentrism, can result in enormous misunderstanding and disappointment.

Charles and Amy butted heads from the first day of their service learning assignment for their Global Studies class. Their team wanted to put together a discussion panel with representatives from various religions and present it in a community forum as a fundraiser for the Center for Tolerance. Charles proposed that the panel members debate on the merits of each of their religions; he felt like some friendly competition was the best way to bring out the highlights of each religious philosophy. Amy was appalled at his proposal; she thought a question and answer panel would provide a more positive experience for everyone involved. Even during their team's meetings there was a clear distinction in Charles and Amy's preferred styles of communication. Amy's priority was that all team members felt comfortable and that there was peace amongst the group, demonstrating a feminine style of communication. Charles wanted to challenge each member and play devil's advocate when anyone presented an idea, clearly showing a more masculine style of communication. By the end of their project Charles and Amy despised each other. Rather than seeing their problem as a difference in communication style based on their genders, they employed egocentrism, assuming the other's method was "wrong."

COMMUNICATION BEHAVIORS TO PRACTICE

Now that you have a sense of how not to communicate in service learning environments, let's look at more productive ways to interact.

Be Clear

To be effective means that your message must achieve its intended goal. For this to happen your message must be understood, meaning that it should be clear, not ambiguous. If you feel like you are frequently misunderstood by the people with whom you are working, you should review the skills from the chapter on verbal communication, including:

■ Replace abstract language with behavioral descriptions.

For example, instead of telling your group member that her choice of clothes for today's project is "interesting," tell her that her skirt is probably too revealing for working with young kids who are so impressionable.

■ Try to make factual statements as opposed to opinion statements based on inferences.

For example, instead of saying, "These people are so poor they probably can't even buy Christmas presents for their kids" try being more accurate by saying something like, "Parents who make low wages have very little disposable income for things like gifts and entertainment."

Your effectiveness is largely determined by your appropriateness: You will not be effective if you are inappropriate. To be appropriate, your message should consider the receiver, the time, place, and the overall context in which your communication is occurring. To be appropriate, remember these additional skills:

- Recognize emotive language, words that sound as if they are describing something when they are really expressing an opinion.

  For example, instead of viewing assertive males and females the same, people will often use words like "opinionated" or "uppity" to describe an assertive woman.

- Only use evasive language when necessary.

  For example, when dealing with other groups you may be faced with a clash in worldviews that would only anger either party if it were addressed. Sometimes you can give an equivocation, a deliberately vague statement, or use a euphemism, a pleasant term substituted for an unpleasant one, to avoid unnecessary conflict.

Adapt and Accommodate

Adaptability requires that you abandon any prescription for communication, and instead modify the way you communicate depending on how the conversation unfolds. One student describes the necessity for adaptability when working with different cultures, but not in the way you would expect:

> *I thought I had mastered every intercultural theory before my communication class headed to Japan for our service learning experience working with Japanese high schools. We were taught that Japan is a high-context culture, where feelings and opinions are not stated directly. Furthermore, we learned that the culture is collectivistic, meaning nobody wants to stick out. But what our textbook didn't teach us was that the up and coming generation of teenagers in Japan are a hybrid between their traditional culture and what they learn from exposure to western ideals through the media. I've never seen kids who were more individualistic and outspoken! At first I tried to communicate in a high-context manner, recalling recommendations from our textbook and lectures. But I quickly noticed that they didn't respond to me treating them like aliens, assuming they were so different from American teenagers. Once I relaxed and just talked to them like I would to kids at home we were able to really connect.*

Establishing common ground with the people you are serving is one pathway to competent communication. In this text you learned about communication accommodation theory, which suggests that we subconsciously adapt our communication to those with whom we are interacting depending on our goals. If we want to build solidarity with others, we match our verbal and nonverbal styles to theirs. Social scientists call this convergence. On the other hand, when we want to distinguish ourselves from others, we practice divergence by speaking and acting differently.

It follows that one ingredient of an effective service learning experience is convergence to the style of the community group where you are serving. In our example of the project at the retirement home, the students should avoid slang that an older generation may not understand, they should eliminate profanity or any other offensive language they may use amongst their peers, and even possibly slow down their speech to accommodate to the elders.

As you strive to accommodate your communication to the people you are serving, be careful to not go overboard and act in ways that aren't authentic. In the example above, students may run the risk of sounding patronizing or disrespectful if they slow down their speech too much. They

may appear uncomfortable or awkward if they are trying to use the dialect of an older generation. People can usually tell when others are trying too hard, so the goal is to be considerate, but real. Converge as much as possible while still allowing your own identity to shine through.

FINDING AND CREATING SERVICE LEARNING OPPORTUNITIES

You may be thinking that a service learning experience sounds great, but finding the right one for you may seem like a daunting task. The information in this chapter on service learning can only be utilized if you find your way to a good project. The rest of the chapter will present some methods for finding opportunities that already exist, as well as recommend strategies for creating new service learning projects.

Now that you know a little about what it means to get involved in service learning, you may want to start looking for a project that meets your learning objectives. There are many outlets for discovering pre-established projects and finding out how you can contribute.

UTILIZE CAMPUS RESOURCES

The first place to check for service learning projects is through your college. Most campuses have an office, center, or webpage dedicated to helping students find service-oriented classes and projects.

The campus listings you find may mingle service learning projects with volunteer programs and community service events. By reviewing the characteristics outlined at the start of the chapter that distinguish service learning from other types of service, you can sort out the ones that truly have a learning orientation.

If your campus doesn't have a center dedicated to service projects then you might want to ask a guidance councilor if there are any classes on campus that have a service component.

Along with resources specifically focused on service learning, your school almost certainly has clubs and other organizations that may provide opportunities for service learning projects. One example is Sigma Chi Eta, the official community college honor society of the National Communication Association (NCA). The society, founded in 2000, was designed to stimulate interest in the field, encourage professional development, and provide a forum for discussion and exchange of ideas between students in communication. Many chapters accomplish these objectives by creating and implementing service projects. Most local chapters hold monthly meetings where they assess community needs and work together with local organizations to serve and learn. If your school does not already have a chapter, it's fairly easy to start one: all you need is the support of an enthusiastic faculty member and a few interested students. See www.natcom.org for more information on how to get started.

FIND ESTABLISHED ORGANIZATIONS

Several organizations offer a variety of service learning opportunities. United Way is a large non-profit organization that works with more than 1,300 offices throughout the U.S. in helping to meet community needs. United Way works with local government agencies, religious organizations,

schools, businesses, financial institutions, and neighborhood associations to use a community's strengths to overcome its weaknesses. You can log on to the United Way homepage for information on specific projects at www.liveunited.org. For opportunities around the world, you can search United Way International.

Rotary International (www.rotary.org) is another organization that helps people get involved in service learning projects. The organization is comprised of over 32,000 community-based Rotary Clubs all over the globe. The purpose of the Rotary Club is to bring community members together for the common goal of serving, promoting goodwill, and encouraging ethical business practices. Rotary members in each chapter help decide which service projects to take on.

You can find additional established organizations by searching the Internet. Be aware that if you perform an Internet search you're likely to come up with a lengthy list of organizations that range from service learning to volunteerism. Take a look at the following short list of some useful web pages to start you off:

- **National Campus Compact** is a national coalition of more than 800 college and university presidents committed to the civic purposes of higher education. www.compact.org

- **Learn and Serve America** supports the service learning community in higher education, kindergarten through grade twelve, community-based initiatives and tribal programs, as well as all others interested in strengthening schools and communities using service learning techniques and methodologies. www.servicelearning.org

- **National Service Learning Clearinghouse** is an aggregation of the search pages of primary online resources on service learning and civic engagement research in K-12 education, teacher education, and higher education. gsn.nylc.org

USE PERSONAL NETWORKS

Relationships with people in your community, can help you find causes that will benefit from a service learning approach. Beyond the people in your immediate networks, potential leads for opportunities may come from people they know. Asking your contacts to spread the word can lead to an abundance of opportunities. An example illustrates the power of networking: Members of one student team had no idea where to find a service learning project. Each team member committed to telling ten people of their desire to find a community group that needed help. The results were exponential: each person they told mentioned it to a few others, and before they knew it they had at least a dozen possibilities for organizations to work with.

CREATE AN OPPORTUNITY

Working with established organizations is an easy way to get involved with service learning. However, you may want to exercise more creativity and design a project of your own. If you plan to create a project from scratch, the following information will be useful.

Creating a service learning project from scratch can be a big undertaking. To get the ball rolling you can ask your professors whether they might be interested in adding a service learning component to their course, or if they could help you design a project based on specific course concepts. Some classes require a team project but are flexible with the topic. Don't be afraid to ask your instructor

if your group could incorporate a service component into the topic you choose to investigate. For example, students in a business communication course were required to demonstrate their presentation skills by completing a team presentation on a business topic of their choice. One group chose to spend a few days serving a local non-profit organization and then created a presentation on communication skills unique to non-profit work.

TURN A VOLUNTEER EXPERIENCE INTO SERVICE LEARNING

As its name makes clear, service learning has two components: service and learning. Whether you join an existing program or plan your own, you can turn almost any volunteer or service experience into service learning by establishing clear goals and connecting your learning to your course objectives. Make sure you answer each of the following questions in deciding whether a project will qualify as service learning:

1. Is the goal clear?

    Similar to a mission statement or vision, a successful experience has to have a clear intention. To assess your goals, ask yourself:

    - What knowledge will be demonstrated or applied?

    - What is the expected result from this experience?

    - How will this experience augment my learning in the traditional classroom?

2. Are you prepared for the service being rendered?

    Make sure you enter the experience with enough knowledge and skill to make the project successful. For example, if the goal is to study intercultural communication by teaching English to school children in Japan, participants should understand basic intercultural concepts and theories before they test them in a real-life setting. In addition, general information about the community where participants will work is essential. This information can be covered in an orientation or a series of pre-service meetings.

3. Is there an emphasis on reflection?

    If you are designing your own program, you should work reflection time into the structure. This includes setting aside time during participation when learners will get together for discussion about their experience. Questions for reflection should be given in advance, and should weigh the actual outcomes against expectations, and observe how expectations change as the experience unfolds.

    Examples of reflection questions that may provide a good start include:

    - If you could have used one communication skill more effectively, what would it have been?

    - What major communication challenge did you have during this experience?

    - What did you learn about communication that you could not have learned in the classroom?

As long as you set out clear goals for what you expect to learn, and reflect on whether these goals were met, almost any experience can be turned into a service learning project to enhance your traditional classroom education.

REFERENCES

[342]Mintz, S.D. & Hesser, G.W. (1996). Principles of good practice in service-learning. In B. Jacoby (Ed.) *Service learning in higher education: Concepts and practices*. San Francisco, CA: Jossey-Bass. p. 76.

Glossary

accommodation: a conflict style characterized by giving in to the demands of others, often at the expense of meeting your own needs

account: an explanation or excuse made by the person who committed a behavior that is in question

acculturation: the process through which an individual acquires new approaches, beliefs, and values by coming into contact with other cultures

acknowledgement: the most basic level of response that is simply recognition of the speaker's existence

acquiescent responses: can be considered either direct or indirect responses to hurtful communication, and can include crying, conceding, or apologizing

action-oriented listeners: a listening style that prefers information that is organized, to the point, and accurate

active listening: the conscious process of responding mentally, verbally, and nonverbally to a speaker's message

active perception: observations that occur when we are motivated to select particular information

active verbal responses: are verbal and direct responses to hurtful communication, which can include counterattacks, self-defense statements, sarcastic statements, and demands for explanations

adaptors: kinetic behaviors that help a person to adapt to situation by channeling their energy, such as excitement or nervousness, through a bodily movement

advising: telling the speaker how he or she can solve a problem

affect displays: nonverbal behaviors that communicate emotion

affection: the interpersonal need to give and receive physical affection and verbal praise and approval

Agape: selfless altruistic love such as the love a mother feels for a child; this style is care taking in nature

aggressiveness: communication behavior aimed at expressing one's own needs while denying the needs and rights of others

agreement: the second level of response, which communicates that you think the other person is right about something to which he or she has brought your attention

allness: the tendency to use language to make sweeping and often untrue generalizations about a person or situation

altruism: a concern for other people that overrides concern for oneself

analyzing: a response whereby the listener tries to work with the speaker to see different angles of his or her problem

anxious-preoccupied attachment style: people with this style of attachment seek high levels of intimacy, approval, and responsiveness from their partners, which often results in over-dependency

apologies: the type of response that occurs when there is no justification or overt claim of responsibility, but rather an acknowledgment of the offense

appearance: a category in the nonverbal channels that describes communication through how you look

arousal cues: nonverbal behaviors that show involvement and excitement

artifacts: anything in addition to your own physical body that communicates something about you

assertiveness: communication that expresses your own needs while also considering the needs of the other

attachment theory: a theory that attempts to predict how particular types of childhood attachments affect information processing about relationships in adulthood

attending: the second step in the listening process whereby the listener focuses on the sound he or she has selected

attitudes: favorable or unfavorable predispositions to a person, situation, or thing

attribution: the explanation we make for another person's behavior

attribution theory: a theory that suggests that in trying to understand the world around us, we attempt to explain people's motives for their actions

autopilot: a term used to describe when communicators do not consider how they construct their own realities through their own thought patterns, and therefore tend to repeat the same ineffective communication behaviors

avoidance: a conflict style characterized by trying to work around the conflict and not doing anything to resolve or manage it

avoiding stage: the stage of relational de-escalation in which the couple engages in fewer interactions and there is an increase of physical, emotional, and psychological distance

beliefs: concepts of what is true and what is false

bilateral dissolutions: both parties are predisposed to ending the relationship and simply need to go over the details

bold-faced lies: outright falsifications of information intended to deceive the receiver

bonding stage: the relational stage characterized by a social commitment and/or ritual that signifies the intention to continue the relationship indefinitely

business/organizational communication: communication that occurs in the workplace, which can include many of the other types of communication, such as small group and public communication

bypassing: confusion that occurs when the same words mean different things to different people

centralized power: a societal structure whereby power is in the hands of a small number of people

channel: the pathway through which the messages are sent

circumscribing stage: the stage of relational de-escalation in which information exchange decreases in both breadth and depth

co-culture: a distinct cultural group within a larger culture

cognitively complex: a term used to describe people who do not categorize others easily or quickly

cognitively simple: a term used to describe individuals who have very few categories for understanding others so that they tend to see the world in extremes

collaboration: a conflict management style characterized by using a creative and thoughtful approach to achieve the most positive solution for both people involved

collectivism: a cultural value which views conformity positively, and one is expected to sacrifice personal desires and aspirations if necessary for the good of the group

communibiological approach: a theoretical perspective that suggests peoples' communication behavior can be predicted based on personal traits and characteristics that result from their genetic makeup

communication: the process of acting on information

communication accommodation theory: a theory that suggests that people adapt their verbal and nonverbal styles to seem either similar or dissimilar to the person with whom they are interacting

communication apprehension: the fear or anxiety associated with either real or anticipated communication with other people

communication style: the habitual way we communicate with others

competition: a style of conflict management characterized by seeking to win, often at the expense of the other person involved

compromise: a conflict management style characterized by attempting to find a middle ground

confirmation bias: a perceptual tendency where you attend to information that confirms what you already believe, and therefore manage to find all the evidence you need to support your expectations

conflict emergence/frustration awareness stage: the stage of conflict where at least one person becomes aware that the differences in the relationship are causing increased internal turmoil

conflict escalation: active conflict during which one or both people make their frustrations explicit to the other

conflict style: the learned and consistent pattern or approach we use to manage disagreements with others

connotative meaning: the relationship dimension of communication, which conveys feelings and includes the personal or subjective meaning of the verbal and nonverbal behavior

conscious competence: when you are aware of how to improve and you actively employ these strategies with effort

conscious incompetence: when you are aware about the areas in which you lack skills, but are not sure how to improve

constructive conflict: conflict that ultimately helps build new insights into the relationship and establishes new patterns of communication

contact hypothesis: a theory suggesting that negative stereotypes between two groups can be reduced simply by increasing interaction between the groups

contempt: an exaggerated form of criticism intended to hurt and psychologically abuse the partner, often in the form of insults, name-calling, hostile humor, mockery, or eye-rolling

content analysis: a method of study whereby a researcher looks at communication to find certain behaviors or patterns

content-oriented listeners: a listening style that focuses on facts, intricate details, and evidence in a message

context: the particular environment within which the communication takes place

control: the interpersonal need for some degree of dominance in our relationships as well as the need to be controlled

controllability: the attributional dimension that assesses the extent of control or choice a person had over their behavior

convergence: communication behavior that occurs when we accommodate to be similar to the verbal and nonverbal style of the person with whom we are interacting to emphasize our similarities

conversational management: the process of initiating, maintaining, and closing a conversation with another person

conversational narcissism: when a self-absorbed listener focuses on his or her own personal agenda

criticism: an attack on a person's character or personality

criticizing the speaker: a listening barrier that occurs when the listener is distracted by characteristics of the speaker that he or she doesn't like

cues-filtered-out theory: a theory that suggests that emotional expression is severely restricted in online communication no matter how good you are at it

cultural context: the degree to which meaning is communicated through explicit language or through nonverbal cues

cultural elements: things that represent aspects of a culture such as music, art, food, and social institutions such as schools and government

cultural values: what a given group of people values or appreciates according to Hofstede; cultural values tend to range on five dimensions: comfort with uncertainty, degree of power distance, individual or group orientation, gender orientation, and concept of time

culture: a learned system of knowledge, behaviors, attitudes, beliefs, values, and norms that is shared by a group of people

culture shock: feelings of loss, confusion, and even anger, which stem from a loss of the cultural cues and social rules to which one is accustomed

de-escalation stage: the stage of conflict when emotions calm down and each person is willing to work to resolve the conflict

decentering: the cognitive process in which you take into account another person's thoughts, feelings, values, background, and perspective

deception by commission: the intentional presentation of false information

deception by omission: often called concealment, this type of lying involves intentionally holding back some of the information another person has requested or that you are expected to share

decoding: interpreting ideas, feelings, and thoughts that have been translated into a code

defensiveness: responding to a complaint with blame or criticism rather than addressing the issue

denotative meaning: a word's literal meaning that would be found if you looked it up in the dictionary

destructive conflict: conflict that dismantles rather than strengthens a relationship

differentiating stage: the stage of relational de-escalation in which partners start to prefer autonomy over connection and tend to start to define their lives more as individuals and less as a couple

direct perception checking: a process that involves asking straight out if your interpretations of a perception are correct

discrimination: unfair or inappropriate treatment of other people based on their group membership

dismissive-avoidant attachment style: people who have this attachment style desire a high level of independence and tend to seek less intimacy with relationship partners, which often appears as an attempt to avoid attachment altogether

display rules: implicit rules we use to measure the appropriateness of different nonverbal behaviors

dispute settlement: the stage of conflict where both individuals try to either manage or resolve the conflict entirely by suggesting approaches or solutions

divergence: communication behaviors that occur when you differentiate yourself verbally and nonverbally from the person with whom you are interacting

dominance cues: nonverbal behaviors that communicate status, position, importance, and control

downward social comparison: occurs when a person evaluates themselves with a comparison group who they believe are worse off than they are

dyadic phase: the stage of relational de-escalation when internal contemplations about the relationship progress to an actual confrontation about the issues

ego conflict: conflict that arises because neither will let go of his or her personal position; often include personal attacks from one or both people, which puts the other person on the defensive

egocentric blindness: the natural tendency not to notice facts or evidence that contradict our favored beliefs or values

egocentric communicators: communicators who are so wrapped up in their goals and needs that they create messages without giving much thought to the person who is listening

egocentric hypocrisy: the natural tendency to ignore glaring inconsistencies between what we claim to believe and the actual beliefs indicated by our behaviors, otherwise known as a double standard, whereby the standards to which we hold ourselves are inconsistent with those we expect from others

egocentric infallibility: the natural tendency to think that our beliefs are true simply because we believe them

egocentric memory: the natural tendency to "forget" evidence that does not support our current way of thinking and to "remember" evidence and information that supports what we already believe

egocentric myopia: the natural tendency to think in absolutes, or black and white, within one's narrow point of view

egocentric oversimplification: the natural tendency to ignore the complexities of the world in favor of overly simplistic explanations if consideration of those complexities would require us to change our belief system

egocentric righteousness: the natural tendency to feel superior due to our confidence that we know the truth

egocentrism: the belief that our perceptions, beliefs, and methods are correct and superior to those of others

electronically mediated communication (EMC): communication transmitted through electronic devices

emblems: bodily cues, often in the form of hand gestures, that have a specific and commonly understood meaning in a given culture and may even substitute for a word or phrase

emotional contagion theory: suggests that emotional expression is contagious; people can "catch" emotions just by observing each other's emotional expressions

emotional noise: emotional arousal that interferes with communication effectiveness

empathy: the feeling that occurs when you experience the emotional reaction that is similar to the reaction being experienced by another person

encode: to translate ideas, thoughts, and feelings into a code, such as words or even nonverbal cues

enculturation: the process of communicating a group's culture from one generation to the next

endorsement: a response that shares the enthusiasm communicated by the other

episode: any communication encounter during which there is a source, receiver, and message

epistemology: theory of knowledge that addresses how we know what we know

equivocation: an intentionally evasive statement that can be interpreted in many ways

Eros: a love style characterized by a passionate physical and emotional love

ethical standards: a set of values by which you determine what you should and should not do

ethnicity: a social classification based on a variety of factors that are shared by a group of people who also share a common geographic origin or location

ethnocentrism: when we view and judge other cultures only from our own cultural frame of reference

etiology: an account of the world's origins and constructions

euphemism: a term that acts as a substitute for a word that may not be socially acceptable in a given context

exaggeration: also known as embellishing, is a type of deception used when one makes a smaller or bigger claim than what is true

excuse: a response that occurs when the offender admits the act was bad, but includes that it was caused or influenced by an external source

expectancy violation theory: a theory that suggests that people develop expectations about the verbal and nonverbal communication of others, and when these expectations are violated it causes attention to shift toward the communicator and the relationship

experiment: a method for conducting research, used when a researcher wants to control a situation to see how individuals react

experimenting stage: a stage of relational escalation that is characterized by some specific nonverbal indicators, including little physical contact and a social distance

explanation: description of how the world operates

explicit: concepts, ideas, or rules about which there has been some verbal agreement

external noise: the literal noise of sounds in the environment

facework: the use of communication to maintain a certain image of yourself and others

facial cues: the channel of nonverbal behavior from which you are able to communicate by producing over 250,000 different expressions

fact-inference confusion: the tendency to respond to inferences as if they were factual

fearful-avoidant attachment style: this style expresses mixed feelings about close relationships: they desire to have emotionally close relationships, but they tend to feel uncomfortable with emotional closeness

feedback: the ongoing verbal or nonverbal responses to a message sent, which can be intentional or unintentional

feminine cultures: a term used to describe cultures where priorities include the family, personal relationships and the quality of life

fundamental attribution error: the tendency to underestimate the situational causes for others' negative behavior and instead blame the actor

futurology: beliefs and descriptions of where the world is headed

gender: psychological and emotional characteristics that cause people to feel and/or express themselves as masculine, feminine, or non-binary

generation: a group including all people born in a limited span of consecutive years, whose length approximates the span of a phase of life (approximately 22 years) and whose boundaries are fixed by location in history, which helps define their personalities

grave-dressing phase: the phase of breakup where one or both partners create the "tombstone" of the relationship, telling how and why it ended and making summarizing statements about it

gunny sacking: bringing up old problems and issues from the past

halo effect: a perceptual tendency that involves attributing a variety of positive attributes to someone we like without confirming the existence of these qualities

haptics: nonverbal channel through which we communicate meaning through touch

hearing: the physiological function of receiving sound

heuristics: shortcuts in our mental processing

high power distance: a cultural value used to describe cultures where there is a larger social "distance" between people with different levels of power

high-context cultures: cultures that derive most communicative information from nonverbal cues, such as space, eye contact, and body movement

horn effect: a perceptual tendency that involves attributing a variety of negative qualities to people simply because we do not like them

hubris: exaggerated self-pride, which often comes in the form of overconfident speech or behavior

human communication: the process of making sense out of the world and attempting to share that sense with others

hypothesis: a prediction about what a researcher expects to find

I Language: using language that lets go of blaming others for "making" you feel a certain way, and instead acknowledge that your perception of their behavior is what is upsetting you

illustrators: nonverbal behaviors that accompany a verbal message and either contradict, accent, or complement it

immediacy cues: nonverbal behaviors that communicate friendliness, attraction, and liking

impersonal communication: communication that occurs when you treat people as objects or relate to them based on their role

impersonal responses: responses that attempt to take an objective or intellectual approach to the other person's need

impervious responses: responses that fail to acknowledge an attempt by the other to communicate

implicit: concepts, ideas, or rules that are unspoken but mutually understood

implicit bias: an inclination in judgement and/or behavior that occurs at a subconscious level

implicit personality theory: a theory that explains how we each have a mental framework of personality traits in our minds which are clustered together, so that once we learn a few details about someone we infer other traits that are "clustered" with the traits we observe

impression management: our attempt to control how others see us

impressions: collections of perceptions about others that we maintain and use to interpret their behaviors

inclusion: the interpersonal need to be sought out, considered, and included in social activities and the need to seek out and include others

incoherent responses: responses that are inconsistent with the accompanying nonverbal behavior

indirect perception checking: a process that involves seeking additional information through observation to either confirm or refute your interpretations

individualism: a cultural value that measures a person's worth by his or her ability to excel at their pursuits and accomplish things

information overload: a listening barrier that occurs when you are faced with an onslaught of information that is too intense in quality or quantity, and therefore you either miss important pieces or block out the message entirely

ingroup: a group with whom you associate and consider yourself a member

initiating stage: a stage of relational escalation in which interaction is typically routine, both people stick to safe and superficial topics and are presenting a "public self" to the other person

integrating stage: the relational stage during which the dyad is clearly a unit; each person has a clearer definition of their roles and of the relationship than ever before; nonverbal indicators of the integrating stage include even more synchronization of nonverbal behaviors: both individuals may start to dress, talk, and even look and sound alike

intensifying stage: a stage of relational escalation characterized by a new set of nonverbal behaviors that evolve as the dyad becomes increasingly comfortable; nonverbal indicators of the intensifying stage include touch, distance, and body orientation

interactional synchrony: the process of engaging in behaviors that mirror the posture or behavior of others

intercultural communication: communication that occurs specifically between people from two different cultures

interdependence: a characteristic of interpersonal relationships that describes how the relationship is constantly negotiated between two parties that are both affected in some way by its outcome

intergroup communication: communication between people from two different social, cultural, or demographic groups (such as different ages, genders, or teams), when those group memberships are somehow salient

intergroup empathy bias: a perceptual bias that causes us to be less likely to have empathy for outgroup members than for ingroup members

intergroup interactions: interactions in which communication is driven by each person's respective memberships in various social groups or categories, and not much affected by the unique personal relationships between the people involved

interpersonal communication: the process of two individuals interacting and mutually influencing each other simultaneously, usually for the purpose of managing relationships

interpersonal conflict: an expressed struggle that occurs when interdependent people cannot agree on a way to meet their needs and achieve their goals

interpersonal interaction: interactions in which the communication between two or more individuals is fully determined by their interpersonal relationships and individual characteristics, and not driven by the social groups or categories to which they respectively belong

interpersonal perception: the process of observing and interpreting the behaviors of other people

interpersonal relationships: the ongoing connections we maintain through interpersonal communication with the important people in our lives

interrupting responses: responses that imply that what one person has to say is more important than what the other was saying

intimate space: the zone of personal space most often reserved for personal or intimate interactions, ranging from zero to one and one-half feet from the individual

intra-psychic phase: the stage of relational de-escalation when one partner reaches a threshold of dissatisfaction and starts to focus on the other's problematic personality traits and negative behaviors in order to gather evidence that will ultimately justify withdrawing from the relationship

***intra*personal communication:** communication with yourself, otherwise known as thinking or self-talk

invulnerable responses: indirect responses to hurtful communication, such as ignoring the message, laughing, or being silent

irrelevant responses: responses that show that the other person was not listening, which is indicated when the response has nothing to do with what the other has said or asked of them

jargon: vocabulary that is shared by members of a particular group, but that others outside that group may not understand

journal: a publication that features several articles by different people

justification: a response that occurs when there is no denial of responsibility on the part of the offender; he or she claims the behavior is good, sensible or permissible

kinesics: the study of human movement and gesture

knowledge component: the information you need to know in order to understand how you and others communicate, and what it means to communicate effectively

latent conflict stage: the first stage of conflict, in which one or both people become aware that there are important differences between you

leakage cues: nonverbal behaviors that indicate that someone might be lying

linguistic determinism: a perspective that describes how the use of language determines or influences thoughts and perceptions

linguistic intergroup bias: a phenomenon that occurs when positive behavior displayed by an ingroup member is described in relatively abstract terms, whereas the same behavior shown by an outgroup member will be described in relatively concrete terms

linguistic relativity: the idea that each language includes some unique features that are not contained in other languages

listening: a complex process of selecting, attending to, creating meaning from, and responding to verbal and nonverbal messages

listening styles: your preferred ways of making sense out of the spoken messages you hear

locus of control: the attributional dimension that determines the degree to which someone's behavior is caused by internal attributes of the actor or by external circumstances

long-term oriented: a term used to describe societies where future is the focus, and thrift and perseverance are valued

looking glass self: the part of your self-concept that you learn based on your interaction with others who reflect your self back to you

low power distance: a cultural value used to describe cultures where there tends to be a smaller "distance" between people with different levels of social power

low-context cultures: cultures that derive much information from the literal, or denotative meaning words, and they tend to pay less attention to information from nonverbal and environmental cues

Ludus: a style of love that is played as a game or sport; this is the "conquest" approach to love

maintenance strategies: communication behaviors aimed at keeping a relationship healthy, such as telling someone when they've hurt your feelings or made you mad, or even making sure you fulfill the mutually expected amount of time together

malapropism: the confusion of one word for another word that has a different meaning but sounds similar

Mania: a love style characterized by a highly volatile love verging on obsession, which is fueled by low self-esteem

masculine cultures: a term used to describe cultures that prioritize achievement, success, and material possessions

mass communication: the type of communication that occurs when one person sends the same message to many people at once, with little or no opportunity for listener feedback

material self: total of all the "artifacts" you possess

mediated communication: communication with others through media, such as email, phone, IM or text rather than through face-to-face encounters

mere exposure hypothesis: states that the more exposure we have to a stimulus, the more positively we evaluate it

message: the cumulative written, spoken, and unspoken elements of communication to which people assign meaning

Message Creation Model: the most recent model of communication, which shows human communication as a transaction; this model shows that feedback never stops, and each person is both the sender and receiver simultaneously

Message Exchange Model: the second communication model, which gets closer to reality by showing human communication as an interaction; this model includes feedback from the receiver to the source of the message, and shows the influence of noise on message transmission and reception

Message Transfer Model: the first communication model, which showed human communication as an action

metacommunication: communication about the way we communicate

methodology: a theory of action that directs us on how to attain goals

microaggressions: unwelcome comments or insulting behaviors directed at members of marginalized groups, such as women, People of Color, and LGBTQ folks, among others.

microexpressions: momentary "real" expressions that a liar quickly hides with a fake expression

mindfulness: operating in a way that is self-reflective, open-minded, and unattached to communicative outcomes.

minimal group paradigm: a conceptual framework describing the phenomenon that occurs when even a random categorization of people into two or more distinct groups can produce ingroup favoritism and outgroup discrimination

mixed methods: research that incorporates both quantitative and qualitative methods; is often ideal for finding information that can be generalized but also considers how individuals may vary across different contexts

monochronic: a time orientation whereby time is viewed as limited and linear

motivational component: the desire to improve your communication

narcissism: a trait characterized by inflated but fragile self-esteem indicated by such characteristics as vanity, conceit, and self-centeredness

Negative Sentiment Override: a climate whereby negative feelings create a negative filter through which a dyad interprets events resulting in more destructive communication behavior

noise: anything that interferes and keeps a message from being understood completely and achieving its intended effect

non-assertive communication: communication that aims to address others' needs only, possibly at the risk of your own

nonverbal communication: any communicative behavior other than written or spoken language that creates meaning for someone

norms: ideas held by most members of the society about what is appropriate and expected behavior

objective self-awareness: the ability to be the object of one's own thoughts and attention

oculesics: the study of eye behavior, including but not limited to eye contact and gaze, and expressions made with the eyes

olfactics: the study of the impact of smell in human communication

ontology: descriptive model of the world and its parts

other-oriented communication: communication in which you consider the needs, goals, desires, and motives of your partner when sending a message

outgroup homogeneity effect: a perceptual bias that makes us perceive outgroup members as more similar to each other than are the unique individuals within our ingroups

outgroup: a group with whom you have little association and of which you do not consider yourself to be a member

paradigm: a common way of understanding and organizing reality that is collectively agreed upon by a society to such a degree that it is unquestioned

paradigm shift: what occurs when what was formerly considered an ultimate truth is questioned, doubted, or disproved, causing a society to undergo some fundamental change

paraphrasing: a verbal summary of the key ideas of your partner's message that helps you check the accuracy of your understanding

passive perception: observations that occur simply because our senses are in operation

peer-reviewed journal: a journal that only publishes articles once they have been approved by a panel of experts on the article's topic

people-oriented listening: a listening style that tends to focus around listening to the feelings, emotions, and perspectives of others

perception: the process of experiencing the world around you and making sense out of what you experience

personal space: the zone of personal space normally used in a conversation with friends, families, colleagues, and even sometimes strangers, which ranges from one and one-half to four feet from the individual

personality: the reaction to one's environment based on a set of enduring internal predispositions and behavioral tendencies

phonological rules: rules that dictate how words should sound when they are pronounced

physical environment: the space and objects around us that communicate information nonverbally, including nature, structures, and placement of objects

physical noise: an external sound, such as a car driving by, that distracts from listening

polarization: the use of extreme language, whereby you describe and evaluate what you observe in terms of black and white

polychronic: a time orientation whereby time is viewed as cyclical and plentiful

positive distinctiveness: the desire for your ingroup to compare in a favorable light to relevant outgroups

positive reappraisal: the process of perceiving negative experiences as opportunities for personal growth and development

Positive Sentiment Override: a climate whereby overall positive feelings lead to more positive conflict behaviors such as compromise, soft start-ups, soothing and verbal or physical affection

post-conflict stage: the aftermath of a conflict when each person is assessing how the conflict has affected the overall dynamic, and trying to get the relationship back on track

power distance: a cultural value that refers to a culture's perception of the distance on the social hierarchy that separates people who have different roles in society

Pragma: a love style characterized by rationality and good decision-making; pragmatic love is practical, and thus dictated by the head, not the heart

pragmatic rules: rules based on the meanings interpreted between the sender and receiver of messages

prejudice: a judgment or opinion of someone formed before you know all of the facts or background of that person

principle of parsimony: a principle which states that the simplest explanation is usually the correct one

principles: fundamental ideas that are assumed to be true from which all other knowledge derives

proxemics: the study of personal distance

pseudo conflict: conflict triggered by miscommunication or misunderstanding

pseudo listening: responsive behavior in which the listener shows all the signs of active listening when he or she really isn't listening at all

psychological noise: internal noise, such as preoccupation, fears, or thoughts of any kind

public communication: the communication that occurs when a speaker addresses a large audience in person, for example when giving a presidential address

public space: the distance most often used in a one-to-many interaction, such as public speaking, which extends twelve feet or more from the individual

punctuation: how we make sense out of stimuli by grouping and dividing information into time segments with beginnings and ends

qualitative: methods of research that are more interested in explaining the reasons behind human behavior and therefore often allow for the interpretation of the researcher to be included in the findings

quantitative: research analyses using samples of people who are considered to represent the population

quasi-courtship behaviors: behaviors that show readiness to engage in an interpersonal relationship

questioning: a response that includes gathering more information from the speaker

race: a classification based on the genetically transmitted physical characteristics of a group of people

receiver: the person who attempts to make sense of the message from the source

reference groups: people to whom you can realistically compare yourself, such as people of your same age, gender, and social class

referent: the thing that a symbol represents

regulators: nonverbal messages that help to control the flow of communication between people during an interaction

relational de-escalation: the movement that occurs when a relationship decreases in intimacy

relational dialectics theory: suggests that as a relationship increases in intimacy it becomes increasingly important to be aware of and manage naturally occurring tensions in the relationship;

these tensions come in the form of three sets of contrasting needs: autonomy/connectedness, privacy/transparency, and novelty/predictability

relational empathy: a perspective that permits varying degrees of understanding rather than requiring complete comprehension of another's culture or emotions

relational escalation: the process of moving through these stages toward interpersonal intimacy

relational transgressions: occurrences that can threaten the future of a relationship, which are usually based on violations of implicit or explicit rules between people in relationships

relational violence: refers to any destructive behaviors aimed at emotionally, psychologically, or physically hurting another person, including physical abuse, aggressiveness, and threats

remembering: recalling information

reproach: a message that a failure event has occurred, which can be communicated directly or indirectly

research questions: questions about the topic of study that have no proposed answer

resolution stage: the stage of conflict when one or both individuals try to either manage or resolve the conflict entirely by suggesting approaches or solutions

responding: confirming your understanding of a message

responsiveness: the tendency to be aware of and sensitive to the needs of others

rule: a prescription that indicates what behavior is obligated, preferred, or prohibited in certain communication situations or contexts

rumination: the continual thinking about an unpleasant event after it has occurred, such as an argument with another person, which distracts people from focusing on the present moment

salience: relative importance of some idea or trait, based on the context in which it is being considered

Sapir-Whorf hypothesis: a perspective that is based on the principles of linguistic determinism, suggesting that the words we select and use create the world we see around us

scarcity: an economic model that causes us to believe that there are only a limited number of resources to go around

schemata: the web of interconnected ideas and knowledge that you learn from experiencing the world

secure attachment style: an attachment style that stems from a positive view of the self and a positive view of others

selecting: the first step in the listening process whereby the listener chooses one sound amongst various sounds competing for attention

selective exposure: our tendency to put ourselves in situations that reinforce who we think we are and the outcomes we expect

selective perception: observations that occur when we direct our attention to specific details and consequently ignore other pieces of information

selective recall: when we remember things we want to remember and forget or repress things that are unpleasant, uncomfortable, or unimportant to u

self: the sum total of who a person is

self-awareness: your consciousness of your "self"

self-concept: your subjective personal description of who you think you are

self-disclosure: the process of revealing personal information to the other for the purpose of developing intimacy and understanding

self-esteem: self-worth, or an evaluation of personal value

self-fulfilling prophecies: outcomes that occur when our predictions about how things will turn out come true because we subconsciously make them come true

self-monitoring: trying to control the impression you make on others

self-serving bias: when we believe when things go right it's because of our own skills and well-doing, rather than partially caused by others or the circumstance

short-term oriented: a term used to describe societies that focus on the past and the present through respect for tradition, fulfilling social obligations, and protecting one's "face"

shyness: the behavioral tendency not to talk or interact with other people

simple conflict: conflict that stems from real differences in ideas, definitions, perceptions, or goals

six identities: the identities present in any interpersonal interaction, which include 1) who you think you are, 2) who you think the other person is, 3) who you think the other person thinks you are, 4) who the other person thinks they are, 5) who they think you are, and 6) who they think you think they are

skills component: the set of behaviors, often learned, that you can employ to improve your communication with others

slang: unique vocabulary used by people who share similar interests and experience

small group communication: an area of study which attempts to analyze communication between three to fifteen people who meet to interact with a common purpose, to solve a problem, make a decision, or just have fun

social comparison: the process of noticing how you compare and contrast to other individuals with whom you interact

social exchange theory: posits that people seek the greatest reward with the least amount of cost when it comes to relationships

social identity: the part of your self-concept that is derived from your group memberships

social identity theory: a theory explaining how one's social identity is the part of an individual's self-concept derived from his or her membership in a social group combined with the emotional significance attached to that membership

social information-processing theory: a theory that suggests that we can communicate relational and emotional message via the Internet, but it just may take longer to express messages that are typically communicated with facial expressions and tone of voice

social learning theory: a theoretical perspective that suggests that while biology plays a large role in how we each behave, we adapt and adjust our behavior toward others based on our own personal experiences

social media: communication channels that allow for mediated interactions between multiple people and an infinite amount of receivers for the purpose of information exchange and social interaction

social penetration theory: states that as a relationship develops, the partners share more aspects of the self through an exchange of information, feelings and activities; breadth is the array or variety of topics that are shared, and depth is the amount of information shared about each topic

social phase: the stage of relational de-escalation when there is usually a mutual agreement to end the relationship and both partners begin to inform the members of their social circle

social self: the part of you that interacts with others

social space: the zone of personal space typically used during group interactions, ranging from four feet to twelve feet

socialization: the acquisition of the norms of your culture through experience with its members

source: the originator of a thought or emotion

speech-thought differential: the difference between how quickly you can think and how quickly you can speak

spiritual self: the part of yourself that consists of internal thoughts about your values, moral standards, and beliefs, which includes your spiritual and philosophical perspectives

stability: the attributional dimension that assesses the degree to which the cause of someone's behavior is a stable characteristic of the actor that is consistent over time

stage-hogging: using someone else's story or comments to go off on a tangent about your own personal story

stagnating stage: the stage of relational de-escalation that is characterized by scripted communication occurring in predictable and habitual patterns

stalemate stage: the stage of conflict during which both parties are stuck in their perspectives and attitudes

statistics: numbers derived from samples that are supposed to apply to the larger population

stereotype threat: a situation where people feel at risk of conforming to negative stereotypes about their social group, often causing them to fulfill the stereotype

stereotypes: beliefs about a person based solely on the fact that they belong to a certain group

stonewalling: when one partner tries to talk about difficult issues, and the other refuses to engage in the discussion

Storge: an affectionate love that slowly develops from friendship and is based on similarity, shared interests, and feeling understood

subjective self-awareness: the ability that people have to differentiate themselves from their environment, to see themselves as autonomous agents interacting with the world around them

superimposing: filling in information that is not there based on our assumptions

support: the third level of response that shows that you are willing to help the other achieve his or her needs

survey: a method of research by which a researcher composes questions that ask a respondent to report their own behavior

symbol: a word, sound, or visual device that represents an image, concept, or experience

symbolic interaction theory: a theory that explains that people make sense of the world through their interaction, which involves co-creating meaning and negotiating identities through symbols such as language

symbolic self-awareness: our ability not only to think about the self, but also to use language (symbols) to communicate about ourselves to others

sympathy: compassion, or acknowledgment that someone may be feeling bad

syntactic rules: rules that govern the way symbols can be arranged to create the intended meaning

systems theory: an approach that acknowledges that parts of a system are synergistic; rather than being a sum of its parts, a relationship is a complex system of intertwined pieces that each affects the other

tangential responses: responses that acknowledge what the other person said, but do not meet his or her need because they are only slightly related to the topic at hand

termination stage: the stage of relational de-escalation when there is an overt decision to eliminate further interaction as a couple

thought: the mental process of imagining an image, concept or experience triggered by a referent or symbol

time orientation: the importance a culture places on the future versus the past and the present

time-oriented listeners: a listening style that prefers communication be efficient

triadic model: a framework that proposes that people with similar attributes and opinions will be influential to each other because of their social relevance

triangle of meaning: a model that explains the relationships between referents, thoughts, and symbols

trigger words: highly individual words that cause an emotional or physiological reaction in the listener

trolling: making intentionally offensive or provocative online posts with the goal of upsetting a specific person or group of people

uncertainty avoidance: a cultural value that describes a culture's tolerance for uncertainty

uncertainty reduction theory: suggests that a primary motivation for interacting at all is to reduce uncertainty about the world around you

unconscious competence: when you are so used to using your learned skills that they come naturally

unconscious incompetence: when you are not aware of the deficits in your skill set

understanding: the third step in the listening process whereby the listener assigns meaning to what he or she has heard

unilateral dissolutions: only one person desires the breakup

upward social comparison: occurs when individuals compare themselves to others who they consider socially better in some way

values: enduring concepts of good and bad, right and wrong

vocalics: the tone, rate/speed, pitch, and volume of your words; anything included in "how" you say what you say

white lies: dishonest statements that only deviate from the truth in a minor or inconsequential way

willingness to communicate: describes an individual's tendency to be shy or apprehensive about communicating with others

worldview: the framework through which you interpret the world, including everyone you meet and everything that happens to you

Index